WAR, THE STATE AND INTERNATIONAL LAW
IN SEVENTEENTH-CENTURY EUROPE

War, the State and International Law in Seventeenth-Century Europe

Edited by

OLAF ASBACH
University of Hamburg, Germany
and
PETER SCHRÖDER
University College London, UK

First published 2010 by Ashgate Publishing

Published 2016 by Routledge
2 Park Square, Milton Park, Abingdon, Oxon OX14 4RN
711 Third Avenue, New York, NY 10017, USA

Routledge is an imprint of the Taylor & Francis Group, an informa business

Copyright © The editors and contributors 2010

Olaf Asbach and Peter Schröder have asserted their right under the Copyright, Designs and Patents Act, 1988, to be identified as the editors of this work.

All rights reserved. No part of this book may be reprinted or reproduced or utilised in any form or by any electronic, mechanical, or other means, now known or hereafter invented, including photocopying and recording, or in any information storage or retrieval system, without permission in writing from the publishers.

Notice:
Product or corporate names may be trademarks or registered trademarks, and are used only for identification and explanation without intent to infringe.

British Library Cataloguing in Publication Data
War, the state and international law in seventeenth-century Europe.
 1. International relations—History—17th century. 2. Europe—Foreign relations—Law and legislation—History—17th century. 3. State governments and international relations—Europe—History—17th century.
 I. Asbach, Olaf, 1960– II. Schröder, Peter.
 327.4'009032—dc22

Library of Congress Cataloging-in-Publication Data
War, the state, and international law in seventeenth-century Europe / edited by Olaf Asbach and Peter Schröder.
 p. cm.
 ISBN 978-0-7546-6811-4 (hardcover : alk. paper) 1. International relations—History—17th century. 2. International law—History—17th century. 3. Europe—Politics and government—17th century. I. Asbach, Olaf, 1960– II. Schröder, Peter.

JZ1330.W37 2009
327.4009'032—dc22

2009018786

ISBN 13: 978-0-7546-6811-4 (hbk)

Contents

List of Figures	*vii*
List of Contributors	*ix*
Acknowledgements	*xiii*

PART I INTRODUCTION

1 War, the State and International Law in Seventeenth-Century Europe 3
   Olaf Asbach and Peter Schröder

PART II MODERN STATE AND WAR – AN INTERNAL NEXUS?

2 Wars of States or Wars of State-Formation? 17
   Johannes Burkhardt

3 Revisiting the "War-Makes-States" Thesis: War, Taxation and Social Property Relations in Early Modern Europe 35
   Benno Teschke

PART III MODERN LAW OF NATIONS – FROM SPANISH SCHOLASTICS TO GROTIUS

4 The Law of Nations and the Doctrine of *Terra Nullius* 63
   David Boucher

5 Taming the Fox and the Lion – Some Aspects of the Sixteenth-Century's Debate on Inter-State Relations 83
   Peter Schröder

6 War, Diplomacy and the Ethics of Self-Constraint in the Age of Grotius 103
   Harald Kleinschmidt

7 Liquefied Sanctity: Grotius and the Promise of Global Law 131
   Bertram Keller

PART IV STATE AND INTERNATIONAL RELATIONS – FROM MACHIAVELLI TO HOBBES

8 The Anatomy of Power in International Relations: The Doctrine of Reason of State as a "Realistic" Impact 155
   Peter Nitschke

9 Security as A Norm in Hobbes's Theory of War: A Critique of Schmitt's Interpretation of Hobbes's Approach to International Relations 163
Luc Foisneau

10 Hobbes on the Concepts of the State and Political Sovereignty 181
Christine Chwaszcza

PART V WAR AND STATE IN THE EXPANDING EUROPEAN STATE SYSTEM

11 Peace Impossible?: The Holy Roman Empire and the European State System in the Seventeenth Century 197
Christoph Kampmann

12 Hegemon History: Pufendorf's Shifting Perspectives on France and French Power 211
David Saunders

13 Colonial Design in European International Law of the Seventeenth Century 231
Andrea Weindl

PART VI CONCLUSIONS AND PERSPECTIVES

14 Dynamics of Conflict and Illusions of Law: Making War and Thinking Peace in the Modern International System 249
Olaf Asbach

Index 267

List of Figures

2.1a	"Europa Regina"	19
2.1b	"Europa Regina"	20
2.2	"Gustav Adolf auf dem Siegeswagen Ausschnitt aus der dreiteiligen Flugblattserie Schwedischer Beruf"	21
2.3a	"Neuer Auß Münster ... abgefertigter ... Postreuter"	23
2.3b	"Danck-Gebet, für den ... nunmehr geschlossenen Frieden"	24
2.4	"AUGURIUM PACIS" (= Augsburger Friedenswagen)	25
2.5a	"Böhmische Krone"	28
2.5b	"Niederländischer Löwe"	29

List of Contributors

Olaf Asbach, Dr. phil., Professor for Political Science, Heisenberg-Chair "Europe and Modernity", University of Hamburg, Germany. Research areas: History of Political Ideas; Modern Concepts of State, Democracy and (Inter-)National Law. His publications include: *Die Zähmung der Leviathane. Die Begründung einer internationalen Rechts- und Friedensordnung bei Abbé de Saint-Pierre und Rousseau* (2002), *Staat und Politik zwischen Absolutismus und Aufklärung* (2005), *Vom Nutzen des Staates. Staatsverständnisse des Utilitarismus: Hume – Bentham – J. St. Mill* (2009).

David Boucher, Ph.D., F.R.Hist.S. Head of the School of European Studies, Professor of Political Philosophy and International Relations, Director of the Collingwood and British Idealism Centre, Cardiff University. Adjunct Professor of International Relations, University of the Sunshine Coast, Australia. Research areas: Modern Political Theory, Theory of International Relations, Human Rights, Popular Culture. Recent publications: *Political Theories of International Relations: From Thucydides to the Present* (1998), "The Rule of Law and the Modern European State: Michael Oakeshott and European Enlargement", in: *European Journal of Political Theory* (2005), *The Limits of Ethics in International Relations: Natural Law, Natural Rights and Human Rights in Transition* (2009).

Johannes Burkhardt, Dr. phil., Professor Emeritus of Early Modern History, University of Augsburg, Germany. His continuing research explores War, Peace and German Federalism in Early Modern Europe. His publications include: *Die Friedlosigkeit der Frühen Neuzeit. Grundlegung einer Theorie der Bellizität Europas*, in: *Zeitschrift für Historische Forschung* (1997), *The Thirty Years' War: Central Europe*, in: *A Companion to the Reformation World* (2004), *Vollendung und Neuorientierung des frühmodernen Reiches 1648–1763* (2006).

Christine Chwaszcza, Dr. phil., Professor of Social and Political Philosophy, European University Institute, Florence, Italy. Research areas: Political Philosophy (contemporary, early modern), Philosophy of Action, Philosophy of Social Sciences. Recent publications: *Moral Responsibility and Global Justice. A Human Rights Approach* (2007), "Beyond Cosmopolitanism: Towards a Non-ideal Account of Transnational Justice", in *Ethics and Global Politics 1/3* (2008), "The Unity of the People, and Migration in Liberal Theory", in *Citizenship Studies 13/5* (2009), "Staat und politische Philosophie in David Humes *Essays*", in: Olaf Asbach (ed.): *Vom Nutzen des Staates* (2009).

Luc Foisneau, Dr., Director of research at the Centre National de la Recherche Scientifique/ Ecole des Hautes Etudes en Sciences Sociales, Paris, France. Research areas: History of Modern Political Thought, Contemporary Political Philosophy. Recent publications: (co-editor) *Leviathan after 350 Years* (2004), (ed.) *Dictionary of Seventeenth-Century French Philosophers*, 2 vols (2008), *Governo e Soberania. O Pensamento politico moderno da Maquiavel a Rousseau* (2009).

Christoph Kampmann, Dr. phil., Professor of Early Modern History, University of Marburg, Germany. Research Areas: International Relations in Early Modern Europe; Comparative Constitutional History; Political Concepts, Historical Thought and "Memoria" in Early Modern Europe; Religion and Politics in Early Modern Europe. Recent publications: *Europa und das Reich im Dreißigjährigen Krieg. Geschichte eines europäischen Konflikts* (2008), "Ius Gentium and International Peace Order. The Treaty of London (1518) and The Question of Continuity in International Law", in: Marauhn, Steiger, *Universality and Continuity in International Law* (2009), (co-editor) *Bourbon – Habsburg – Oranien: Konkurrierende Modelle im dynastischen Europa um 1700.* (2008).

Bertram Keller studied law and philosophy in Heidelberg, Cambridge, UK, Paris and Vienna. Since 2006 he has been the editor responsible for *polar*, a biannual journal for politics, theory and art. Recent Publications: *Rechtsphilosophische Kontroversen der Gegenwart* (1999), *Im Taumel der Freiheit. Demokratie und Repräsentation bei Jürgen Habermas, in: Der Staat* (2000), "Streit um Konsens. Alternative Konfliktlösung im diskursiven System des Rechts", in: G. Kreuzbauer et al. (ed.): *Der Juristische Streit* (2004).

Harald Kleinschmidt, Dr. phil., Professor at the University of Tsukuba, Japan, Graduate School of Humanities and Social Sciences. Research areas: History of International Relations, specifically, History of International Theories, History of Migration, History of Human Security. Recently publications: *Charles V. The World Emperor* (2004), *Ruling the Waves. Emperor Maximilian I, the Search for Islands and the Transformation of the European World Picture c. 1500* (2007), *Migration und Identität. Studien zu den Beziehungen zwischen dem Kontinent und Britannien zwischen dem 5. und dem 8. Jahrhundert* (2009).

Peter Nitschke, Dr. phil., Professor for Political Science, University of Vechta, Germany. Research areas: Political Theory and the History of Political Ideas, European Integration and New Terrorism. Major publications: *Politische Philosophie* (2002), (ed.) *Globaler Terrorismus und Europa. Stellungnahmen zur Internationalisierung des Terrors* (2008), (ed.) *Politeia. Politische Verfasstheit bei Platon* (2008).

Benno Teschke, Dr. phil., Senior Lecturer, Department of International Relations, University of Sussex, UK. Research interests: International Relations Theory, International History and Historical Sociology, Social Theory and Marxism; Recent Publications: *The Myth of 1648: Class, Geopolitics and the Making of Modern International Relations* (2003), "Marxism and International Relations", in: Christian Reus-Smit and Duncan Snidal (eds), *The Oxford Handbook of International Relations* (2008), "The Many Logics of Capitalist Competition", in: *Cambridge Review of International Affairs 20* (2007).

David Saunders, Professor Emeritus in the Socio-Legal Research Centre at Griffith University, Australia. His continuing research explores consequences of historical religious settlements for modern European political-legal orders. His publications include: *Anti-lawyers: Religion and the Critics of Law and State* (1997); *Natural Law and Civil Sovereignty: Moral Right and State Authority in Early Modern Political Thought* (co-editor) (2002), *Samuel Pufendorf: The Whole Duty of Man According to the Law of Nature* (co-editor) (2003).

Peter Schröder, Dr., Senior Lecturer in Early Modern History, University College London. Research interests: History of Political Thought, esp. Natural Law, international relations and concepts of sovereignty and civil liberty. His publications include: *Christian Thomasius zur Einführung* (1999), *Naturrecht und absolutistisches Staatsrecht* (2001), *Niccolò Machiavelli* (2004).

Andrea Weindl, Dr. phil., Member of the research group on European peace treaties, Institute of European History, Mainz, Germany. Research interests: History of the Atlantic system, Globalization in Early Modern Times, International Law in Early Modern Times. Recent publications: *Wer kleidet die Welt? Globale Märkte und merkantile Kräfte in der europäischen Politik der Frühen Neuzeit* (2007), "The asiento de negros and the International Law", in: *Journal of the History of International Law* (2008).

Acknowledgements

This volume emerged as a product of the conference *War, the State and International Law in Early Modern Europe* held at the German Historical Institute, London, in June 2008. We should therefore like to begin by thanking all the speakers, discussants and participants for their contributions. As often with such projects, not all contributions to the conference made it into the volume, for very different reasons. The range of themes and material covered at the conference is thus not fully reflected here. In particular, some of the contributions on the international and global dimensions that broached a stimulating debate beyond "Eurocentric" discussions of early modern inter-state relations could not be completed in time for publication. However, given that the early modern world system of the *Jus Publicum Europeaum* was itself a result of European domination and order, we believe that the focus of the volume rightly reflects and explores this Eurocentric bias.

We are glad to acknowledge the financial assistance of the *Deutsche Forschungsgemeinschaft* (German Research Foundation) and the unfailing support well beyond financial help of the German Historical Institute, London. Its director Professor Andreas Gestrich and his staff ensured that the conference was not only an intellectually stimulating but also a very pleasant event. In preparing the chapters for publication we are grateful for the assistance of Dr. Jonathan Uhlaner. Finally, we would like to thank all the contributors for working to a pressing schedule that made possible the publishing of the proceedings so shortly after the conference.

The Editors

PART I
Introduction

Chapter 1
War, the State and International Law in Seventeenth-Century Europe[1]

Olaf Asbach and Peter Schröder

From the Seventeenth to the Twenty-First Century – and Back

The seventeenth century is of particular importance for the study of the theory and practice of the modern state, of the system of international relations and of the question of war and peace. The pivotal significance of the developments of this time may be seen, for example, from the large number of studies and debates in political and cultural science, international law, philosophy, and social, economic and cultural history that have taken it as their subject.[2] It is striking that they often draw an open or implicit relation between developments and problems then and now. This became especially clear a few years ago in the commemoration of the 350th anniversary of the Treaties of Münster and Osnabrück, which brought the Thirty Years War to an end in 1648.[3] The peace settlement signalled the end of an era of state-building and confessional wars in that the following period saw the establishment of new structures and institutions that re-ordered social and international relations by means of modern state power.[4] Of the research and debates occasioned by this anniversary the same may be said as of those brought forth by the anniversary a few years before, celebrating the publication of Immanuel Kant's *Zum ewigen Frieden* in 1795. Both observances initiated a wave of writings, conferences and projects on

---

[1] Translated from the German by Jonathan Uhlaner.

[2] This pivotal significance may also be seen in the fact that most comprehensive historical interpretations take 1648 as a caesura and thus both reflect and reproduce the prevalent "mental map". In distinctive contrast to this is Heinz Schilling's treatment of the period between 1250 and 1750 in *Die neue Zeit. Vom Christenheitseuropa zum Europa der Staaten* (Berlin, 1999).

[3] Cf. Heinz Duchhardt (ed.), *Der Westfälische Friede. Diplomatie – politische Zäsur – kulturelles Umfeld – Rezeptionsgeschichte* (Munich, 1998); Meinhard Schröder (ed.), *350 Jahre Westfälischer Friede. Verfassungsgeschichte, Staatskirchenrecht, Völkerrechtsgeschichte* (Berlin, 1999); Olav Moorman van Kappen, Dieter Wyduckel (eds), *Der Westfälische Frieden in rechts- und staatstheoretischer Perspektive* (Berlin, 1999); Heinz Duchhardt (ed.), *La Paix de Westphalie: de l'événement euopéen au lieu européen de mémoire?* (Sigmaringen, 1999); James A. Caporaso (ed.), *Continuity and Change in the Westphalian Order* (Oxford, 2000).

[4] Heinz Schilling, "Der Westfälische Friede und das neuzeitliche Profil Europas", in Heinz Duchhardt (ed.), *Der Westfälische Friede. Diplomatie – politische Zäsur – kulturelles Umfeld – Rezeptionsgeschichte* (München, 1998), pp. 3–32.

questions of the institutional and normative re-thinking of international law and peace that continues to have an effect today in interdisciplinary efforts and at the international level.[5] In spite of their often historico-political content and frequent instrumentalisation of their subjects, or precisely because of this, both these focal points of political, historical and philosophical debate are extraordinarily instructive. For after all, they are applicable and capable of being updated in a historico-political and ideological respect only because we can discuss through them fundamental problems of the present, whether in order to conceive these problems rationally or to transform them ideologically.

The forms and configurations of political, social, cultural and legal institutions and structures, especially as they developed and were consolidated in the Europe of the seventeenth century and were globalised in the second half of the eighteenth century, make up the common factual reference point of these scholarly and political debates.[6] Anglophone research in particular sums up these developments and transformations under the term "Westphalian order". Here the Peace of Westphalia is a symbol for a specific set of new social and political actors, institutions and dynamics, and for the political, legal and philosophical forms in which they are to be conceived and framed. And it is precisely these structural and functional connections that have come to stand increasingly at the centre of current debates. It is this constellation, so the general tenor of articles on this debate show, that has been fundamental to modern and global relations into the second half of the twentieth century, but that in recent decades has fallen into a crisis of truly epochal character. For when basically new actors, structures and dynamics shape political, socio-economic and cultural action, all the forms, institutions and criteria used to organise, analyse and evaluate them must also be completely reconceived.

These connections among the structures and dynamics of the state, international relations and war in the seventeenth century, which are constitutive

---

[5] On the debates over Kant, cf. Reinhard Merkel, Roland Wittmann (eds), *"Zum ewigen Frieden" – Grundlagen, Aktualität und Aussichten einer Idee von Immanuel Kant* (Frankfurt am Main, 1996); Matthias Lutz-Bachmann, James Bohman (eds), *Perpetual Peace. Essays on Kant's Cosmopolitan Ideal* (Cambridge, Mass., 1997); Klaus Dicke, Klaus-Michael Kodalle (eds), *Republik und Weltbürgerrecht. Kantische Anregungen zur Theorie politischer Ordnung nach dem Ende des Ost-West-Konflikts* (Weimar; Köln, Wien, 1998); Gerd Wehner (ed.), *Von der ewigen Suche nach dem Frieden. Neue und alte Bedingungen für die Friedenssicherung* (München, 2000); Eric S. Easley, *The War over Perpetual Peace: An Exploration into the History of a Foundational International Relations Text* (Houndmills, Basingstoke, 2004).

[6] Cf. Heinz Duchhardt, "'Westphalian System'. Zur Problematik einer Denkfigur", *Historische Zeitschrift* 269 (1999): 305–15; Olaf Asbach, "Die Globalisierung Europas und die Konflikte der Moderne. Dynamiken und Widersprüche in der Theorie und Praxis der internationalen Beziehungen in der frühen Neuzeit", in Sven Externbrink (ed.), *Der Siebenjährige Krieg (1756–1763): Ein europäischer Weltkrieg im Zeitalter der Aufklärung* (Berlin, 2008).

for an understanding of the relations and developments of the future as well as the present, may be exemplified by three, frequently interwoven strands of contemporary debate and research. Focused on these strands, the seventeenth century, and the turn of the twentieth century, appear to be both the beginning and the end of a specific historical epoch.

From the Birth of the "Leviathan" to the End of the Nation-State

Many current debates revolve round the question of the change or decline of the state and state sovereignty brought about by the process of globalisation. From the perspective of these studies and diagnoses (sometimes in combination with a more or less clear practical-political orientation), the seventeenth century in general and the symbolic year "1648" in particular stand for the establishment of the "modern state". The crisis that followed upon the dissolution of the feudal-corporative order, overarched by imperial rule and *christianitas*, and the numerous resultant political, economic, socio-cultural and religious conflicts and wars, led to implementing the state as a new, centralised institution. The state now lay claim to an exclusive monopoly on legislation and the use of force, and justified its internal and external sovereignty with the competence to guarantee general conditions of law, freedom, peace and order; this was the foundation upon which social stability and the secure pursuit of individual and collective interests was to be made possible.[7]

In the eyes of many observers, this organisational form of social coherence, which has decisively determined political structures for centuries, has today fallen into a crisis or even come to an end.[8] Under the catchword of "globalisation"[9],

---

[7] Cf., for example, Hendrik Spruyt, *The Sovereign State and its Competitors. An Analysis of Systems Change* (Princeton, 1994), p. 27; Heinz Schilling, "Formung und Gestalt des internationalen Systems in der werdenden Neuzeit – Phasen und bewegende Kräfte", in Peter Krüger (ed.), *Kontinuität und Wandel in der Staatenordnung der Neuzeit. Beiträge zur Geschichte des internationalen Systems* (Marburg, 1991), p. 37.

[8] Representative of this view, but with clearly differing reasons and diagnoses, are Joseph A. Camilleri, Jim Falk, *The End of Sovereignty? The Politics of a Shrinking and Fragmenting World* (Aldershot, 1994); John Hofman, *Beyond the State* (Cambridge, 1995); Martin Albrow, *The Global Age: State and Society Beyond Modernity* (Cambridge, 1996); Peter Evans, "The Eclipse of the State? Reflections on Stateness in an Era of Globalization", in *World Politics* 50 (1997), pp. 62–87; Martin L. van Creveld, *The Rise and Decline of the State* (Cambridge, 1999); Stephan Leibfried, Michael Zürn (eds), *Transformations of the State?* (Cambridge, 2005); David J. Eaton (ed.), *The End of Sovereignty? – A Transatlantic Perspective* (Münster, 2006). A comparsion of relevant contributions to this debate has been undertaken by Stefan Lange, "Diagnosen der Entstaatlichung. Eine Ortsbestimmung der aktuellen politischen Zeitdiagnostik", *Leviathan* 30 (2002), pp. 454–81.

[9] On the boom in the use of the term "globalisation" since the 1990s, cf. Andreas Busch, "Die Entwicklung der Debatte. Intellektuelle Vorläufer und ausgewählte Themen",

they have discussed all those developments and processes that seem seriously to undermine the organisational, regulatory and directive institutions of the national state, from the globalisation of production and finance capital, the development of new sub and transnational actors and institutions, to ecological problems that are no longer amenable to the regulatory power of nation-states.

From the Westphalian Order to the New World (Dis)Order

From the mid-seventeenth century on, the establishment of the sovereign state generated a new system of international relations.[10] Its central figures are states that confront one another with the claim to sovereignty and no longer acknowledge an overarching legal and normative instance such as emperor and pope. This radically transforms, and in a specific sense rationalises and secularises, the theory and the practice of the international system: both become the object of a purely rational calculus of interests that seeks to secure the policies and wealth, position and goals of each individual state by the use of political, military, economic, financial and other sources of power. On the one hand, as a correlate of reasons of state in foreign policy so to speak, the concepts and political strategies of a *balance of power* and of a politics of interests gain the ascendancy; on the other hand, a new kind of *international law* emerges that is primarily understood as the *law of states*. Together, these tendencies come to form the fundament of political and international thought and action in the new system, first in Europe and then across the globe.[11] From this results the secular character of the present crisis of the international system.

---

in Stefan A. Schirm (ed.), *Globalisierung. Forschungsstand und Perspektiven* (Baden-Baden, 2006), pp. 35–53.

[10] Benno Teschke summarily sketches the relevant assumptions of what he understands to be "a constituting founding myth within International Relations" in *The Myth of 1648: Class, Geopolitics and the Making of Modern International Relations* (London, 2003; German transl. Münster, 2007), pp. 1–4. For a critical discussion of various variants of this position, cf. *ibid.*, chap. 1, and Matthias Zimmer, *Moderne, Staat und Internationale Politik* (Wiesbaden, 2008), pp. 37–53.

[11] Cf. Roland Axtmann, "The State of the State: The Model of the Modern Nation State and its Contemporary Transformation", in *International Political Science Review* 25 (2004), pp. 264–81. Of the vast literature on the theory and practice of political and legal operations in the modern state system, cf. for example Heinz Duchhardt, *Gleichgewicht der Kräfte, Convenance, Europäisches Konzert. Friedenskongresse und Friedensschlüsse vom Zeitalter Ludwigs XIV. bis zum Wiener Kongreß* (Darmstadt, 1976); Wilhelm G. Grewe, *The Epochs of International Law* (Berlin and New York, 2000); Arno Strohmeyer, *Theorie der Interaktion. Das europäische Gleichgewicht der Kräfte in der frühen Neuzeit* (Wien, Köln and Weimar, 1994); Michael Sheehan, *The Balance of Power. History and Theory* (London and New York, 1996); Lucien Bély (ed.), *L'Europe des traités de Westphalie. Esprit de la*

When today, under catchwords like the "end of the Westphalian state system",[12] scholars detect an upheaval in international relations, they are noting the end of fundamental structures of an order that has been in effect for more than three centuries and that dominates contemporary institutions and outlooks.[13] This is a matter not merely of a quantitative increase in new international actors alongside states, or a growing complexity of power relations and problem-solving strategies, but rather of the perception that we are living through the collapse of the entire political and socio-cultural, institutional and conceptual framework that has emerged since the seventeenth century.[14] The manifold efforts to create transnational forms of integration and cooperation as well as new regional and global institutions and mechanisms, and thereby to achieve a re-determination of international private and public law, represent attempts to reformulate international relations and international law. Opinions differ widely, however, as to whether this is a supplement to or a surrogate for the hitherto state-centred world and legal order.

From the Nationalisation of War to the Unleashing of New Wars

The upheavals within the classical "Westphalian order" come to the fore with particular clarity in the current discussions of (the at least supposedly) "new wars". In early modernity, the establishment of the new state system, for whose territorially defined organisation of rule the claim to external sovereignty was constitutive, went hand in hand with nationalisation of war. The Westphalian

---

diplomatie et diplomatie de l'esprit (Paris, 2000); Arnaud Blin, *1648 – La Paix de Westphalie ou la naissance de l'Europe moderne* (Paris 2006).

[12] Joachim Hirsch, "Die Internationalisierung des Staates. Anmerkungen zu einigen Fragen der Staatstheorie", *Das Argument* 236 (2000), p. 329.

[13] Cf. John Darwin, *After Tamerlane. The Global History of Empire since 1405* (London, 2007), p. 8: "the international states system, with its laws and norms, reflects the concepts and practice of European statecraft, and territorial formatting on the European model".

[14] Cf., for example, the following diverse assessments: M. Gene Lyons, Michael Mastandundo (eds), *Beyond Westphalia?* (Baltimore and London, 1995); Susan Strange, *The Retreat of the State. The Diffusion of Power in the World Economy* (Cambridge, 1996); Michael Zürn, *Regieren jenseits des Nationalstaates. Globalisierung und Denationalisierung als Chance* (Frankfurt am Main, 1998); Ulrich Menzel, "Die postwestfälische Konstellation, das Elend der Nationen und das Kreuz von Globalisierung und Fragmentierung", in *ibid.* (ed.), *Vom Ewigen Frieden und vom Wohlstand der Nationen* (Frankfurt am Main, 2000), pp. 158–87; and Ulrich Beck, Edgar Grande, *Das kosmopolitische Europa* (Frankfurt am Main, 2004). Huntington's thesis of a "clash of civilizations" also rests on the diagnosis of a transition to a new epoch shaped by cultures with their own traditions, values and religions; cf. Samuel Huntington, *Clash of Civilizations. Remaking of World Order* (New York, 1996).

Peace was, as it were, a symbol for a new international system that made states alone the legitimate actors in the declaration, conduct and ending of wars.[15] We might speak of a downright symbiosis between the state and war in modern times, although the views that underlie the interpretations of the foundations of and relations between these two phenomena are based on very heterogeneous evidence, both empirical and theoretical. War and the rules of war became exclusively an affair of the state. The upshot of this "nationalisation process", however, was quite ambivalent: historically and systematically it harboured the opportunity for a "civilising", "managing" and "juridification" of the *ius ad bellum* and *ius in bello* as well as the potential for an extraordinary increase and intensification of the use of organised violence.[16]

The increasingly often used designation of "new wars" indicates the diagnosis of a basic breach of this "Westphalian order".[17] On this view, the previously mentioned processes of the "de-nationalisation", pluralisation and globalisation of actors, resources and structures of conflict lead to shelving the well-rehearsed forms in which wars have hitherto been thought of, explained and politically and legally legitimated. They are now being replaced by completely new – or perhaps better, completely old – organisational forms, modes of thought and strategies of legitimation, such as were known *before* the forming of the Westphalian order and which are marked by a basic pluralising and "privatising" of the use of violence.[18]

---

[15] Cf., for instance, Otto Kimminich, "Die Entstehung des neuzeitlichen Völkerrechts", in Iring Fetscher, Herfried Münkler (eds), *Pipers Handbuch der politischen Ideen, Bd. 3: Neuzeit: Von den Konfessionskriegen bis zur Aufklärung* (Munich, 1985), p. 93; Carl Schmitt, *The Nomos of the Earth in the international Law of the Jus Publicum Europaeum*, translated by G.L. Ulmen (New York, 2004), pp. 140–51; Wilhelm Janssen, "Krieg", in *Geschichtliche Grundbegriffe. Historisches Lexikon zur politisch-sozialen Sprache in Deutschland*, ed. by Otto Brunner, Werner Conze and Reinhart Koselleck, vol. 3, Stuttgart 1982, pp. 576–83; Grewe, *The Epochs of International Law*, pp. 203–21.

[16] Cf. Ekkehard Krippendorff, *Staat und Krieg. Die historische Logik politischer Unvernunft* (Frankfurt am Main, 1985), pp. 277–82.

[17] Cf. Mary Kaldór, *New and Old Wars: Organized Violence in a Global Era* (Stanford, 1999; 2nd 2007); Mark Duffield, *Global Governance and the New Wars: The Merging of Development and Security* (London, 2001); Bernhard Zangl, Michael Zürn, *Frieden und Krieg. Sicherheit in der nationalen und post-nationalen Konstellation* (Frankfurt am Main, 2003); Bernhard Zangl, Monika Heupel, "Von 'alten' und 'neuen' Kriegen – Zum Gestaltwandel kriegerischer Gewalt", *Politische Vierteljahresschrift* 45 (2004): pp. 346–69; Martin Kahl, Ulrich Teusch, "Sind die 'neuen Kriege' wirklich neu?", *Leviathan 32/3* (2004): 382–401; Herfried Münkler, *The New Wars* (Cambridge, 2005); Ibid., *Der Wandel des Krieges. Von der Symmetrie zur Asymmetrie* (Weilerswist, 2006); Siegfried Frech, Peter I. Trummer (eds), *Neue Kriege. Akteure, Gewaltmärkte, Ökonomie* (Schwalbach, T., 2005).

[18] Cf. Mark Duffield, "Post-modern Conflict: Warlords, Post-adjustment States and Private Protection", *Civil Wars* 1/1: 65–102; Michael Riekenberg, "Warlords. Eine

Thus the emergence of the modern state system in the seventeenth century throws up the fundamental questions of war and peace, of international relations, international law and the rules of war, with a radicality comparable to our own day. September 11, 2001 was not necessary in order to prove that these questions have become significantly more urgent in view of the present degree of the global interlinking of political, economic and ecological problems, and the manifoldly increased potential for destruction.

The disciplinary and methodological perspectives, conceptions, diagnoses and assessments that appear in the previously mentioned studies and debates exhibit a broad spectrum of themes in each of the three indicated fields. The question whether the theoretical and empirical assumptions, methods and consequences of the various positions are objectively appropriate has aroused intense controversies. Precisely this heterogeneity of positions and the vehemence of the related debates attests to the need and the urgency of coming to grips with the historical and systematic foundations of the state, war and international relations as they came to be formed and consolidated in the seventeenth century, and have today become the quintessence of that which is understood under the label of the "Westphalian order". Quite apart from whether we refer to the idea of the "Westphalian order" positively or critically, this order has constituted the central reference point of debates that are of extraordinary relevance not only for the scholarly, but also for the political process of agreement about the basic structures of past and present international relations and conflicts, and of our knowledge of them.

Towards a New Approach to the Seventeenth-Century International System

The aim of this volume is to present new studies and approaches in the investigation of the historical, systematic and contemporary meaning of the structures and developments of the state, war and international law in and since the seventeenth century, and to afford new accesses to these subjects. The previous reflections on the complexity of the related factual and methodological themes and dimensions show that current research is confronted by at least two challenges.

On the one hand, one desideratum of this research is a further, and particularly a methodologically reflective, study of the presuppositions, forms and consequences of the development of the modern state system, its political and (international) legal forms of organisation and the intellectual forms in which it is reflected. This requirement arises not least from the danger of being taken in by widespread anachronistic ideas of a "Westphalian order" such as

---

Problemskizze", *Comparativ* 5/6 (1999): 187–205. The current debate on the "war on pirates" is only the most recent reminder of the comeback of well-known phenomena from early modernity.

may be seen in not a few historical, political and social studies, especially in the field of International Relations. One does not always resist the temptation of constructing as a backdrop to the (supposedly) completely new developments and challenges of the present a schematic idea of the (supposedly) completely different conditions and structures of the state, international relations and war that have prevailed since the beginning of modernity, and that are assumed to have no longer anything to do with contemporary historical reality and its practical and systematic-theoretical significance.

To guard against this danger, on the other hand, requires a much stronger interdisciplinary approach, that is to say, the systematic awareness and taking into account of the factual and methodological developments in other disciplines and contexts of research. Although in recent years and decades there have been numerous new approaches to and studies of the forming of modern society and the state system, and to questions of international law, war and peace, the various branches and perspectives of research have had the tendency to become isolated and independent of each other in spite of the fact that in the end they treat the same subject. Precisely the progress and differentiations within the various disciplines have led to highly specialised studies and debates that hardly admit to taking cognisance of other studies and approaches, and, if so, then only in stereotypical form. This is well illustrated by research on the development of the state, international relations and war in early modernity. Here scholars have devoted studies to international relations and their history, to international political economy and the "new political history", to a highly differentiated social and cultural history influenced by numerous new methodological approaches, to international law and philosophical and historical-systematic investigations, which also often pursue various national and regional *Sonderwege*;[19] yet a real exchange and learning process seldom takes place, and this can lead to mutual incomprehension of results that representatives of various disciplines and methodological perspectives have obtained about one and the same subject and set of questions.

---

[19] On new methodological developments and perspectives, cf. John Macmillan, Andrew Linklater (eds), *Boundaries in Question. New Directions in International Relations* (London, 1995); Wilfried Loth, Jürgen Osterhammel (eds), *Internationale Geschichte. Themen – Ergebnisse – Aussichten* (Munich, 2000); Gunilla Budde, Sebastian Conrad et al. (eds), *Transnationale Geschichte. Themen, Tendenzen und Theorien* (Göttingen, 2006); Barbara Stollberg-Rilinger (ed.), *Was heißt Kulturgeschichte des Politischen?* (Berlin, 2005); Ronald G. Asch, Dagmar Freist (eds), *Staatsbildung als kultureller Prozeß* (Köln, 2005); Peter Burke, *History and Social Theory* (Ithaca, N.Y., 2005); Christine Chwaszcza, Wolfgang Kersting (eds), *Politische Philosophie der internationalen Beziehungen* (Frankfurt am Main, 1998); and Peter Niesen, Benjamin Herborth (eds), *Anarchie der kommunikativen Freiheit. Jürgen Habermas und die Theorie der internationalen Beziehungen* (Frankfurt am Main, 2007).

For these reasons, this volume hopes to make a contribution to stimulating an enlarged inter- and trans-disciplinary discussion of the developments and problems at the centre of current scholarly and political debates on the state, war and international relations in the seventeenth century and their historical and contemporary significance. We have placed particular importance on including research that is based on interdisciplinary and international approaches and has given a fresh stimulus in this direction. We have therefore gathered studies by scholars who cover a correspondingly broad spectrum of themes. Coming from diverse disciplines and countries, they present new perspectives on various aspects of the state, war and international relations in early modernity. The studies represented here come from disciplines such as history and social science, cultural and political science, philosophy and jurisprudence, and originated in very different national and regional traditions of scholarship, so that each contains a specific angle on its subject. In this way, reading these articles affords some initial hints of possible differences, connections, and opportunities for mutual learning.

It is especially important to test the scope and compatibility of the new methodological approaches and perspectives with which the various disciplines or national scholarly traditions and practices view the early modern development of the state and international relations, and the ways in which they have been reflected upon theoretically. A particularly interesting example for this purpose is the various methodological approaches that have been developed for the presentation, analysis and explanation of the emergence of modern state structures, the international system and operative conflicts and dynamics of war. The contributions to this volume present and convey social, political, socio-economic, cultural historical, discourse and intellectual historical approaches, and they begin at various levels, the national and European level as well as the global, just as the formation of the new world system of early modernity began. Exemplary of this is the discussion between Johannes Burkhardt and Benno Teschke on the controversy over the connection between the state and war in early modernity that was sparked by Otto Hintze, Michael Mann and Charles Tilly, in which the "state-makes-war-thesis" is confronted by the "war-makes-states-thesis". Their articles illuminate the debate from the point of view of the historical sciences, political science, international relations theory and international political economy.[20]

---

[20] Both scholars have already written much-discussed studies on this question. Johannes Burkhardt has, since the 1990s, been developing a "theory of the bellicosity of the modern state's formation" (cf. "Die Friedlosigkeit der Frühen Neuzeit. Grundlegung einer Theorie der Bellizität Europas", *Zeitschrift für Historische Forschung* 24 (1997): 509–74), while Benno Teschke, in his *Myth 1648* (see note 9), has made a theoretically ambitious contribution to the scholarly appraisal of the seventeenth century. For a discussion of Teschke's work, see the articles in *International Politics* 43/5 (2006).

This is a fundamental debate to which the other collected articles constantly refer directly or indirectly. It is joined by articles here that analyse, from a historical, systematic and comparative perspective, the international relations and the structure and conflict-generating elements that emerged in early modernity in a twofold respect: on the one hand, with a view to how these were perceived and theoretically conceived; on the other, with a view to how these were practically and politically organised. These articles give an impetus to renew the discussion of seventeenth-century modes of thought and concepts of action and organisation that are still of considerable relevance today and often recur in contemporary discourses.

They discuss the forming of a new concept of international law and the rules of war, of diverse tendencies and their forms of political and diplomatic institutionalisation in various regions and traditions; this discussion concerns debates in international law about positive and universal law, about the decline of traditional concepts such as those of the just war and external sovereignty, and about normative constraints on state action: (cf. the articles by Keller, Kleinschmidt, Kampmann, Schröder, Foisneau, Chwaszcza and Asbach).

At the same time, the articles discuss the development of modern political concepts such as the "balance of power" and "reasons of state". They attempt to elucidate the specifically new forms and to conceive the international relations that emerged in modernity under the state-organised conditions of power competition that are often referred to in various traditions of discourse under rubrics such as "Machiavellian power and interest politics" (cf. the articles in section IV and those by Kleinschmidt, Boucher, Kampmann, Saunders and Asbach).

The articles also discuss relations among the new national and international political, social and economic actors, the interests and goals that developed in the seventeenth century and have been fundamental for the later political thought and conceptions of international law. Here it is a question (again being intensely discussed in contemporary discourses of crisis) of relations between individual states and problems and interests that stand athwart and transcend them, and of the interplay of national, European and global developments in the wake of early modern processes of expansion and globalisation. This set of questions applies both at the European and at the global level, and is discussed by (for instance) the articles by Weindl, Boucher, Teschke and Asbach.

All the articles are united by a common interest in questions such as the extent to which there were regional or national "Sonderwege" along which seventeenth-century international relations in war and peace were shaped in theory and organised in practice. Geographically, therefore, they focus on conditions in various central regions of early modern developments in politics and international law, particularly Spain and the Netherlands, England, France and the Holy Roman Empire. At the same time, however, this volume also points beyond

Europe and discusses global aspects of theoretical and practical developments in the seventeenth century. It is our hope that the articles gathered here will throw light on major concepts, consequences and perspectives of seventeenth-century developments in their systematic and historical significance, and stimulate further studies.

PART II
Modern State and War – An Internal Nexus?

Chapter 2
Wars of States or Wars of State-Formation?

Johannes Burkhardt

Is there an internal nexus between the formation of the modern state and war in early modern history? Many historians take this for granted. Their work forms a long line, ranging from the classical historian Otto Hintze's treatment of the Prussian state up to Wolfgang Reinhard's initial study "Das Wachstum der Staatsgewalt",[1] which was enriched with half a dozen additional items in his masterly monograph "On the History of Statehood".[2] Yet it is one thing to found state-formation in war, the Hintze-Reinhard "war-makes-states" thesis, and quite another to explain war as the result of state-formation, the "states-make-war" thesis. The latter thesis is that of the political scientist Ekkehard Krippendorf.[3] In his provocative study "Staat und Krieg", he stressed that the machinery of state itself has repeatedly and automatically caused wars – and continues to do so. The consequence is clear enough: in order to abolish war, you will have to abolish the state.

Krippendorf's colleague Herfried Münkler protested against this thesis, producing Thomas Hobbes as his political crown witness, who described the stateless condition as the *bellum omnia contra omnes*.[4] Later, Münkler invented "die neuen" or "asymmetrischen Kriege" (the new or asymmetrical wars) conducted without (or at least partly without) a state.[5] This thesis, however, is the result of a restricted Eurocentric perspective, as the historian Dieter Langewiesche has recently demonstrated.[6] These wars are "new" only to our belated cognisance of

---

[1] Wolfgang Reinhard, "Das Wachstum der Staatsgewalt", *Der Staat*, 31 (1992): 59–79.
[2] Wolfgang Reinhard, *Geschichte der Staatsgewalt. Eine vergleichende Verfassungsgeschichte Europas von den Anfängen bis zur Gegenwart* (München, 1999).
[3] Ekkehard Krippendorf, *Staat und Krieg. Die historische Logik politischer Unvernunft* (Frankfurt am Main, 1985).
[4] Herfried Münkler, "Staat, Krieg und Frieden. Die verwechselte Wechselbeziehung. Eine Auseinandersetzung mit Ekkehard Krippendorf", in Reiner Steinweg (ed.), *Kriegsursachen* (Frankfurt am Main, 1987), pp. 135–44.
[5] Herfried Münkler, *Über den Krieg. Stationen der Kriegsgeschichte im Spiegel ihrer theoretischen Reflexionen* (Weilerswist, 2002); Herfried Münkler, *Der Wandel des Krieges. Von der Symmetrie zur Asymmetrie* (Weilerswist, 2006).
[6] This thesis was the subject of Dieter Langewiesche's lecture at the conference "Macht und Recht. Völkerrecht in den Internationalen Beziehungen" organised by the

them. Nevertheless, it remains true for Europe and European history that "Europe has invented the State (*Europa hat den Staat erfunden*)",[7] as Wolfgang Reinhard declared at the very beginning of his monumental *Geschichte der Staatsgewalt*. One of Europe's greatest inventions is the State, and one of the centuries most important for its rise was undoubtedly in the seventeenth century.

This century was not only a century of the state, but at the same time one of war. It was an epoch of many wars in the early modern period: "an early modern densification of war", as I have put it in a monograph on the Thirty Years' War.[8] This coincidence of more wars and more state is a strong argument for the assumption that there must be a relevant connection. And surely the state is the systematic point that explains the bellicosity of the century. My thesis, however, is that we have to do here not with state wars, but with wars of state-building or state formation.[9] That is to say, the unfinished state makes war, and an unfinished international state system causes war. And both do so because they are unfinished.

What does "unfinished" mean here? To explain this not uncomplicated constellation, I have developed a model that enumerates three classes and seven elements of respective deficiencies. A first version of the model was published in 1997, shortly after and in reaction to Krippendorf's book.[10] Here I shall expound principally the first class, because it comprises the most urgent problems of state-building in the seventeenth century, and because contemporary leaflets furnish material for visualising the problems and their solutions. Then, in a second part, I present a summary of the full theory.

Iconic Approach

Monarchia Universalis

Let us begin by considering a broad map of Europe before the Thirty Years' War (Fig. 2.1a). In general, as it is the case here, political frontiers were not marked on

Otto-von-Bismarck-Stiftung in Friedrichsruh and supported by the Gerda-Henkel-Stiftung on 27–8 March 2008.

[7] Reinhard, *Geschichte der Staatsgewalt*, p. 15.

[8] Johannes Burkhardt, *Der Dreißigjährige Krieg* (Frankfurt am Main, 1992, 7. ed. 2006), pp. 9–28. Revised English Summary: Johannes Burkhardt, "The Thirty Years' War", in Ronnie Po-Chia Hsia (ed.), *A Companion to the Reformation World* (Malden, 2004), pp. 272–90.

[9] Burkhardt, *Der Dreißigjährige Krieg*, pp. 20–28; Johannes Burkhardt, "Der Dreißigjährige Krieg als frühmoderner Staatsbildungskrieg", *Geschichte in Wissenschaft und Unterricht*, 45 (1994): 487–99.

[10] Johannes Burkhardt, "Die Friedlosigkeit der Frühen Neuzeit. Grundlegung einer Theorie der Bellizität Europas", *Zeitschrift für Historische Forschung* 24 (1997): 509–74.

European maps in the sixteenth and seventeenth centuries. We can identify the characteristic geographic shape of northern Scandinavia, of southern Italy and of Spain, but Europe as a whole is represented as an undivided unit.

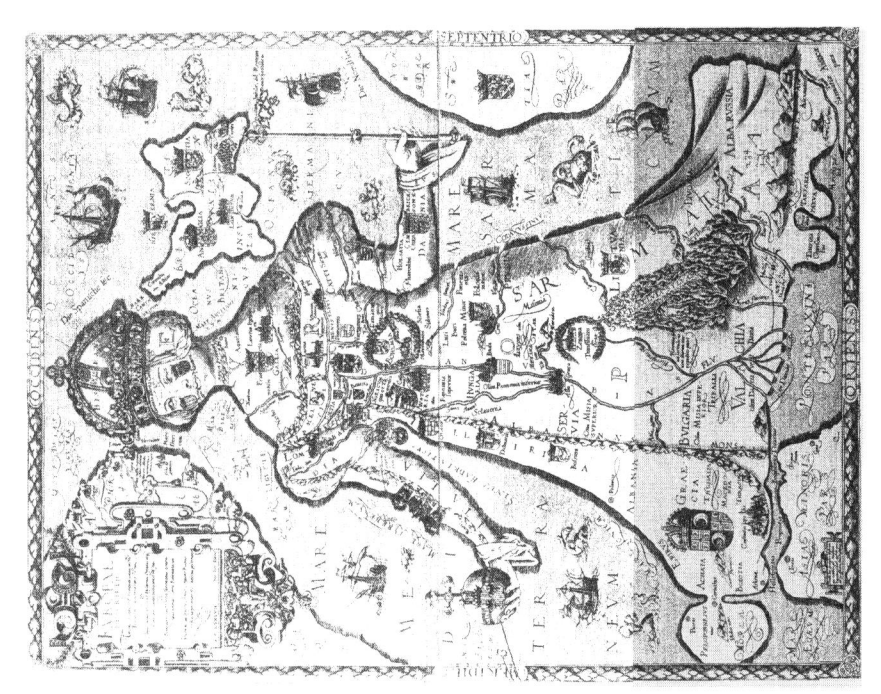

Figure 2.1a   "Europa Regina"

And yet this was a political map: Europe is presented as a political unit. If the map is turned around, Europe takes on the form of a woman (Fig. 2.1b). The crowned "head" of Europe is Spain, and the "heart" Bohemia (under the ruler-ship of Emperor Rudolf II, who made Prague his capital). In other words, the map symbolises the claim to power over all Europe by the House of Habsburg.

Similar rulership symbolism was developed in both words and pictures by the competing power of France: the "First Crown of Christendom" (this being the meaning of the French royal title *Roi tres chrétien*) and "Head of all Princes of Europe". And the Swedish king Gustav Adolf, who crossed the Baltic Sea and landed on the German coast, also cultivated such symbolism. His propaganda presented him as the Protestant hero come to save the German princes. But invoking his Goth ancestors who once conquered the Roman Empire, he marched on to southern Germany and attempted to seize the imperial crown of the new Holy "Roman Empire" (Fig. 2.2).

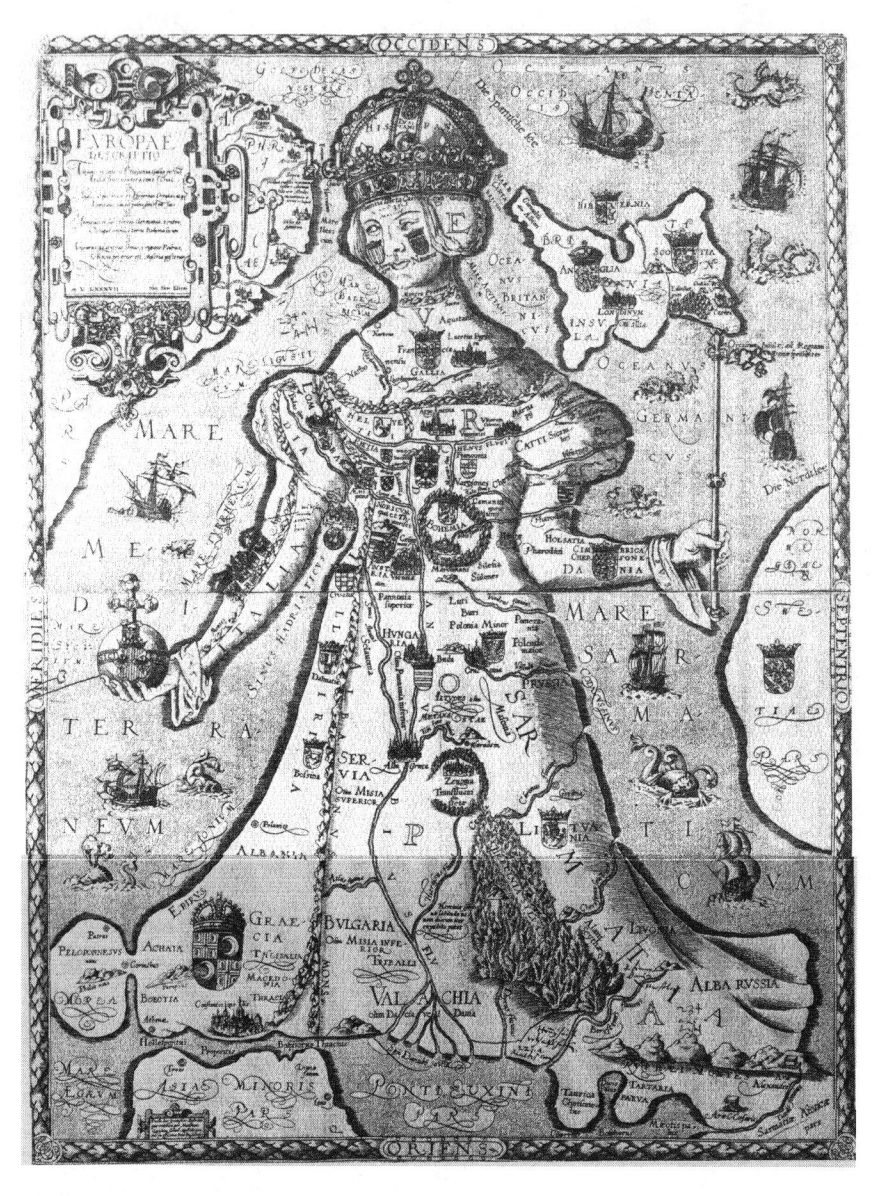

Figure 2.1b "Europa Regina"

Figure 2.2 "Gustav Adolf auf dem Siegeswagen Ausschnitt aus der dreiteiligen Flugblattserie Schwedischer Beruf"

This Europe was obviously not a state system, but rather a battlefield for universal rulership: the ruler-ship of, or pre-eminence in, Europe or the known world – a struggle that intensified during the Thirty Years' War in which the three named powers were engaged. These images, accompanied by terms such as *monarchia universalis*, *imperium* and *Christianitas*, expound a hierarchical model portraying Europe as an universal unit in which a ruler or a dynasty was to assume the elevated position of a universalist power.[11]

Westphalian System

We first meet with a completely different visual concept of Europe within the context of the Treaty of Westphalia.[12]

This may be seen in the picture of the famous messenger spreading word of a peace settlement (Fig 2.3a). He is riding over a stylised map of Europe to Vienna, Paris and Stockholm. The map no longer depicts a universalist-hierarchical order, but rather the equality of the future European capital cities by means of a horizontal arrangement.

Other pictures show the contracting parties – the Emperor, the French king and the Swedish queen – shaking hands while standing on a three-leaved shamrock made of mussels (Fig. 2.3b). The Emperor is represented as somewhat larger than Louis XIV (still a minor) and the child queen Christine, but in principle all three are portrayed as equal. While in representations of earlier peace treaties it was invariably only one party that appeared as the peacemaker or even the victor, here we see that a personified plurality of states has entered the picture.

This plurality becomes even clearer in the image of the "chariot of peace" published in an Augsburg broadsheet (Fig. 2.4). The allegorical figure of peace in the chariot is being drawn by four horses, which appear as a team of European powers

---

[11] Franz Bosbach, *Monarchia Universalis. Ein politischer Leitbegriff der frühen Neuzeit* (Göttingen, 1988); Burkhardt, Der Dreißigjährige Krieg, pp. 30–62.

[12] Cf. Burkhardt, "Auf dem Weg zu einer Bildkultur des Staatensystems. Der Westfälische Frieden und die Druckmedien", in Heinz Duchhardt (ed.), *Der Westfälische Friede. Diplomatie, politische Zäsur, kulturelles Umfeld, Rezeptionsgeschichte* (Munich, 1998), pp. 81–114. See also Hans-Martin Kaulbach, "Das Bild des Friedens – vor und nach 1648", in Klaus Bußmann and Heinz Schilling (ed.), *1648 – Krieg und Frieden in Europa* (3 vols, Münster and Osnabrück, 1998), vol 2. "Kunst und Kultur", pp. 593–603; the research report Johannes Burkhardt, "Das größte Friedenswerk der Neuzeit. Der Westfälische Frieden in neuer Perspektive", *Geschichte in Wissenschaft und Unterricht* 49 (1998): 592–618; Johannes Arndt, "Ein europäisches Jubiläum. 350 Jahre Westfälischer Friede", *Jahrbuch für Europäische Geschichte*, 1 (2000): 132–58; and Helmut Neuhaus, "Westfälischer Frieden und Dreißigjähriger Krieg. Neuerscheinungen aus Anlaß eines Jubiläums", *Archiv für Kulturgeschichte* 82 (2000): 455–75.

Figure 2.3a "Neuer Auß Münster ... abgefertigter ... Postreuter"

Figure 2.3b "Danck-Geber, für den ... nunmehr geschlossenen Frieden"

Figure 2.4 "AUGURIUM PACIS" (= Augsburger Friedenswagen)

in the form of coats-of-arms – from left to right, France, Sweden, the Emperor and a now separated Spain. In these initial pictorial testimonies of the state system, the former universalist powers and aspirants to such power revoke their claims and enter into a pluralist order of egalitarian co-existence. This transformation, which I have presented by means of expressive contemporary images and which is of course no less manifest in historical sources, concepts and literature, was in fact a longer-term and sophisticated change in the prevailing political model.

What then did this change signify for war and peace?[13] It was only because of the change in political model that peace in Europe had an opportunity of success. Universal empires can be effectual as peaceful empires only if several individual powers are not competing for leadership. As long as Europe was regarded as a universalist-hierarchical unit in which only one of the contenders could take up the position at its head, there was virtually a compulsion to fight for rulership if one power did not want to risk that another would stake a claim and become predominant. Originally, there was nothing improper about this struggle, as the position at the top was intended for someone and had to be filled. Accordingly, the beginnings of the state system were viewed with suspicion as being merely an interregnum or anarchy. However, after it was recognised during the Thirty Years' War that no single power would be able to achieve the goal of the universalist ideal, it was necessary for all powers to dissociate themselves from this earlier model in order to attain a peaceful compromise. Only a new concept of order, founded on the avant-garde ideal of equality, facilitated the acceptance of a co-existence of homogeneous states in a lasting, peaceful order. Thus the Thirty Years' War was not a war conducted by states, but rather a war, which resulted in plurality of states.

The struggle for pre-eminence among individual powers, however, was not a problem only during the Thirty Years' War, but also during the whole of the early modern period. In the wars between the Emperor Charles V and the French kings in the sixteenth century it was already a question of the *Monarchia universalis* or a "duel for Europe".[14] Nevertheless, even after the Treaty of Westphalia, wars of state-formation continued to occur. That they did was owing, in the first instance, to relapses to the old system and unresolved issues dating from the time of the universalist wars over Europe, the effects of which continued to be felt in the early

---

[13] Johannes Burkhardt, "Das größte Friedenswerk der Neuzeit. Der Westfälische Frieden in neuer Perspektive", *Geschichte in Wissenschaft und Unterricht* 49 (1998): 592–618. Johannes Burkhardt, "Vollendung und Neuorientierung des frühmodernen Reiches 1648–1763", Gebhardt. *Handbuch der deutschen Geschichte* (Stuttgart, 2006), pp. 25–54; Heinz Duchhardt, "Westphalian System. Zur Problematik einer Denkfigur", *Historische Zeitschrift* 269/2 (1999): 305–16.

[14] Bosbach, Monarchia Universalis; Johannes Burkhardt, *Das Reformationsjahrhundert. Deutsche Geschichte zwischen Medienrevolution und Institutionenbildung* 1517–1617 (Stuttgart, 2002), pp. 136–99.

modern state system. The most spectacular relapse was witnessed in the case of Louis XIV, the *Roi soleil*, who did not want his sun to shine only on an absolutist France, but also on the whole of Europe. The situation was subsequently remedied by the powers within the state system that were responsible for its balance of power. The remedy, of course, was again war. A "Second Thirty Years' War" (1667–97) ensued (a term I have introduced to summarise the four individual wars that culminated in the "Nine Years' War"), and then in the next century, for instance, the "War of the Spanish Succession".[15]

Thus the first half of the early modern period was spent at war trying to discover the egalitarian principle of the state-system, and the second half in enforcing this principle against intransigents. But the British claim to the position of European arbiter and to an "Empire of the Seas" stemmed from the same universalist roots,[16] as did Moscow's idea of itself as the "Third Rome" and Peter the Great's restoration of the title of Russian Emperor.[17] In many respects an excellent comparison would be the Ottoman Empire, with its claims to supremacy reaching into Europe. It required many bloody lessons before the universalist legacy of European history really became history and the state system of the eighteenth century could be established.

State Building from Below

An additional problem concerning state formation from below was that of emergent states. The formation of three states, which separated from the universalist Habsburg Empire and were for the most part of corporate origin and composed of particularist units, kept Europe well provided with war.

First, there were the Swiss Confederates (*Confoederatio helvetica*), which composed its inner and outer conflicts in the fifteenth and sixteenth centuries and gained recognition of statehood in 1648. Second, there was the Bohemian Uprising. This led to the formation of a federal state composed of five countries, the *Confoerderatio bohemia*, which lost its war of state-formation at the Battle of the White Mountain and then caused the Thirty Years' War. Finally and above all, there were the Dutch, who freed themselves from the Habsburgs, but only at the cost of an eighty-year war of independence, the last phase of which coincided with the Thirty Years' War.

There are two images from the Thirty Years' War that especially typify this kind of state-formation from below.

---

[15] Heinz Duchhardt, "Vorwort", in Heinz Duchhardt (ed.) *Der Friede von Rijswijk 1697* (Mainz, 1998), pp. VII–VIII.

[16] Christoph Kampmann, *Arbiter und Friedensstiftung. Die Auseinandersetzung um den politischen Schiedsrichter im Europa der Frühen Neuzeit* (Paderborn, 2001).

[17] Burkhardt, "Die Friedlosigkeit der Frühen Neuzeit", p. 523.

In the Bohemian case, there is an official copper plate of the newly elected royal couple Frederick V of the Rhineland-Palatinate with his English princess, who are to convey European recognition to Bohemia as a state (Fig. 2.5a). The true bearers of statehood, however, are revealed on a commemorative coin as five confederated hands. It is a kingdom "by the Grace of God and the Estates".

Figure 2.5a "Böhmische Krone"

In a final image one can see the image opposing the figure of Europa Regina at first glance: the Dutch lion arising from the universalist empire of the Habsburgs (Fig. 2.5b). In a similarly personified form, the right of the individual sovereign state composed of provinces is placed in opposition to the to the universalist Europe of the House of Habsburg.

There were other belligerent emergent states such as Savoy and especially Prussia. The latter was in fact the Reichsstand Brandenburg, along with a few other

Figure 2.5b "Niederländischer Löwe"

imperial territories and a Prussian Duchy, now elevated to the status of a kingdom, located outside the Reich on the periphery of Europe. The kingdom of Prussia had little chance of entering the state system already developed by the eighteenth century. Nevertheless, Frederick the Great forced the emergence of Prussia as a European state by means of three wars – in one of which, the Seven Years' War, there were particularly heavy in casualties, costing half a million people their lives. After the three continental powers Austria, France and Russia failed, despite a costly alliance, to "overthrow"[18] this trouble-maker and spoilsport in a kind of police operation, they too were forced to concede a long-lasting recognition of this state-formation. Only then did the state system become more peaceful.

Thus on the one hand we have to do with unresolved difficulties resulting from a universalist past, and on the other hand with latecomers seeking statehood who prevented the process of European state formation, which was a constant source of war, from coming to an end for almost 300 years. The destabilising incompleteness of the state system was not, however, purely a result of the continuing deficiency in equality and mutual recognition, but also of internal imperfections and weaknesses in the process of state-formation that presented a risk to security and caused conflicts during this developmental stage.

A Typological Theory of Bellicosity

At this point we have to enlarge the iconic approach and take into account a more elaborate theory of bellicosity of the early modern period [19] that I have developed only recently and that has been discussed by German and Japanese historians of this epoch.[20] In addition to the previously analysed first group pertaining to equality, I now include two further classes of structural deficiencies and dangers to early modern statehood, each of which posed a particular risk of war. The European states demonstrated deficiencies of equality, institutionalisation and autonomy. Correspondingly, wars can be explained in terms of conflicts over equality of status, crises of institutional stability and side-effects of state-creation.

A summary of this thesis yields the following typological model of deficiencies and their bellicose effect.

---

[18] A quotation from Kaunitz: "Übern Haufen werfen"; cf. *Denkschrift vom August 1755*, in Gustav Berthold Volz and Gerhard Küntzel (ed.), *Preußen und Österreich. Acten zur Vorgeschichte des Siebenjährigen Krieges* (Osnabrück, 1995), p. 145.

[19] Cf. Burkhardt, "Die Friedlosigkeit der Frühen Neuzeit".

[20] Edgar Wolfrum, *Krieg und Frieden in der Neuzeit. Vom Westfälischen Frieden bis zum Zweiten Weltkrieg* (Darmstadt, 2003), pp. 35–7, 67–9. See also the Japanese Translation of Burkhardt, "Die Friedlosigkeit der Frühen Neuzeit", in *TOIN Law Review* 8 (2002): 197–254.

Lack of Equality: Conflicts in the Emergent State System

What has been hitherto elucidated is encapsulated in in this first point:

1. Competition between and reduction of the universal powers.
2. The struggle for recognition for specific estate-based state formations from below.

To summarise, the modern state system was based on the principle of equality.

It was constructed on the principle of the territorial contiguity of uniform and equal-ranking political units, which recognised each other's sovereignty. Older European estate-based societies, which embodied the principle of inequality and a hierarchical order, found it difficult to accept this juxtaposition of plurality as a legitimate European order. On the one hand, universal claims to the whole of Europe, relating to supra-state legitimating authorities, continued to be voiced; on the other hand, Europe experienced numerous wars for recognition fought by specific estate-based state-formations from below. A long and warlike learning-process was necessary before everyone recognised that the future European political order would be based on neither super-ordination nor subordination, but on the egalitarian co-existence of large political units. Until well into the eighteenth century, old universalist claims and aggressive latecomers continued to disturb the peace.

Lack of Institutionalisation: the Risk to Stability Posed by Incomplete Statehood

In the early modern period a second factor that promoted war was the institutional incompleteness of states. The early modern state was not yet the thoroughly regulated and stable institution of today. Although administrative systems were developed further in the modern period, they still contained destabilising and organisational weak points and failings. Two of these institutional shortcomings prove to be particularly important for the investigation of war: the instability at the head of the monarchic-dynastic leadership, and a military organisation that was only partly administered by the state.

Dynastic instabilities   The early modern state was so strongly identified with its ruler that it had to share the full risks posed by the warlike tradition of the aristocracy from which rulers were drawn and those inclinations inherent in individual personalities – without Frederick the Great there would have been no Frederician wars.[21] Most importantly, however, whenever rulers changed and there was any uncertainty about the succession, Europe was threatened with a state crisis. This naturally applied to elective monarchies, but even the dynastic principle did not guarantee state stability. Marriages within the higher European nobility, partitions and personal unions as well as uncertainties about the female succession, led to a series of wars of succession. Not primogeniture, the law, contracts, nor wills was able to avert the risk of war when a ruler changed.[22]

Military instabilities   As far as military organisation is concerned, state-maintained standing armies would naturally have been a stronger force for keeping the peace than the seasonal armies composed of mercenaries who lived by fighting and who needed war as a work-creation programme. But standing armies were not fully integrated into the state. They half remained the ruler's private army, as the long separate co-existence of army and state administrations shows. The older defence forces, on the contrary, had been integrated through the estates and could be used only within their own country. Yet standing armies, which could be called out at any time, which had no defensive commitments, and which were not bound to the state but were available for the ruler's personal use, undoubtedly constituted a provocation to war.[23]

Thus it was actually the ruler's position, which was not yet fully integrated into the state, that undermined the institution of the state both dynastically and militarily, and had belligerent consequences in the early modern period.

Lack of Autonomy: Props for the State with Belligerent Side-effects

In the early modern period the institutionally unfinished states sought outside help. Religion, the economy, and political culture were particularly important props in the development of the state, but unfortunately all three had side effects, which encouraged war.

Religion   In the area of religion, it was "formation of confessions" (*Konfessionsbildung*)

---

[21] Johannes Burkhardt, "Vom Debakel zum Mirakel. Zur friedensgeschichtlichen Einordnung des Siebenjährigen Krieges", in Helmut Neuhaus and Barbara Stollberg-Rilinger (ed.), *Menschen und Strukturen in der Geschichte Alteuropas: Festschrift für Johannes Kunisch zur Vollendung seines 65. Lebensjahres* (Berlin, 2002), pp. 299–318, and Dennis Showalter, "Roi-Connétable und Kriegsherr. Friedrich II. (1712–1786)" in Stig Förster, Markus Pöhlmann and Dierk Walter (ed.), *Kriegsherren der Weltgeschichte. 22 historische Porträts* (Munich, 2006), pp. 147–67.

[22] Johannes Kunisch, *Staatsverfassung und Mächtepolitik. Zur Genese von Staatenkonflikten im Zeitalter des Absolutismus* (Berlin, 1979).

[23] Burkhardt, "The Thirty Years' War", pp. 281–4.

and the consequent "confessionalisation" of the state that opened up new opportunities for legitimating rule and strengthening identity, for expanding administrative competence and for homogenising and disciplining subjects. This meant that the structural lack of tolerance displayed by all early modern confessions, each of which claimed to represent the whole and only Christian truth, became a concern of the state, bringing with it the danger of religious wars, or at least of confessional-ideological conflicts, from the sixteenth to the beginning of the eighteenth century.[24]

Economy In the economy, the emergent state combined with the capitalist commercial world of the early modern period. But states themselves suffered the backlash against aggressive mercantilism, which aimed at re-distributing the presumed static wealth of the world in its own favour, and they became involved in conflicts over distribution and trade wars.[25]

Historic-political culture In political culture, history played a large part in legitimating the rule of the states, but it also legitimated exaggerated claims and hereditary enmities. In the early modern understanding, history was largely based on examples that were enshrined as behavioural models. Hence the many historical examples of war legitimated future conflicts.[26]

Thus all three props of the early modern state also increased the risk of war.

Conclusion

The historical theory presented here is not meant of course to resolve all the issues of state-and-war-problems in the seventeenth century, and it needs to be complemented by still closer investigations that are now in full swing in studies

---

[24] Burkhardt, *Das Reformationsjahrhundert*, pp. 77–135.
[25] Johannes Burkhardt, article on "Wirtschaft", in Otto Brunner, Werner Conze and Reinhart Koselleck (ed.), *Geschichtliche Grundbegriffe. Historisches Wörterbuch zur politisch-sozialen Sprache in Deutschland* (8 vols, Stuttgart, 1972–92), vol. 7, pp. 511–13, 550–94, and Johannes Burkhardt and Birger P. Priddat (ed.) *Geschichte der Ökonomie. Vierhundert Jahre deutscher Wirtschaftstheorie in 21 klassischen Texten – aus den Quellen herausgegeben und kommentiert* (Frankfurt am Main, 2000).
[26] Johannes Burkhardt (ed.), *Krieg und Frieden in der historischen Gedächtniskultur. Studien zur friedenspolitischen Bedeutung historischer Argumente und Jubiläen von der Antike bis in die Gegenwart* (München, 2000).

on peace treaties and political theory being conducted by the leading German-speaking centres of early modern peace research.[27]

But the model proves this much: the thesis of the state as war-maker is not historically correct. The bellicosity examined in the early modern models did not stem from the complete, fully developed state, but rather from the state's imperfections, failings and shortcomings. It is not the institution that is bad and that ought to be abolished so as eventually to attain peace: rather it was the incomplete formation of the institution that was responsible for wars. Trouble during puberty need not determine character traits in later life. The early modern process of state-formation will come to a close only when no more wars are waged. There may be new problems and new solutions, but history proves that it was not the institution of the state itself which stood in the way of a more peaceful world. Perhaps quite the contrary.

---

[27] Institut für Europäische Geschichte Mainz in cooperation with the Institut für Europäische Kulturgeschichte der Universität Augsburg; Institut für Kulturgeschichte der Frühe Neuzeit der Universität Osnabrück; Sonderforschungsbereich "Kriegserfahrungen. Krieg und Frieden in der Neuzeit" der Universität Tübingen; and the Japanese-German project "Synthetische Forschung über den Krieg des frühneuzeitlichen Europas" at the Shimane University and University of Tokyo in cooperation with the Augsburgian Institute.

Chapter 3
Revisiting the "War-Makes-States" Thesis: War, Taxation and Social Property Relations in Early Modern Europe

Benno Teschke

Introduction: War and State-Formation in Early Modern Europe

The broad consensus and widespread unanimity across the disciplines of history, historical sociology and International Relations on the significance of the internal nexus between war – or, more broadly, geopolitical competition – taxation and early modern state-formation constitutes an exceptional rarity in the field of human enquiry. Seldom a year passes without the appearance of major publications that review and re-assert the centrality of military rivalry and the attendant pressures of novel forms of revenue-extraction for the construction of the institutions of the modern state – absolute sovereignty, exclusive territoriality, public military monopoly, modern bureaucracy. This idea of a self-reinforcing dynamics between war and state-formation constitutes a long-standing, ongoing and powerful theoretical preoccupation, going back at least as far as Otto Hintze's comparative studies on international rivalry, military organisation and constitutional development.[1] Its overall intellectual thrust – the emphasis on the primacy of geopolitics – constitutes a direct attack on both liberal as well as Marxist conceptions of modern state-formation. For "nothing could be more detrimental to an understanding of this whole process than the old liberal conception of European history as the gradual creation and extension of political rights".[2] Similarly, and reacting against the "sociological proclivity to absorb the state into society", the charge is that "classical Marxism failed to foresee or adequately explain the autonomous power, for good and ill, of states as administrative and coercive machineries embedded in a militarised international

---

[1] Otto Hintze, *Staat und Verfassung: Gesammelte Abhandlungen zur Allgemeinen Verfassungsgeschichte*, edited by Gerhard Oestreich, third edition (Göttingen, 1970) and Otto Hintze, "The Formation of States and Constitutional Development: A Study in History and Politics" [1902], in Felix Gilbert (ed.), *The Historical Essays of Otto Hintze* (New York, 1975), pp. 159–77.

[2] Charles Tilly, "Reflections on the History of European State-Making", in Charles Tilly (ed.), *The Formation of National States in Western Europe* (Princeton, NJ, 1975), p. 37.

states system".[3] Thus positioned beyond Liberalism and Marxism, the neo-Hintzean research programme constitutes a far-reaching paradigm-shift in the disciplines of History and Historical Sociology, recasting the research agenda in decisive ways. More recently and over the years, this literature has become highly diversified, increasingly sophisticated and supplemented by the incorporation of other spheres of determination into the geopolitical matrix. Still, while the exact modalities of causation, timing and regional variations can diverge, the unifying core premise, *grosso modo*, is never revoked: war made states.

This chapter mounts a critical review of the literature and argues that, while its emphasis on geopolitics has identified and addressed a significant weakness in liberal and Marxist historiography, the Neo-Hintzean perspective is itself riddled with empirical and theoretical problems that cannot be rectified from within this tradition. The chapter then provides elements for a theoretical recasting of how to conceive of the relation among economics, politics and geo-politics – revenue extraction, state formation and war – in pre-capitalist early modern Europe, revolving round contested social property relations. This recasting also has important implications for re-conceptualising early modern "international" history and "international" relations by problematising the anachronistic meaning of the very notion of the "international" in seventeenth-century Europe. The explanatory potential of this revised Marxist perspective is then exemplified by means of a long-term and large-scale reconstruction, set in a geopolitical context, of the radically diverging trajectories of class and state formation in medieval and early modern France and England. This generates a new interpretation of how the bellicosity of early modern Europe – what I call "geopolitical accumulation" – is structurally premised on pre-capitalist social property relations, as this interpretation shows how conflicts over property relations affected fiscal-military performance, differential state development and inter-state rivalry. Finally, this perspective leads to an alternative understanding of how these processes affected the formation of the modern system of states. The chapter concludes with a short reflection on the relation between capitalism and the interstate system.

The Rise and Rise of the Neo-Hintzean Perspective: the Primacy of Geopolitics?

The neo-Hintzean literature diverges regarding different ultimate sources of causation, broadly suspended between a military techno-determinism, revolving round the autonomous development of military technology and strategic innovations, and a systemic geopolitical determinism, revolving round the behavioural constraints imposed by the anarchical nature of the European system

---

[3] Theda Skocpol, *States and Social Revolutions: A Comparative Analysis of France, Russia and China* (Cambridge, 1979), pp. 28 and 292.

of states. Yet it dovetails in the final outcome: the growth and centralisation of modern state power.

Michael Roberts's original thesis on the seventeenth-century "Military Revolution", arguing that it consisted of innovations in offensive and defensive armaments, tactics, army organisation and strategy, was extended by Richard Bean, who suggested a co-constitutive relation between war and the birth of the nation state.[4] This was broadly confirmed by Michael Duffy and others, tracing how the administrative requirements subsequent to the Military Revolution led to a revolution in government culminating in the eighteenth-century modern state.[5] Charles Parker drew even broader conclusions, suggesting that "the key to the [success of] Westerners" in creating the first truly global empires between 1500 and 1750 depended upon precisely those improvements in the ability to wage war which have been termed the "Military Revolution".[6] Similarly, Paul Kennedy's influential thesis on uneven economic development, military rivalry, revenue-raising capacities, "imperial overstretch", and hegemonic succession, locates the *differentia specifica* of "Europe's Miracle" in the continent's original condition of geopolitical fragmentation, if not in geography itself.[7] "The lack of any such supreme authority in Europe and the warlike rivalries among its various kingdoms and city-states stimulated a constant search for military improvements, which interacted fruitfully with the newer technological and commercial advances that were also being thrown up in this competitive, entrepreneurial environment".[8] The systemic exigencies of war in a multi-polar geo-strategic context, in conjunction with revenue-enhancing institutional innovations (the "Financial Revolution"), constituted the central *explanans* of early modern state-formation and, ultimately, Europe's successful outward expansion.[9] John Brewer, in an equally seminal study, took exception to the timing and causality of the Military Revolution for English state formation, objecting that the financial requirements generated by military pressure led only after the Glorious Revolution to a decisive series of institutional

---

[4] Michael Roberts, "The Military Revolution, 1560–1660", in Michael Roberts, *Essays in Swedish History* (London, 1967), pp. 195–225; Richard Bean, "War and the Birth of the Nation-State", *Journal of Economic History*, 33 (1973): 203–21.

[5] Michael Duffy (ed.), *The Military Revolution and the State, 1500–1800* (Exeter, 1980).

[6] Geoffrey Parker, *The Military Revolution: Military Innovation and the Rise of the West, 1500–1800* (Cambridge, 1988), p. 4. For a survey of this debate, see Clifford J. Rogers (ed.), *The Military Revolution Debate: Readings on the Military Transformation of Early Modern Europe* (Boulder, Col., 1995).

[7] Paul Kennedy, *The Rise and Fall of the Great Powers: Economic Change and Military Conflict from 1500–2000* (London, 1988), p. 17.

[8] Ibid., pp. xvi–xvii.

[9] Ibid., pp. 70–139.

innovations – generalised taxation, public finance, modern public administration – which were encapsulated in the notion of an effective Stuart-Hannoverian "fiscal-military state".[10] Still, he concurs broadly that "the most important innovations in the workings of eighteenth-century government occurred, in the first instance, in its relations with other states – in the spheres of war, finance and diplomacy".[11] Here, even the traditionally least "militaristic" case of state formation, the prime example of the traditional liberal society-centred view, was brought into the Neo-Hintzean fold.

This orientation, coupled with a Schumpeterian comparative fiscal sociology, also constitutes the research-organising idea of the recent multi-volume series on *The Origins of the Modern State in Europe*, edited by Wim Blockmans and Jean-Philipe Genet. It starts from the assumption that "interstate rivalries and conflicts were at the heart not only of demarcations of territories, but also of the ever-growing need to mobilize resources for warfare" – a research premise amply confirmed in the three volumes that bear most directly on the war-state nexus.[12] According to Wolfgang Reinhard, editor of *Power Elites and State Building*, "war was the father of all things. In its decisive phase of growth the modern state is a war state, which expands its administration and taxation mainly in order to be able to wage war".[13] Equally, Philippe Contamine's special volume on *War and Competition between States* concludes that "surely, war was the most powerful element in the development of states, or rather of 'the state'".[14] In a *hors series* companion volume on the *Rise of the Fiscal State in Europe*, Richard Bonney, while emphasising European variations, concurs that "the gradual emergence of the 'fiscal-military state' is now a truism for the evolution of European states in general". He concludes that "military need was the driving force for the recrudescence of more developed fiscal systems in Europe" – an essential property of the modern state.[15]

Parallel to these developments in historiography, the field of historical sociology has further refined, in a theoretically more sustained and systematic way, this Neo-

---

[10] John Brewer, *The Sinews of Power: War, Money and the English State, 1688–1783* (New York, 1988), p. xvii.

[11] John Brewer, "The Eighteenth-Century British State: Contexts and Issues", in Lawrence Stone (ed.), *An Imperial State at War: Britain from 1689–1815* (London, 1994), p. 57.

[12] Philippe Contamine (ed.), *War and Competition between States* (Oxford, 2000), p. v.

[13] Wolfgang Reinhard (ed.), *Power Elites and State Building* (Oxford, 1996), p. 9.

[14] Contamine, *War and Competition between States*, p. 2.

[15] Richard Bonney (ed.) (1999), *The Rise of the Fiscal State in Europe, c.1200–1815* (Oxford, 1999), pp. 9–10. See also Richard Bonney, "The Eighteenth Century II. The Struggle for Great Power Status and the End of the Old Fiscal Regime", in R. Bonney (ed.), *Economic Systems and State Finance* (Oxford, 1995), pp. 336–45.

Hintzean orientation.[16] These authors differ, however, in their competing accounts of explaining variations in the timing and results of state building. Moving away from earlier uni-linear explanations to the effect that all polities followed similar developmental trajectories, temporally and institutionally, historical sociologists have generally "opened up" their geopolitical model to domestic determinations, especially to variations in the modalities of taxation and class-coalitions. While the idea of the primacy of geopolitical competition is generally maintained, there is a broader move towards a causal pluralism, if not eclecticism, in order to capture the regional specificities of different cases.

This body of literature has perhaps found its most vocal and visible expression in the work of Charles Tilly, encapsulated in his famous dictum that "war made the state, and the state made war".[17] Within this general geopolitical matrix and adopting a classical Weberian definition of the modern state, he argues that rulers responded to the strategic imperatives of military competition by adopting differential strategies to supply revenues and manpower, depending on regionally different socio-economic arrangements. Coercion-intensive regions, defined by the absence of cities and agricultural predominance (states like Brandenburg and Russia), are distinguished from capital-intensive regions, defined by cities and commercial pre-dominance, where rulers entered into temporary coalitions with capitalists (like the Italian city-states and the Dutch republic). Both are, in turn, set apart from capitalised coercion-intensive regions (like France and England), where rulers incorporated capitalists into state structures (representative assemblies) in order to build up standing armies and rationalise bureaucracies, producing "fully-fledged national states" by the seventeenth century.[18] Instead of uni-linearity, we see multi-linearity – a multi-linearity, however, whose differential

---

[16] Apart from the three authors discussed here, further important contributions in the Weber–Hintze tradition include Brian Downing, *The Military Revolution and Political Change: Origins of Democracy and Autocracy in Early Modern Europe* (Princeton, NJ, 1992), Hendrik Spruyt, *The Sovereign State and its Competitors* (Princeton, NJ, 1994), Thomas Ertman, *Birth of the Leviathan: Building States and Regimes in Medieval and Early Modern Europe* (Cambridge, 1997), Wolfgang Reinhard, *Geschichte der Staatsgewalt: Eine Vergleichende Verfassungsgeschichte Europas von den Anfängen bis zur Gegenwart*, second ed. (München, 2000), pp. 24 and 305 passim, and Victoria Tin-bor Hui, *War and State Formation in Ancient China and Early Modern Europe* (Cambridge, 2005).

[17] Tilly, "Reflections on the History of European State-Making", p. 42.

[18] Note Tilly's differentiation between capitalists and capitalism:

Capitalists are people who specialize in the accumulation, purchase and sale of capital. They occupy the realm of exploitation, where the relations of production and exchange themselves yield surpluses, and capitalists capture them. Capitalists have often existed in the absence of capitalism, the system in which wage-workers produce goods by means of materials owned by capitalists. Through most of history, capitalists have worked chiefly as merchants, entrepreneurs, and financiers, rather than as the direct organizers of production.

lineages eventually converge between the seventeenth and nineteenth centuries on the successful capitalised-coercion model.[19]

In her comparative study on interstate war, fiscal crises, social revolutions and the growth of bureaucratic state power, Theda Skocpol has formulated arguably the most analytically rigorous and ambitious version of the model. Based on the observation that "recurrent warfare within the system of states prompted European monarchs and statesmen to centralize, regiment, and technologically upgrade armies and fiscal administrations", she re-defines "nation-states as organizations geared to maintain control of home territories and populations and to undertake actual or potential military competition with other states in the international system".[20] This leads her to argue for state autonomy over and against social interests derived from geopolitical exigencies.[21] In striking contradistinction to the Weber-Hintze mainstream, and due to her preoccupation with the impact of externally-induced military-fiscal crises on pre-capitalist agrarian class structures in *anciens régimes*, she conceives of military conflict not as the key driver of specifically modern state formation, but rather as the key dynamics in generating crises and, ultimately, the breakdown of old regimes (France, Russia and China). These precipitate social and political revolutions that result in the post-revolutionary growth of bureaucratic state power. Notwithstanding this significant divergence from the Weber-Hintze mainstream, she concludes that "the international states system as a transnational structure of military competition was not originally created by capitalism. Throughout modern world history, it represents an analytically autonomous level of transnational reality – interdependent in its structure and dynamics with world capitalism, but not reducible to it".[22] Thus, while Skocpol rates the causal effects of military competition on state formation in early modern Europe in diametrical opposition to the neo-Hintzean mainstream, she also conceives of military competition as an independent and overriding level of determination. This insight results in a theoretical pluralism of pre-existing macro-structures that interact only externally.

Michael Mann's (projected) trilogy on the "History of Social Power" starts from the axiomatic assumption that historical development can be conceived in terms of four analytically independent, yet constantly interacting, trans-historical sources of social power (ideological, economic, military and political). Their

---

Tilly, Charles (1990), *Coercion, Capital and European States, AD 990–1992* (Cambridge, Ma., 1992), p. 17.

[19] *Ibid.*, p. 31.

[20] Theda Skocpol, *States and Social Revolutions: A Comparative Analysis of France, Russia and China* (Cambridge, 1979), pp. 21–2.

[21] While the argument for state autonomy over and against domestic social interests due to external pressures may be plausible, it raises the question of how much autonomy states had in relation to these external pressures.

[22] *Ibid.*, p. 22.

relative preponderance changes over time and space, yet none is fully reducible to any other, undergirding Mann's generic position of multi-causal pluralism. His account of the "European dynamic" behind the ascendancy of "Europe" traces the interrelation between capitalism, the modern state, and the modern states-system through three successive and cumulative phases: 800–1155, 1155–1477, and 1477–1760. By the late eighteenth century, at the latest, the modern state and the modern states-system are held to have been established. Mann detects the origins of capitalism in the first phase. The "acephalous" structure of feudal political authority created opportunities for profit-oriented economic behaviour. Urban revival and the resumption of long-distance trade combined with technological developments, intensive agriculture, and the normatively pacifying framework of Christianity. The origins and interrelations of these power-networks that drove the "European miracle" were a "gigantic series of coincidences".[23] The only necessary condition is deemed to have been Christianity (ideology), which distinguished Europe from rival civilizations. In the second phase, two further accidents, one internal and one external, conditioned development. Internally, ecological (soil fertility) and geo-commercial (Baltic-Atlantic navigational opportunities) factors contributed to agricultural intensification and commercial expansion. Simultaneously, the rise of "co-ordinating states" (territorial federations that co-ordinated powerful domestic social groups) went hand in hand with the Military Revolution and growing intra-European geopolitical pressures, precipitating the transition from feudal political fragmentation to a multi-state system. "By 1477 these power networks were developing into their simpler, modern form: a multistate, capitalist civilization".[24] Externally, Islam blocked eastern expansion, since the conquest of Constantinople (1453) meant the end of Orthodox Christianity. The closure of the East and the opportunities provided by the West ensured that "power" travelled towards the Atlantic. The third phase was characterised by a rapid intensification of military rivalry, driving spiralling military expenditures, creating new modes of fiscality and administration, and generalizing the "organic state". Polities that failed to compete militarily were eliminated. While differences between French absolutism and the post-1688 British constitutional monarchy are recognised, they are quickly subsumed under the ideal-typical "organic state". Absolutist regimes, like France, were "mobilized states" that enjoyed "despotic power" over "civil society" and "a measure of financial and manpower autonomy" in a territory rich in manpower and poor in wealth.[25] Constitutional regimes, like England and Holland, were "fiscal states" with little despotic power but strong "infrastructural powers" in territories poor in manpower but rich in wealth. Yet these differences in regime type are conflated within a single category – the "organic state", subject

---

[23] Michael Mann, *The Sources of Social Power*, vol. 1 (Cambridge, 1986), p. 505.
[24] *Ibid.*, p. 510.
[25] *Ibid.*, p. 437.

to identical competitive pressures that produced identical state-responses. Mann concludes that "the growth of the modern state, as measured by finance, is explained primarily not in domestic terms but in terms of geopolitical relations of violence".[26] More sharply: "States and the multistate civilization developed primarily in response to pressures emanating from the geopolitical and military spheres".[27] The wider theoretical conclusion is that the modern state and the modern inter-state system are not reducible to capitalism. Similar to Skocpol, Mann holds that "nothing in the capitalist mode of production (or the feudal mode if that is defined economically) leads of itself to the emergence of many networks of production, divided and at war, and of an overall class structure that is nationally segmental".[28]

Irrespective of internal differentiations, there is a broad agreement in the "geopolitical competition" literature on the primacy of interstate rivalry for re-thinking early modern state-formation. Summed up in an ideal-typical manner, the following schematic chain of causation emerges:

> Geopolitical rivalry → war → military-technological and military-institutional innovations → cost increases → increased public resource extraction → new modes of taxation, fiscality, and public finance → bureaucratisation → state centralisation and rationalisation → state monopolisation of the means of violence → modern sovereignty.

The geopolitical competition model defines the modern state as a *Machtstaat* whose *raison d'être* resides primarily in *Machtpolitik* (power politics) driven by external imperatives. On this view, European state-formation is overwhelmingly determined by geopolitical imperatives, precipitating a neo-evolutionary process of geopolitical competition, institutional adaptation and selection. In this scenario, rulers had to monopolise, centralise and rationalise their military capacities. In addition to state collapse, this led *à la longue* to a European-wide institutional isomorphism of state-forms converging on the modern, sovereign state. Overall, the tendency is to assume a relative long-term uniformity in the war-driven outcomes of state-formation: the modern state defined as a "military-fiscal machine", to use John Brewer's term. Reversing the traditional liberal and Marxist perspectives, Neo-Hintzeans adopt an essentially outside-in and above-below explanation.

---

[26] *Ibid.*, p. 490.
[27] *Ibid.*, p. 511.
[28] *Ibid.*, p. 515. For comprehensive critiques of Mann's work, see Perry Anderson, "Michael Mann's Sociology of Power", in Perry Anderson, *A Zone of Engagement* (London, 1992), pp. 76–86 and Robert Brenner, "From Theory to History: 'The European Dynamic' or from Feudalism to Capitalism?", in John A. Hall and Ralph Schroeder (eds), *An Anatomy of Power: the Social Theory of Michael Mann* (Cambridge, 2006), pp. 189–232.

Preliminary Objections

This line of reasoning has become a ruling orthodoxy in historical sociology, providing a powerful counter-narrative and theoretical challenge to the traditional Marxist (and liberal) literature, associated with authors like Immanuel Wallerstein, Barrington Moore or Perry Anderson. For it broaches the problem of recognising, explaining and incorporating the insertion of early modern polities into a wider system of states characterised by military rivalry, and the effects this had on the trajectories of state-development, into a revised Marxist perspective. If we can agree that the Marxist tradition has largely failed to come to terms with a geopolitical deficiency that was already built into the original Marxist research programme due to its preoccupation with the socio-economic and internalist premises intrinsic to the paradigm of "bourgeois revolution", it does not necessarily follow that Marxism is inherently incapable of rising to this theoretical and empirical challenge.[29] Yet prior to a theoretical recasting, several *prima facie* objections can be raised.

First, the very nature of late medieval and early modern Europe as a geopolitical pluriverse (that is, its character as a proto-states-system) is taken as a given. This original multi-territorial condition for geopolitical rivalry is never explained and lies outside the model's theoretical reach. For Paul Kennedy, for example, the fundamental reason for military rivalry lies in "Europe's original geographical condition" – a politically decentralised region never subject, after the Roman Empire, to imperial unification.[30] In other words, a theoretically controlled and empirically informed reconstruction of Europe's medieval and early modern configuration as a political pluriverse is not provided. Consequently, the Neo-Hintzean model falls back on a naturalised geo-topological determinism, beyond all socio-political interrogation. The absence of a continent-wide empire is noted, yet the presence of geopolitical multiplicity is not explained.[31]

Second, what actually accounts for geopolitical rivalry in this model? What explains the frequency, intensity and duration of early modern wars? Why do we see the rise of the "permanent war-state"? As a rule, the argument for early modern

---

[29] This argument is set out in Benno Teschke, "Bourgeois Revolution, State Formation and the Absence of the International", *Historical Materialism: Research in Critical Marxist Theory*, 13/2 (2005): 3–26 and Benno Teschke, "Marxism and International Relations", in Christian Reus-Smit and Duncan Snidal (eds), *The Oxford Handbook of International Relations* (Oxford, 2008), pp. 163–87.

[30] Kennedy, *The Rise and Fall of the Great Powers*, pp. 16–22.

[31] For a detailed reconstruction of the socio-political dynamics that led to the disintegration of the Carolingian Empire and the subsequent consolidation of a plurality of feudal kingdoms in the eleventh and twelfth centuries, see Benno Teschke, *The Myth of 1648: Class, Geopolitics and the Making of Modern International Relations* (London, 2003), chap. 3.

Europe's bellicosity jumps from the mere fact of co-existing contiguous polities to the analytical conclusion that it is this that explains geopolitical rivalry. If there is a theoretical argument, it tends to resort either to (i) the neo-realist theorem of a security-dilemma in an anarchical situation (*si vis pacem para bellum*), or (ii) to the classical realist idea of a subjective *animus dominandi* of rulers – (as power-holders, rulers want to expand by definition), or (iii) to technological breakthroughs in military equipment and organisation in the context of an arms-race. In the first case, the interstate system is essentially naturalised as a pre-social "state of nature" in which foreign policy behaviour is a function derived from the system's anarchical structure. In the second case, the pursuit of power is reified – the autonomy of politics as the quintessential quest for power. In the third case, pressures for military innovations are anchored in an autonomous military techno-determinism. In short, the model lacks a social theory of war.

Third, and returning to Tilly's central thesis on "war-makes-states", to what degree did warfare actually *make* the state in the specifically modern sense of the term? If, in line with the Neo-Hintzean orthodoxy, we deploy Max Weber's standard definition of the modern state – abstract state power, legitimate and public monopoly in the means of violence, consolidated state-territory, separation of bureaucrats from their means of administration – which early modern polity in the seventeenth or even eighteenth century actually complied with these criteria? Where do we see the classical modern separation between public authority and civil society, the economy and the state, private and public power during this period? As will be set out below, the *effects* of military rivalry had, at least in the French case (and this is something that can be generalised for the Continent), precisely the *opposite result* of what the geopolitical competition model asserts. Rather than driving an incremental and linear process of successful modern state-formation, leading to a rationalised, centralised and de-personalised state-form, warfare exacerbated the social conflicts within Old Regime France, undermined its fiscal-military health, exhausted its economic performance, and shaped a distinct process of "unsuccessful", "irrational" (in terms of outcome, not in terms of interests and strategies pursued by historically situated actors) and "involuntary" state-formation that actually weakened the French state over time.[32] These processes combined to lead, especially during and after the Seven

---

[32] The vocabulary of "strong" vs. "weak" states may be inadequate to describe the situation. It may be better to say that the French state apparatus became "heavier" over time in terms of the numbers of officers that reproduced themselves through the state, and "weaker" in its ability to absorb the financial costs associated with each war, since royal debt-accumulation and the need to retrieve income through office-proliferation meant a loss of state control over its fiscal and financial system and therewith its capacity to rationalise French society for military purposes. "Efficient" and "inefficient" states may be a better pairing.

Years' War, to a permanent state of fiscal crisis and, finally, to state-collapse under the geopolitical pressure exerted by a qualitatively distinct and comparatively superior capitalist state and society complex: post-1688 England. In this respect, Bonney's concluding statement that by 1815 "only one state, Britain, had reached the more advanced stage of a 'fiscal state'", and its logical corollary concerning the reasons Britain's continental rivals had failed to reach this stage, requires sustained reconsideration.[33]

Finally, what was the role of capitalism? Some historical sociologist advance the further claim that the war-driven pressures towards the rationalisation of public fiscal systems for revenue-procurement decisively promoted the development of capitalism. There are three variants of this argument. First, state-led mercantilist strategies of economic growth started to penetrate society at large, including the rationalisation of production (especially in military, infrastructural and luxury goods), with the twin objectives of harnessing capital-accumulation for military spending and deploying capitalist methods of production for vital public security goods. Second, mercantilist colonialism established overseas markets that fostered inter-continental long-distance trade which expanded the division of labour, providing not only incentives for intensified and taxable commerce, but also for market-oriented production. Colonialism also provoked large-scale investments overseas. Third, more rationalised modes of regularised and monetarised taxation (rather than wilful seigniorial dues in kind or labour) provided incentives to reorient (agricultural) production to urban markets, leading to specialisation and greater economies of scale. Thus, capitalism is either conceived of as a by-product of state-led revenue-procurement or, alternatively, as a pre-existing and not further specified phenomenon that is selectively mobilised, usually in terms of compacts between the Crown and mercantile financial circles, for the provision of war finance. Whatever the precise modalities of different explanations and the exact definition of capitalism adopted, capitalism is here either a derivative of war making or only contingently related to the story of early modern state-formation.

Relations of Domination in Pre-Capitalist Europe: Re-Conceiving the Relation between the Political and the Economic

Approaching the issue from a wider, epistemological angle, these contributions are united by an under-problematised deployment of analytical categories – be they levels of determination, sources of social power or mere factors – for large-scale and long-term historical analysis. The axiomatic assumption that any particular moment in world history can be read in terms of the variable configuration and

---

[33] Bonney, *The Rise of the Fiscal State in Europe*, p. 14.

interaction between pre-existing and universalised spheres of determination – the ideological, economic, military, political or, alternatively, the state, the market and the economy, society, war, the domestic, the international and so on – assigns an unfounded *a priori* existence and autonomy to these phenomena and ascribes, simultaneously, a timelessness to an analytical vocabulary that is essentially abstracted from a specific historical context (let us call it "European modernity") – and projected back onto history at large. Thus semantically neutered, these supra-historical abstractions generate analytical anachronisms. This facile transhistorical pluralism has been repeatedly and convincingly challenged from both ends of the politico-theoretical spectrum, exemplified by Otto Brunner's warnings against the temptations of "disjunctive thinking" in his analysis of the constitution of medieval polities and by Jürgen Habermas's historical inquiry into the rise and transformation of a public sphere in early modern Europe.[34]

These and many others writings have drawn our attention to a proper historicisation of social phenomena and a corresponding sensibility to their context-specific semantics. More directly, they have insisted on the essential unity of the economic and the political – their non-differentiation – in pre-capitalist times. But as "the state", "economy" and "society" are quintessentially modern concepts, the historicisation of these concepts will also allow us to re-problematise the historical construction and differentiation between "the domestic" and "the international", with important implications for how to conceive of "international history" and of "geopolitics" in medieval and early modern Europe.[35] Central to this theoretical and semantic recasting is the focus on *Herrschaftsverhältnisse* – relations of domination – in "Old Europe", spanning the period 1000–1800.[36] This term conceptualises nothing less than the thesis that the political relations of domination (rights and privileges) constitute simultaneously the economic powers of exploitation. Any expansion of rights of domination is tantamount to the expansion of rights of exploitation – the political constitution of

---

[34] Otto Brunner, *Land and Lordship: Structures of Governance in Medieval Austria*, transl. from the fourth rev. edn by Howard Kaminsky and James van Horn Melton (Philadelphia, 1992 [1939]) and Jürgen Habermas, *The Structural Transformation of the Public Sphere: An Inquiry into a Category of Bourgeois Society*, transl. by Thomas Burger (Cambridge, Ma., 1989 [1965]). The *locus classicus* remains Karl Polanyi (ed.), *Trade and Market in the Early Empires: Economies in History and Theory* (Glencoe, Ill., 1957). For a spirited defence of a semantically sensitive approach to medieval politics, see Rees Davies (2003), "The Medieval State: The Tyranny of a Concept?", *Journal of Historical Sociology*, 16/2, pp. 280–300.

[35] Teschke, *The Myth of 1648* and Benno Teschke, "Debating 'The Myth of 1648': State Formation, the Interstate System and the Emergence of Capitalism in Europe – A Rejoinder", *International Politics*, 43 (2006): 531–73.

[36] Dietrich Gerhard, *Old Europe: A Study of Continuity, 1000–1800* (New York, 1981).

economic reproduction. In this sense, politics and economics are fused or non-differentiated.

The Marxist tradition has approached this nexus less through an institutional or constitutional lens than primarily with reference to Karl Marx's notion of "extra-economic compulsion", interpreted through a philosophy of internal relations.[37] This term captures the idea that in all pre-capitalist communities social interdependence – and the transfer of surplus from producers to non-producers – relies primarily on direct relations of personal dependence or, alternatively, social bonds of obligation. Robert Brenner, in turn, suggested that these *Herrschaftsverhältnisse* are institutionalised in politically constituted and contested property relations, the nodal points of intersection in which power relations shape social relations.[38] The focus thus shifts towards the historical and geographical specificity of social property relations – the configuration between power and property – and the social conflicts over the modalities of surplus transfer (dues and taxes) that are at the centre of differential trajectories of state-development in medieval and early modern Europe. In this, the distinction between capitalist and non-capitalist property relations is central. The argument is that in social property regimes where direct producers are in possession of their means of reproduction, non-producers tend to re-invest in the means of appropriation and coercion – rather than in the means of production – to secure the extraction of surplus and so to accumulate wealth. Hence accumulation was primarily a political process: Marx's "extra-economic compulsion". And this process of political appropriation vis-à-vis the peasantry also internally divided the ruling class in terms of conflicts over property rights, the terms of appropriation and the distribution of surplus. As this process divided elites domestically, it also drove an inter-lordly and inter-dynastic conflict over the expansion and control of "land and people" – territory and labour. I call this process "geopolitical accumulation". Consequently, warfare and re-investment in the means of coercion (pressures towards military innovations) were not a geopolitical imperative in pre-capitalist seventeenth Century Europe, but a normal ruling class strategy of expanded reproduction, driven by the social and domestic needs of (geo-) political accumulation. In

---

[37] Karl Marx, *Capital: A Critique of Political Economy*, vol. 3, trans. by David Fernbach (London, 1981 [1894]), pp. 926–7.

[38] Robert Brenner, "The Agrarian Roots of European Capitalism", in T.H. Aston and C.H.E. Philpin (eds) *The Brenner Debate: Agrarian Class Structure and Economic Development in Pre-Industrial Europe* (Cambridge, 1985), pp. 213–27; Robert Brenner, "The Social Basis of Economic Development", in John Roemer (ed.), *Analytical Marxism* (Cambridge, 1986), pp. 23–53. Compare also Ellen Wood, "The Separation of 'The Economic' and 'The Political' in Capitalism", in Ellen Wood, *Democracy Against Capitalism: Renewing Historical Materialism* (Cambridge, 1995 [1981]), pp. 19–48.

this sense, the early modern "permanent war-state" institutionalised the social imperatives of political accumulation.

The next section gives examples of how these theoretical premises, revolving around the regionally specific development of social property relations, may be translated into a reconstruction of the diverging trajectories of state-formation in early modern France and England. This reconstruction directly challenges the Neo-Hintzean "war-makes-states" thesis, not by denying the efficacy and prominence of military rivalry, but by providing an alternative explanation, and so rejects Tilly's and Mann's thesis that both states can be subsumed under the same regime-type. At the same time, it should be noted that this revised Marxist perspective breaks with some central assumptions of classical Marxism, including the idea of historical teleology, economic structuralism or a technological determinism, as it also breaks with the understanding of capitalism that defines it (following Adam Smith or Immanuel Wallerstein) as the widening of the division of labour driven by commercial expansion, that is, trade. As the following sections attempt to demonstrate, the equation of capitalism with capitalists pursuing profits (essentially commerce and finance) is not helpful in understanding the actual fundamental difference between "commercial capitalism" – the political maintenance and exploitation of price-differentials in long-distance trade – and capitalism understood as a social relation between producers and non-producers. Whereas commercial capitalism refers to the principle of "buying cheap and selling dear", connecting different markets without integrating them (which characterised the Italian and Dutch experiences and later, in the form of mercantilism, the French and English experiences) so as to reap windfall profits in the sphere of circulation, "capitalism" refers to a social relation in which all factors of production, including most crucially labour, are commodified, leading to market-dependency by both producers and non-producers.[39] This type of property regime emerged in early modern times in only one country: England.

Social Property Relations, Fiscal-Military Performance, State Variations and Geopolitics: France and England

Why did class conflict and its strategic dimension – geopolitics – lead in France to an absolutist property regime, an "inefficient" pre-modern polity, and the relative decline of France's international position, whereas they led in England and Britain to a capitalist property regime, an "efficient" and modern state, and Britain's rise to global primacy?

---

[39] It should be clear that this definition constitutes an ideal-type which requires concretisation for specific instances.

France: from Feudalism to Absolutism

A full reconstruction of the French trajectory has to start with the outcome of the "feudal revolution" around the year 1000 that left a territorially fragmented social property regime (the multiplicity of banal lords) that was slowly and gradually centralised by the Capetian and, later, Valois monarchies.[40] Here, in contrast to England, competition between regional lords and royal power created room for a policy of peasant protection. In the course of the crisis beginning in the fourteenth century, the feudal rent-regime between lords and bonded peasants was undermined and finally replaced, after the seventeenth-century crisis, by an absolutist tax-regime between the king and free peasants in possession of their lands, creating wide-spread peasant small-holding.[41] Peasant communities had benefited from competition between the monarchy and local nobles with respect to their surplus, gaining freedom in the process and establishing inheritable tenures that owed fixed dues which subsequently lost value with inflation. In this process, the old sword-carrying and independent nobility lost many of its feudal powers and became either impoverished or absorbed into the court society of the Old Regime through office venality and other channels of privilege. Simultaneously, the monarchy actively promoted the creation of a new "office nobility" that started to administer public power (taxation, justice and war). In this process, the demilitarisation of the old feudal nobility and the loss of their autonomous feudal powers of domination and appropriation implied their domestication and their need to re-organise their privileges and powers of extraction in relation to the royal state.

The class-distinctions between the bourgeoisie and the aristocracy had become blurred, as members of both classes made the most of their wealth from landholdings and lucrative state offices. But the income from these landholdings was generated through pre-capitalist sharecropping and not from asserting direct control over production.[42] Additionally, both classes reproduced themselves from fees collected in their capacity as office-holders, investment in state loans and royal largesse. Agrarian capitalism did not develop in France since neither peasants, who formed subsistence communities based on unmediated access to their means of reproduction, nor the upper classes (noble and bourgeois), which reproduced themselves through land-rents and the spoils of political offices, were subject to capitalist imperatives.

---

[40] Jean-Pierre Poly and Eric Bournazel, *The Feudal Transformation: 900–1200* (New York, 1991).
[41] Brenner, "The Agrarian Roots of European Capitalism".
[42] Stephen Miller, *State and Society in Eighteenth-Century France: A Study of Political Power and Social Revolution in Languedoc* (Washington, D.C., 2008).

By the mid-seventeenth century, the demise of independent feudal centres of power finally meant that territoriality became internally more consolidated, since the French polity was no longer a fragmented ensemble of lordships that defined the "parcellised sovereignty" of the medieval polity, but a kingdom in which the Crown was sovereign. It would be a fundamental mistake, however, to confound "absolutist" with modern sovereignty, for the relations of exploitation remained politically constituted, if now in the form of the "tax/office state" (the *Steuer – und Ämterstaat*).[43] This meant that the process of political accumulation continued to rest on practices of domination, revolving round the personalised sovereignty of the ruling dynasty: *L'État, c'est moi*. In the context of this social property regime, a separation of public and private realms, of the political and the economic, could not be carried through. As the king regarded the realm as his patrimonial property, *raison d'État* meant *raison de roi*. "Divine kingship" became the dominant mode of legitimation rather than a secularised discourse and praxis of "popular sovereignty" or "the national interest".

But "absolutism", as the revisionist literature has confirmed, never implied unlimited or unchecked royal power, but rather institutionalised a new and ultimately unstable *modus vivendi* between king and privileged groups, most notably the sword and office nobility and the higher clergy.[44] The relations of

---

[43] Heide Gerstenberger, *Impersonal Power: History and Theory of the Bourgeois State*, transl. by David Fernbach (Leiden and Boston, 2007 [1990]).

[44] It should be noted that my account of French "absolutism" is consonant with the findings, but not with the explanation, of the dominant revisionist interpretation of absolutism, Marxist and non-Marxist alike, in historiography. See, for example, William Beik, *Absolutism and Society in Seventeenth-Century France: State Power and Provincial Aristocracy in Languedoc* (Cambridge, 1985); Philip T. Hoffman, "Early Modern France, 1450–1700", in Philip T. Hoffman and Kathryn Norberg (eds), *Fiscal Crises, Liberty, and Representative Government, 1450–1789* (Stanford, 1994), pp. 226–52; David Parker, *Class and State in Ancien Régime France: The Road to Modernity?* (London, 1996); Ronald Asch and Heinz Duchhardt (eds), *Der Absolutismus — ein Mythos? Strukturwandel Monarchischer Herrschaft in West- und Mitteleuropa (ca.1550–1700)* (Köln, 1996) and Mark Potter, "War Finance and Absolutist State Development in Early Modern Europe: An Examination of French Venality in the Seventeenth Century", *Journal of Early Modern History*, 7/1–2 (2003): 120–47. Note that Ertman, *Birth of the Leviathan*, and Hui, *War and State Formation in Ancient China and Early Modern Europe*, arrive at similar conclusions regarding the overall trajectory of French state-formation. In a recent survey, William Beik nuances minor parts of the dominant revisionist thesis, particularly with respect to specific French provinces. See William Beik, "The Absolutism of Louis XIV as Social Collaboration", *Past & Present*, 188 (2005): 195–224. However, he strongly confirms the view of absolutism as "social collaboration" in contrast to the outdated Tocquevillian account of a triumphant monarchy-led project of state modernisation, centralisation and rationalisation that erased all intermediary bodies.

exploitation between the Crown and the nobility and between the ruling class and the peasantry remained governed throughout the *ancien régime* by political conflicts over access to and distribution of the total peasant-produced output. Consequently, taxation became the key arena of domestic conflict. In this context, every war tested and re-negotiated the balance of power between Crown and nobility, as the monarchy tried to meet its financial needs by higher taxes, the artificial creation and selling of venal offices, or by loans advanced by private financiers who were often themselves tax-farmers. But while the nobility was, as a rule,[45] exempted from taxation and therefore not represented in a national forum (the Estates General met for the last time before the French Revolution in 1614), the monarchy's reliance on the nobility for financial support translated into an entrenchment of its position in the venal 'bureaucracy' in the provincial estates and other regional corporate bodies, and into a flowering of indirect and informal deals that individual financiers struck in the clientelistic system of the court at Versailles. To remain financially afloat and pacify the office nobility, French monarchs sold and auctioned off public offices in ever greater numbers. Over time, venal offices were held in perpetuity and heredity and so became a privatised source of income. The Crown thus lost control over its fiscal and financial administration. It failed to establish a central bank or secure lines of credit, while being forced to borrow on short-term loans at high interest rates from a class of wealthy financiers, who were themselves tax-farmers. Especially the recourse under Louis XIV to office venality persistently strengthened the private property rights of office holders. In this way, the pretension to absolutism was belied by the progressive loss of control by the monarchy over the state apparatus as it was re-privatised by an office nobility of heterogeneous (including bourgeois) social origins.

While war thus increased the absolutist claims of French monarchs over their subjects, it simultaneously paralysed their long-term financial and administrative capacity to rule. In short, there was a direct correlation between the intensification of warfare and office proliferation, the pursuit of international geopolitical accumulation and the domestic hollowing out of state power. Caught between spiralling military expenditures, its inability of radical administrative reform due to deeply entrenched vested interests, and the excessive and punitive taxation of the peasantry that further undermined relative low rates of productivity, pre-capitalist

---

[45] There were some successful, but always intermittent, attempts to tax the privileged through, for example, the *capitation* (head tax) and the *dixième* (income tax). "The serious fiscal pressure of the last years of the War of the Spanish Succession was bitterly resented by the privileged classes, who made it clear that their consent to the *dixième* had been for the duration of the war only: the regent conceded its withdrawal in 1717." Bonney, "The Eighteenth Century II. The Struggle for Great Power Status and the End of the Old Fiscal Regime", p. 325.

France underwent a series of fiscal crises.[46] This downward spiral, precipitated by the rising costs of warfare, royal debt-accumulation, office creation and sub-letting, over-taxation and inability to repay loans, contributed to the increasing dissatisfaction of a class of private financiers and office-holders that finally led to a general crisis within the ruling class over the form of the state, exploding at last in the French Revolution.[47] The conclusion is that the class dynamics and geopolitics of the *ancien régime* could not and did not lead to a rationalised, efficient, and "modern" bureaucratic state. In fact, military rivalry reinforced and intensified rather than resolved the pre-capitalist class tensions that structured Old Regime France. In a reversal of Charles Tilly's dictum that "war-made-states-and-states-made-war", it seems more plausible to argue that pre-capitalist states made war, and that war unmade these states.

Westphalian Geopolitics

These domestic dynamics had their correlate in early modern "international" relations. The replication of similar, though by no means identical, processes of "absolutist" state-formation across most regions of the Continent gave rise, *mutatis mutandis*, to a European system of "states" in which dynastic rulers acted as gigantic (geo-) political accumulators. It was this pre-capitalist complexion that gave the early modern continental system of "states" its over-militarised and bellicose character.[48]

Although the seventeenth century witnessed the rise of a territorially more sharply defined inter-state system (even though territoriality remained a fluid and exchangeable appendix of dynastic property rights of domination), this system still consisted of pre-capitalist "states", in which sovereignty continued to be personalised and tied to dynasties, rather than a de-personalised abstract notion of statehood. The inter-dynastic system remained defined by very specific foreign policy practices: the war-driven accumulation of territories; the predatory and compensatory logic of dynastic equilibrium (*convenance* rather than power-balancing); control over exclusive and monopolistic trading-routes secured by politico-military means; the elaborate dynastic strategies of territorial

---

[46] Hoffman, "Early Modern France, 1450–1700"; Kathryn Norberg, "The French Fiscal Crisis of 1788 and The Financial Origins of the Revolution of 1789", in Philip T. Hoffman and Kathryn Norberg (eds), *Fiscal Crises, Liberty, and Representative Government, 1450–1789* (Stanford, 1994), pp. 253–98.

[47] Comninel, George C., *Rethinking the French Revolution: Marxism and the Revisionist Challenge* (London, 1987).

[48] "Over-militarised" both in its quantitative sense regarding the frequency of war and its qualitative sense regarding the catastrophic ratio between war expenditures and fiscal income – the economic sustainability of war.

aggrandisement through marital policies; the resulting dynastic unions and composite monarchies and their flip-side, the endemic wars of succession, including a general drive towards territorial empire-building. In short, it was these very specific patterns of conflict and co-operation that characterised the logic and dynamics of "Westphalian Geopolitics". This interpretation relegates the Peace Treaty of Westphalia, consistently regarded in the discipline of International Relations as the founding moment of the modern inter-state system, to a pre-modern compact between pre-dominantly "absolutist" polities, irrespective of the special status of the Holy Roman Empire and the independence achieved by the Netherlands and Switzerland.

England: from Feudalism to Capitalism

If continental patterns of property relations, state-development and warfare seemed to generate a breakthrough neither to capitalist economic development nor to modern state-formation, why and how did the English trajectory so radically diverge? How did the rise of capitalist property relations in the agrarian economy affect the institutional changes in the British polity, and how did these changes re-position Britain in the international system?

Returning to the millennium and the Norman Conquest, a tight feudal hierarchy of Crown magnates and lords was carried over after 1066 from ducal Normandy, in which the King retained the royal ban. This enabled a form of close, though not of course conflict-free, intra-ruling class co-operation that led to the enserfment of large sections of the English peasantry (a portion of the peasantry remained free-holders) while ruling out the complete geographical fragmentation of power in eleventh-century France, characterised by the multiplicity of banal lords. Correlatively, this tight feudal hierarchy reduced inter-lordly competition over peasant surplus, so that the French pattern of royal support for peasant freedom and peasant property in order to turn lordly rents into royal taxes failed to develop. Instead, while English serfs were able to achieve personal freedom during the feudal crisis of the fourteenth century, they failed to secure property rights to their lands in striking contrast to their counterparts in France. Backed by royal justice, English lords transformed relatively secure copyholds (the customary form of peasant land use that was inscribed into manorial rolls) into competitive leaseholds for which they charged market rents while levying high entry fines.[49] In the process, the regulation of land use through customary law was replaced by Common Law. This resulted in the gradual dispossession of the peasantry, the consolidation of larger estates and the market-driven need by capitalist tenant-farmers to raise productivity in order to maintain their leases in a competitive

---

[49] Brenner, "The Agrarian Roots of European Capitalism".

land market. By the mid-seventeenth century, we see the large-scale emergence of peasant wage-labour, capitalist tenant-farmers and a socio-politically homogeneous class of entrepreneurial landlords – the overall consolidation of agrarian capitalism. This process was accompanied and intensified by the enclosure movement.

The English transition to agrarian capitalism led to a class-constellation in which an entrepreneurial aristocracy (supported by the new "interloping merchants") entered into a period of conflict with the monarchy, the old colonial merchant class and surviving feudal magnates over the form and control of the English state.[50] While the Stuarts tried to establish absolute authority, the capitalist aristocracy sought to construct a state that was responsive to the needs of private property protection, limited taxation and capital accumulation, encapsulated in the programmatic call for "political liberties". This conflict between "court" and "country" culminated in the Glorious Revolution and the new notion of the "King-in-Parliament" – a formula that essentially codified the Crown's concession of crucial powers to Parliament, which became the locus of British sovereignty. Between 1688 and 1715, the parliamentary classes consolidated their power by passing a series of fundamental constitutional acts – the Triennial Act, the Bill of Rights and others. Agrarian capitalism had generated a social property regime in which the political conflicts amongst the members of the ruling class over the distribution and terms of the rights of political accumulation were increasingly replaced by private forms of economic exploitation in the sphere of production, though this hardly took place overnight. The shift from personalised forms of domination and appropriation to de-personalised forms generated the formal, not substantive, separation between the economic and the political. Market and state, private and public, came to be increasingly differentiated.[51]

This new form of sovereignty, no longer personal-dynastic, but abstract-national sovereignty, drove the concomitant revolution in public administration – the Fiscal Revolution, the Financial Revolution, and the Military Revolution in particular. Core departments of government – the Treasury, the Excise and the Navy – turned from being patrimonial to being modern bureaucracies,[52] while public finance was drastically modernised through the establishment of the Bank of England and the "public debt".[53] This combination of revolutionary institutional innovations (Britain's naval superiority and exceptional fiscal-financial responsiveness in

---

[50] Brenner, Robert, *Merchants and Revolution: Commercial Change, Political Conflict, and London's Overseas Traders, 1550–1653* (Cambridge, 1993).

[51] Ellen Wood, *The Pristine Culture of Capitalism: A Historical Essay on Old Regimes and Modern States* (London, 1991).

[52] Brewer, "The Eighteenth-Century British State: Contexts and Issues".

[53] Peter Dickson, *The Financial Revolution in England: A Study in the Development of Public Credit, 1688–1756* (London, 1967); Cain, P.J. and Hopkins, A.G., *British Imperialism: Innovation and Expansion, 1688–1914* (London, 1993), pp. 58–84.

the face of external military pressure on the basis of a self-sustaining capitalist economy) gave the Hanoverian state the decisive *comparative economic, fiscal, and military advantage* over its continental competitors – British exceptionalism.[54] The re-organisation of public power conferred upon Britain a very special, in fact revolutionary, position within the European system of absolutist-dynastic states: a system that can now be regarded as "capitalism plus modern sovereignty in one country", surrounded by a sea of pre-capitalist polities.

It seems therefore insufficient to derive the character of the post-1688–1707 British state as a "fiscal-military" machine from the exigencies of geopolitical rivalry, as John Brewer has suggested,[55] without reconnecting state-development with domestic social dynamics and, in particular, social property relations. The post-1688 British state responded to military competition as vigorously and successfully as it did only on the back of a capitalist economy that generated the resources to finance war without the constant threat of bankruptcy and royal defaulting on debts which was so characteristic of France. And the unique fiscal responsiveness of the British polity was secured through the self-taxation of the capitalist aristocracy and merchants, which passed laws in Parliament that made tax-levels not only sustainable and tax-collection effective, but also made both socio-politically far less divisive compared with absolutist France.[56]

We cannot, however, simply extrapolate from the successful capitalist revolution the liberal idea of a "state-lite" embraced by the venerable Whig historiography. A liberal night-watchman state could not be realised in an international context that forced the British state to spend between seventy-five and eighty-five per cent of its annual expenditures between 1680 and 1780 on the army, navy and debt

---

[54] British fiscal exceptionalism is clearly recognised, but not sufficiently explained, by historians who otherwise subscribe to the geopolitical competition model. Patrick O'Brien, "Inseparable Connections: Trade, Economy, Fiscal State and the Expansion of Empire, 1688–1815", in P.J. Marshall (ed.) *The Oxford History of the British Empire, 2: The Eighteenth Century* (Oxford, 1998); Patrick O'Brien, "Fiscal Exceptionalism: Great Britain and its European Rivals from Civil War to Triumph at Trafalgar and Waterloo", in D. Winch and P. O'Brien (eds), *The Political Economy of British Historical Experience: 1688–1914* (Oxford, 2002); Patrick O'Brien, Patrick and Phillip A. Hunt, "England, 1485–1815", in R. Bonney (ed.) *The Rise of the Fiscal State in Europe, c.1200–1815* (Oxford, 1999), pp. 53–100; most recently Leandro Prados de la Escosura (ed.), *Exceptionalism and Industrialisation: Britain and its European Rivals, 1688–1815* (Cambridge, 2004).

[55] Brewer, "The Eighteenth-Century British State: Contexts and Issues", p. 56.

[56] It is therefore no "potent irony" (Hoffman and Norberg, *Fiscal Crises, Liberty, and Representative Government*, p. 310) to find that rates of taxation in absolutist states (Spain and France) were relatively light compared to states with representative institutions (Netherlands and post-1688 Britain). But none of this can be fully understood without relating the presence or absence of representative institutions to differential constellations of class relations and social property regimes.

servicing related to war.[57] Consequently, the militarisation of the British state was largely externally driven, not by international anarchy *per se*, but by a very specific inter-state order whose complexion remained defined by geopolitically accumulating pre-capitalist states. Thus there was what may be described as a geopolitical feedback-loop that massively continued to shape the construction of the British state: the making of a military super-power.

Still, the transformation of public power, property and class relations changed the position of Britain in the interstate system, forcing it to redefine and adapt its role to this wider strategic context. The Glorious Revolution not only started to rationalise the English state, but also occasioned a revolution in British foreign policy. This was characterised by a shift from dynastic to parliamentary foreign policy-making, no longer defined by the whims of dynasticism but rather by the "national interest", as articulated by the propertied classes in Parliament (the Hanoverian stemlands in Germany were regarded by Parliament as a constant source of irritation). As a result, Parliament adopted a very distinctive "dual foreign policy strategy" based, on the one hand, on power-balancing versus its rivals on the continent (a policy driven first and foremost by British "security interests") and, on the other hand, on unlimited commercial and colonial expansion overseas – the so-called "blue water policy".[58] Power balancing, with Britannia holding in her hand the scales, implied the disengagement from the continental dynastic game of territorial geopolitics with its endless wars of succession, political marriages and dynastic unions. After the Peace Treaty of Utrecht (1713–15), Britain largely withdrew from direct territorial aspirations on the Continent, yet started to regulate the states-system by means of rapidly changing alliances, hence giving rise to the image of "perfidious Albion", with its monetary subsidies and mercenary expedition corps to smaller powers always ready to counter any emergent continental hegemony, usually, of course, French. The Seven Years' War (1756–63) ideally

---

[57] Brewer, "The Eighteenth-Century British State: Contexts and Issues", p. 57; Bonney, "The Eighteenth Century II. The Struggle for Great Power Status and the End of the Old Fiscal Regime".

[58] Daniel A. Baugh, "Great Britain's Blue-Water Policy, 1689–1815", *International History Review*, 10/1 (1989): 33–58. Although Britain's commercial policy retained throughout the eighteenth century a mercantilist character, due to its international strategic context, its distinctiveness compared with the mercantilist policies of its continental rivals lay in two areas. "The first was the commercial flexibility and efficiency of the private economic sector in Britain compared with the state-run, rather rigid, mercantilism of some other western European powers. The second area was contextual and built around the state support provided by naval power and government taxes and loans – the 'fiscal-military state' – that allowed oceanic commerce to flourish in an era of international warfare." Kenneth Morgan, "Mercantilism and the British Empire, 1688–1815", in D. Winch and P. O'Brien (eds) *The Political Economy of British Historical Experience: 1688–1914* (Oxford, 2002), p. 167.

exemplifies British blue water strategy. While heavily subsidising Prussia in its struggle against Austria, France and Russia, Britain defeated France overseas and incorporated Canada, Florida, Louisiana and ex-French territories in India into her expanding colonial empire. To put it metaphorically, Britain started to "drop out" of the operative logic of continental "Westphalian" geopolitics while steering it by "remote control". Simultaneously, it built up its colonial empire overseas and rose to global hegemony by the end of the Seven Years' War, a position fortified for another century by Waterloo and sealed by the Vienna Settlement.

Ironically, it may well be the core theorem of the realist theory of international relations, namely the balance of power, that needs to be re-interpreted: not as the timeless regulator of "grand strategy" between great powers, but as the specific conduit for the unintended expansion of capitalism throughout the Continent during the nineteenth century and beyond. For it was through power-balancing, indeed through the adoption of the role of the balancer, that Britain was able to distribute military pressure on continental states. In response, continental states were forced to design political counter-strategies that would secure their military viability and fiscal-financial health so as to survive in the states-system. But these strategies always involved intense political conflict, both intra-ruling-class and inter-class, over the redefinition of the state and the re-arrangement of class relations, as either old forms of tax extraction were intensified or new modes of taxation and property relations introduced, with regionally highly specific outcomes. In the French case, Britain's naval superiority and power balancing finally cracked the shell of French "absolutism" and its pre-capitalist reproductive logic, and this is really the inner meaning of the Seven Years' War and the War of American Independence, which paved the way for 1789.[59]

Conclusion: Beyond the "War-Makes-States" Thesis

To conclude by way of returning to the central question: Was there an internal nexus between war and modern state-formation in the seventeenth century? Certainly, war was central to patterns of state-formation. The intensity, frequency

---

[59] For revealing figures on Anglo-French divergences with regard to war expenditures, public debts, costs of debt-servicing, taxation rates, tax compliance, interest rates and revenue-debt ratios, see Bonney "The Eighteenth Century II. The Struggle for Great Power Status and the End of the Old Fiscal Regime", pp. 336–45. Bonney attributes the inferior fiscal performance of pre-1789 France and its repeated failures in fiscal reform to "institutional obstacles", as if Old Regime institutions were not direct manifestations of definite social interests that reflected the specific configuration of very resilient social-property relations, but unspecified presences that had no social rationale. See also Cain and Hopkins, *British Imperialism*, p. 64.

and duration of warfare, however, cannot simply be derived from systemic geopolitical competition in a naturalised international context or from an autonomous techno-military determinism, but needs to be grounded in the domestic dynamics of social property regimes. Warfare was a social phenomenon and not a derivative of geopolitical imperatives or a function of technical innovations. Furthermore, the effects of warfare did not lead, in a straightforward or linear way, to a general strengthening and rationalisation of state power – at least not in regimes that we would like to refer to as "absolutist", and certainly not in the direction of the Weberian definition of the modern state. If anything, the crippling costs of warfare, despite repeated attempts to broaden the tax basis, to invent new and more centralised modes of taxation, and to rationalise public administration, usually met with stiff resistance by entrenched social interests – leading, at least in the French case, to the hypertrophic growth of a partly re-privatised state-apparatus, revolving round office venality and clientelism. Given that social property relations, regime types and the temporalities of development varied quite dramatically in early modern Europe (even though the dominant state-form was "absolutist"), there is a greater need to account for European variations and specificities such as the Holy Roman Empire, the Polish "crowned aristocratic republic", oligarchic merchant republics, city-leagues, and others. This especially raises the need to reconsider the ability of smaller states with a smaller tax-basis to survive in an otherwise hostile international environment. War cannot have been the "great selector" that either led to functionally equivalent "conflict-units", nor could it invariably have "crowded out" smaller polities that failed to comply functionally with the imperatives of international rivalry by transforming themselves into institutional "fiscal-military" states. Across Europe, modern state-formation was a very uneven and geopolitically mediated process, which began with the formation of capitalism in late medieval and early modern England and its effects on the post-1688 British state and did not extend to continental states until the nineteenth century and beyond. This history, in its proper geopolitical context, remains to be written. The theoretical conclusion is that, while all early modern polities were drawn into the vortex of international rivalry, social property relations and the associated struggles over power determined to a large degree state-development, fiscal-military performance and state-collapse.

Still, the Neo-Hintzean literature has made one important argument that requires reflection. Both Mann and Skocpol have argued that capitalism in and of itself cannot account for Europe's multi-territorial complexion. There is no direct generative link from capitalism to a system of states. But the *historical* observation that a states-system preceded capitalism does not warrant the *theoretical* conclusion that such a system represents a trans-historically independent or autonomous structure (level of analysis) which affirms the call for theoretical pluralism. Quite the contrary, a territorially preconfigured pre-capitalist multistate system was the result of a long history of class conflicts over sources of income (land and people) that began in the eleventh and intensified in the fourteenth and the seventeenth centuries, crystallising into a recognisable multi-territorial order during the early modern period. It was not "states" that competed against each other for power and security, but ruling classes organised in territorially centralising communities that struggled over their relative international share of territory and other sources of income. The fragmentation of the European ruling class into multiple and separately organised states was neither theoretically necessary nor historically contingent, but it is nevertheless retrospectively intelligible. Capitalism and a political pluriverse are chronologically and causally not coeval, but pre-capitalist geopolitical accumulation and a pluriverse are. Capitalism and the states-system are the diachronic *disiecta membra*, synchronised in one contradictory totality.

PART III
Modern Law of Nations – from Spanish Scholastics to Grotius

Chapter 4
The Law of Nations and the Doctrine of *Terra Nullius*

David Boucher

Pope Benedict XVI, responsible under Pope John Paul II for counteracting the dangerous tendencies in Liberation Theology, addressed the Bishops of Latin America in Brazil on 13 May 2007. Pope Benedict thanked God for bestowing the great gift of the Christian faith upon the indigenous peoples, which had served for five centuries to animate the continent. Its significance, he argued, consisted in the coming of that God whom their ancestors had been in search of, unknowingly, in their own religious quests. To compound the insult, Pope Benedict XVI added that at no point had the introduction of Christianity alienated the pre-Columbian cultures. Nor had it been the imposition of a foreign culture. Authentic cultures, he argued, are open and receptive to other cultures, "hoping to reach universality through encounter and dialogue with other ways of life".[1] Pope Paul III had been of a similar mind almost five centuries earlier. In 1537, he announced that "the Indians are truly men and ... they are not only capable of understanding the Catholic faith, but, according to our information, ... desire exceedingly to receive it".[2]

The seventeenth century in Europe was a time of an immense opening of horizons, in which the new continent of America was firmly embedded in considerations of the territorial expansion of the state related to what was permissible under natural law and the law of nations. At the heart of conceptualising the relationship between Europe and the Americas was the issue of property, an issue absolutely essential to defining one's political *persona* from wherever one might hail. The capacity to own and cultivate land, the obligation to conform to natural law, violation of which provided grounds for waging just war, and the opportunity for Europeans to enslave American Indians and to appropriate their lands with or without their consent, afforded numerous criteria that the Indians could rarely, or barely, meet.

---

[1] Pope Benedict, "Apostolic Journey of his Holiness Benedict XVI to Brazil on the Occasion of the Fifth General Conference of the Bishops of Latin America and the Caribbean: Address of his Holiness Benedict XVI" (Rome, 2007) 1–2 (http://www.vatican.va/holy_father/benedict_xvi/speeches/2007/may/ documents/hf_ben-xvi_spe_20070513_conference-aparecida_en.html).

[2] Lewis Hanke, *The Spanish Struggle for Justice in the Conquest of America* (Philadelphia, 1949), p. 73.

In this chapter I should like to explore the practical implications of European ideas of natural law, natural rights and the law of nations with specific reference to the idea of *terra nullius*. The cases of the European encounters with the American Indians and Australian Aborigines provide an excellent illustration of how such abstract doctrines, with their universal standards and applicability, led to widely differing conclusions when translated into concrete social and political contexts requiring practical prescriptions and imperative injunctions, and ultimately could provide justifications for occupation and ownership even among apologists for the Indians. I want to suggest that while the idea *terra nullius* was closely allied with the right to husbandry, it was more fundamentally the duty to cultivate the land to its utmost capacity that provided the moral justification for appropriating "wasteland" and under-cultivated land. Of ultimate importance, however, was the fact that despite appearances even the concession of land rights to indigenous peoples did not at the same time concede sovereignty. Even more humanitarian Europeans from the seventeenth to the twentieth century believed that Indians were primitive, but that with proper training in the Christian religion, European agricultural methods and literacy they could become civilized.

The Idea of *Terra Nullius*

The Latin *terra* means land, earth, or ground, and *nullius* means no one's; hence vacant or empty land, or at least unoccupied by anyone who qualifies as capable of ownership. The idea of *terra nullius* has become increasingly prevalent in recent discussions of the legitimacy of European expansionism, but especially so in the context of the "history wars" in Australia. I want to suggest that while ideas that constitute the "doctrine" of *terra nullius* were important, and while most natural law jurists acknowledged a right to take possession of vacant lands, there were other much more fundamental arguments that justified European expansionism in America, Australia and Africa, namely that the indigenous peoples were in dereliction of their duty to God to cultivate the land and make it as productive as possible.

This contention rests upon a number of propositions:

1. That universal principles were used as instruments of oppression, and instead of conferring rights and duties upon all, were the preserve of only those who qualified. In other words, universal rights were almost invariably special rights.
2. That theories of property and just war were fundamental to the application of the principles of natural law, natural rights and the law of nations.

3. That, contrary to the widespread contention that the likes of Grotius, Pufendorf and Rachel secularised the natural law and natural rights traditions, these traditions rested on the obligation to obey the natural law principally as a duty to God.[3] The Indians therefore had a duty to God to cultivate their land, which they singularly failed to fulfil.

The third proposition is probably most contentious because it denies current orthodoxy, as expressed, for example, by Arthur Nussbaum, A.S. McGrade and James Griffin. Arthur Nussbaum firmly believes that both Grotius and Pufendorf may justifiably have laid claim to secularising natural law.[4] Griffin, for example, contends that the use of reason as the means of discovering natural law and as the ground of our obligation to obey it is the hallmark of modern natural rights theory. In my view, he is wrong to attribute these ideas to thinkers such as Grotius, Puffendorf and Locke.[5] A.S. McGrade is representative of the prevailing view in suggesting that during the period encompassing John of Salisbury (c. 1115–76), Richard Hooker (1554–1600) and Francisco Suarez (1548–1617), the theory of natural rights arose out of the religious view of society. After this time, McGrade suggests, the politics of right more or less dispensed with religion.[6]

It is my contention, however, that even natural rights theorists who are said to have secularised the tradition, such as Hugo Grotius (1583–1645), Samuel von Pufendorf (1632–94), John Locke (1632–1704) and Johann Wolfgang Textor (1638–1701), retain such a heavy residue of absolute theological presuppositions that their arguments would be unsustainable without the religious outlook upon which they depend. It is not my contention that all natural law and natural rights thinkers ultimately rely on God as the ground of obligation.[7] My claim is more modest: those thinkers who have been most identified with secularising natural

---

[3] This proved to be a particularly contentious issue at the conference and I therefore go to some pains to substantiate it. I would particularly like to thank Thomas Pink and Kees van der Pijl for their comments. I have elaborated some of the themes in this chapter in my book *The Limits of Ethics in International Relations: Natural Law, Natural Rights, Human Rights in Transition* (Oxford, 2008).

[4] Arthur Nussbaum, *A Concise History of the Law of Nations* (New York, 1953).

[5] James Griffin, *On Human Rights* (Oxford, 2008), pp. 10–12.

[6] A.S. McGrade, "Rights, Natural Rights, and The Philosophy of Law", in N. Kretzmann, Antony Kenny, J. Pinborg (eds), *The Cambridge History of Later Medieval Philosophy: From the Rediscovery of Aristotle to the Disintegration of Scholasticism 1100–1600* (Cambridge, 1982), p. 739.

[7] Thomas Pink, "Natural Law and the Theory of Moral Obligation", in Jill Kraye and Risto Saarinen (ed.) *Moral Philosophy on the Threshold of Modernity* (Dordrecht, 2005), pp. 31–50. Thomas Pink, "Moral Obligation", in Anthony O'Hear (ed.), *Modern Moral Philosophy* (Cambridge, 2004), pp. 159–86.

law and natural rights tended *not* to abandon God as the ultimate source of obligation. Why, indeed, would they want to, given the contemporary conditions of belief?

It is important to distinguish in the classic writers between the method or means by which we come to know natural law and the grounds for our obligation to obey it. My view is that in the earlier thinkers who are significant for the development of natural law and the law of nations, reason enables us to know the law and God ultimately obliges us to obey it. Emer Vattel (1714–67) saw this distinction very clearly and was aware of what was at stake. He differed from those who wished to posit God as the foundation of obedience to natural law, preferring instead a complicated combination of motive, interest and reason.[8] He says that "In no way does it detract from the authority of God to say that everything he ordains for us in natural laws is so *fine* and *useful* in itself that we would be *obliged* to adopt it, even if God had not ordered it".[9] For revealed laws such as those we find in the Scriptures, Vattel does not deny that God is the source of obligation. For natural laws, however, we know them to be the will of God only "by the *reasons* for these laws".[10] This hardly constitutes a secularisation of the tradition. Indeed, it still inhabits the same universe of discourse as those who posit *Him* as the foundation of obligation.

As Charles Taylor has argued, belief in God was almost unchallenged because the "conditions of belief" made it axiomatic that alternative views were inconceivable for most people. Owing to a transformation in those conditions of belief, it is no longer axiomatic to believe in God because there are evident alternatives that make it more difficult to sustain faith.[11] In the seventeenth century, if a philosopher did not rely at some stage in his argument on God as the ultimate foundation of obligation, sometimes alongside other compelling reasons, we would need to seek an explanation for the omission; in contemporary society, it is the inclusion of such grounds that demands an explanation.

From the time of the early Christians to the seventeenth century and beyond, the dominant view was that all authority ultimately derives from God. It is difficult to see what would give moral and intellectual force not only to the arguments but also to the obligations and rights that individuals and nations have under the natural law had God not willed it so. St. Paul, for example, contends that "No authority exists save by God's sanction; such as do exist have been appointed

---

[8] Emer D. Vattel, "Essay on the Foundation of Natural Law and on the First Principle of Obligation Men Find Themselves Under to Observe Laws", in Béla Kappossy and Richard Whatmore (ed.), *The Law of Nations* by Emer D. Vattel (Indianapolis, 2008), pp. 747–71.

[9] Vattel, "Essay on the Foundation of Natural Law", p. 760.

[10] Vattel, "Essay on the Foundation of Natural Law", pp. 757–8.

[11] See Charles Taylor, *A Secular Age* (Cambridge, Mass., 2007).

by God".[12] It is common during the later medieval period explicitly to invoke God as the ground for obedience to the natural law. Gratian, for example, in *The Decretum Gratiani* (c. 1140), contends that any principle that can be determined as a pre-conventional natural right must be regarded to be a reflection of divine wisdom and will. He declares that "nothing is commanded by natural right except that which God wishes to be done, and nothing forbidden except that which God forbids to be done".[13]

Grotius, Pufendorf, Textor and Rachel suggest that the law of nature pertains only to humans, and is obligatory in its force. An indubitable and immutable human nature provides the foundation for natural law. Starting from the basis of our natural sociableness, Grotius, for instance, suggests that proofs of the natural law are almost as self-evident as the data we receive through the senses.[14] Natural law is so inextricably tied to human nature that even if God did not exist, and He had no interest in the welfare of humanity, the law would remain valid.[15] This has often been taken to be Grotius's secularisation of the natural law. Such a view is anachronistic.

When one examines Grotius's argument closely, it is evident that his statement is partially rhetorical, and what lies at the heart of our obligations is God: as Jean Barbeyrac comments in his notes to Grotius's text, "the Duty and Obligation, or the indispensable Necessity of conforming to these Ideas, and Maxims, necessarily supposes a superior Power, a supreme Master of Mankind, who can be no other than the Creator, or supreme Divinity".[16] Jean Jacques Burlamqui, the author of *The Principles of Natural Law* writes in a similar vein. He argues that it is obvious from Grotius's mode of expression that Grotius did not wish to exclude the divine will from natural law. While reason is a source of obligation, "it could never produce of itself so effectual an obligation, as when it is joined with the divine will".[17]

Grotius, in fact, explicitly contends that there are compelling reasons for ascribing the principles of the natural law to God. God has made them so evident and clear even to those "less capable of strict Reasoning" that He forbids us to give in to impetuous passions which are contrary to our own and others' interests and

---

[12] St. Paul, The Letters of St. Paul to seven churches and three friends, with the Letter to the Hebrews, trans. Arthur S. Way (London, 1926), Romans, XIII, p. i.

[13] Cited in Jean Porter, "Custom, Ordinance and Natural Rights in Gratian's *Decretum*", in Amanda Perreau-Saussine and James Bernard Murphy (eds), *The Nature of Customary Law: Legal, Historical and Philosophical Perspectives* (Cambridge, 2007), p. 89.

[14] Hugo Grotius, *The Rights of War and Peace* (1625), trans. Jean Barbeyrac, three books, edited with an introduction by Richard Tuck (Indianapolis, 2005), Book II, chap. xxiii, I.

[15] Grotius, *Rights of War and Peace*, Book I, Preliminary Discourse: § 11.

[16] Grotius, *Rights of War and Peace*, Preliminary Discourse, ns 1 to § XI.

[17] Jean-Jacques Burlamaqui, *The Principles of Natural and Politic Law* (Indianapolis, 2006), p. 191.

which divert us from conforming to the rules of reason.[18] In the *Mare Liberum* (*The Free Sea*) Grotius goes further and suggests that God directly insinuates certain precepts into men's minds, which are "sufficient to induce obligation even if no reason is apparent".[19]

It is true that Pufendorf did not believe that God had inscribed the natural law in men's hearts. He believed himself to be in conformity with orthodoxy when he said, "Most are agreed, that the Law of Nature is to be drawn from Man's Reason; flowing from the true Current of that Faculty, when unperverted".[20] Yet not only does God endow us with the reason we use for coming to know the natural law; the reason that we are obliged to follow natural law is because it is God's "Will and Command we should act according to that Law".[21]

Despite the fact that Pufendorf is acknowledged to derive the natural law from God, and explicitly rejected the tentative Grotian suggestion that the natural law would retain its force even if God did not exist, Nussbaum argues that in practical terms Pufendorf is so little influenced by theological and religious sentiments that he has come to be "considered the true founder of a secular law of nature".[22] This flies completely in the face of the evidence. Pufendorf explicitly states that the dictates of reason do not alone achieve the power and dignity of laws. A higher principle must be invoked in order to instil an immutable obligation. There can be no law without a sovereign and, as sovereign of the universe, God is the creator and enforcer of natural law. Natural law, from which our natural rights derive, is the creation of God, who, should we transgress against it, punishes our actions. Pufendorf argues that "the obligation of Natural Law proceeds from God himself, the great Creator and supreme Governor of Mankind; who by Virtue of his Sovereignty hath bound Men to the observation of it".[23]

The same can be said for Rachel, Textor and Burlamaqui. For Rachel, it is not reason that gives natural law its obligatory force. The source of natural law is divine providence, and its obligatory force derives from the same source: "For if the obligation of every law derives its authority in paramount fashion from God, Natural Law receives its authority in the highest possible degree from that same source".[24] Johann Wolfgang Textor perhaps has a stronger claim to having secularised

---

[18] Grotius, *Rights of War and Peace*, Preliminary Discourse, § 13.
[19] Hugo Grotius, *The Free Sea*, trans. Richard Hakluyt, with an Introduction by David Armitage (Indianapolis, 2004), p. 105.
[20] Pufendorf, *The Law of Nature and Nations*, Book II, chap. iii, § XIII.
[21] Pufendorf, *The Law of Nature and Nations*, Book II, chap. iii, § XIII.
[22] Nussbaum, A Concise History of the Law of Nations, p. 148.
[23] Pufendorf, *Law of Nature and Nations*, Book II, chap. iii, § 20.
[24] Samuel Rachel, *Dissertations on The Law of Nature and of Nations* [1676], trans. John Pawley Bate, with an introduction by Ludwig von Bar (Washington D.C., 1916), Diss. I, § xlv.

the natural law. He follows and modifies the theories of Grotius and Hobbes. The law of nature for him issues directly from natural reason. God, however, implants this reason in men and one of the self-evident laws of nature is that we must fulfil our obligations to God. Without God, whose existence Textor goes to some pains to prove, there is no basis for obligation and civil society would collapse.[25]

Even in the mid-eighteenth century, natural law was still being inextricably linked to God's authority. Jean Jacques Burlamaqui (1694–1748), an influential Swiss jurist whose chief works are *Principles of Natural Law* (1747) and *Principles of Political Law* (1751), set out to demonstrate the efficacy of natural law by relating it to its original source in God's rule, and to human reason and moral instinct. International and domestic law were, for him, based on natural law. Burlamaqui contends that the law of nature consists in certain principles of right reason that teach us what is right and wrong according to the extent to which this law agrees or disagrees with man's rational and sociable nature. Hence God, the author of nature, commands or forbids those actions. The obligation to obey the natural law, then, is ultimately a duty to God.

> As soon as we have acknowledged a creator, it is evident that he has a supreme right to lay his commands on man, to prescribe rules of conduct to him, and to subject him to laws; and it is no less evident that man for his part finds himself, by his natural constitution, under an obligation of subjecting his actions to the will of this supreme being. [26]

In essence the rationalist who believes that the natural law is right because it is rational, and the voluntarist who believes it is right because God wills it so, on the whole maintain that obligations to obey it rest on God.

The Implications for *Terra Nullius*

I want now to look at the idea of *terra nullius* and how what I have just argued has a bearing on it. The doctrine of vacant or unoccupied lands, available for others to acquire and appropriate was a central pillar in conceptualising relations between European and non-European nations, that is, between civilized and barbarous and savage societies. It was an important issue because "unoccupied" did not literally merely mean "uninhabited", it also came to mean under-used, uncultivated or

---

[25] Johann Wolfgang Textor, *Synopsis of the Law of Nations* [1680], trans. John Pawley Bate, with an introduction by Ludwig von Bar (Washington D.C., 1916), VI, pp. 1–28.
[26] Jean-Jacques Burlamaqui, *Principles of Natural and Politic Law* (ed.) Peter Korkman (Indianapolis, 2006), Part I, chap. 1, § xi, p. 129. Cf. Part II, chap. 5, §§ vi and vii, pp. 168–9.

under-cultivated land available for appropriation, and in this respect it was an important consideration in the partition of Africa.

The term *terra nullius* itself has come to be emblematic of some of the more pernicious acts of Europeans perpetrated upon Australian Aboriginals after they took possession of the continent.[27] The idea that vacant land may be occupied through necessity, for example, was well established among the Greeks and Romans. In order to alleviate overpopulation in the polis or city, establishing a colony elsewhere provided a practical solution to a pressing problem.

Michael Connor and Merete Borch deny that there is evidence of any body of opinion that regarded indigenous lands as *terra nullius*. Connor simply rejects international juristic and philosophical opinion as having no legal substance and irrelevant to his claim that the term itself was not used by government officers and settlers in the eighteen century or before.[28] To say that it has no legal substance, however, is to overstate the case. Michael Connor accuses Henry Reynolds,[29] a leading proponent of the *terra nullius* thesis, of fabricating the doctrine on the grounds that it had no basis in British nor European law, and that his use of Vattel to substantiate his case was illegitimate in that Vattel was "not making up rules of law for men to follow, he was a writer, a publicist, a theorist".[30] Merete Borch has suggested that "it is difficult to see that any of the frequently quoted international jurists provided argumentation for seeing indigenous land as *terra nullius* either during the eighteenth century nor before it".[31] This view, I think, is mistaken.

Connor's criticism assumes an excessively positivistic conception of international law, and Borch's is simply contrary to the evidence. The law of nations, or *ius gentium*, was not a law enacted by an international legislature nor was it enforced in international courts; it was legal in the sense that it was inferred from the accepted practice of "civilised" states as either directly derivative from the natural law or from international custom, but also from the opinions of learned theologians, philosophers and jurists. It was a law that comprised a curious amalgam of moral, political and legal arguments in the justification of state and individual practice.

There was no doubting its existence, as Suarez suggests, because it "is assumed by all authorities to be an established fact, or so we gather from their very frequent use of

---

[27] Stuart Banner, "Why *Terra Nullius*? Anthropology and Property Law in Early Australia", *Law and History Review*, 23 (2005): 1.
[28] Michael Connor, *The Invention of Terra Nullius: Historical and Legal Fictions on the Foundation of Australia* (Sydney, 2003), p. 4.
[29] Henry Reynolds, *The Law of the Land* (Ringwood, Melbourne, 1992).
[30] Connor, *The Invention of* Terra Nullius, pp. 23 and 25.
[31] Merete Borch, "Rethinking the Origins of *Terra Nullius*", *Australian Historical Studies*, 117 (2001): 232.

the term".[32] One of its distinguishing features is that its precepts "are not established in written form" and "it consequently differs in this respect from all written civil law, even from that imperial law which is applicable to all".[33] Furthermore, the law of nations differs from natural law in that the latter is truly universal, common to all peoples and accepted by everyone. The law of nature can fail to be observed only by those in error. It may not, however, always be observed by all nations, and what is considered by some to be the law of nations may not be considered so by others, and therefore "without fault fail to be observed".[34] As Samuel Rachel maintains, "the law of nations is employed as a common bond of obligation; and peoples of different forms of government and of different size lie under the control of these rules, which depend for their efficacy upon mutual good faith".[35]

It is incontrovertible that the authorities on the Law of Nations generally acknowledged a right, to the occupation of unoccupied lands, and in some instances even if the lands were under the eminent domain of a recognizable sovereign. The basic premise among jurists and philosophers in the early modern period regarding property rights was that God gave the whole world in common to mankind, and those portions that remained unoccupied or uncultivated, which did not necessarily mean upon which no people resided, were available for legitimate occupation.

Vitoria, Ayala, Suarez, Gentile, Locke, Wolff and Vattel, for example, contend that people have an obligation to cultivate the land, and if they do not they have no right to prevent those who would. Although Vitoria did not as such disagree with the doctrine, he denied that mere discovery, *ius inventionis*, was a legitimate claim to ownership. Occupation of land for him is a manner of appropriating territory that has no owner, that is, *illa quae sunt deserta, quod in nullius bonis est*.[36] For him, under natural law, all men originally had a right to everything. Because of God's premonition of Man's sinfulness, He made provision for private property in permissive natural law in so far as men could come together and agree that "You take this and you this and I will have this".[37] Vitoria was in no doubt that the American Indians had ownership rights and that not all their land was *res nullius*. *Res nullius* is not an exact equivalent of *terra nullius*. The former refers

---

[32] Francisco Suarez, *Selections from Three Works*, translation of the 1621 edition by Gwladys L. Williams, Ammi Brown and John Waldron (Washington, 1944), Book II, chap. XVII, § 1, p. 325.

[33] Suarez, *Selections from Three Works*, Book II, chap. XIX, § 6, p. 345.

[34] Suarez, *Selections from Three Works*, Book II, chap. XIX, § 2, p. 342.

[35] Rachel, *Law of Nations*, Diss. II, § I, p. 157.

[36] Coleman Phillipson, "Franciscus A Victoria (1480–[15]46) International Law and War", *Journal of the Society of Comparative Legislation*, New Ser., 15/2 (1915): 148.

[37] Cited in Brian Tierney, "Permissive Natural Law and Property: Gratian to Kant", *Journal of the History of Ideas*, 62 (2001): 389.

to items in general without an owner, such as buffalo roaming the range, which are common to everyone, or to things that cannot be owned, such as the air we breathe or the oceans we sail.

Balthazar Ayala contends that under natural law, in primitive times, all things were in common and no individual owned anything. Community of goods, however, did not suit man's debased nature. Natural reason informed the law of nations that a system of private property was required to mitigate the sinfulness of mortals.[38] Suarez, using Isidore's *Etymologies* (Bk. V, chap. vi), contends that *ius gentium*, or the natural law, confers upon individuals the right to occupy places not previously occupied by others.[39] Alberico Gentili (1552–1608), starting from the premise that humanity comprises a universal society, claiming Tacitus as an authority, and developing an idea from Thomas More's *Utopia*, concluded that exiles from their own countries were entitled, out of necessity, to wage offensive wars in their quest for habitable territory, and that vacant lands may be colonised by people who need them for their own use. Unoccupied land belongs to no one and those who take it have a right to do so. Nature abhors a vacuum. Under the rule of Spain, he argues, almost all of the New World remains unoccupied. The implication was that the right to occupy it by means of possession was still valid.[40]

Wolff confirms that uninhabited lands may be colonised and appropriated because they are the property of no one. The nation appropriating the vacant land acquires property rights to it and sovereignty over it. Unlike Locke, for example, he acknowledges ownership and sovereignty by nations over the lands they occupy, even if those lands are waste and barren. Nevertheless, since every nation should perfect its condition, such land that lays vacant should be given to foreigners.[41]

Vattel suggests that "Every nation is obliged by the law of nature to cultivate the land that has fallen to its share", and that "The cultivation of the soil … is … an obligation imposed by nature upon man".[42] The land would simply not feed its inhabitants if it were allowed to lay vacant. It may have been all right in primitive

---

[38] Balthazar Ayala, *On the Law of War And on Duties Connected with War And on Military Discipline*, [1582], trans. John Pawley Bate (Washington D.C., 1912), Book II, chap. v, [16], p. 41

[39] Francisco Suarez, *Selections from Three Works*, translation of the 1621 edition by Gwladys L. Williams, Ammi Brown and John Waldron (Washington, 1944), p. 837.

[40] Alberico Gentili, *De Iure Belli Libre Tres*, translation of the edition of 1612 by John C. Rolfe, and introduced by Coleman Phillipson (Oxford, 1933), Book I, chap. xvii, p. 81 [131–2].

[41] Christian Wolff, *The Law of Nations Treated According to Scientific Method in which the Natural Law of Nations is carefully distinguished from that which is voluntary, stipulative and customary* [1764], trans. Joseph H. Drake, with an introduction by O. Nippold (Oxford, 1934), chap. III, § 275– § 292, pp. 40–152.

[42] Vattel, *The Law of Nations*, Book I, chap. vii, § 81, p. 129.

times to live the life of hunting and gathering, but now that the population has greatly increased each nation "is obliged by the law of nature to cultivate the land that has fallen to its share".[43]

There was a distinction to be made, then, between the use of the land by American Indians and ownership, between occupation and possession. Even though this was not the widespread practice in America, it nevertheless informed the famous *Johnson v. M'Intosh* decision, which was itself evidentially supported with reference to the authorities on the law of nations. It is a widespread misperception that Europeans refused to acknowledge Indian land rights, a myth perpetuated by the classic *Johnson v. M'Intosh* (1823) ruling by Chief Justice John Marshall to the effect that, because the English had not recognised the Indians as property owners, neither should the United States.[44] In fact, there was widespread acknowledgment of Indian property rights, often for the benefit of the settlers who ruthlessly exploited them, rather than from any altruistic motives or moral conscience. Even when land rights were granted to indigenous peoples, governments felt little compunction in seizing them if their value became reassessed.

Prior to this decision, however, perception had already deviated from the fact. It came to be a widespread belief that Indians were hunter-gathers, and for centuries the law of nations had not acknowledged that they owned the land on which they hunted. Indeed, if agriculturalists settled on the same land, it was they who were deemed its owners.[45]

In Grotius's view, for example, God had given the world to man in common, but also made provision for the acquisition of property through individual labour and industry as long as this acquisition conformed to two primary conditions, or natural laws. These were, first, that everyone may use common things without causing harm to others, and second that everyone be content with his portion and abstain from coveting another's.[46] For Grotius there is a difference between "occupation" (*occupation*) and "ownership" (*dominium*). Occupation is a natural right that pertains to self-preservation. There is a rudimentary form of private property, in owning one's body, for example, and that extends to the appropriation of things such as fruit and animals for preserving that body. "Ownership" (*dominium*) is an institution created by civil society and is the result of agreement.

---

[43] Vattel, *The Law of Nations*, Book I, chap. vii, § 81, p. 35.
[44] Stuart Banner, *How the Indians Lost Their Land: Law and Power on the Frontier* (London, 2005), p. 11.
[45] Banner, *How the Indians Lost Their Land*, p. 168.
[46] Hugo Grotius, *The Free Sea*, trans. Richard Hakluyt, with an introduction by David Armitage (Indianapolis, 2004), p. 6.

Various legal cases, including *Johnson versus M'Intosh* (1823) in the United States, served to reinforce the distinction between occupation and ownership. They reaffirmed the belief that when John Cabbot discovered and symbolically occupied North America in 1497, he delivered full proprietary title to Henry VII and the natives either became trespassers or attained some other title. They, and other aboriginals, were deemed licensees of the Crown, allowed rights of occupancy on sufferance, but not of ownership unless explicitly given such title by the Crown.[47] The implication is an affirmation of Grotius's point. If the Crown or government conferred land rights, then those rights qualify them for protection by the legal system just as the rights of any other American, Canadian or Australian who derived his titles from the government or Crown. What the idea of vacant land effectively meant for Grotius was that proprietary or ownership rights were deemed to have validity only within the context of a system of law.

There was a distinction to be made, then, between the use of the land by American Indians and ownership, between occupation and possession. Thomas Hobbes (1588–1679), although less fulsome in his discussion, subscribed to the view of More, Gentili and Grotius that the lands of the Americas were plentiful enough to accommodate a people that was still increasing in population and needed to expand into new territories. This did not give settlers a right to massacre the natives, but they could constrain them to live closer together.[48]

The idea of wasteland was to figure prominently in Locke's justification of acquisition. The fact that the land was deemed empty was justification for occupancy, but occupancy in itself did not, in the eyes of many apologists, give sufficient grounds for title or ownership. As with Grotius, occupancy for Locke had to be equated with possession. The principle of appropriating waste territories therefore needed to be supplemented with a theory of property that established a moral title to the ownership of land. Vattel was also quite clear that occupancy was not enough: "The law of nations will, therefore, not acknowledge the property and sovereignty of a nation over any uninhabited countries, except those of which it has really taken actual possession, in which it has formed settlements, or of which it makes actual use".[49]

Various strategies were adopted to effect opportunities of appropriation and ownership. Charles Mills argues that white settlers joined in expropriation contracts, which created societies, with the clear implication that no society had previously existed.[50] James Tully has argued that European theories of property

---

[47] Geoffrey Lester, *Inuit Territorial Rights in the Canadian Northwest Territories* (Canada, Published by Tungavik Federation of Nunavut, 1984), p. 3.

[48] Thomas Hobbes, *Leviathan*, ed. Richard Tuck (Cambridge, 1991), p. 239.

[49] Emer Vattel, *The Law of Nations*, ed. Richard Whatmore (Indianapolis, 2008), Book I, chap. xviii, § 208, p. 215.

[50] Charles W. Mills, *The Racial Contract* (Ithica, 1997), pp. 13, 24 and 49–50.

after settlement served to misrecognise the systems of property and the political organizations of the aboriginal peoples they encountered.[51] Carole Pateman extends these ideas to talk about a specific form of Charles Mill's expropriation contract. This she calls the "settler contract", among whose principal components are the right to husbandry and the establishment of sovereignty where the natives were deemed insufficiently organized and civilized to conceive of, let alone exercise, it. On the strict logic of the settler contract natives were excluded, as in Australia, or on the modified logic were afforded certain concessionary rights and partially accommodated, as in America under English settlement.[52]

Where there was a recognisable social structure and system of authority – and this, of course, never went uncontested, irrespective of religion – the peoples were deemed to have the same rights and duties under natural law as Europeans. From this point of view the universality of the natural law, and of natural rights, appears to work for the benefit of indigenous peoples who conformed to universal (that is, to European) standards of social and political relations. The application of natural law, and the law of nations, uniquely the product of the western political experience, were conceived as universal, local variations on which, at least in terms of fundamental beliefs, were regarded as violations.

Natural law and natural rights were the universal standards employed by Europeans to judge what they encountered and to arrive at answers to the most fundamental of questions. There could be no exceptions to these rational universal standards, but there might be mitigating circumstances, such as invincible ignorance, that made some initial judgments less severe. Few Europeans would have denied that there were natural rights, and that all humans had them by the mere fact of being human: what was at issue was whether the American Indians met the qualifications, or fell short in some way, of being fully human. If they qualified, then like every human they possessed natural rights and participated in the universal community of humankind. This, however, was a doubled-edged sword. Far from offering the American Indians unqualified protections against violations by Europeans, it presented a set of criteria from which deviation constituted a just cause for war, during which many of these rights were in abeyance. There were disputes as to the circumstances that gave rise to just cause, or about practices that invited what we would now call humanitarian intervention, but few would argue that there were no conditions that could not give rise to the justifiable acquisition of territories and dominion in the Americas on the principle of the natural right of *terra nullius* or on grounds of violations of natural rights by the Indians against their own peoples or against Europeans.

---

[51] James Tully, "Aboriginal Property and Western Theory: Recovering a Middle Ground", *Social Philosophy and Policy*, 11 (1999): 158.
[52] Carole Pateman and Charles Mills, *Contract and Domination* (Cambridge, 2007).

The appearance of the universalism of natural rights was undermined in practice by what amounted to an imposition of European Christian standards of conduct and rationality. Fundamentally, Francisco Vitoria's arguments, for example, rest upon universal rights, which take priority over those of specific communities, the contravention of which justifiably legitimates intervention by a foreign state to restore rights and punish the perpetrators of the wrong. Indeed, Vitoria believed in a universal community that was not merely confined to Christians. Each state has a right and a legal obligation to compel rogue states to conform to international law and to the customary law of the *societa gentium*. Vitoria assumed that not only Christians, but also the American Indians, could discover natural law by the exercise of right reason, and that just as the Spanish were obliged to act in a corresponding manner, so too they had the right to expect the Indians to do likewise. The laudable intention to constrain heavily armed Spanish soldiers in their relations with native Indians by reference to the natural law broke down ultimately when the Indians acted in a manner at variance with that law, as Vitoria conceived it.[53] The gospels (Mark 16: 15) command Christians to spread the word throughout the world, and if the Indians obstructed them, or punished the converted, the Spaniards "may take up arms and declare war on them, in so far as this provides the safety and opportunity needed to preach the Gospel".[54]

In addition, despite the variations in the definition of the law of nations and its relation to the law of nature, one aspect of that law, at least, was based upon the usage or custom of "civilised" states, and to which all other nations were subject irrespective of exhibiting signs of consent. As late as 1680, Textor, invoking the example of the American Indians and Africans of the Cape of Good Hope, argued that "if there be a people so wild and inhumane as to live without Law, The Law of Nations, which Reason dictates and Usage affirms, is not on that account any the less the Law of Nations".[55]

By applying the universal standards of natural law and the law of nations, even though this may have protected the Indians from some adverse consequences on grounds of invincible ignorance, justifications could be given for waging war against them. If certain of their internal societal arrangements, such as human sacrifice and cannibalism, were an affront to humanity, intervention to save innocent victims could be justified. Even where such affronts were not acknowledged, transgressing the law of nations provided ample excuse. Impediments to the rights of passage, attempts to prevent the appropriation of "vacant land" or acquire gold from the ground that the world held in common, gave just cause for war. Sepúlveda went as far as to argue that if natural slaves, such as the Indians, resisted the natural

---

[53] James Turner Johnson, *Just War Tradition and the Restraint of War* (Princeton, 1981), p. 77.
[54] Vitoria, *Political Writings*, Q 3, Article 2, § 9–§ 11, pp. 284–5.
[55] Johann Wolfgang Textor, *Synopsis of the Law of Nations*, I, 3.

dominion of their superiors, they gave grounds for just war against them with no more injustice than one would hunt down a wild and savage beast.[56]

The Right to Husbandry and the Duty of Cultivation

There is an aspect of Carole Pateman's "Settler Contract" that deserves further exploration and on which the continuing grounding of obligation in God has significant bearing: the right to husbandry with the associated issues of property rights. There is no doubt, as we have seen, that such a right has strong support in the law of nations that comprises elements of natural law, the customary practice of states, the opinions of philosophers and jurists, and case law.

To focus upon husbandry as a right, however, is to imply that the natives had a duty to allow settlement (from the point of view of the settlers) and to give up lands that were vacant or not fully used. This correlation is certainly to be found in commentaries on the law of nations and nature. Locke's influential argument is emphatic: if American Indians attempt to subject Europeans to their system of rules, or deny them the right to husbandry, it is they who have violated natural law and given just cause for war, in which case the injured parties may punish the transgressors and seek reparations. In conditions of war the injured may justifiably "destroy" the violators as "dangerous and noxious Creatures" bent themselves on destruction.[57]

The emphasis of both Tully and Pateman upon the right of husbandry or of cultivation nevertheless hides from view, or at the very least obscures, the more fundamental moral justification for appropriating native lands. It is the application of a universal principle, against which savages and barbarians are found wanting. It is a principle derived from the natural law, and deeply ingrained in the Christian religion. It is the duty imposed by God upon humanity of self-preservation that requires making the earth productive and bountiful. The more efficiently this is done the better. To optimise productivity of the soil and fulfil man's duty to God requires the development of techniques of cultivation, and just as importantly the establishment of civil society or sovereignty, to ensure good governance and security in order to protect citizens from harm and to allow them to cultivate the land in safety.

To judge indigenous peoples against the universal obligation to cultivate or exploit the land to its optimum meant that they fell short of their moral duty in a number of respects. Hunters and gatherers were deemed to be merely parasitic

---

[56] Lewis Hanke, *Aristotle and the American Indians: A Study in Race Prejudice in the Modern World* (Bloomington, 1959), p. 45.

[57] John Locke, *Two Treatises of Government*, ed. Peter Laslett (Cambridge, 1988), II, §§ 10–11 and § 16.

on the land. Though rudimentary agriculture that exhausted the nutrients in the soil and required abandoning one location for another fulfilled the obligation to a greater degree, it still fell far short of efficient exploitation. Thus cultivation becomes the only recognised form of labour that fulfils the religious obligation. It is the fact that land is not cultivated that makes it no man's land, not the fact that there are no people on it. In other words, a certain type of labour was deemed synonymous with civilization. This deeply and long held conviction was expressed without any compunction by Thomas Arnold (1795–1842), the headmaster of Rugby School: "so much does the right of property go along with labour that civilized nations have never scrupled to take possession of countries inhabited only by tribes of savages – countries which have been *hunted over* but never *subdued* or cultivated". He goes on to suggest that the hunting grounds of the American Indians belonged to no one, and in taking them Englishmen were simply exercising "a right which God has inseparably united with industry and knowledge".[58]

Locke's theory of private property in the state of nature does not require the context of civil society. In addition to Grotius's primitive form of property, in which each has the right to the fruit he or she picks, and of the animals hunted and killed, Locke wants to go further and establish ownership of land. The problem was how to do this without conceding that the American Indians already owned the land. The device he used was to employ a very restricted definition of labour.

Locke's subtle shift from ownership of things to ownership of land is nothing short of masterly. Hunter-gatherers, deep-sea fishermen, bakers or craftsmen in the state of nature are entitled to what they have killed, gathered or made. Land, however, is a different matter. Not all labour generates a property title. Locke recounts that the curse placed upon Adam required men to labour because of their impoverished and destitute condition.[59] Only sustained labour yields the full potential of the fruits of the earth. Neither mere occupation nor appropriation (that is. taking possession) counts as sustained labour.

Locke ingeniously restricts labour and ownership to that type of activity which is associated with cultivation. He argues that "*As much Land* as a man Tills, Plants, Improves, Cultivates, and can use the Product of, so much is his *Property*".[60] In order to secure a property title, then, it is not enough to roam over uncultivated land, engage in hunting and gathering, or to graze one's sheep on it. Locke does not stop here. Not only is private property an entitlement of the special type of

---

[58] Thomas Arnold, 'The Labourers of England', *Englishman's Register*, No. 6, 11 June, 1831, p. 157.
[59] Locke, *Two Treatises*, I, pp. 144–5.
[60] Locke, *Two Treatises*, II, § 32, pp. 290–91. Cf. Jeremy Waldron, *God, Locke, and Equality: Christian Foundation in Locke's Political Thought* (Cambridge, 2002), pp. 164–70.

labour he calls cultivation; Locke also wants to make the much stronger claim that there is a moral obligation to engage in labour. Mixing one's labour in the land by, for example, enclosures, planting trees and crops falls far short of what Locke intended to convey. He wants to say that we are obliged to develop land to its greatest productive capacity. As industrious and rational creatures, men were given the world by God "for their benefit. And the greatest Conveniences of Life they were capable to draw from it".[61]

By implication, the American Indians, and any peoples who fail to cultivate the land to its full productive capacity, failed to exhibit the industriousness and rationality required of them by God and had no good reasons for objecting to those who are more capable of fulfilling God's will. Locke's argument provided the philosophical grounds for the contention that the British had just as much right to settle "wasteland" as those who lived on there but merely roamed over it. In landing in Australia, for example, the British simply exercised a right that they held in common with Aboriginals, and of which the Aboriginals singularly had failed to avail themselves.[62]

For most of the eminent writers on the natural law and law of nations, native peoples, were therefore morally derelict in fulfilling their obligation to God to make the earth bountiful and to establish civil societies so as to ensure efficient exploitation of the soil. Locke, for instance, admonishes hunter gathers for producing one hundredth or even one thousandth of the products for commodious living that their European counterparts produce. Europeans use one tenth, or even one hundredth, less land than American Indians to produce the same or equivalent products.[63]

Vattel was not so specific in quantifying the extent to which native peoples fell short of their obligation, but he was equally admonishing: "Every nation then is obliged by the law of nature to cultivate the land that has fallen to its share", and those which do not "have, therefore, no reason to complain, if other nations, more industrious and too closely confined, come to take possession of part of those lands".[64]

Strategies were pragmatic, of course, and the use of the idea of wasteland, *terra nullius*, was one such strategy to take possession of lands that were not under cultivation. Even Māori, who were deemed to occupy a higher level of civilization than the Australian Aboriginal, and were designated agriculturalists, acknowledged to own the land they cultivated and (unlike the Australian

---

[61] Locke, *Two Treatises*, II, § 34, p. 291. Cf. Herman Lebovics, "The Uses of America in Locke's Second Treatise of Government", *Journal of the History of Ideas*, 47 (1986): 577.
[62] See Stuart Banner, *How the Indians Lost Their Land: Law and Power on the Frontier* (London, 2005), p. 20.
[63] Locke, *Two Treatises*, II, §§ 40–42.
[64] Vattel, *Law of Nations*, Book I, chap. vii, § 81, pp. 129–30.

Aboriginals) were credited with a capacity to alienate it, nevertheless failed to meet the conditions necessary for the full exercise of the universal rights enjoyed by civilized nations. The Māori, and American Indian farmers, were thought rudimentary agriculturalists who had not developed plough technology. When the soil was exhausted, they moved on to new lands. The fact that they were not hunters was used by many to the opposite effect from what one would expect, namely in order to argue that such peoples did not need as much land as hunter gatherers over which to roam in search of game, and that their proprietary rights should be restricted to that land which they actually cultivated and not extended to that which they claimed.[65]

Political Society and Sovereignty

Whether or not indigenous peoples were acknowledged to have private property rights was to some extent secondary to the issue of whether they had the collective right of sovereignty. Even though Indians entered into so called treaties, such arrangements never had the full imprimatur of international law.

It was argued by Locke that the obligations to God of self-preservation and of cultivating the earth, in order to make it more productive and conducive to self-preservation, are better discharged within a political society. The implication of Locke's arguments is that the American Indians fell far short of adequately discharging their obligations to God. They still lived outside political society in a state of nature and they failed to add to the common stock of mankind by improving the productivity of the land. In so doing, they had no claim on vast territories in the Americas that "*lie waste*".[66] Locke's was not the only view. Grotius makes the distinction between property and jurisdiction. Jurisdiction remains with the "ancient nation" even when strangers justifiably lay claim to wasteland. Pufendorf's position was that nations exercise eminent domain, or sovereignty, even over those tracts of land that appear to "lie waste", and the seizure of such lands is therefore contrary to the laws of nature and nations, a position ostensibly endorsed by Christian Wolff.[67] Wolff contended that the original position of

---

[65] Mark Hickford, "'Decidedly the Most Interesting Savages on the Globre': An Approach to the Intellectual History of Māori property Rights, 1837–53", *History of Political Thought*, xxvii (2006): 123. Further evidence that the central idea to focus upon is the failure to exploit the potential productive capacity of the land is the fact that this argument was used to justify European trusteeship in Africa in the latter part of the nineteenth century. See William Bain, *Between Anarchy and Society: Trusteeship and the Obligations of Power* (Oxford, 2003), p. 62.

[66] John Locke, *Two Treatise*, II, § 38, p. 295.

[67] Wolff, *Law of Nations*, chap. VII, § 866.

land in common was modified by families or communities jointly coming to hold territory as a proprietary right. The use of the land made no difference to ownership. Land belonging to such families or communities cannot be taken or occupied by others coming into the territory.[68] Those who occupy the sovereignty of a territory also exercise eminent domain over property and persons.[69] This would seem to imply that Native Americans owned and had sovereignty over the lands they occupy. For Locke, they still lived in a state of nature. Just as earlier theorists tried to disqualify American Indians on grounds of their lacking full human attributes, or because of their sinfulness, or because they engaged in the wrong sort of labour, Wolff applies stringent criteria for what constitutes a nation. He argues that "it denotes a number of men who have united into a civil society, so that therefore no nation can be conceived of without a civil sovereignty. For groups of men dwelling together in certain limits but without civil sovereignty are not nations".[70] For Adam Smith, nations of hunter-gatherers, whose society could not sustain or maintain an army for self-defence, could properly be considered neither a commonwealth nor sovereign.[71]

In practice even when it was acknowledged that native peoples exercised ownership rights, the colonising country laid claim to the rights of eminent domain and denied sovereignty to native peoples on the grounds of conquest or secession. Even where the natural right of individuals to property was acknowledged, community rights under the law of nations were denied because the indigenous peoples were not deemed fully sovereign nations. Indeed, although treaties paid lip service to Indian sovereignty, there was no suggestion of equality. During the eighteenth century in the Americas it became common practice among British officials to acknowledge the land rights of the Indians while emphasizing that sovereignty had been ceded.[72] Joseph Story articulates the principle well when he commented on the Indians that "As infidels, heathens, and savages, they were not allowed to possess the prerogatives belonging to absolute, sovereign and independent nations".[73] Christian Wolff, for example, confirms that uninhabited lands may be colonised and appropriated because they are the property of no one. The nation appropriating the vacant land acquires property rights in it and

---

[68] Also see Borch, "Rethinking the Origins of *Terra Nullius*", p. 234.
[69] Wolf, *Law of Nations*, chap. VII, § 866.
[70] Wolff, *Law of Nations*, chap. III, § 309, pp. 156–67.
[71] Adam Smith, *An Inquiry into the Nature and Causes of the Wealth of Nations*. Volumes I and 2 (The Glasgow Edition of the Works & Correspondence of Adam Smith), (Indianapolis, 1976), p. 690.
[72] See Borch, "Rethinking the Origins of *Terra Nullius*", p. 229.
[73] Joseph Story, *Commentaries on the Constitution of the United States with a Preliminary Review of the Constitutional History of the Colonies and States Before the Adoption of the Constitution* (Boston, 1833), Book 1, chap. XVI, § 152).

sovereignty over it. He acknowledges ownership and sovereignty by nations over the lands they occupy, even if those lands are waste and barren. Nevertheless, since every nation should perfect its condition, such vacant land should be given to foreigners.[74]

Conclusion

Most of the great early modern and enlightenment philosophers, who are hailed as champions of reason and liberalism, were complicit in the use of universal standards to dispossess peoples of their lands, oppress them, deny them sovereignty and condemn them to permanent exclusion from the international society of nations. It was an exaggeration to contend that the American Indians did not engage in agriculture. Colonists frequently reported agricultural activity throughout eastern North America, and it was well known that parts of what is now North Carolina had extensive cultivated fields. It was the growing acknowledgement that Indians farmed the land that contributed to the recognition of their right to property.[75] Whether indigenous peoples were deemed to own the land over which they "roamed", or whether they merely had a use right in common, they were not deemed to have entered into a social contract among themselves and were therefore not deemed to have instituted sovereign political societies. These arguments were almost invariably sustained by invoking the authority of God who obliges us to conform to the natural law, which includes cultivating the land to its productive capacity.

---

[74] Wolff, chap. III, §§ 275–92, pp. 140–52.
[75] Banner, *How the Indians Lost Their Land*, p. 38.

Chapter 5

Taming the Fox and the Lion – Some Aspects of the Sixteenth-Century's Debate on Inter-State Relations[1]

Peter Schröder

At the end of the sixteenth century Alberico Gentili was perhaps the first political thinker who fully realised that the fundamental problem of the relationship between sovereign states was that the very nature of their sovereignty seemed to undermine any pacification of this anarchical society. After the Council of Trent (1545–63) had failed to reunite Christianity,[2] politics in Europe and beyond were never to be the same, and any pacification of inter-state relations had to take into account the existence of antagonistic theologies and the apparently mutually exclusive confessions. Any basis of universally accepted religious principles, even among Christian states, seemed impossible. Moreover, the implications of these antagonistic positions undermined the arguments about legitimate sovereignty. Gentili, however, challenged the justifications of religious strife, and one aim of his, *De Iure Belli* (1598), may certainly be seen in the attempt to banish religion from the international scene as a reason for going to war. In his *De Legationibus* (1585) he had already warned: "let sovereigns be careful of their actions when they use the pretext of religion in dealing with embassies".[3] Clearly, more was needed than such a simple appeal to political rulers. It was truly an immense task to deny religion the prominence it commanded as a reason for conflict in the late

---

[1] I would like to express my particular thanks to Olaf Asbach, Nick Johnstone and Angus Gowland for their helpful comments and criticism. I also want to acknowledge the support of the British Academy, which enabled me to do necessary research on the Huguenots whilst abroad.

[2] The emperor Charles V aimed at uniting Christianity by means of a council, but when he eventually managed to bring it into existence, the Protestants refused their participation. The council met in three different sessions, which were interrupted because of conflicting European politics. It was crucial for reforming and regenerating the Catholic Church and inaugurated the Counter-Reformation. See J. Bossy, "The Counter Reformation and the people of Catholic Europe", *Past and Present* 47 (1970): 51–70; D.M. Luebke, *The Counter-Reformation* (Oxford, 1999); M. Mullet, *The Catholic Reformation* (London, 1999). A.D., Wright, *The Early Modern Papacy* (Harlow, 2000).

[3] A. Gentili, *Three Books on Embassies*, ed. by G.J. Laing (New York, 1924), p. 91.

sixteenth century, given that among Christian states all major conflicts seemed fuelled by religious controversies. The Dutch Revolt against the Spanish crown, the French wars of religion or the antagonism between Elizabeth and Philip II, are only the most prominent examples at the time Gentili wrote his major work.

This humanist was well-read in the different currents of political philosophy. He was not only one of the most remarkable jurists of his time, but also equally acquainted with the literature on *reason of state*, notably Machiavelli and Guicciardini. Furthermore, he was clearly also well-versed in the literature of French political thought, which had emerged in the context of the Huguenots' struggle for recognition of their reformed faith. After the massacres of St Bartholomew's Day, this literature had considerably changed its tone and strategy: the argument now explored whether and to what extent resistance was legitimate even against the monarch. The most notorious and wide-spread argument along these lines was advocated in the *Vindiciae contra Tyrannos* (1579).

Thus the French Protestants threatened to undermine Gentili's theory from a quarter which should have been a natural ideological ally to his own position, because the ideological and epistemological positions of the Huguenots should have tallied well with Gentili's own convictions in favour of religious liberty. This chapter will argue that Gentili perceived the change of argument in Huguenot political writing as a menace to the European inter-state order. As has been convincingly shown by Diego Panizza, Gentili argued against, among others, the Dutch Protestant Justus Lipsius, who was involved in yet another of the dominant religious-political struggles for freedom of conscience and religious toleration.[4] Gentili denied the validity of Lipsius' argument which, according to him, culminated in the assertion that religious unity was essential for social cohesion and stability. Gentili argued on the contrary that to enforce religious unity was more a reason for sedition and strife than a factor of stability. Thus far Gentili should not have any reason for concern regarding the Huguenot theory. But after the St Bartholomew's Day massacres, the Huguenot community felt betrayed by the French Crown. Until this dramatic event, despite some drastic rhetoric and the repeated outbreak of open civil war, the Huguenots' position had always been that they needed to address a wrong which had been done by over-zealous advisers of the Crown, but not by the Crown itself. It is important to stress that this change in the Huguenot attitude was preceded by gleeful Catholic propaganda about the massacres, such as the anonymously published *Allegresse chrestienne* and *Discours contre les Huguentoz*. These aggressive anti-Huguenot writings were seconded by semi official pamphlets by Legier du Chesne or Claude

---

[4] See notably D. Panizza, "Il pensiero politico di Alberico Gentili. Religione, virtù e ragion di stato", in D. Panizza (ed.), *Alberico Gentili Politica e religione nell'Età delle Guerre die Religione* (Milan, 2002), pp. 57–213, esp. p. 75 and pp. 88–9.

Nouvelle, to name only two other authors.[5] The fundamental change and obvious threat to political stability in France was arguably still perceived by Gentili in the fact that the *Vindiciae contra Tyrannos* and other Huguenot political writings openly discussed and endorsed resistance against the monarchy.[6]

Gentili's attempt to provide a framework for and thus restrictions to the wars which threatened to tear Europe apart was fundamentally based on the concept of sovereign states, that is to say, the order and stability of princely or republican government. Any theory advocating resistance against the foundations of government must therefore also undermine the attempt to organise inter-state relations with reference to this established inner-state order. It is true to say that "Gentili ... non possedeva compiutamente il concetto moderni *sovranità*, ma monstrava un chiaro senso della distinzione dei due ordini di realtà, quella di interna e quella di internazionale".[7] I have argued elsewhere that the idea of sovereign states poses a challenge to and at the same time the solution for organising inter-state relations in Gentili's view.[8]

---

[5] Anonymous, *Allegresse chrestienne de l'heureux succes des guerres de ce royaume* (Paris, 1772); *Discours contre les Huguentoz, auquel est contenue et déclarée la source de leur damnable religion* (Lyon, 1573). L. du Chesne, *Exhortation au Roy, pour vertueusement poursivre ce que sagement il a commencé contre les Huguenots, avec les Epitaphes de Gaspar de Colligny etc.* (Paris, 1572); C. Nouvell, *Ode trionfale au roy, sus l'equitable justice que sa majesté feit des rebelles, la veille et jour de sainct Loys* (Paris, 1572). See F.J. Baumgartner, *Radical Reactionaries: The Political Thought of the French Catholic League* (Geneva, 1975) and R. Birely, *The Counter-Reformation Prince: Anti-Machiavellism or Catholic Statecraft in Early Modern Europe* (London, 1990).

[6] Cf., for example, anonymous, *Remonstrance d'un bon Catholique françois aux trois estats de France* (n.p., 1576). This good Catholic is, of course, anything but a good Catholic. Like the *Vindiciae contra Tyrannos*; the main thrust of the argument here claims that Machiavelli's odious teachings are to blame for the massacre. The anonymously published *De furoribus Gallicis, horrenda et indigna amirallij Castillionei, nobilium atque illustrium virorum caede* (Basle, 1573), which is now attributed to Hotman, argued in a similar vein. See also F. de La Noue, *Discours politiques et militaires* (Basle, 1687). Particularly instructive on the St Bartholomew's Day Massacres are R.M. Kingdon, *Myths about the St Bartholomew's Day Massacres 1572–1576* (Cambridge, Mass., 1988); A. Soman (ed.), *The Massacre of St Bartholomew. Reappraisals and Documents* (The Hague, 1974). On the French Wars of Religion more generally, see M. Yardeni, *La conscience nationale en France pendant les guerres de religion, 1559–1598* (Paris, 1971); M.P. Holt, *The French Wars of Religion, 1562–1629* (Cambridge, 1995), and J.H.M. Salmon, *The French Religious Wars in English Political Thought* (Oxford, 1959).

[7] D. Panizza, 'Il pensiero politico di Alberico Gentili', p. 158.

[8] Two forthcoming papers prepare and complement the argument I explore in this chapter.

The idea of a world sovereign as potential arbiter, a role such as the Pope had indeed claimed and assumed most famously in the Treatise of Tordesillas in 1494,[9] would deny the very notion of a sovereign state and was therefore, on this general account alone, not a feasible option. Where conflicts between states ensued, the principle of *ipse-iudex* was in place, and if they could not be solved politically, war would necessarily ensue. For Gentili "war" is thus "a just and public contest of arms", and more importantly the warring parties are seen on an equal legal footing. Right at the beginning of chapter two of *De Iure Belli*, where he gives his definition of war, he states that "*hostis* is a person with whom war is waged and who is the equal of his opponent".[10]

His assertion that "it is the nature of wars for both sides to maintain that they are supporting a just cause"[11] thus paid tribute to the emergence of the concept of sovereignty and fundamentally challenged and revolutionised the classical just-war theory. For him, states fighting each other as enemies are thus both morally and politically justified in waging war in order to obtain their political ends as long as they have a just cause. This, in a nutshell, is the first aspect of his argument, which is of course well known and has rightly attracted attention among scholars.[12]

The focus of my analysis of Gentili will be on what one may consider the second aspect of his argument, and it is precisely here that the Huguenot political writings, and the *Vindiciae contra Tyrannos* in particular, were most unsettling for Gentili's own position. Needless to say, the intellectual engagement and ideological challenge found in Gentili's writings are much more complex and multi-layered than the focus of my analysis might suggest. The focus of this chapter is already complicated enough, however, given that the shadow of Machiavelli looms large and somewhat unspoken over Gentili's endeavour to argue against the Huguenot theory of resistance without at the same time abandoning religious toleration, and indeed the Protestants' right of coexistence in a political world dominated by Catholics. In the preface of the anonymously published *Vindiciae contra Tyrannos*, the rhetorical ploy was to accuse the advisers of the French Crown once again of plotting against the Huguenots:

---

[9] See F. de Vitoria, "On the American Indies", in *Vitoria, Political Writings*, ed. by A. Pagden and J. Lawrence (Cambridge, 2003), p. 285.

[10] A. Gentili, *The Three Books on the Law of War*, ed. by J.C. Rolfe (Oxford, 1933), p. 12. See also Cicero, *On Duties*, ed. by M.T. Griffin and E.M. Atkins (Cambridge, 2006), I–37, p. 16.

[11] Gentili, *The Three Books on the Law of War*, p. 31.

[12] C. Schmitt, *The Nomos of the Earth in the International Law of the Jus Publicum Europeum* (New York, 2003), p. 122, was perhaps the first modern scholar who drew attention to "the great advance of modern international law among European states", which he saw as consisting "in substituting the doctrine of the juridical equality of *justi hostes* for the doctrine of *justa causa*".

> You princes of men, I consider that these investigations [undertaken in the *Vindiciae contra Tyrannos*] are able to contradict both the Machiavellians and their books, by whose wicked counsels the commonwealth is divided by so many civil dissensions, factions, and disturbances.[13]

To what extent the *Vindiciae contra Tyrannos* effectively engaged with Machiavelli's *Principe* is still a matter of controversy.[14] It is certainly true that despite the ardent rhetoric in the preface the main body of the text only once explicitly mentions Machiavelli, but there are many allusions to the Florentine (to which I shall turn later in this chapter) that will have been clear enough to contemporary readers. Gentili's engagement with Machiavelli and the *Vindiciae contra Tyrannos* demonstrates the extent to which the arguments advanced in these texts were perceived as tackling the unsettling core issues of sixteenth-century political and moral theory. Gentili was clearly a close and attentive reader and, it would be fair to say, also a great admirer of Machiavelli. What I have previously called the second aspect of Gentili's theory thus provides at the same time a means to discern more clearly how Gentili perceived and reacted to the various competing theories and where he placed, and to what extent he appropriated, Machiavelli in this rhetorical and political struggle. Given the anti-Machiavellian rhetoric of the *Vindiciae contra Tyrannos* and Gentili's own intellectual engagement with and debt to Machiavelli's theory,[15] it will become clear that Gentili tried to re-work the existing political theories in view of a coherent theory of inter-state relations, and that his particular understanding of Machiavelli was a crucial starting point for the problems Gentili perceived and meant to address.

Machiavelli bequeathed one fundamental question to Gentili and all other political thinkers who reflected on inter-state relations and politics in general. In chapter XVIII of his *Principe*, Machiavelli asked if princes should keep their word. The beginning of the chapter poses the problem in unambiguous terms:

---

[13] S.J. Brutus, *Vindiciae contra Tyrannos or, concerning the legitimate power of a prince over the people, and of the people over a prince*, ed. and trans. by G. Garnett (Cambridge, 1994), p. 10.

[14] Cf. E. Barker, *Church, State and Study* (London, 1930), esp. pp. 72–108. Pertinent and most comprehensive is G. Garnett, "Editor's Introduction", in S.J. Brutus, *Vindiciae contra Tyrannos*, esp. pp. XXI–XXII. S. Mastellone, *Venalità e Machiavellismo in Francia (1572–1610)* (Florence, 1972), pp. 58–60, suggests that Innocent Gentillet might be the author of the preface. But this seems merely an interesting speculation, lacking substantial proof, and I am rather inclined to doubt this.

[15] Panizza, "Il pensiero politico di Alberico Gentili", p. 126 characterises "Machiavelli [next to Aristotle as] l'altra autorità paradigmatica dell'universo teorico-politico di Gentili".

> Everyone knows how praiseworthy it is for a ruler to keep his promises, and live uprightly and not by trickery. Nevertheless, experience shows that in our times rulers who have done great things are those who have set little store by keeping their word, being skilful rather in cunningly confusing men; they have got the better of those who have relied on being trustworthy. ... Therefore, a prudent ruler cannot keep his word, nor should he, when such fidelity would damage him, and when reasons that made him promise are no longer relevant. This advice would not be sound if all men were upright; but because they are treacherous and would not keep their promises to you, you should not consider yourself bound to keep your promises to them.[16]

It was, of course, this kind of advice given in the *Principe* that caused Catholics and Protestants alike to react to Machiavelli in such strong terms. In 1589, Gentili's countryman Giovanni Botero, who had left the Jesuit order in 1581, published his critique of Machiavelli, *Della ragion di stato*, four years after Gentili's *De Legationibus* of 1585 and nine years before his *De Iure Belli* of 1598. The Spanish Jesuit Pedro Ribadeneyra published his *Tratado de la religion y Virtudes que deve tener el Principe Christiano, para governar y conservar sus Estados*. This explicit attack on Machiavelli and the *politiques* appeared first in 1595, was widely circulated and reprinted in several editions.[17] These writings, together with the *chef d'œuvre* of Justus Lipsius and Jean Bodin, and the earlier polemical writings that dominated the immediate aftermath of the St Bartholomew's massacres,[18]

---

[16] N. Machiavelli, *The Prince*, ed. by Q. Skinner and R. Price (Cambridge, 1988), pp. 61–2.

[17] R.W. Truman, *Spanish Treatises on Government, Society and Religion in the Time of Philip II* (Leiden, 1999), esp. pp. 277–314 and Birely, *The Counter-Reformation Prince*, esp. pp. 111–35.

[18] The most important were Innocent Gentillet's *Anti-Machiavel* and the notorious *Vindiciae contra Tyrannos*. Given that Gentili was one of the few writers who dismissed Gentillet's criticism of Machiavelli and defended the latter against the charges issued against him in the anonymously published *Anti-Machiavel*, I shall focus on the *Vindiciae contra Tyrannos* rather than on the *Anti-Machiavel* when assessing Gentili's interpretation of Huguenot writings on religion, state and resistance. Gentili makes his own position on the *Anti-Machiavel* abundantly clear:
"The fact that some claim that he was a man of no learning and of criminal tendencies makes no difference to me. It is his remarkable insight that I praise; I do not defend his impiety or his lack of integrity, if actually he had such faults. And yet if I, reviewing *the book issued against him* [my emphasis], take into consideration his position, if I give a just estimate of his purpose in writing, and if I choose to reinforce his words by sounder interpretation, I do not see why I can not free from such charges the reputation of this man who has now passed away. He was not understood by the person who wrote against him and he has been calumniated in many ways. There is no doubt that Machiavelli is

provide the wider intellectual context for assessing Gentili's own theory.[19] It was thus in this context that Gentili had to position himself rather than in the natural law tradition, which was still largely dominated by Catholic scholastics.[20] This might explain why Gentili rather half-heartedly embraced that line of thought. Only with Grotius did the Protestants fully explore and reshape the natural law doctrine.[21] It is certainly true that there were "two rival political moralities" which "were now confronting each other in every commonwealth of late sixteenth-century Europe. One was the natural law theory ... the other was the theory of 'Machiavelli and the *politiques*'".[22] Yet despite this predominant intellectual divide, it is also evident that among the natural law tradition as well as among the *politiques* there existed not just one homogeneous strand of thought within

---

a man who deserves our commiseration in the highest degree" (Gentili, *Three Books on Embassies*) p. 156.

[19] This is, of course, still a very limited selection of a much more complex ongoing debate. For the Jesuit's engagement with Machiavelli, see H. Höpfl's masterful study, *Jesuit Political Thought The Society of Jesus and the State, c. 1540–1630* (Cambridge, 2004), esp. pp. 84–90 and 164–7. See also C. Benoist, *Le Machiavellisme* (Paris, 1936); A.M. Battista, "Sull'antimachiavellismo francese del secolo XVI" *Storia e Politica 1* (1962): 412–447; G. Procacci, *Machiavelli nella cultura Europea dell'età moderna* (Rome, 1995). S. Anglo, *Machiavelli. The First Century* (Oxford, 2005), esp. pp. 229–414 is, despite its focus on Gentillet, helpful on the wider Catholic and Huguenot context, but adds hardly anything on Gentili.

[20] An excellent study of early Protestant natural law theories is M. Scattola, *Das Naturrecht vor dem Naturrecht. Zur Geschichte des* ius naturae *im 16. Jahrhundert* (Tübingen, 1999). A competent analysis of natural law theories in the Spanish scholastic is to be found in A. Brett, *Liberty, Right and Nature: Individual Rights in later Scholastic Thought* (Cambridge, 1997). See also M. Scattola, "Before and after natural law: Models of natural law in ancient and modern times", in T. Hochstrasser and P. Schröder (eds), *Early Modern Natural Law Theories: Contexts and Strategies in the Early Enlightenment* (Dordrecht, 2003), pp. 1–30.

[21] See notably J. Sauter, *Die philosophischen Grundlagen des Naturrechts Untersuchungen zur Rechts- und Staatslehre* (Frankfurt am Main, 1966), and F. Grunert, *Normbegründung und politische Legitimität. Zur Rechts- und Staatsphilosophie der deutschen Frühaufklärung* (Tübingen, 2000). Despite the obvious similarities between Grotius and Gentili, Richard Tuck does not appreciate the fundamental differences on which both men based their argument. It seems problematic to deny categorically the influence of previous natural law theorists like Vitoria and Suárez on Grotius; this in turn blurs the understanding of Gentili's specific approach, which relies much more on the tradition of the politiques than on the natural law tradition. Cf. R. Tuck, *War and Peace. Political Thought and the International Order from Grotius to Kant* (Oxford, 1999), esp. p. 108.

[22] Q. Skinner, *The Foundations of Modern Political Thought*, vol. 2 (Cambridge, 1978), p. 172. Quentin Skinner discusses this notably with reference to Pedro Ribadeneyra's *Religion and the Virtues of the Christian Prince against Machiavelli*.

these distinguishable traditions, but also several competing doctrines of political thought. Gentili was part of this tradition and contributed to the different tendencies amongst the *politiques*, which becomes particularly clear in Gentili's position towards Machiavelli and some of the most prominent contemporary criticism of the Florentine's doctrine, which Gentili in turn also addressed in his political writings.

The ideological and political agenda Gentili pursued in his interpretation of Machiavelli reveals how he addressed the relationship between politics and religion. He explored the scope, and in his view the necessity, of toleration at the same time as he discussed the status of sovereign state power, or in other words, the issue of sovereignty and resistance. He was clear that this had profound implications for his main attempt to provide a framework for regulating the relations between inter-confessional states.[23] I would like to argue here that Gentili's twofold strategy in addressing these issues can be grasped in his groundbreaking assertion that every enemy is a just enemy, which he later qualifies and restricts by introducing the all-decisive proviso that there exist certain unjust enemies as well.

> For the word *hostis*, "enemy", while it implies equality, like the word "war" ... is sometimes extended to those who are not equal, namely to pirates, proscribed persons and rebels; nevertheless it cannot confer the rights due to enemies, properly so called, and the privileges of regular warfare.[24]

If my interpretation is correct, Gentili is not contradicting himself, because the notion of an unjust enemy was comprised in the term pirate, which in turn became *the* all-decisive criterion of either inclusion or exclusion in his system of organising the relations between sovereign states. This is the second and complementary aspect of Gentili's argument. He thus argued first that "the Spaniards [waged a war] against violators of the law of nature and of common law, against cannibals, and monsters of lewdness. It is right to make war against pirates".[25] Second, he applied the term "pirate" to atheists, because:

---

[23] For the crucial controversy between Gentili and the orthodox theologians at Oxford University, see D. Panizza, *Alberico Gentili giurista ideologo nell'Inghilterra elisabettiana* (Padua, 1981), and Panizza, "Il pensiero politico di Alberico Gentili", esp. p. 116.

[24] Gentili, *The Three Books on the Law of War*, p. 25.

[25] Gentili, *The Three Books on the Law of War*, p. 124. Contrast this with Francesco Vitoria's view: Vitoria, "On the American Indies", esp. p. 286 or with B. De Las Casas, *A short Account of the Destruction of the Indies* (London, 2004), p. 70: "The Spanish also prove blind to their own wickedness in persisting in waging war (even though such a course of action is condemned by all the laws known to man) on a people on whom they have previously inflicted unpardonable wrongs and towards whom they have behaved in an evil and wicked fashion. On the contrary, they now proclaim and record for posterity their

some kind of religion is natural, and therefore if there should be any who are atheists, destitute of any religious belief, either good or bad, it would seem just to wage war upon them as we would upon brutes. For they do not deserve to be called men, who divest themselves of human nature, and themselves do not desire the name of men. And such a war is a war of vengeance, to avenge our common nature.[26]

Third, he turned this same argument at least partly and potentially against the Turks.[27] Although Gentili realised that the Ottoman Empire could not be ignored in the attempt to establish an international society whose members would follow certain rules in their behaviour towards each other, he nevertheless remained insistent that only states that share a certain set of values are in the end sufficiently trustworthy to conduct their conflicts along the lines suggested in his work. How the Turks – *the* perceived threat and enemy to Europe at the time[28] – should be treated, is not a question for theologians but for people like Gentili.

According to him the decisive question is whether the Ottomans qualify as trustworthy enemies and thus deserve to be considered as falling under the idea of a just enemy – that is, an enemy who will observe certain rules and who will thus remain calculable to a certain degree. Gentili seems absolutely straightforward on this point:

> War is not waged on account of religion, and war is not natural either with others or even with the Turks. But we have war with the Turks because they act as our enemies, plot against us, and threaten us. With the greatest *treachery* [my emphasis] they always seize our possessions, whenever they can. Thus we constantly have a legitimate reason for war against the Turks. We ought not break with them; no! We ought not to make war upon them when they are quiet and keeping the peace, and have no designs upon us; no! But when do the Turks act thus? Let the theologians keep silence about matters which is outside of their province.[29]

---

conviction that the 'victories' they continue to enjoy over an innocent local population, by dint of massacring them, come from God, and that their wicked campaigns in the New World amount to a just war". See also A. Pagden, *The fall of natural man: The American Indian and the origins of comparative ethnology* (Cambridge, 1982), pp. 67–108.

[26] Gentili, *The Three Books on the Law of War*, p. 125.
[27] Cf. Gentili, *The Three Books on the Law of War*, p. 332.
[28] W. Schulze, *Reich und Türkengefahr im späten 16. Jahrhundert. Studien zu den politischen und gesellschaftlichen Auswirkungen einer äußeren Bedrohung* (München, 1978); V. Aksan and D. Goffman (eds), *The Early Modern Ottomans: Remapping the Empire* (Cambridge, 2007); D. Goffman, *The Ottoman Empire and Early Modern Europe* (Cambridge, 2002).
[29] Gentili, *The Three Books on the Law of War*, p. 57.

Towards the Ottoman Empire his position is thus at least ambivalent. Gentili's constant appeal to custom serves to prompt (Christian) states to have faith in these rules and institutions and to observe them in their dealings with other (Christian) states.[30] None of these groups mentioned may thus be considered just enemies; all fall outside the established customs between states and international law. The discrimination of these groups is an attempt to provide an answer to the all-decisive question of how trust and faith among sovereign states might be maintained. Because Gentili believed that those he had singled out could not be trusted, even the slightest basis for trust and mutual good faith towards them was impossible and hence, in classical Machiavellian terms, politically inadvisable. Gentili thus restricts his concept of a just enemy to sovereign states who do seem to share certain general moral values. Among these there will always be a residue of understanding and mutual trust. This is why he also demands that one should not deal with the enemy too harshly, because one cannot anticipate "what becomes of good faith, which is the essence of the law of nations and of embassies".[31] Trust and good faith therefore play a large role in Gentili's concept of providing rules and customs on how to engage with the enemy. His legal and political theory only works on the basis of this cardinal assumption. Hence it is crucial to assure that all those who potentially undermine this assumption, because they do not share the fundamental moral values, are excluded from the system of equality between states. Here we can see that the differences of Christian confessions may be allowed to come in the way of this concept. If this part of Gentili's argument is to work, he must show that, despite Machiavelli's advice in the *Principe*, trust and good faith in the domain of politics is possible and even sensible. Obviously religious strife was even more of a threat to this concept, because it profoundly undermined any basis of reconciliation. The explosive mixture of simplified Machiavellian concepts in connection with religious strife was thus the fundamental obstacle that Gentili had to surmount.

Interestingly, Pedro Ribadeneyra seems to argue in a similar vein when he attacks Machiavelli and encourages the Christian Prince not to follow Machiavelli's advice:

> because Machiavelli teaches that sometimes the Prince should break his word and his faith, ... it is very fitting that the Christian Prince be very attentive and

---

[30] This is why his constant appeal to custom is certainly much less naïve than it might otherwise appear. See, for example, his assertion that "to show the prevalence of the custom is of service. For by doing this we establish firmly the right of such embassies". And in a similar vein: "But what purpose do I serve in citing these and other examples which I might collect? It is to show that the institutions of embassies, with their maintenance, rights, and dignity, has existed among all nations". Gentili, *Three Books on Embassies*, p. 19 and p. 50.

[31] Gentili, *Three Books on Embassies*, p. 87.

greatly consider first what he says, promises, and swears; but afterwards that he be constant and firm in fulfilling what before God he has promised and sworn. And let him know for certain that the keeping of his faith and word is very important for the conservation of his State and for being better thought of, richer, better obeyed, and feared.[32]

The underlying issue here is again the question about the reasonable expectation of mutual trust and faith. Ribadeneyra argues that Machiavelli's theory simply undermines all possibility of trusting in the promises and declarations of others, notably because of the lack of religion and thus of fundamental moral values. But Gentili obviously drew on a different reading of Machiavelli, which is closely related to his republicanism. Machiavelli had elaborated on the political and military organisation of the republic reflected in the need for education and military reform, and the need for engagement and participation of the citizenry. This whole argument is in turn closely related to Machiavelli's deliberations about the German free imperial cities. His anti-clericalism and a new concept of civic religion provide the ideological heart of this republican theory. Machiavelli's republican ideal finds its place in the tradition from Tacitus to Rousseau, and it is certainly more than a coincidence that all three thinkers find similar praise of *Teutonic liberty*. Political survival in a precarious political world is far from self-evident. Machiavelli singles out the republican virtue inspired by adherence to civil religion, uncorrupted by clerical machinations, as the underlying foundation of republics:

> In the province of Germany it is quite clear that goodness and respect for religion are still to be found in its peoples with the result that many republics there enjoy freedom and observe their laws in such a way that neither outsiders nor their own inhabitants dare to usurp power there. ... This goodness is the more to be admired in these days in that it is so rare. Indeed, it seems to survive only in this province. This is due to two things. In the first place the towns have but little intercourse with their neighbours, who seldom go to visit them, or are visited by them, since they are content with the goods, live on the food, and are clothed with the wool which their own land provides. The occasion for intercourse, and with it the initial step on the road to corruption, is thus removed, since they have no chance of taking up the customs either of the French, the Spaniards or the Italians, nations which, taken together, are the source of world-wide corruption.[33]

---

[32] P. Ribadeneyra, *Religion and the Virtues of the Christian Prince – against Machiavelli*, ed. by G.A. Moore (Washington, 1949), p. 303.

[33] N. Machiavelli, *The Discourses*, ed. by B. Crick (London, 2003), I–55, pp. 244–5.

This somewhat surprising praise of German frugality and moral righteousness is meant to foster republican civic virtue. Contrast this with Machiavelli's outright attack on the corrupted clergy:

> owing to the bad example set by the Court of Rome, Italy has lost all devotion. ... The first debt that we owe to the Church and to priests, is that we have become irreligious and perverse. But we owe them a yet greater debt, which is the second cause of our ruin. It is the Church that has kept, and keeps Italy divided.[34]

Why? Because the Papacy was too weak to assume full sovereign power and to unite Italy, but too strong not to play politics in temporal matters and, most importantly, get other powers involved. Italy as a whole and the Italian republics and city states live under precarious conditions. Germany, by contrast, is much more fortunate: "That the republics of Germany have ... lasted a considerable time, is due to the conditions which prevail in that country and are not found elsewhere, conditions without which it is impossible to maintain this type of polity".[35]

This kind of republicanism, which goes hand in hand with Machiavelli's political realism and pragmatism, were the intriguing aspects of his doctrine for Gentili. Machiavelli did not advocate ruthless behaviour among states. On the contrary, when discussing the acquisition of princely power by wicked means, he already insisted that "it cannot be called virtue to kill one's fellow-citizen, to betray one's friends, to be treacherous, merciless and irreligious; power may be gained by acting in such a way, but not glory".[36] In the *Discorsi*, he complemented and substantially qualified the advice given in the *Principe* in the following way:

> Although to use fraud in any action is detestable, yet in the conduct of war it is praiseworthy and glorious. And a man who uses fraud to overcome his enemy is praised, just as much as is he who overcomes his enemy by force. ... I do not mean that a fraud which involves breaking your word or the contracts you have made, is glorious; for although on occasion it may win for you a state or a kingdom ... it will never bring you glory.[37]

Success is thus also for Machiavelli an ambiguous criterion, and he was himself apparently very much concerned with the problem he had presented in such

---

[34] Machiavelli, *The Discourses*, I–12, p. 144.
[35] Machiavelli, *The Discourses*, II–19, p. 336.
[36] Machiavelli, *The Prince*, p. 31. Cf. Cicero's discussion of glory: *On Duties*, II–31, p. 74.
[37] Machiavelli, *The Discourses*, III–40, p. 513. Cf. Cicero, *On Duties*, I–62, p. 26.

radical terms when he attacked Cicero, the authority of humanist moral and political thought, maintaining that "a ruler must know how to act like a beast".[38]

It is worthwhile to recall that Cicero had famously claimed in *De Officiis* that:

> injustice may be done, either through force or through deceit; and deceit seems to belong to a little fox, force to a lion. Both of them seem most alien to a human being; but deceit deserves the greater hatred. And out of all injustice, nothing deserves punishment more than that of a man who, just in a time when they are most betraying trust, act in such a way that they might *appear* [my emphasis] to be good.[39]

To highlight the fundamental problem, Machiavelli had turned this assertion deliberately on its head when he gave his advice to princes. A ruler:

> should imitate both the fox and the lion .. one could give countless modern examples ... and show how many peace treaties and promises have been rendered null and void by the faithlessness of rulers; and those best able to imitate the fox have succeeded best. But foxiness should be well concealed: one must be a great feigner and dissembler.[40]

The question of trustworthiness was also quite clearly of major concern to Machiavelli, but he was not prepared to ignore that many rulers simply preferred political success to faithful and honourable conduct. As previously quoted, Machiavelli said himself that his "advice would not be sound if all men were upright; but because they are treacherous and would not keep their promises to

---

[38] Machiavelli, *The Prince*, p. 61.
[39] Cicero, *On Duties*, I–41, p. 19.
[40] Machiavelli, *The Prince*, pp. 61–2. Cicero was not the first classical author who used this famous dictum about the fox and the lion. Since Machiavelli's notorious inversion, many polemicists and political thinkers referred in one way or another to this dictum. Besides the references below, cf. for instance, the Jesuit Ribadeneyra, *Religion and the Virtues of the Christian Prince*, p. 259 and p. 279 and the Huguenot La Noue, *Discours politiques et militaires*, p. 77, who both refer to the image of the fox to denounce Machiavellian treachery. La Noue explicity refers to Plutarch as the ancient source of this dictum. Anglo, *Machiavelli*, provides more references to contemporary sources with a similar anti-Machiavellian thrust not considered in this chapter, and Lysander yet another ancient source: pp. 251, 267, 280, 291, 347, 349 and 387. See also M. Stolleis, "Löwe und Fuchs. Eine politische Maxime im Frühabsolutismus", in M. Stolleis, *Staat und Staatsräson in der frühen Neuzeit* (Frankfurt am Main, 1990), pp. 21–36; J. Barlow, "The Fox and the Lion: Machiavelli replies to Cicero", *History of Political Thought 20* (1999): 627–45; M. Colish, "Cicero's De officiis and Machiavelli's Prince", *Sixteenth Century Journal 9* (1978): 80–93.

you, you should not consider yourself bound to keep your promises to them".[41] Gentili is taking Machiavelli as the thinker who highlighted the problem, and not as the one who created it because of the advice apparently given against Cicero in the *Principe*. But perhaps there is much more common ground between Cicero and Machiavelli than the quotations might suggest.

Cicero discussed the *problematique* of faith most prominently in the context of war, which in itself was one of the crucial parts of his discussion of justice in *De Officiis*. Underlying this discussion was his concern for the Roman Republic, which had crumbled under the civil war and Cesar's rise to dictatorial power. "In my opinion, our concern should always be for a peace that will have nothing to do with treachery. If I had been followed in this we would still have some republican government (if perhaps not the best); whereas now we have none".[42] Another equally notorious aspect in which Machiavelli apparently turns Cicero's political advice on its head concerns Cicero's assertion that "there is nothing at all more suited to protecting and retaining influence than to be loved, and nothing is less suited than to be feared".[43] The reason for taking this position may be seen in Cicero's belief that there can be no trust and hence no reliable intercourse between the different parties. "For those who wish to be feared cannot but themselves be afraid of the very men who fear them".[44] As is well known, Machiavelli had infamously claimed "that it is desirable [for a Prince] to be both loved and feared; but it is difficult to achieve both and, if one of them is lacking, it is much safer to be feared than loved".[45] The ruler should not depend on other peoples' sentiments or promises, but "only rely on what is under his own control".[46] It is thus in the nature of princely rule, in contrast to the concept of a republic shared by both Cicero and Machiavelli, in which every citizen has a stake and interest in the common good, that it be isolated, always precarious and under potential threat. Cicero had already suggested the connection between a well-ordered republican government and the appreciation of love, and dictatorial rule and the appreciation of fear, as the leading and motivating principles in society. "The republic we have lost. And we have fallen into this disaster ... because we prefer to be feared than to be held dear and loved".[47] In spite of the rhetoric directed against Cicero, it seems that Machiavelli is taking Cicero's thought one step further and spelling out even more clearly the autocrat's dependence on fear, in contrast to a less conflictual and more virtuous republican government. There is simply no one

---

[41] Machiavelli, *The Prince*, pp. 61–2.
[42] Cicero, *On Duties*, I–35, p. 15. See also I–57, pp. 23–4.
[43] Cicero, *On Duties*, II–23, pp. 70–71.
[44] Cicero, *On Duties*, II–24, p. 71.
[45] Machiavelli, *The Prince*, p. 59.
[46] Machiavelli, *The Prince*, p. 61.
[47] Cicero, *On Duties*, II–29, p. 74.

whom an autocrat could trust. Thus "rulers should have two main worries: one is internal, and concerns the subjects; the other is external, and concerns foreign powers".[48] Stability can thus never be had. Any alliance with other powers must necessarily remain fickle, as does the internal tranquillity of the commonwealth which is only possible through permanent princely vigilance and potential threat to the subjects. Machiavelli argued at length that a republic should and could rely on its citizen militia and does not need fortresses.

This argument is well known,[49] but so far it seems not to have been observed that it is also closely related to the question of trust. A well-governed republic can trust in its institutions and hence in its citizens. No coercion or force need be exercised against the citizen. Such an exercise of power was amply symbolised, and de facto exercised by the princely fortresses that dominated Renaissance cities. For this reason Machiavelli could maintain that "so long as Rome enjoyed freedom and was loyal to her ... constitution she never held either cities or provinces by means of fortresses".[50] They are militarily and politically useless for a well-constituted republic. For princes, however, who find themselves in tense relations with their subjects, fortresses might serve a purpose. They are, according to Machiavelli, useless against external enemies, but "if a ruler is more afraid of his own subjects than of foreigners, he should build fortresses".[51] The fortress thus becomes the signum of the prince's fear of his own subjects. Where there is no scope for mutual trust, there will be the attempt to coerce people into submission. In a republic, this is not necessary and would be counterproductive. In this respect it seems, despite the first impression made by the textual evidence, that Cicero and Machiavelli effectively share common ground. According to both thinkers, a republican government can and actually needs to rely on the citizens' love, but not so the prince.

Interestingly, this is exactly how Gentili interpreted both Cicero and Machiavelli. For him they were republicans who not only gave general political

---

[48] Machiavelli, *The Prince*, p. 64.

[49] H. Münkler, *Machiavelli. Die Begründung des politischen Denkens aus der Krise der Republik Florenz* (Frankfurt am Main, 1982). See generally M.E. Mallett, *Warfare in Renaissance Italy* (London, 1974), and M.E. Mallett, "The theory and practice of warfare in Machiavelli's republic" in G. Bock and Q. Skinner (eds), *Machiavelli and Republicanism* (Cambridge, 1990), pp. 173–80. For my own position on the complexity and originality of Machiavelli's political thought, see P. Schröder, *Niccolò Machiavelli* (Frankfurt am Main, 2004).

[50] Machiavelli, *Discorsi*, II–24, p. 352.

[51] Machiavelli, *The Prince*, p. 75. Giovanni Botero reiterates Machiavelli's view of the usefulness of fortresses for the ruler in subduing his subjects, but he also accords them a place in the defence against external enemies. Cf. the English translation of his *Della Ragion di Stato*: G. Botero, *Practical Politics*, trans. and ed. by G.A. Moore (Washington, 1949), p. 131.

advice, but also were both engaged in a concrete struggle for preserving, or rather attempting to re-establish, the republican constitution of their commonwealth. Well before Rousseau's famous dictum about Machiavelli's *Principe*, Gentili effectively anticipated Rousseau when he hailed Machiavelli as "an eulogist of democracy, and its most spirited champion. ... It was not his purpose to instruct the tyrant, but by revealing his secret counsels to strip him bare, and expose him to the suffering nation".[52] Gentili thus implies that, for Machiavelli, the crucial question about trustworthiness had already been how to tame the fox and the lion in the realm and intercourse of politics.[53] Gentili implied that, if there were only states which were governed under a republican constitution, then even Machiavelli would have conceded his provocative political advice would not be necessary.[54] In his appropriation of Machiavelli, Gentili does not discuss the fact that republics could also be, and in the case of Rome certainly had been, expansionist. His reading of the *Discoursi* and the *Principe*, however, still seems to have a point in clearly highlighting the *problematique* of trust and appropriating the arguments found in Machiavelli to the sphere of inter-state relations.

Had Machiavelli not hinted at this himself in the *Principe*, when he asserted that:

> it must be understood that a ruler, and especially a new ruler, cannot always act in ways that are considered good because, in order to maintain his power, he is often forced to act treacherously, ruthlessly or inhumanely, and disregard the precepts of religion. Hence he must be prepared to vary his conduct as the winds of fortune and changing circumstances constrain him and ... not deviate

---

[52] Gentili, *Three Books on Embassies*, p. 156. Cf. J.-J. Rousseau, "Of the social contract", in J.-J. Rousseau, *Political Writings*, ed. by V. Gourevitch, Cambridge 2003, III–6, p. 95: "While pretending to teach lessons to Kings, he [Machiavelli] taught great lessons to peoples. Machiavelli's *Prince* is the book of republicans". A similar, though less ardent and certainly less known argument in defence of Machiavelli had already been made before Gentili in Florence. Cf. M. Toscano, *Peplus Italiae* (Paris, 1578) and R. Pole, *Apologia Reginaldi poli ad Carolum V.*, ed. A.M. Quirini (Brescia, 1744), p. 151. I am indebted for these references to Anglo, *Machiavelli*, p. 409.

[53] The image of the fox in particular had an ambivalent, positive as well as negative, connotation in early modern political thought. See Stolleis, "Löwe und Fuchs. Eine politische Maxime im Frühabsolutismus" and Barlow, "The Fox and the Lion: Machiavelli replies to Cicero".

[54] I. Kant, "Toward Perpetual Peace", in *The Cambridge Edition of the Works of Immanuel Kant. Practical Philosophy* ed. by M.J. Gregor (Cambridge, 1996), pp. 315–51. Trustworthiness and the existence of a federation of republican states were both central for Kant's concept of international law. Anticipating Kant's position, Gentili already pointed to the importance of these aspects, which then became crucial for Kant's well-known theory.

from the right conduct if possible, but be capable of entering upon the path of wrongdoing when this becomes necessary.[55]

Part of the strength of the republican constitution, for Machiavelli, was that a republic is less dependent on a single person and so less exposed to chance and the whims of the goddess *Fortuna*.[56] Gentili's reading of Machiavelli thus also fans the controversial question of the relationship between the *Principe* and the *Discorsi*, and demonstrates, from a different and not so well-known perspective, the coherence of these works.[57] The similarities between Cicero and Machiavelli should not, of course, obscure the significant differences in style and emphasis of their respective moral and political theories. When Cicero insists that a wise man should always follow what is honourable and his view should not be distorted by expediency, he makes a profoundly un-Machiavellian point. Although he concedes that "it happens that one thing seems beneficial and another honourable", he is quite clear "that is a mistake: for the rule of what is beneficial and of what is honourable is one and the same. If someone has not grasped that, no type of deceit or crime will be beyond him".[58] In Gentili's interpretation, Machiavelli is saying exactly the same thing, only he shows more clearly that political rulers deliberately have recourse to these methods and that, *horribile dictu*, one has to reckon with such ruthless behaviour and conduct in the realm of politics. Gentili's attempt to draw lessons from this kind of political realism, and to use the positive foundations he claimed to have found in Cicero and Machiavelli alike, are set out in his *De Iure Belli*. His endeavour to transfer the *problematique* already tackled by Cicero, and so provocatively extended by Machiavelli especially to the sphere of inter-state relations in a period when (as Hobbes later put it) "the interpretation of a verse in the Hebrew, Greek, or Latin Bible, is oftentimes the cause for civil war",[59] made even more unlikely the establishment of a universally accepted basis for mutual trust. Thus, as has already been stated at the beginning of this chapter, Gentili had to engage with quite a wide range of considerably different writers in order to defend his position. Clearly the religious polemicists of Catholic and Huguenot confession alike had a much easier task than Gentili, who wanted and

---

[55] Machiavelli, *The Prince*, p. 62.
[56] Cf. Schröder, *Niccolò Machiavelli*, pp. 83–6; M. Viroli, *Machiavelli* (Oxford, 1998), p. 121 and D. Hoeges, *Niccolò Machiavelli. Die Macht und der Schein* (München, 2000), p. 198.
[57] Cf. H. Baron, "Machiavelli: the Republican Citizen and the Author of *The Prince*", *The English Historical Review* 76 (1961): 217–53.
[58] Cicero, *On Duties*, III–74, p. 128.
[59] T. Hobbes, *Behemoth or the long Parliament*, ed. by F. Tönnies (Chicago, 1990), p. 144.

needed to establish a basis for mutual trust beyond the respective confessional factions in order to make his system effective in bridling war.

In conclusion, we may briefly look again at one prominent example from the prevailing Huguenot and Catholic polemics in order to assess not only the hostile atmosphere against which Gentili had to argue, but also to appreciate fully his innovative approach. One might, indeed, be tempted to believe that Gentili intended to apply the previously cited position that "theologians [should] keep silence about matters which is outside of their province"[60] not just to the Turks, but also to the confessional polemicists, such as Ribadeneyra or the Monarchomachs.

The *Vindiciae contra Tyrannos* effectively equated Machiavelli's *Principe* with a tyrant. It is in this way that the polemic in the preface against the Florentine makes sense and is carried through in the argument. The consideration of the scope and legitimacy of resistance culminates in the third question set out in the *Vindiciae contra Tyrannos* where, in the discussion of who qualifies as a tyrant, Machiavelli's name and obvious allusions to his *Principe* again suddenly figure prominently in the text: "Briefly, the ... tyrant wants to appear to be what the king actually is. Since he knows that men are inflamed by love of virtue. But at any event, however much the fox dissembles, the fox's tail always shows; however much he yelps, the gaping jaws and roar reveal a lion".[61] A tyrant "feigns praise for justice and faith",[62] but the *Vindiciae contra Tyrannos* unmasks the tyrant by showing him to be an adherent of Machiavelli's doctrine. The preface and the central part of the discussion on the legitimacy of resistance against tyrants are in fact closely and very effectively knitted together. The assertion in the preface is that "the Machiavellians [have] laboriously educated them [the tyrants]", who would therefore calumniate the argument of the *Vindiciae contra Tyrannos*, whereas "to a wise, pious, and faithful prince, whom these investigations teach and instruct, it can only be the highest virtue".[63] It is therefore impossible, at least on the premise of this argument, to deny and argue against the findings of the *Vindiciae contra Tyrannos* without at the same time qualifying as a tyrant or a Machiavellian – that is, a "slave ... of tyrants".[64] Resistance was, at least for the magistrates, though not for the individual citizens, clearly legitimate against a tyrant. But it is more than questionable whether such a case can be argued on the grounds of confessional allegiance. Any theory of resistance is necessarily confronted by the crucial question of who might be in the position to make such decision on legitimate grounds. It is obvious that the opposing religious confession would strongly object to any such

---

[60] Gentili, *The Three Books on the Law of War*, p. 57.
[61] Brutus, *Vindiciae contra Tyrannos*, p. 147.
[62] Brutus, *Vindiciae contra Tyrannos*, p. 147.
[63] Brutus, *Vindiciae contra Tyrannos*, p. 12.
[64] Brutus, *Vindiciae contra Tyrannos*, p. 10.

claim and that there is consequently no ground for mutual trust once politics is mixed with confessional claims.[65]

The Jesuit Mariana also advocated tyrannicide, but his position was rejected by the Jesuits themselves, who condemned resistance to legitimate government, especially in its most extreme form of tyrannicide.[66] If we turn again to Ribadeneyra, we see that he faced the same problematic issue of trustworthiness once he denounced Protestants as heretics – although it seems that, for him, secular politicians, the *politiques*, are even worse than heretics, because heretics at least believe in some kind of religion and will therefore adhere to certain moral values. This argument of a Jesuit political thinker is considerably closer to Gentili's own position than are most Huguenot political writings, in particular the *Vindiciae contra Tyrannos*. Ribadeneyra argued that:

> the heretics, though they are lightening from hell and enemies of all Religion, profess some Religion; and among the many errors that they teach mix some truths. The politicians and the followers of Machiavelli have no religion, nor make distinction whether the religion be false, or true, except that it is proper for their political thinking.[67]

As previously quoted, Gentili indeed said almost the same thing when he discussed the concept of a *just enemy*. Those without any religion were not to be trusted and could not be just enemies. Both authors adhere to a certain political realism, especially in inter-state relations, and both discriminate against atheists. The fundamental difference, however, is that Gentili does not count Machiavelli among the atheists, whereas for Ribadeneyra Machiavelli is obviously the principal thinker responsible for introducing atheism into political theory:

> because there is no doubt that men, and kings more so, live among enemies, and that there are many who with the art of Machiavelli and a fine hypocrisy try to deceive them ... it is well that they consider how they ought to conduct themselves with the other Princes when there are false friends and true enemies; that on the one hand they be not deceived and the sincerity of their simplicity and truth be not mocked, and on the other hand by taking care with these they do not go against the law of God. When one walks among enemies it is necessary that one go armed, and with deceivers, to use some dissimulation; but

---

[65] Apart form the previously mentioned literature on religious strife and the St Bartholomew's Day massacres in particular, see also the still valid study by A. Elkan, *Die Publizistik der Bartholomäusnacht* (Heidelberg, 1901).

[66] See Höpfl, *Jesuit Political Thought. The Society of Jesus and the State* and H.E. Braun, *Juan de Mariana and Early Modern Spanish Political Thought* (Aldershot, 2007).

[67] Ribadeneyra, *Religion and the Virtues of the Christian Prince*, p. 251.

they should look well how far it is to continue without God being offended, and the limits and bounds that their care and artifice have to observe, in order that, being Christian Princes and disciples of Christ, they do not make themselves disciples of Machiavelli.[68]

Gentili had clearly and, given the circumstances of his time, courageously contradicted such a position, which was widely held by Protestants and Catholics alike. But he must have been aware that he could not fully answer the problem of trust in inter-state relations once he had allowed Machiavelli's *realism* into his argument. In the end he was unable to provide more than a precarious status for the binding force of the laws and customs he so laboriously unearthed and tried to systematise in his works. This is why, towards the end of his *De Iure Belli*, the issue of taking hostages is discussed at some length. This was, of course, only a makeshift argument, not designed to replace but rather to second the painstaking attempt to provide a basis for mutual trust in inter-state relations. "Hostages", he argued with reference to Baldus and other earlier jurists, "are those who are given to a sovereign or to the leader of an army for the purpose of *binding public faith* [my emphasis]".[69] Religion was thus crucial for Gentili's concept of "faithfulness, the most precious of possessions" in inter-state relations,[70] in order to foster moral values as the crucial basis for trust. But confessional strife must necessarily undermine this idea and had to be excluded from the realm of politics. "The pretext of religion" had thus to be banned from politics, and banned as a reason for going to war, as the only way of establishing reasonable ground to believe in the possibility that conflicting or warring parties would still observe a minimum of mutual trust and good faith towards each other, and that on this basis the laws of war might be observed by both parties. If one of them failed to do so, they would clearly not qualify for justifiable recourse to these laws, because "the laws of war are not observed towards one who does not himself observe them; one vainly implores the aid of the law who offends the law".[71] In this respect Gentili successfully took up some of the most unsettling concerns of Machiavelli's political theory in a much more constructive way than the religious polemicists of both confessions.

---

[68] Ribadeneyra, *Religion and the Virtues of the Christian Prince*, p. 280.
[69] Gentili, *The Three Books on the Law of War*, p. 241.
[70] Gentili, *The Three Books on the Law of War*, p. 243.
[71] Gentili, *The Three Books on the Law of War*, p. 272.

Chapter 6

War, Diplomacy and the Ethics of Self-Constraint in the Age of Grotius

Harald Kleinschmidt

Introduction: History, Theory and the History of International Relations Theory

What is the logical status of international relations theories? Many theorists distinguish theory from thought and confine theory to the arcane realm of academe. They position academe as an exclusive, if not the sole, theory-making institution, while denying to political decision-makers the originality to theorise.[1] This position, however, is far from obvious. As no one can deny that the doings of political decision-makers have been couched in current patterns of thought, the confinement of theorising to academe has the consequence of artificially partitioning theory (as the supposedly grand synthesising or analytical achievement) from thought (as the seemingly unreflected, rough-and-ready utilisation of convenient bits of ideology). The resulting gap between theory and practice is unfortunate, for the denial of original theorising to political decision-makers is ideological in its own right and, more importantly, rests on specific theoretical assumptions that cannot be generalised, since they relate to period-specific perceptions of international relations. The core assumption, informing the partition of theory from thought, is Edward Hallett Carr's time-honoured realist insistence that, while the doings of foreign-policy decision-makers such as diplomats may be tainted by political pressures or be totally unreflective, the theory-based study of international relations, categorised as international politics, is to be systematic, scientific and subject to critical scrutiny.[2]

By consequence, the history of international relations theories makes explicit some of the theoretical assumptions about international relations widely shared by contemporary actors. These assumptions are to be examined not merely on the high grounds of academic theorising but also in the lowlands of political practice. More importantly, theories of international relations may have existed

---

[1] Michael Joseph Oakeshott, *Lectures in the History of Political Thought*, eds Terry Nardin and Luke O'Sullivan (Exeter, 2006). Oakeshott, *Hobbes on Civil Association* (Indianapolis, 2000). James Tully (ed.), *Meaning and Context. Quentin Skinner and His Critics* (Cambridge, 1988).

[2] Edward Hallett Carr, *The Twenty-Years' Crisis. 1919–1939*, reprint (London and Basingstoke, 1981), pp. 9–10.

even at times when academics did not provide now extant records of theorising on international relations. Separating theory from thought in the study of international relations is thus tantamount to the unwarranted and untenable postulate that there was no theory of international relations theories before St Thomas Aquinas took up his pen.

Moreover, in looking at the change of international relations theories, historical research in these theories traces aspects of changes in the perception of the world enshrined in international relations theories. Specifically, international relations theories have featured changing statements about what has been referred to as an international system, whether this refers explicitly to Europe since the beginning of the seventeenth century or earlier and elsewhere *avant la lettre*. Consequently, ranking international relations theories among the perceptions of the world implies the assumption that an international system exists in the realm of perceptions. From an historical point of view, then, theorists claiming that the international system has the status of an objective, quasi-tangible entity in the world,[3] adhere to one or other particular brand of objectivist international relations theories that have flourished at certain times and places.

An inquiry into the history of international relations theories will seek to determine the factors for and conditions of the establishment, acceptance and criticism of certain perceptions of the world and the international relations conducted therein. In other words, in placing international systems into the realm of perceptions, the study of the history of international relations theories seeks to describe and explain the change of international systems as part and parcel of broader socio-cultural changes.

What are, in general terms, the differences between sixteenth- and seventeenth-century and twentieth- and twenty-first-century European or, for that matter, western perceptions of international relations? The question, as I shall argue, relates to differences, in terms of epistemology, in models used to describe and analyse the international system; in terms of metaphysics, of assumptions about the origin of order as the core feature of the international system; and in terms of pragmatics, to the conceptualisation of actors within the international system. Regarding epistemology, the question is well illustrated by a recent comment from 2004 on the apparent lack of explanatory capacity of balance of power theory that refers

---

[3] For examples, see Bartholomäus Keckermann, *Systema systematum* (Hannover, 1613), p. 891; Samuel Pufendorf, "Systema ciuitatum", in Pufendorf, *Dissertationes academicae selectiores* (Uppsala, 1677), pp. 210–61; Joachim Erdmann Schmidt [resp.], *Exercitatio politico-historica de ciuitatis origine ciuitatumque systematis*, LLD. Diss. (University of Jena, 1745); Ernst Carl Wieland [resp.], *Dissertatio politica de systemate civitatum*, Ph.D. Diss. (University of Leipzig, 1777), p. V; Hans Joachim Morgenthau, *Politics among Nations*, 5th edn (New York, 1975), p. 4; and Kenneth Neal Waltz, *Theory of International Politics* (Reading, MA, 1979), pp. 161–2.

to "the notion that states seek to survive as independent entities. They also seek power in the anarchical global system".[4] The statement focuses on the metaphor of survival, lending expression to the view that states can be personalised into dynamic entities which live and can be put to "death".[5] In other words, present systems analysis in International Relations proceeds through the use of a biologistic model, drawn from the human body. This is not an entirely new phenomenon, specific only to the early twenty-first century, for biologism has informed debate among international relations theorists of various branches for about two hundred years.[6] The statement is in line with biologistic international relations theory in articulating the general and non-historical claim that states have always been quasi-personal actors no matter when and where they existed. In laying claim to a general truth where reference is in fact made to a specific perception of the international system, the statement papers over the difficulty that systems analysis can, and did, proceed without resort to biologistic models elsewhere in the world and in former periods of European history. International relations theories operating under the assumption that systems analysis can be based on an inalterable epistemology are, at the very least, at a loss to explain how and why models of analysis can change and have changed. In other words, the epistemological dimension of the question about the differences between present and past perceptions of the international system brings to the fore the changing impacts that analytical models can have on the conceptualisation of the international system.

In categorising the international system as "anarchical", the quoted statement also reveals a disposition of current international relations theorists concerning metaphysics. Categorising the international system negatively as "anarchical" implies the ascription of defects, specifically the absence of institutions of rule or agencies of governance providing for order in the international system. This negative ascription or, differently stated, the unfulfilled expectation that the international system should (but perhaps cannot) have order-providing institutions or agencies, reveals the belief that human actors should in principle be seen as capable of establishing order-providing institutions or agencies. Admittedly, not all international relations theorists share the sceptical view that human actors, in establishing the international system, have failed to equip the system with order-providing institutions or agencies. Nevertheless, while such scepticism is typical of theorists in the realist camp, rival theorists, among them functionalists in the

---

[4] T.V. Paul, "Introduction. The Enduring Axioms of Balance of Power Theory and Their Contemporary Relevance", in T.V. Paul, James J. Wirtz and Michael Fortmann (eds), *Balance of Power. Theory and Practice in the 21st Century* (Stanford, 2004), pp. 1–25, p. 3.

[5] For a more explicit statement of this form of biologism, see Tanisha M. Fazal, *State Death. The Politics of Conquest, Occupation and Annexation* (Princeton, 2007).

[6] For a survey, see Harald Kleinschmidt, *The Nemesis of Power. A History of International Relations Theories* (London, 2000), pp. 21–44.

early twentieth century, and neo-liberal institutionalists in the later part of the century, operated on the common metaphysical assumption that human actors should be credited with the capability of providing for order in the international system. The perception of a gap between basic human capability and the lack of actual success in implementation is thus based on the metaphysical belief that order in the world flows from human action and can not be regarded as a given. However, this belief is far from self-evident from a cross-cultural and long-term perspective, which illustrates the different belief that order in the world in general and the international system in particular is divinely willed. Hence the metaphysical dimension of the question about the difference between past and present perceptions of the international system places an emphasis on changing assumptions about the origins of order in the international system.

Concerning pragmatics, current international relations theories appear still to be based on the recognition of the state as the major type of actor in the international system. Thus theorists are prone to draw on the ascription of anarchy and to refer to the conventional balance-of-power theoretical hypothesis "that states act rationally to maximize their security or power in anarchic systems without a higher authority to regulate disputes".[7] In doing so, these theorists admit only "states" as actors in the international system, equate states with governments and, for the purpose of theory-making, exclude all other types of potential or manifest actors. The problem with this approach primarily results not from its rigidity, but from the conventional prioritising of states as the only seemingly regular actors in the international system in distinction to apparently irregular, and thus once again negatively categorized, "non-state actors". The distinction draws on the convention of vesting the conduct of foreign policy and international relations in state rulers or governments and their appointed diplomatic representatives. This convention has been the property of what has somewhat loosely been labelled the "Westphalian" state system.[8] Surprisingly, the convention has continued to flourish despite the often reiterated observation that "Westphalia" has become the property of historians. Even within the so-called Westphalian system, however, actors other than rulers or governments of states, among them long-distance trading companies, were perfectly regular agents.[9] Hence there is hardly anything new about "non-state actors" and this

---

[7] Jack Levy, "What Do Great Powers Balance Against and When?", in T.V. Paul, James J. Wirtz and Michael Fortmann (eds), *Balance of Power. Theory and Practice in the 21st Century* (Stanford, 2004), pp. 29–51, p. 34.

[8] Gene M. Lyons and Michael Mastanduno, "Introduction", in Gene M. Lyons and Michael Mastanduno (eds), *Beyond Westphalia? State Sovereignty and International Intervention* (Baltimore, 1995), pp. 3–6.

[9] For an articulate view that the so-called "Westphalian sovereignty" has been rendered at least problematic, see Stephen D. Krasner, *Sovereignty. Organized Hypocrisy* (Princeton, 1999), pp. 118–21; James N. Rosenau, "Sovereignty in a Turbulent World", in

type of actor is also far from irregular. In conclusion, the pragmatic dimension of the question about the difference between past and present perceptions of the international system focuses on changes in the notion of actorship.

In the following analysis, I intend to use the three categories of system, order and actorship to specify the characteristic features of European sixteenth- and seventeenth-century perception of the international system. I shall describe the interconnectedness of war with diplomacy at the time that Grotius was writing. The description of practical actions by military people and practitioners of diplomacy will serve the purpose of demonstrating that sixteenth- and seventeenth-century theorists analysed the international system in a mechanistic and static, not in a biologistic and dynamic, way.

War and Diplomacy: The Eighty Years War in Context

Professionals versus Militiamen

In terms of military history, the major military confrontations over the Netherlands were contests between Spanish *Tercios*, professional warrior bands on the one side, and locally conscribed Dutch militiamen and English "Trained Bands" on the other. The strategic advantage of the deployment of professional warrior bands was that they could be dispatched anywhere and were thus ready for combat on distant battlefields, where they would be able to demonstrate their fighting prowess in dual combat. The predominant threat potential emanating from these professional warrior bands resulted from their professionalism, which placed a premium on willingness to fight to the very end and imposed heavy sanctions against desertion, insubordination and defiance of given orders. Hence the recruitment of professionals was expensive, even if they did as a rule bring their own weapons, but usually they were fairly disciplined, easy to handle, quick to deploy and could be used to impress local people in enemy territory when appearing in large numbers. By contrast, militia forces lent themselves mainly to combat *pro aris et focis*, as they were recruited for defensive purposes and manned by practitioners of civilian professions. Militia combatants would, as a rule, receive no pay, since they were conscripts, and did not bring their own weapons. Being summoned to war, they were usually unfit for dual combat and had to be trained

---

Gene M. Lyons and Michael Mastanduno (eds), *Beyond Westphalia? State Sovereignty and International Intervention* (Baltimore, 1995), pp. 191–227; Mark Zacher, "The Decaying Pillars of the Westphalian Temple", in James N. Rosenau (ed.), *Governance without Government* (New York, 1992), pp. 58–101; and Karl-Heinz Ziegler, "Pluralisierung und Autorität im europäischen Völkerrecht des Spätmittelalters und der Frühen Neuzeit", *Zeitschrift für Historische Forschung*, 30 (2004): 533–53.

to do battle, exercised in the handling of weapons and ordered into battalions remaining intact in the course of battle. As war was not their source of income, they had to be furnished with a specific motive to fight. As a rule, this motivation was drawn on the insistence by some legitimate institution of government, such as the military commander, that war was inevitable to repel an alien aggressor and safeguard the welfare of the residents.

In consequence, on the various occasions when militia forces were organised, the organisers drew on what they considered successful cases recorded in military history. Down to the eighteenth century, the legacy of warfare in Greek and Roman antiquity played by far the most important role as the provider of models for the organisation of militia forces.[10] Against the massive weight of cases recorded by the ancients, specifically Polybios and Sallust, but also of Ailianos, Frontinus and Vegetius, the few late medieval instances of successful militia warfare faced an uphill struggle, receiving recognition most notably in Machiavelli's theory of war.[11] At the turn of the seventeenth century, the Italian scholar Francesco Patrizi[12] and the Dutch philologist Justus Lipsius[13] were foremost in promoting Greek and Roman warfare as the model for militia-based military organisation. These theorists advocated the deployment of militia forces for defensive purposes and demanded that rulers should take proactive attitudes to warfare, namely by making preparations for war in times of peace or truce. As militia forces were not ready for battle immediately after recruitment, planning war became the essential prerequisite for their use, regardless of the weapons technology used. As planning requires theory, the organisation of militia forces has tended to be connected with efforts to lay down in writing thoughts on warfare. Grotius's legal theory of war thus needs to be understood against contemporary Dutch military practice.[14]

The need to plan war, if militia forces were to be deployed, ushered in a conservative approach to weapons technology. In the entire time spanned by the fourteenth, fifteenth, sixteenth and seventeenth centuries, there was only one case of a weapons-driven practice of training warrior bands, both professionals and militia men. This case related to the English longbowmen, for whom government-

---

[10] Jean-Charles Chevalier de Folard, *Histoire de Polybe. Enrichi de notes critiques et historiques* (6 vols, Amsterdam, 1753), vol.1.

[11] Niccolò Machiavelli, *L'arte della guerra* (Verona, 1979). For a study of this, see Martin Hobohm's still indispensable work, *Machiavellis Renaissance der Kriegskunst* (2 vols, Berlin, 1913).

[12] Francesco Patrizi, *La militia Romana* (Ferrara, 1583). Patrizi, *De paralleli militari* (2 vols, Rome, 1594–95).

[13] Justus Lipsius, *De milicia Romana libri quinque* (Antwerp, 1595). Lipsius, *Poliorceticon* (Antwerp, 1596).

[14] Hugo Grotius, *De jure belli ac pacis libri tres*, lib. II, cap. 1 (Paris, 1625).

stipulated training measures are already on record from the fourteenth century.[15] The effective use of the longbow by lightly armed, poorly protected combatants required pre-combat training and repetitive exercises under government control and the composition of tactical formations made up from longbowmen and heavily armed cavalry capable of giving support to and willing to serve the archers.[16] Fifteenth-century Italian warfare provided evidence that this unique type of military organisation could be used outside England only under the command of English kings, as at Agincourt,[17] or by commercially operating English commanders.[18] By the middle of the sixteenth century, the longbowmen provided the model for the regularised Trained Bands as characteristically English fighting forces.[19] The English Trained Bands had a heavy impact on combat in the course of the Eighty Years War, both through their direct participation as subsidiaries to the Dutch side and by providing the empirical record for the salience of training warriors and planning war at times of peace.[20]

Private and Public Actors in International Relations

The Eighty Years War, however, does not only present the case of a contest between two rival types of military organisation, but also a record of the diversity of actorship in international relations. While the conduct of war against the Spanish armed forces, deployed in and to the Netherlands, was considered as the legitimate activity of Dutch ruling institutions, private trading companies were thought to act on their own behalf and at their own risk in relations with rulers or states in Africa and Asia. During the latter part of the Eighty Years War, the VOC, incorporated from six local trading companies and chartered with a monopoly of trade between the Netherlands and places east of the Cape of Good Hope and west of the Straits of Magellan in 1602, became the most successful of these trading companies, ousting Portuguese traders from some of their positions along the coasts of Africa and Asia, intervening heavily in the inner Asian trade and establishing a monopoly of trade between Japan and Europe. The charter also gave license to the VOC to conclude treaties with rulers in the areas assigned to it, to build fortresses, secure places, appoint governors and deploy armed forces,

---

[15] Edward III, [Ordonnance, dated 1 June 1363], in Thomas Rymer (ed.), *Foedera, conventions, literæ conventiones cujuscunque generis act publica inter reges Angliae et alios quosuis imperatores, reges … habita aut tractata* (The Hague, 1740), vol. 3, pt 2, p. 79.
[16] See Jim Bradbury, *The Medieval Archer* (Woodbridge, 1992).
[17] See Alfred Higgins Burne, *The Agincourt War*, new edn (Ware, 1999), pp. 76–96.
[18] Geoffrey Trease, *Die Condottieri* (Munich, 1973), pp. 41–3.
[19] Roger Acham, *Toxophilus* (London, 1545), pp. 32, 33, 53, 55, 58, 59, 60–62.
[20] For further references, see Harald Kleinschmidt, *Tyrocinium militare* (Stuttgart, 1989), pp. 32–5.

to maintain order and administer justice in its own capacity. In other words, the States General as the government of the United Netherlands used their then self-claimed sovereignty to equip the VOC with essentially sovereign rights, thereby constituting the company as an international actor in the areas and seaways assigned to it. The VOC used its privileges to conclude contracts with the Shah of Iran and various rulers in the Indonesian archipelago.[21] The admission of traders as regular actors in international relations had a strong impact on the conduct of war where war occurred at all.

The common effect of the deployment of militia forces and the admission of traders as international actors was the imposition of constraints on warfare. Organisers of militia forces would be subject to the demand that militiamen should not be exposed to life-threatening campaigns unless these campaigns were warranted by the demonstrable need for the defence of the realm.[22] In the course of the Eighty Years War, the VOC managed to conduct its military operations without reducing stakeholder profits from the trade, while the House of Orange as the leaders of the military resistance against the Spanish government succeeded in mobilising a fighting force that, though not taken seriously at first by its opponents, would eventually pave the way for Spanish withdrawal from the northern Netherlands. By the same token, the Dutch military leaders licensed the VOC to maintain its own armed forces because they assigned to the company the task of driving its Portuguese-Spanish competitors away from their strongholds on the coasts of the Indian Ocean. The Eighty Years War thus imposed diverse and irreconcilable demands on both conflicting parties. The Oranian decision to

---

[21] For the charter, see the edition and translation in Ella Gepken-Jager, Gerard van Solinge and Levinus Timmermann (eds), *VOC 1602–2002. 400 Years of Company Law* (Deventer: Kluwer, 2005), pp. 23–4 (original), pp. 34–5 (translation). The charter gave expression to the monopoly in the legal form of barring entry to any ship not belonging to the company (except for ships holding a temporary license that had previously been issued and retained validity until the date of its expiration) to the areas and seaways assigned to VOC. The charter thereby prevented the States General from dispatching its own vessels to seaways east of the Cape of Good Hope. Hence the granting of the monopoly was consistent with chartering of the company to conduct its own affairs in the areas and seaways assigned to them. For the treaties, see Jan Ernst Heeres (ed.), *Corpus diplomaticum Neerlandico-Indicum* (The Hague: Nijhoff, 1931), vol. 1, passim, especially pp. 370–80 (nr CXLVI), pp. 31–3 (nr XIV) (Bijdragen tot de Taal-, Land- en Volkenkunde van Nederlandsch-Indië. 87.) Hugo Grotius, *Mare liberum. Sive De iure quod Batavis competit ad Indicana commercia* [written 1604–1605] (Leiden, 1618), pp. 15–20, 64–5.

[22] For studies see Christian Anton Krollmann, *Das Defensionswerk im Herzogtum Preußen* (2 vols, Berlin, 1904–1909); Rolf Naumann, *Das kursächsische Defensionswerk* (Leipzig, 1916); and Rainer Wohlfail, "Das Heerwesen im Übergang vom Ritter- zum Söldnerheer", in Johannes Kunisch and Barbara Stollberg-Rilinger (eds), *Staatsverfassung und Heeresverfassung in der europäischen Geschichte der frühen Neuzeit* (Berlin, 1986), pp. 107–27.

organise the war as the collective self-defence of the resident population against an allegedly illegitimate and tyrannical alien government forced the Spanish side to conduct its attacks with troops and supplies shipped to the battlefields in the Netherlands from far-away locations in Spain and other parts of Europe. As the Spanish side could hope to crush the Dutch resistance merely through the massive deployment of professional troops with heavy weaponry, the most challenging task was the provision of such warriors and supplies. By contrast, the most demanding challenge for the Oranian side was to limit the size of the Dutch fighting forces, so as not to impose constraints on the economy and retain the capability of drilling the militiamen. While the organisation of the so-called Spanish Road has received some attention among historians,[23] the Oranian militia reforms have attracted few scholars outside the Netherlands and Germany, even though their significance for the analysis of seventeenth-century warfare is far greater than that of their foes.[24] This is so because the Oranians created a set of tactical schemes aimed at reducing the number of combatants without jeopardising fighting power and systematised the tactical formations inherited from the English longbowmen. Foremost among the tactical schemes were the practice of rolling fire (as even Parker has recently admitted) and the evolution of the drill to perform it (which Parker has continued to underrate, although it was the essential precondition for the implementation of the tactic).[25] Rolling fire was a significant innovation because it allowed the continuing use of firearms by small battalions whose size permitted mobility and thus allowed commanders to shift units across the battlefield in the course of combat. Rolling fire could only be accomplished if combatants were trained to perform the necessary movements with their weapons and position themselves variously within their battalion while under enemy fire. In other words, the drill was not an accidental oddity added to Oranian warfare, but its essential precondition.

The Mechanicism Informing the Oranian Reforms

It seems that the military reformers in the House of Orange, supplementing Lipsius's work on the Roman military, drew on three sources for their drill commands, namely ancient Greek military training manuals, lansquenet tradition

---

[23] Geoffrey Parker, *The Army of Flanders and the Spanish Road* (Cambridge, 1972). René Quatrefages, *Le Tercio*. Thèse (Université de Paris IV, 1975) [Spanish version (Madrid, 1983)].

[24] The major source on the Dutch military reforms is Werner Hahlweg (ed.), *Die Heeresreform der Oranier. Das Kriegstagebuch des Grafen Johann von Nassau-Siegen* (Wiesbaden, 1973).

[25] Geoffrey Parker, "The Limits to Revolutions in Military Affairs. Maurice of Nassau, the Battle of Nieuwpoort (1600) and the Legacy", *Journal of Military History*, 71 (2007): 331–72.

recorded from the late fifteenth century and the practice of the English Trained Bands. The combination of these three sources constituted the beginning of Dutch military drill practice in the 1590s. By the first decade of the seventeenth century, the practice was becoming systematised to the degree that drill manuals went into print displaying drilling warriors and listing commands. The result, to cut a long and complicated story short,[26] was a well-organised armed force composed of small battalions that could be moved on the battlefield. War, as the Oranians conceived it, was to follow man-made rules, to become subject to pre-combat planning and to be conducted by fighting forces as if they were mobile machines.[27] Yet, once constructed, the machines signified the regularity of process and the continuity of structure. The machines would not change at their own discretion and through their own will. As Hobbes would say: "The Machine was an artificial Man".[28]

The mechanistic model associated with war did not arise as a mere contingency at the turn of the seventeenth century, since contemporary political thinkers emphasised human action as a condition for the coming into existence of institutions of rule and political order within and across states. They did so with increasing frequency in the course of the seventeenth century. The insertion of human will in the making and transformation of institutions of rule has long been accepted as the core characteristic of rebellions organised by local neighbourhoods seeking to assert their freedom against an outside authority.[29] The number of records of violent protest among rebellious neighbourhood groups increased dramatically from the sixteenth century onwards.[30] The unrest spreading in the Netherlands during the second half of the sixteenth century was merely one case, but one that has been given importance because it spilt over from a domestic neighbourhood protest into a war against the then globally operating predominant European military power. In other words, it was not primarily the mobilisation of neighbourhood resistance capability that has boosted the significance

---

[26] Kleinschmidt, *Tyrocinium militare*, pp. 96–149.

[27] Johann Jakobi von Wallhausen, *Progamma schola militaris* (Frankfurt, 1616), pp. 17–23, specifically nos V, X, XII.

[28] Thomas Hobbes, *Leviathan*, Introduction (London, 1651), p. 1. Newly ed. Richard Tuck (Cambridge, 1991), p. 9.

[29] See Peter Blickle and Elisabeth Müller-Luckner (eds), *Theorien kommunaler Ordnung in Europa* (Munich, 1996); Blickle (ed.), *Resistance, Representation and Community* (Oxford, 1997); Blickle, *Kommunalismus* (2 vols, Munich, 2000); Blickle, "Die ‚Consociatio' bei Johannes Althusius als Verarbeitung kommunaler Erfahrung", in Blickle, Thomas Otto Hüglin and Dieter Wyduckel (eds), *Subsidiarität* (Berlin, 2002), pp. 215–35; František Graus, *Struktur und Geschichte; Drei Volksaufstände im mittelalterlichen Prag* (Sigmaringen, 1971); Knut Schulz, *Denn sie lieben die Freiheit so sehr. Kommunale Aufstände und die Entstehung des europäischen Bürgertums im Hochmittelalter* (Darmstadt, 1992).

[30] Andreas Würgler, Unruhen und Öffentlichkeit Städtische und ländliche Protestbewegungen im 18. Jahrhundert (Tübingen, 1995).

of the Dutch Revolt, but its effect on the conduct of international relations within and beyond Europe. The leaders of the Dutch Revolt successfully asserted their willingness not merely to restore autonomy to their government, but also to manifest themselves as privately operating institutional actors across the international system. In both respects, the legal mechanism used to accomplish these goals was the contract. Although conjurations have been recorded since the eighth century,[31] and even though the idea of making a contract to establish legitimate government was already used in the urban foundation charters of the twelfth century,[32] it was the Dutch Revolt that provided the first record of willingness to organise neighbourhood resistance against a perceived alien ruler on the basis of a written and formally approved contract.[33] Whereas since the fourteenth century contractualism had been employed as a theory legitimising monarchical government,[34] and continued to be used in the sixteenth[35]

---

[31] See Otto Gerhard Oexle, "Gilden als soziale Gruppen in der Karolingerzeit", in Herbert Jankuhn, Walter Janssen, Ruth Schmidt-Wiegand und Heinrich Tiefenbach (eds), *Das Handwerk in vor- und frühgeschichtlicher Zeit* (Göttingen, 1981), pp. 284–354.

[32] For instance, see the early twelfth-century Freiburg town privilege, ed. Friedrich Keutgen, *Urkunden zur städtischen Verfassungsgeschichte* (Berlin, 1899), Nr 133. For further evidence, see Charles Petit-Dutaillis, *Les communes françaises* (Paris, 1947), S. 26–36; Christoph Dartmann, "Innere Friedensschlüsse in den italienischen Stadtkommunen. Öffentliche Interaktion und schriftliche Fixierung", *Frühmittelalterliche Studien*, 38 (2004): 355–69; Gerhard Dilcher, *Bürgerrecht und Stadtverfassung* (Cologne, Weimar and Vienna, 1996); and Dilcher, "Bürgerrecht und Bürgereid als städtische Verfassungsstruktur", in Rainer Christoph Schwinges (ed.), *Neubürger im späten Mittelalter. Migration und Austausch in der Städtelandschaft des alten Reiches (1250–1550)* (Berlin, 2002), pp. 83–97.

[33] Explicitly in the Pacification of Gent of 1576, the Union of Utrecht of 1579 and the edict of the States General of 1581. Printed in *Texts Concerning the Revolt of the Netherlands*, edited by Ernst Heinrich Kossman[n] and Albert Fredrik Mellink (Cambridge: Cambridge University Press, 1974), pp. 126–35, 165–73, 216–28.

[34] Willem P. Blokmans, "Du contrat féodal à la souveraineté du peuple", in *Assemblee di stati e istituzioni rappresentative nella storia del pensiero politico moderno* (Rimini, 1983), pp. 135–50; Yves Marie-Joseph Congar, "Quod omnes tangit ab omnibus tractari et approbari debet", *Revue historique de droit français et étranger*, 6 (1958): 210–259; Antonio Marongiu, "Das Prinzip der Demokratie und der Zustimmung", *Studia Gratiana*, vol. 8 (1962): 555–75; Werner Näf, "Herrschaftsverträge und die Lehre vom Herrschaftsvertrag", *Schweizer Beiträge zur allgemeinen Geschichte*, 7 (1949): 26–52; Näf (ed.), *Herrschaftsverträge des Spätmittelalters* (Bern, 1951); Gerhard Oestreich, "Die Idee des religiösen Bundes und die Lehre vom Staatsvertrag", in Wilhelm Berges (ed.), *Zur Geschichte und Problematik der Demokratie. Festgabe für Hans Herzfeld* (Berlin, 1958), pp. 11–32; Gaines Post, "A Romano-canonical Maxim 'Quod omnes tangit' in Bracton", *Traditio*, 4 (1946): 197–251; Post, "A Roman Legal Theory of Consent", *Wisconsin Law Review* (1950): 66–78.

[35] Richard Hooker, *Of the Lawes of Ecclesiasticall Politie. Eyght Bookes* (London, 1594), pp. 70–73. Juan de Mariana, *De rege et regis institutione libri III*, lib. I, cap. 1 (Toledo, 1599), pp. 21–2.

and seventeenth centuries,[36] the ideologues supporting the Dutch Revolt went further. They used the institution of the conjuration not merely to establish the legitimacy of government, but also to charter contractual private trading companies and to equip them with the privilege to conduct international relations on their own.[37]

In short, while political decision-makers at the turn of the seventeenth century deemed human action capable of provoking transformations of power relations, they perceived the structure and composition of the international system as unchangeable and beyond the reach of human will.[38] Without himself employing balance-of-power arguments, Grotius followed suit in demanding that, in pursuit of legitimate self-interest, rulers should not make use of all available and not even of all legitimate strategies, whether in preparations for or in the conduct of wars.[39]

Military and International Relations Theory: The Ethics of Self-Constraint, the Law of War and the Preservation of Stability

The Impacts of Political Aristotelianism and Augustinian Peace Theology

The decades around 1600 witnessed an unprecedentedly high density of printed works on politics, mostly but not exclusively drawing on the philosophy of Aristotle.[40] While some authors, such as Crucé,[41] Althusius[42] and Arnisaeus,[43] have received a good deal of attention among historians of political thought, the general attitude towards authors writing between Machiavelli and Hobbes has been one of neglect, as these authors have been judged mainly merely to restate conventions. While this verdict is fair to the extent that many authors of

---

[36] Johannes Althusius [praes.], Hugo Pelletarius [resp.], *Disputatio politica de regno recte instituendo et administrando* (Herborn, 1602), theses 6–56. Althusius, *Politica methodice digesta*, lib. I, cap. 2, lib. I, cap. 7, lib. IX, cap. 12, lib. XIX, cap. 12, third edn (Herborn, 1614) [newly ed. Carl Joachim Friedrich (Cambridge, 1932), pp. 15, 16, 90, 161].

[37] For the text of the VOC charter, see above, note 21.

[38] Keckermann, *Systema*, p. 901. Theorists seconded and proclaimed that form of government as the best that would be least likely of succumbing to change.

[39] Grotius, *De iure belli*, lib. II, cap. 18, 19.

[40] For the context, see Wilhelm Bleek, *Geschichte der Politikwissenschaft in Deutschland* (Munich, 2001), pp. 62–4.

[41] Emeric de Crucé, *Le nouveau Cynée* [1623] (Paris, 1976). English version s. t.: *The New Cineas* [1623] (Philadelphia, 1909).

[42] Althusius, *Politica methodice digesta*, passim.

[43] Henning Arnisaeus, *Doctrina politica in genuinam methodum quae est Aristotelis reducta* (Frankfurt, 1612). On Arnisaeus, see Horst Dreitzel, *Protestantischer Aristotelismus und absoluter Staat. Die Politica des Henning Arnisaeus* (c. 1575–1636) (Wiesbaden, 1970).

the later sixteenth and the earlier seventeenth centuries wrote within the confines of Aristotelianism and a few derived their position from the Younger Stoa,[44] the verdict should not be used to deny that authors like Bartholomaeus Keckermann in Gdansk and Justus Lipsius in Leiden wielded considerable influence in their own time and should therefore be taken seriously as propagators of political thought. Of these, the Calvinist Aristotelian polymath Keckermann had the widest influence across the disciplines, ranging from theology to geography.[45]

---

[44] Cf. Günter Abel, *Stoizismus und Frühe Neuzeit* (Berlin and New York, 1978); Albertine Maria van de Bilt, *Lipsius' De Constantia en Seneca*, Ph.D. Diss. (Catholic University of Nimwegen, 1946); Julien Eymard d' Angers, "Le Stoicisme en France dans la première moitié du XVIIe siècle", *Etudes franciscaines*, N. S., vol. 2 (1952), pp. 287–97, 389–400, vol. 3 (1953), pp. 5–20, 133–57; Leonard Forster, "Lipsius and Renaissance Neostoicism", in Anthony Stephens, Harold Leslie Rogers and Brian Coghlan (eds), *Festschrift for Ralph Farrell* (Bern, 1977), pp. 201–20; Martin van Gelderen, "The Machiavellian Moment and the Dutch Revolt. The Rise of Neostoicism and Dutch Republicanism", in Gisela Bock, Quentin Skinner and Maurizio Viroli (eds), *Machiavelli and Republicanism* (Cambridge, 1990), pp. 205–23; Gelderen, "Holland und das Preußentum", *Zeitschrift für Historische Forschung*, 23 (1996): 29–56; Simone Hopchet, *Le Stoicisme de Juste Lipse*, Ph. D. Thesis (University of Louvain, 1942); Jacqueline Lagrée, *Juste Lipse et la restauration du Stoicisme* (Paris, 1994); Jacqueline Lagrée (ed.), *Le Stoicisme aux XIVe et XVIIe siècles* (Caen, 1994); Bo Lindberg, *Stoicism och stat. Justus Lipsius och den politiska humanism* (Stockholm, 2001); Eco O.G. Haitsma Mulier, "Neostoicisme en het vroegmoderne Europa", *Theoretische geschiedenis*, 5 (1978): 69–82; Mulier, "Het neostoicisme in de zeventiende eeuw", *Theoretische geschiedenis*, 9 (1982): 130–33; Gerhard Oestreich, "Der römische Stoizismus und die oranische Heeresreform", *Historische Zeitschrift*, 176 (1953): 17–43; Oestreich, "Die antike Literatur als Vorbild der praktischen Wissenschaften", in Robert Ralph Bolgar (ed.), *Classical Influences on European Culture* (Cambridge, 1976), pp. 315–24; Oestreich, *Neostoicism and the Early Modern State*, ed. Brigitta Oestreich and Helmut Georg Koenigsberger (Cambridge, 1982), especially pp. 13–27, 39–55, 57–75, 76–89, 90–117; Oestreich, *Antiker Geist und moderner Staat bei Justus Lipsius*, ed. Marianne Elisabeth Henriette Nicolette Mout (Göttingen, 1989); John Hearsey McMillan Salmon, "Stoicism and Roman Example. Seneca and Tacitus in Jacobean England", *Journal of the History of Ideas*, 50 (1989): 199–225; Petrus Hermannus Schrijvers, "Justus Lipsius. Over standvastigheid bij algemene rampspoed", *Lampas*, 16 (1983): 107–28; Carl Siedschlag, *Der Einfluß der niederländisch-neustoischen Ethik in der politischen Theorie zur Zeit Sullys und Richelieus* (Berlin, 1978); Werner Welzig, "Constantia und barocke Beständigkeit", *Deutsche Vierteljahresschrift für Literaturwissenschaft und Geistesgeschichte*, 35 (1961): 416–32; Leontine Zanta, *La Renaissance du Stoicisme au XVIe siècle* (Paris, 1914).

[45] For studies on Keckermann, see Manfred Büttner, "Die Neuausrichtung der Geographie im 17. Jahrhundert durch Bartholomäus Keckermann", *Geographische Zeitschrift*, 63 (1975): 1–12; Büttner (ed.), *Wandlungen im geographischen Denken von Aristoteles bis Kant* (Paderborn, Munich, Vienna and Zurich, 1979), pp. 153–72; Friedrich Goedeking, *Die "Politik" des Lambertus Danaeus, Johannes Althusius und Bartholomäus Keckermann*. DD Thesis, typescript (University of Heidelberg, 1977); and Willen Henrdik Zuylen, *Bartholomäus Keckermann. Sein Leben und sein Werk*, Ph.D. Thesis (University of Tübingen, 1934).

Keckermann's posthumously published two-volume *Systema systematum* represents a grand attempt at cross-disciplinary analysis, wherein politics, together with economics and ethics, found its place in the discipline of Practical Philosophy. Keckermann assigned to politics the task of analysing the "happiness or civil beauty of several humans ... consociated in a house".[46] Although the house metaphor for the state suggests human building activity as the basic condition for state-making, Keckermann positioned monarchy as the best form of government because he ranked it as the most stable. According to Keckermann, this was so because monarchy was best ordered and most difficult to divide, since under the government of a divinely ordained ruler it had the most solid unity.[47] Keckermann thus ranked the absence of change as the prime condition of happiness. The preservation of the status quo as a condition of happiness required the permanence of order, which Keckermann deemed most easily accomplished if there was only one divinely instituted ruler and a clear distinction between the giver and the recipients of commands.[48] In suggesting that human actors have the capability of choosing among a variety of forms of government, Keckermann implicitly surmised that forms of government were neither givens nor divinely willed. Thus he was more Aristotelian than some of his fourteenth-century predecessors.[49] However, he argued that human beings should reasonably opt for that form of government which, he thought, most contributed to maintaining the divinely willed stability of the world. Thus, in his quest for stability, Keckermann was in line with authors theorising on the justice of war at the time of the Eighty Years War.

In essence, just war theories were elaborations of the Augustininan theological paradigm that prevailed into the late Scholastic law theories of the sixteenth century,[50] which admitted solely the restitution of previously received injustice as a legitimate war aim and sought to constitute just war as a means of restoring peace in a more stable constitution. In promoting the sequence of peace – war – peace, the Augustininan theological paradigm positioned war as a sinful temporary human infringement of the divinely willed condition of peace, while also boosting the

---

[46] Keckermann, *Systema*, pp. 890, 891. "Consociatio" is a Lipsian term, also appearing in Althusius, *Politica*.

[47] Keckermann, *Systema*, p. 901.

[48] Keckermann, *Systema*, p. 900.

[49] Cf Engelbert of Admont, "De ortu et fine Romani imperii", cap. 2, ed. Melchior Goldast of Haiminsfeld, *Politica imperialia* (Frankfurt, 1614), p. 755, and John Quidort of Paris, *De potestate regia et papali*, cap. 1, ed. Fritz Bleienstein (Stuttgart, 1969), pp. 75–8. Engelbert regarded universal rule as divinely instituted.

[50] See Francisco de Vitoria, "Relectio de potestate civili [1528]", in Vitoria, *Relectiones morales* (Cologne, 1696), p. 5.

quest for strategies towards perpetual peace.[51] Thus, at the time of the Eighty Years War, pamphleteer Emeric de Crucé took up the fifteenth-century plea in favour of taking deliberate government action for the purpose of effectively ending war through the formation of some federation of states and their rulers.[52] Crucé's idea that governments should purposefully agree to end all wars, thereby reconstituting the divinely willed peace, was not entirely speculative. In 1518, several European rulers, most likely induced by Erasmus of Rotterdam's peace tract *Querela pacis* of 1517, and including Emperor Maximilian I, had already signed an actual treaty instituting a general peace in Europe and obligating the signatory parties to refrain from resorting to war and instead to submit their controversies to an institution of arbitration.[53] The treaty had obvious limitations. It was confined to the Christian rulers of Europe and had an aggressive background in that it was concluded for the purpose of facilitating a crusade against the Ottoman Turkish Empire. Moreover, the treaty failed to accomplish its goal, since the institution of arbitration was not put into action. Nevertheless, the treaty remained on the agenda of diplomats until 1525, albeit mainly as the focal point of accusations that it had been broken.[54] Thus the treaty provided evidence to the effect that just war theories were not confined to the arcane realm of pure theory, but could actually have an impact on the practical conduct of international relations.

Lipsius's Ethics of Self-Constraint and Grotius

The influence of just war theories was restricted neither to setting the agenda for diplomatic quibbles nor to establishing the conditions for ending specific wars in a particular part of the world. Instead, the metaphysics informing just war theories promoted the construction of a framework of norms and rules positioned above

---

[51] Kurt von Raumer, *Ewiger Friede. Friedensrufe und Friedenspläne seit der Renaissance* (Freiburg and Munich, 1953), pp. 2–3.

[52] Cruce, *Cineas*. Previous proposals in the same direction were made by George of Podiebrad, King of Bohemia, in the 1460s, and contemporaneously with Crucé by Maximilien de Béthune de Sully, *Sully's Grand Design of Henry IV* [1607], ed. David Ogg (London, 1921).

[53] The text of the peace treaty has been edited by Thomas Rymer, *Foedera, conventions, litteræ et cujusque generis acta publica inter reges Angliae et alios quosvius imperatores, reges, pontifices, principes vel communitates* (London, 1714), vol. 13, pp. 624–9 [reprint (Farnborough, 1967)], and by Jean Dumont, Baron de Carels-Croon, *Corps diplomatique universel* (The Hague, 1726), vol. 4, pt 1, No. 125, pp. 269–75. Adler restated the proposal in 1944: Mortimer Jerome Adler, *How to Think about War and Peace* [1944] (New York, 1995), pp. 158–9.

[54] On the treaty and its aftermath, see Harald Kleinschmidt, *Charles V. The World Emperor* (Stroud, 2005), pp. 94–102. Garrett Mattingly, "An Early Non-Aggression Pact", *Journal of Modern History*, 10 (1938): 1–30. Mattingly, *Renaissance Diplomacy* (London and Boston, 1955).

rulers and the states under their control. The gist of the writings of Justus Lipsius on political theory and the theory of international relations consists of specifying the metaphysical origin of universally applicable norms and rules for the conduct of international relations. While Lipsius drew on medieval contractualism for his theory of the legitimacy of government, he appears to have been the first theorist to apply the legacy of contractualism in the context of the Dutch Revolt, in the aftermath of the Union of Utrecht.[55] It thus made sense for Lipsius to specify that the hypothetical contract between the ruled and their appointed ruler consisted in the dualism of the ruler's obligation to provide security for the ruled and the obligation of the ruled to supply loyalty to the ruler.

Advising rulers on what he considered to be proper behaviour before and during a war, Lipsius wrote:

> [N]ever make any attack that is not permitted by custom, and reason. For war, like peace, has its laws: and you must wage war no less justly than courageously. And indeed in every commonwealth the laws of war must be especially upheld. Because rashly to go to war, and join battle with the enemy, is something heinous and close to beastly behaviour. And if we allow it to happen, what else will there be than wars between all nations? And shall we, after the manner of Barbarians, avenge killing with killing and blood with blood? We should not. And may the following ideas never penetrate your mind: Justice is a question of arms, and everything belongs to him who is strong.[56]

Through his demand that rulers should constrain their rightful competence to resort to war, Lipsius established an ethics of self-constraint. Despite his declared

---

[55] For Lipsius's editions and commentaries, see especially Justus Lipsius, [Cornelii Taciti] *Historiarum et Annalium libri qui exstant … eiusdem Taciti liber de moribus Germanorum, Iulii Agricolae vita, Dialogus de oratore* (Antwerp, 1574); Lipsius, *Ad Annales Cornelii Taciti liber commentaries sive notae* (Antwerp, 1581); Lipsius, *Animadversiones in Tragoedias quae L[ucio] Annaeo Senecae tribuntur* (Leiden, 1588); Lipsius, *Lucii Annaei Senecae Philosophi Opera quae exstant* (Antwerp, 1605). For his work on political philosophy see Justus Lipsius, *Politicorum sive de doctrina civilis libri sex* (Leiden, 1589), English version, *Six Bookes of Politickes or Civil Doctrine*, ed. William Jones (London, 1594) [reprint (Amsterdam and New York, 1970)]. Newly ed. Jan Waszink (Assen, 2004). I have used Waszink's translation with modifications. Lipsius, *De constancia libri duo* (Antwerp, 1584). For contractarian statements within the political theory of the Dutch Revolt see *Copie eens sendtbriefs der Ridderschap, Edelen ende Steden van Holland* (Dordrecht, 1573), p. A III. *Discours contenant le vray entendement de la Pacification de Gand* (1579), p. 23.

[56] Lipsius, *Politicorum*, p. 128; ed. Waszink, p. 540. It is noteworthy that Lipsius, contrary to some of his more politically minded contemporaries, spotted "barbarians" in antiquity, not in the Americas.

sympathy for the realist aspects of Machiavelli's political doctrines,[57] Lipsius argued that rulers should subject themselves to moral constraints in accordance with reason and act in accordance with such constraints even in the extreme circumstances of war. Following Aquinas, he demanded that moral laws of war should be accepted by all contending parties for the purpose of reducing the likelihood of wars and the amount of violence committed in their course. In addition to this, he maintained that humankind existed as a metaphysical unity overarching the multifarious antagonistic warring territorial polities and urban communities and was manifest as such in a universal ethics. In this respect, he agreed on principle with the sixteenth-century proponents of international law, but emphasised more strongly than they the necessity that universal ethics should and could be accepted voluntarily:

> If we respect the whole nature of man, all these earthly countries are vain and falsely so termed, except only in respect of the body and not of the mind or soul which, descending down from that highest habitation, deem all the whole earth as a gaol or prison. But heaven is our true and rightful country, whether let us advance all our cogitations that we may freely say with Anaxagoras to such as foolishly ask us whether we have no regard to our country? Yes, verily, but yonder is our country, lifting our finger and mind up towards heaven.[58]

In this passage, Lipsius employed a series of conventions. He drew on ancient Greek philosophy for the juxtaposition of the body and the soul and joined to it the imagery of heaven and earth. Yet, unlike the authors of his Greek sources, Lipsius was not interested in ontology. Instead, he used the conventional phrases in the context of his international theory in order to demonstrate that the manifestly existing pluralism and particularism of territorial polities and urban communities stood, as antagonistic spaces of regular communication, in opposition to the theoretical postulate of the moral unity of humankind as a whole. Hence, when relieved of the fusion of the Platonic body-versus-soul dichotomy with the Anaxagorean earth-versus-heaven imagery, Lipsius's international theory made explicit the demand that the idea of humankind should overarch the multitude of antagonistic spaces of regular communication in the world.

Lipsius justified this demand on the grounds of reason. He defined reason metaphorically as "a true sense and judgment of things human and divine"[59] and

---

[57] Lipsius mentioned Machiavelli twice briefly in *Politicorum*, ed. Waszink, pp. 230, 508. He praised Machiavelli's plea for fraud with the qualification that fraud needs to remain confined within the limits of prudence. The papal censor Peregrinus, commenting on Lipsius's work, objected to this position, accusing Lipsius of having pleading for fraudulent conduct. See Laelius Peregrinus, [Report], ed. Waszink, pp. 712–4.

[58] Lipsius, *Constancia*, p. 98. [spelling and punctuation have been modernised].

[59] Lipsius, *Constancie*, p. 79 [spelling and punctuation have been modernised].

accepted it as the ultimate source from which the principles governing humankind as a whole were to be derived. Lipsius argued that reason leads to "patience", the "true mother of constancie" which, in turn, he prescribed for rulers as "a right and immovable strength of the mind, neither lifted up nor pressed down with external or casual accidents". If necessary, "the mind must be changed, not the place".[60] On this basis, he could conclude that only acting in accordance with reason could usher in "constancie" or steadfastness and thus contribute to the well-being of territorial polities and urban communities.

Although Lipsius pleaded for flexibility in the conduct of politics he equated "constancie" with *stabilitas loci*, the willingness to remain where one is, and with *tranquillitas animi*, the stability of the mind, the latter of which he expressed through the technical model of the scales. In the context of international relations, this meant that the several rulers representing the diversity of antagonistic territorial polities and urban communities could commit themselves to the maintenance of the status quo as the condition of stability and peace if and as long as they remained guided by reason. Lipsius was aware, however, of the difficulty that rulers had the option of acting unreasonably and could not be prevented from doing so. They would do so, he thought, out of neglect of the polities entrusted to their rule. Thus Lipsius had to create a juncture between humankind as a universal moral entity and the pluralism of co-existing rival polities. To that end, he drew on the contractualism argued by fourteenth-century political theorists:

> I confess, I say, that every one of us has an inclination and good will to his lesser country. The causes whereof I perceive are to you unknown. You would have it from nature. But the truth is, it grows of custom or of some decree and ordinance. For after that men forsook their wild and savage manner of living and began to build houses and walled towns, to join in society and to use means offensive and defensive. Behold then a certain communion necessarily began among them and a social participation of diverse things. They parted the earth between them with certain limits and bounds. They had temples in common, also market places, treasuries, seats of judgment. And principal ceremonies, rites, laws. All which things our greediness began in time so to esteem and make account of as if they were our own in particular? And so be they in some sort, for that every private citizen had some interest in them, neither did they differ from private possessions saving that they were not wholly in one man's power. This consociation and fellowship gave the form and fashion to a new erected state which now we call properly the commonwealth or our country.

---

[60] Lipsius, *Constancie*, pp. 77–9. Similarly in the letter on travelling. See Justus Lipsius, "De ratione cum fructu peregrinandi et praesertim in Italia. Epistola ad Ph. Lanyum", in Lipsius, *Epistolarum selectarum tres centuriae* (Antwerp, 1691), no. XXII, pp. 23–9 [first published (Antwerp, 1581).

> Wherein when men saw the chiefest stay of each person's safety to consist, laws were enacted for the succour and defence thereof. Or at least such customs were received by tradition from the predecessors to their posterity that grew to be of like force as laws. Here hence it comes to pass that we rejoice at the good of the commonwealth and be sorry for her harm. Because our own private goods are secure by her safety and are lost by her overthrow.[61]

Lipsius used contractualism to demarcate the conceptual boundary between the public and the private spheres and provided an argument in support of his position that the security of the private sphere cannot be established in separation from the security of the public sphere.[62] He did so in order to defend the existence of territorial polities and urban communities as institutions for the legitimate safeguard of private property, and emphasised the voluntarism with which human actors enter into a contract and renounce some of their natural freedom. Admittedly, Lipsius did not employ the fully fledged phraseology of contractualism which Juan de Mariana,[63] Francisco Suarez,[64] Richard Hooker[65] and Johannes Althusius[66] were to use shortly after him. But voluntarism was inherent in his concept of "consociation" (which Althusius would later borrow from Lipsius). It was from this rationalist notion of "consociation" that Lipsius derived the "commonwealth" through custom or decree and ordinance and neither from the divinely ordained world order nor (as his fellow Aristotelians would do) from some natural sociability of human beings. The notion of "consociation" displays Lipsius's efforts to disentangle customary and statutory law as the appurtenances of voluntaristically established spaces of regular communication from the moral norms pertaining to humankind as a whole.

As Lipsius composed his international theory in the United Netherlands, it was appropriate for him to avail himself of such contractualism. This was because the United Netherlands had been established as a polity through an actual contract laid down in a charter. This agreement was signed at Utrecht in 1579 in the form of a union treaty among the councils of towns and cities and rural aristocrats who were trying to free themselves from Spanish rule.[67] The constitutions of the

---

[61] Lipsius, *Constancie*, pp. 95–6 [spelling and punctuation have been modernised].
[62] For earlier sixteenth-century allusions by theorists to contractualism see Vitoria, "Relectio", p. 5. Marius Salamonius, *De principatu libri septem* (Rome, 1544), p. 38.
[63] Mariana, *De rege et regis institutione,* lib. I, cap. 1, pp. 21–2.
[64] Francisco Suarez, *De legibus (III 1–16): de civili potestate,* III/ii, 4–6, ed. L. Pereña and V. Abril (Madrid, 1975), pp. 24–7.
[65] Richard Hooker, *Of the Lawes of Ecclesiasticall Politie. Eyght Bookes* (London, 1594), pp. 70–73 [reprint (Amsterdam and New York, 1971)].
[66] Althusius, *Politica*.
[67] Printed in Ernst Heinrich Kossman[n] and Albert Fredrik Mellink (eds), *Texts Concerning the Revolt of the Netherlands* (Cambridge, 1974), pp. 165–73.

Dutch towns and cities, like towns and cities elsewhere in Europe, provided the best possible empirical support for contractualist political theories. Even though Lipsius regarded monarchy as the best form of government, he was far from a wholehearted supporter of the Dutch Revolt and may have left Leiden in 1591 in protest against what he perceived as a radicalisation of the revolutionary momentum. The established contractualism enabled Lipsius to juxtapose his ethical view of humankind as a lasting and stable moral entity to his legalistic perception of the diversity of "commonwealths" as local, law-governed but antagonistic, competitive and constantly changing institutions of legitimate rule established for the defence of the specific property and interests of private individuals.[68]

---

[68] For the debate on Lipsius's attitude towards the Dutch Revolt, see J.A.C. Lancée, "De pennestrijd tussen Lipsius en Coornherr", *Spiegel historiael*, 12 (1977): 671–6; Francine de Nave, "De polemiek tussen Justus Lispius en Dierck Volckertsy. Coornherr (1590). Hoofdoorzaak van Lipsius vertrek uit Leiden", in *De Gulden Passer*, 48 (1970): 1–39. Against Nave, Marianne Elisabeth Henriette Nicolette Mout, "In het schip. Justus Lipsius en de Nederlandse opstand tot 1591", in Simon Groenveld, Marianne Elisabeth Henriette Nicolette Mout and Ivo Schöffer (eds), *Bestuurdes en geleerden. Opstellen over onderwerpen uit de Nederlandse geschiedenis van de zestiende, zenevtiende ende achttiende eeuw, aangeboden aan Professor Jan Juliaan Woltjer bij zijn afschied als hoogleraar van de Rijksuniversiteit te Leiden* (Amsterdam, 1985): 55–64, argued that it was not the specific polemic with one of his adversaries that induced Lipsius to leave Leiden but general disgruntlement with the process of the revolt. See also Mout, "Justus Lipsius and Leiden University", in Aloïs Gerlo (ed.), *Juste Lipse (1547–1606). Colloque international* (Brussels, 1988), pp. 84–99; Mout, "Ideales Muster oder erfundene Eigenart. Republikanische Theorien während des niederländischen Aufstands", in Helmut Georg Koenigsberger and Elisabeth Müller-Luckner (eds), *Repliken und Republikanismus im Europa der Frühen Neuzeit* (Munich, 1988), pp. 169–94; H.T. Oberman, "Van Leiden naar Leuven. De overgang van Justuis Lipsius naar eende Roomsche universiteit", *Nederlandsch archief voor kerkgeschiedenis*, N.S., vol. 5 (1908): 68–111, 191–227, 269–304. For general studies of Lipsius's life and analyses of his work see Knud Banning, *Justus Lipsius* (Copenhagen, 1975); Ronny Dusoir, Jeanine G. de Landtsheer and D. Imhof (eds), *Justus Lipsius (1547–1606) en het Plantijnse Huis* (Antwerp, 1997); Karl Alfred Engelbert Enenkel, "De neolatijnse Politica. Justus Lipsius, *Politicorum libri sex*", *Lampas*, 18 (1985): 350–362; Enenkel und Christian Lambert Heesakkers (eds), *Lipsius in Leiden. Studies in the Life and Works of a Great Humanist* (Voorthuizen, 1997); Jeanine G. de Landtsheer (ed), *Iam illustravit omnia. Justus Lipsius als lievelingsauteur van het Plantijnse huis* (Antwerp, 2006); *Justus Lipsius (1547–1606). Een geleerde en zijn Europese network. Catalogus van de tentoonstelling in de Centrale Bibliotheek te Leuven, 18 Oktober–20 December 2006* (Louvain, 2006); Marc Laureys (ed.), *The Work of Justus Lipsius. A Contribution Towards His Intellectal Biography* (Rome and Brussels, 1997); Christian Mouchel (ed.), *Juste Lipse (1547–1606) en son temps. Actes du Colloque de Strasbourg 1994* (Paris, 1996); Francine de Nave, "Justus Lipsius, schrijver 'in politicis'", *Res publica*, 11 (1969): 590–622; Viljo Adolf Nordman, *Justus Lipsius als Geschichtsforscher und Geschichtslehrer* (Helsinki, 1932); Théophile Simar, "Notices sur les livres de Juste Lipse", *Revue des bibliothèques*, 17 (1907):

Hence, Lipsius's unequivocal plea for monarchy as the best form of government and his close association with Oranian military leadership, specifically Maurice of Orange, positioned him against radical republicanism. He used the historiographical work of Tacitus, which he had carefully edited, to support his pleas that rulers should use their legitimate power with prudence. In extracting historiographical sources for moral wisdom, Lipsius was in accord with his contemporary humanists. Consequently, Lipsius appreciated Tacitus for what he perceived as the historian's insights into the morality of rulers, rather than as a source of information on Roman politics of the first century A.D.[69]

261–83; Tournoy, J. Papy and Jeanine G. de Landtsheer (eds), *Lipsius en Leuven. Catalogus van de tentoonstelling in de Centrale Bibliotheek te Leuven* (Louvain, 1997); Tournoy, J. Papy and Jeanine G. de Landtsheer (eds), *Iustus Lipsius Europae Lumen et Columen. Proceedings of the International Colloquium Leuven, 17–19 September 1997* (Louvain, 1999); Maurizio Viroli, *From Politics to Reason of State. The Acquisition and Transformation of the Language of Politics. 1250–1600* (Cambridge, 1992); Hans Wansink, *Politieke wetenschappen aan de Leidse Universiteit. 1575–ca. 1650* (Utrecht, 1981); On early modern republicanism see *Estates and Revolutions* (Ithaca, 1971); Helmut Georg Koenigsberger (ed.), *Republiken und Republikanismus im Europa der Frühen Neuzeit* (Munich and Vienna, 1988).

[69] For arguments against Stoicism and in favour of some Tacitism in Lipsius's work, see Waszink, pp. 10–41, 93–8, 148–55. However, Waszink's arguments are far from convincing. They boil down to the observation that Lipsius did not refer explicitly to *constantia* in *De politicorum* (p. 13). While this observation is correct, it by no means supports the conclusion in view of the fact that Lipsius had published an entire book on *Constantia* five years before *De politicorum*. Moreover, associating Lipsius retrospectively with Tacitus rather than with the Stoa neglects that fact that Lipsius's work was received outside the Netherlands in conjunction with the pleas for Stoic positions. This was the case specifically in the context of arguments concerning military reforms and the formulation of ideologies of state institution building. It is noteworthy in this respect that the reception of Lipsius's political theory was not confined to the Dutch Calvinist allies in the Holy Roman Empire but, despite the objections by the Vatican (note 57), extended far into the Catholic world. On the reception of Lipsius's work, see Barbara Bauer, "Jacob Pontanus SJ, ein oberdeutscher Lipsius", *Zeitschrift für bayerische Landesgeschichte*, 47 (1984): 77–120; Karl Alfred Blüher, *Seneca in Spanien. Untersuchungen zur Geschichte der Seneca-Rezeption in Spanien vom 13. bis 17. Jahrhundert* (Munich, 1969); Theodore G. Corbett, "The Cult of Lipsius. A Leading Source of Early Modern Spanish Statecraft", *Journal of the History of Ideas*, 36 (1975): 139–52; Gareth Alban Davies, "The Influence of Justus Lipsius on Juan de Vera y Figueroa's Exbaxador (1620)", *Bulletin of Hispanic Studies*, 42 (1965): 160–73; Martin van Gelderen, *Political Thought of the Dutch Revolt. 1550–1590* (Cambridge, 1992); Hans Hescher, "Justus Lipsius. Ein Vertreter des christlichen Humanismus in der katholischen Erneuerungsbewegung des 16. Jahrhunderts", *Jahrbuch für das Bistum Mainz*, 6 (1954): 196–31; Siedschlag, *Einfluß*; and Michael Stolleis, "Lipsius-Rezeption in der politisch-juristischen Literatur des 17. Jahrhunderts in Deutschland", *Der Staat*, 26 (1987): 1–30. Accusing Lipsius of having remained aloof from the more radical variants

However, contrary to many of his colleagues, Lipsius took a universalist approach to the past and therefore refrained from using Tacitus to fuel proto-nationalist sentiment. Thus Lipsius's praise of Tacitus made him as little into a Tacitist as his praise of Machiavelli made him into a Machiavellian. Instead, the paramount goal of his political theory remained the limitation of warfare to the pursuit of defensive war aims and, in that respect, reflected the contemporary Dutch military experience. Because Lipsius was sceptical that rulers could be prevented from committing immoral actions, he needed to specify the conditions under which such actions could be punished in the interest of humankind and at the level of

---

of contemporary Dutch political theory appears parochial in view of the massive evidence for his popularity. It is correct, however, to say that in praising Tacitus's approving report on the rise of the Batavians against the ancient Romans, Lipsius displayed some degree of opportunism towards the revolutionary authorities. The passage is in Lipsius's comment on Tacitus of 1581 and has been reedited in Justus Lipsius, *Epistolae*, ed. Aloïs Gerlo (Brussels, 1978), vol. 1, p. 81. For sixteenth-century Tacitism, see Peter Burke, "Tacitism, Scepticism and Reason of State", in John H. Burns and M. Goldie (eds), *The Cambridge History of Political Thought. 1450–1700* (Cambridge, 1991), pp. 479–99; Else-Elly Etter, *Tacitus in der Geistesgeschichte des 16. und 17. Jahrhunderts* (Basel, 1966.); Paul Joachimsen, "Tacitus im deutschen Humanismus", *Neue Jahrbücher für das klassische Altertum, Geschichte und deutsche Literatur und für Pädagogik*, 27 (1911): 697–717; Jose Ruysschaert, *Juste Lipse et les Annales de Tacite* (Turnhout, 1949). Kenneth C. Schellhase, *Tacitus in Renaissance Political Thought* (Chicago, 1976); Jürgen von Stackelberg, *Tacitus in der Romania* (Tübingen, 1960); André Stegmann, "Le Tacitisme. Programme pour un nouvel essai de définition", *Il pensiero politico*, 2 (1965): 445–58; Hans Tiedemann, *Tacitus und das Nationalbewußtsein der deutschen Humanisten*, Ph.D. Thesis (University of Berlin, 1913); Enrique Tierno Galván, "El tacitismo en las doctrinas politicas del Siglo de Oro Español", in Tierno Galván, *Escritos. 1950–1960* (Madrid, 1971), pp. 13–93; And Giuseppe Toffanin, *Machiavelli e il "tacitismo". La "political storia" al tempo della controriforma* (Padua, 1921). Waszink has also been correct in insisting that Oestreich's weakness for a strong state and for social discipline had closer connections with the Nazi period than with Lipsius. On Oestreich, specifically his early work before 1945 [Oestreich, "Das persönliche Regiment der deutschen Fürsten am Beginn der Neuzeit", *Die Welt als Geschichte*, 1 (1935): 218–37, 300–316; Oestreich, "Vom Wesen der Wehrgeschicht", *Historische Zeitschrift*, 162 (1940): 231–57], see Stefan Breuer, "Sozialdisziplinierung. Probleme und Problemverlagerungen eines Konzeptes bei Max Weber, Gerhard Oestreich und Michel Foucault", in Christan Sachsse and Florian Tennstedt (eds), *Soziale Sicherheit und soziale Disziplinierung* (Frankfurt, 1985), pp. 45–69; Hans Maier, "Sozialdisziplinierung – ein Begriff und seine Grenzen", in Paolo Prodi (ed.), *Glaube und Eid* (Munich, 1993), pp. 237–40; Ralf Pröve, "Dimension und Reichweite der Paradigmen 'Sozialdisziplinierung' und 'Militarisierung' im Heiligen Römischen Reich", in Heinz Schilling (ed.), *Institutionen, Instrumente und Akteure sozialer Kontrolle und Disziplinierung im frühneuzeitlichen Europa* (Frankfurt, 1999), pp. 65–85; and Mohammed Rassem, "Bemerkungen zur 'Sozialdisziplinierung' im frühmodernen Staat", *Zeitschrift für Politik*, N.F., vol. 30 (1983): 217–38.

international relations overarching the "consociations" of territorial polities and urban communities. Lipsius demanded such punishments as mandatory coercive actions in defence of the moral integrity of humankind against those who wished to ignore the precepts of the ethics of self-constraint. The only available means of enforcing such punishments was, according to Lipsius, warfare. This conclusion was only apparently contradictory because Lipsius, contrary to fourteenth-century contractualists, took into account the absence of institutions of universal rule and thus had to permit resorting to war as a means of enforcing acceptance of the ethics of self-constraint at the level of international relations. Hence he demanded that wars should be limited to the use of force as a means of enforcing sanctions against those who chose to act unreasonably and against the stipulations of the ethics of self-constraint. In order to explicate these views, Lipsius not only devoted the section on international relations in his book on politics to warfare, but also produced two major and widely read works on the theory and practice of war.

Lipsius thus positioned his ethics of self-constraint at the metaphysically constituted level of humankind as a whole, thereby postulating a universal ethics. As this ethics was not enforcible by definition, human actors could sinfully decide to act against its precepts and resort to war. But Lipsius refused to ascribe to human actors the capability of transforming or even annihilating the ethics. His notion of the ethics of self-constraint thus contained a twofold impediment to the resort to war. First and foremost, Lipsius's variant of contractualism made the provision of security one of rulers' highest duties and legitimised attitudes of criticism towards rulers whom the ruled had reason to identify as war mongers. Moreover, Lipsius's universal ethics obliged rulers not merely to avoid war, but also to limit the deployment of military force to what appeared to be required in pursuit of defensive war aims. Like the Oranians, Lipsius conceived of war as a struggle *pro aris et focis*.

Grotius elaborated Lipsius's ethics of self-constraint into a detailed bellicist casuistics of what rulers could, but ought not to do, in war. Grounding the law of war in the law of nature, he applied Lipsius's ethics as a vehicle to reduce the decision-making capability of actors in warfare. In so doing, he established the basis for a tradition of reasoning that would continue until the middle of the eighteenth century and to which Adam Smith still adhered.[70]

The fusion of Aristotelian theories of government, Augustinian peace theology and the Neo-stoic ethics of self-constraint contextualised theories of the law of war within more broadly constituted beliefs about the divinely willed political order of the world which ascribed to human actors no more than a limited capability of affecting that order. While theorists saw human actors as capable

---

[70] For Adam Smith's application of principles of Grotius's theory of the law of war, see Adam Smith, *Lectures on Justice, Poilice, Revenue and Arms. Delivered in the University of Glasgow. Reported by a Student 1763*, ed. Edwin Cannan (Oxford, 1896), pp. 1, 265–80.

of infringing upon the order by acting sinfully and going to war, they concurred with practical political decision-makers in denying that war could jeopardise the texture manifest in the European international system. Theorists took it as their task to outline the conditions under which the European international system and each of its units could attain stability, thereby establishing the framework for actions by political decision-makers.

The Relevance of the Ethics of Self-Constraint in Warfare and Diplomacy

While the Oranians were emerging as successful organisers of military resistance against Spanish power, Protestant as well as Calvinist estates in the Empire had a difficult time coping with the better equipped and more combat-ready forces employed by the Catholic League.[71] Only the partial revision of the Oranian reforms under Gustavus Adolphus of Sweden, who relied heavily on professional warriors, strengthened the Protestant side again.[72] As a result, and in stark contrast to Lipsian speculative political theory, the numbers of combatants increased dramatically, and so did the numbers of war dead. As a consequence, warfare became brutalised, both on the battlefield and against civilian non-combatants as military discipline declined. At Breitenfeld, for instance, 130,000 men were engaged in combat, with roughly half of them dying on the battlefield.[73] Private military entrepreneurs put together their warrior bands at their own expense and sold them to sovereign rulers to do battle for whatever purpose. Contrary to the doings of the long-distance trading companies, the commercialisation of military service within Europe entailed a lack of concern for invalids left after battle. The misery of the invalids became recognisable in the dramatic increase in the number of beggars and the ensuing frequency of government edicts against begging throughout the areas most severely hit by warfare.[74] Seventeenth-century literature depicted

---

[71]   See Rolf Naumann, *Das kursächsische Defensionswerk* (Leipzig, 1916).

[72]   In the wide-ranging debate about the so-called military revolution, Oranian dependence on Lipsius's Neo-stoicism has not been given the attention it deserves, specifically in the intention to limit the scope of warfare that informed the Oranian reforms. For the debate, see Michael Roberts, *The Military Revolution. 1560–1660* [1956], in Roberts, *Essays in Swedish History* (London, 1967), pp. 195–225; Geoffrey Parker, *The Military Revolution. Military Innovation and the Rise of the West. 1500–1800* (Cambridge, 1988); Jeremy Black, *A Military Revolution?* (Basingstoke, 1990); and Clifford J. Rogers (ed.), *The Military Revolution Debate* (Boulder, Col., 1995).

[73]   Cicely Veronica Wedgwood, *The Thirty Years War*, edited by Roy Strong (London, 1999), pp. 259–63.

[74]   For references, see A.L. Beier, *Masterless Men. The Vagrancy Problem in England. 1560–1640* (London, 1985); Robert Jütte, *Abbild und soziale Wirklichkeit des Bettler-*

the professional warrior as the stereotype of the lawless, irresponsible, greedy and brutal suppressor of righteous people and contained outrageous stories of lack of warrior discipline.[75] In a word, the Oranian reforms appeared to be the work of petty ignorant dreamers, who went to militarily inexperienced theoreticians as authorities rather than accepting the seemingly harsh realities of warfare. Even the relatives of the Dutch Oranians in the Empire buried some of the principles of the reform during the early phase of the Thirty Years War. Thus in 1617 Count Johann VII of Nassau-Siegen, who was one of the most insistent reformers in the very early seventeenth century and had founded one of the earliest European military academies at his residence at Siegen in 1613, sacked the academy's first director, Captain Johann Jakobi von Wallhausen, for fear that Wallhausen's teaching and even more his published writings could benefit the hated papists. Eventually, the academy folded in 1621. Obviously, there was no public sphere for debate on military matters in the first half of the seventeenth century equivalent to that of the "Military Enlightenment" of the second half of the eighteenth century.[76] The idea that war could become subject to planning, the ethics of self-constraint and even legal rules seemed very remote from reality at the time.

As civilian government control over the armed forces increased in accordance with the principles of the Oranian reforms, the doings of soldiers acquired a higher domestic significance, since regiments and battalions were no longer disbanded immediately after battle. Armies that remained "standing" turned into instruments of domestic coercion apt to enforce order among the rulers' subjects. Patterns of military behaviour transgressed the confines of the battlefield and the camp as standing armies moved into garrisons stationed in towns. Reviews, parades and other forms of public spectacle made the soldiers part of urban life. The dependent peasant, when drafted as a soldier into a ruler's army, not merely moved from the village into the town but also shifted loyalty from a rural

---

und Gaunertums zu Beginn der Neuzeit. Sozial-, mentalitäts- und sprachgeschichtliche Studien zum Liber vagatorum (1510) (Cologne and Vienna, 1988); Jütte, Poverty and Deviance in Early Modern Europe (Cambridge, 1994); Norbert Schindler, "Die Entstehung der Unbarmherzigkeit. Zur Kultur und Lebensweise der Salzburger Bettler am Ende des 17. Jahrhunderts", Bayerisches Jahrbuch für Volkskunde (1988): 61–130; Ingeborg Titz-Matuszak, "Mobilität der Armut. Das Almosenwesen im 17. und 18. Jahrhundert im südniedersächsischen Raum", Plesse-Archiv, 24 (1988): 9–338.

[75] Cf. Hans Jakob Christoph von Grimmelshausen, *Der abentheurliche Simplicissimus teutsch* [1669], ed. Rolf Tarot (Tübingen, 1967) and Hanns Wilhelm Kirchhof, *Wendunmuth*, ed. Hermann Österely (Stuttgart, 1869).

[76] On this term, see Daniel Hohrath, *Die Bildung des Offiziers in der Aufklärung. Ferdinand Friedrich von Nicolai (1740–1814) und seine enzyklopäischen Sammlungen* (Stuttgart, 1990).

aristocrat to the paramount ruler.[77] Armies were thus converted into instruments for the centralization and bureaucratization of government under the control of a paramount ruler. Only rulers of large territories and economically successful cities could afford the centralization and bureaucratization of government activities through the mediation of lesser rural aristocrats and the subordination of their less powerful neighbours. Thus, as the seventeenth century wore on, smaller principalities, specifically within the Empire and in Northern Italy, gravitated towards a decreasing number of sovereign rulers with dominant military, economic and political capacity. In the long term, the Oranian reforms were significant because the underlying ethics of self-constraint disseminated respect for the law of war, boosted the quest for stability and promoted the belief in the divinely willed continuity of the order of the world. The established pluralism of actors continued as agents other than sovereign rulers were admitted as international actors in Africa, Asia and the seaways thither.

Conclusion

A study of war and diplomacy in the age of Grotius reveals, first and foremost, the specificity of the properties of the European international system at the time. Its features were different from what international relations theorists have taken to be permanent properties of a postulated global international system since the nineteenth century. Whereas theorists have postulated a varying degree of dynamics instigating systemic and even systems change since the nineteenth century,[78] theorists in the age of Grotius took for granted the stability of the system and the entire world around it Whereas theorists since the nineteenth century have emphasised the significance of human action in war and diplomacy,[79] theorists in

---

[77] See Hans Bleckwenn, *Zum Militärwesen des Ancien Régime*, ed. Joachim Niemeyer (Osnabrück, 1987).

[78] Cf. Henry Peter Lord Brougham and Vaux, "Balance of Power", in Brougham, *The Works* (6 vols, London and Glasgow, 1855), vol. 1, pp. 12–13 [the passage was first published anonymously in *Edinburgh Review*, 1 (1803): 353–54] and Johann Gottlieb Fichte, *Reden an die deutsche Nation* [1807–1808], ed. Immanuel Hermann Fichte (Berlin, 1846), pp. 264–79. For a recent restatement, see Andre Gunder Frank and Barry K. Gills (eds), *The World System. Five Hundred Years or Five Thousand* (London and New York, 1996).

[79] John Emerich Edward Dalberg Lord Acton, *History of Freedom and Other Essays*, ed. John Neville Figgis and Reginald Vere (London, 1922); Ernest Renan, "Qu'est-ce qu'une nation?", in *Discours et conférences* (Paris, 1887), pp. 277–310; Woodrow Wilson, *The Public Papers* (New York and London: Harper, 1926), vol. 4, pp. 407–14, vol. 5 (*ibid.*, 1927), pp. 182–3, vol. 6 (*ibid.*, 1927), pp. 309, 362–64; Alexander Wendt, "Anarchy is What States Make of It: The Social Construction of Power Politics", *International Organization*, 46 (1992): 391–425; Wendt and Daniel Friedhelm, "Hierarchy under Anarchy. Informal

the age of Grotius followed the lines set down by their medieval predecessors in subjecting human decisions to divine will. Whereas theorists since the nineteenth century have made actorship a monopoly of rulers and governments of sovereign states,[80] theorists in the age of Grotius assumed not merely that large numbers of actors but also the pluralism of actorship were conducive to the stability of the international system.

Empire and the East German State", in Thomas J. Biersteker and Cynthia Weber (eds), *State Sovereignty as a Social Construct* (Cambridge, 1996), pp. 240–72, pp. 242–5; Wendt, *Social Theory of International Politics* (Cambridge, 1999), pp. 185–6.

[80] Fichte, *Reden*, pp. 264–79.

Chapter 7
Liquefied Sanctity: Grotius and the Promise of Global Law

Bertram Keller

War has many faces today. Iraq has been pacified into a state of guerrilla warfare. Yugoslavia imploded. Terror disseminates stateless fear. China struggles for economic growth. A climate battle looms. What is the position of international law? UN reform is stuck, the ICC ignored, WTO development blocked, the Kyoto Protocol stagnated. Facing a crisis of international law, everyone looks to its origins. Hopes for the future rest on the past.

Prologue – Violating (the Father of) International Law

The Father of International Law

When retracing the path of today's international order, all disciplines stumble over Hugo Grotius, the "father of modern international law". This title corresponds his own estimation: "Many have undertaken to expound ... the civil law ... But few have treated that law that exists between peoples ... and no one as yet has discussed it in a comprehensive and systematic way" [Prol, 1].[1] To be sure, extensive academic debate over the last century has deconstructed Grotius's originality in every detail. His system of natural and international law has been traced to Spanish scholastics.[2] Even Grotius's famous dictum that his argument would

---

[1] Quotations from Hugo Grotius's *De iure belli ac pacis* (1625) are indicated by square brackets [book, chapter, paragraph] in the text and follow the modern English translation of Louis R. Loomis (New York, 1949). I found his colloquial account much more appropriate for my "liquefied" reading of Grotius than the more old-fashioned eighteenth-century translation by John Morrice (originally printed 1715 and 1738), recently re-edited by Richard Tuck (Indiana, 2005), and the careful but cumbersome 1925 translation of Francis W. Kelsey for the Carnegie Endowment (Oxford, 1925). Wherever more rigorous wording is required, I refer to the Latin original in form of the 1919 edition by P.C. Molhuysen (Leyden, 1919).

[2] By Josef Kohler, *Grundlagen des Völkerrechts* (Stuttgart, 1918), p. 41, Otto von Gierke, *Natural Law and the Theory of Society* (Toronto, 1934), p. 36, Quentin Skinner, *The Foundations of Modern Political Thought*, 2 vols (Cambridge, 1978), II, p. 135, and

remain valid "even if … there is no god" (*etiamsi daremus non esse deum*) [Prol, 11] is suspected of having been taken from that source.³ The humanist tradition,⁴ in particular Stoic thought,⁵ is another possible blueprint. Nonetheless, it was *De iure belli ac pacis* that spread the idea of a modern law of nations. The book met the cruel reality of the Thirty Years War, influenced the Peace of Westphalia, and established Grotius as an enduring authority on international law.⁶ Over the centuries it was his name that, among other, changing sources, always appeared as the academic and political reference for the origin of international law.⁷ Grotius could be said to have "founded" modern international law, "if for no other reasons than because he was thought to have done so".⁸ Reputation produced the father.

Modern International Law

Before testing paternity, we might want to know what the child looks like. What does "modern international law" mean?

Knud Haakonssen, "Hugo Grotius and the History of Political Thought", *Political Theory*, 13 (1985): 239.

³ Haakonssen, "Hugo Grotius", p. 248; Leonard Besselink, "The Impious Hypothesis Revisited", *Grotiana*, 9 (1988): 3 contextualizes the *etiamsi daremus* argument in the debate of the time.

⁴ Richard Tuck, *The Rights of War and Peace* (Oxford, 1999) reads Grotius in a humanist tradition, thereby explicitly revising (p. 4) his position in Richard Tuck, *Natural Rights Theories* (Cambridge, 1979).

⁵ Axel Hägerström, *Recht, Pflicht und bindende Kraft des Vertrages*, ed. K. Olivecrona (Uppsala, 1965), p. 44 seq., and recently Benjamin Straumann, *Grotius und die Antike* (Baden-Baden, 2007).

⁶ His prestige in the twentieth century is manifest in the large conferences of renowned international law scholars and judges to celebrate his various anniversaries. Cf. T.M.C. Asser Instituut (ed.), *International Law and the Grotian Heritage* (The Hague, 1985); Alfred Dufour, Peter Haggenmacher and Jirí Toman (eds), *Grotius et l'ordre juridique internationale* (Lausanne, 1985); Hedley Bull, Benedict Kingsbury and Adam Roberts (eds), *Hugo Grotius and International Relations* (Oxford, 1990); in the early twentieth century no less a figure than Harvard Law School Dean Roscoe Pound already praised Grotius as the father of modern law: Roscoe Pound, "Grotius in the Science of Law", *American Journal of International Law*, 19 (1925): 685.

⁷ Durward Sandifer, "Rereading Grotius in the Year 1940", *American Journal of International Law*, 34 (1940): 459, analyses the dissemination of references to Grotius in various disciplines: 26 per cent in religion and theology, 22.5 per cent in law, 20.5 per cent among historians, 11 per cent among writers of literature, 8 per cent in philosophy, 4.5 per cent among political scientists, 2.5 per cent among rhetoricians, and 2 per cent among grammarians.

⁸ Haakonssen, "Hugo Grotius", p. 239.

Modern international law is "international", that is, between nation states (inter nationes). The subjects of modern international law are sovereign states, coordinating their bilateral interactions. Multilateral regulations integrate multiple states in an international system like the United Nations. The term "international" implies the autonomous action of sovereign nation-states.

Modern international law is "law". Law is a hierarchical and enforceable system of rules. A law of nations or peoples defines commitments and subjective rights for the interaction between sovereign states. The UN General Assembly, the UN Security Council and the International Court of Justice form a well-structured and stable legal order. Even if its sanctions are limited, the general claim of modern international law is to establish a homogenous, enforceable legal system.

Modern international law is "modern". Modernity is generally tied to rising individualism, or a subjective perspective, and to secularisation.[9] The recognized sources of modern international law are conventions, custom and general principles.[10] All are considered aggregate common normative standards. Modern international law appeals to shared universal values. The universal claim of human rights, as expressed in the UN Charter or the European Convention on Human Rights, reveals its close relation to the idea of natural law.

Grotian ius Gentium

Grotius outlined all three aspects of modern international law: "[J]ust as there are laws in each state that aim at securing some advantage for that state, so between all or most states (*inter civitates*) some laws could be and indeed have been established by common consent, which look to the advantage not of single communities but of the whole great concourse of states (*magnae illius universitatis*). And this is the law we call the law of nations (*ius gentium*), whenever we distinguish it from natural law" [Prol, 17]. The Grotian *ius gentium* is law between states, that is, inter-national law. Its sources are common consent rooted in a great universal idea. Grotius constructs the law of nations as a multilateral system that allows for closer unions: "So too it may happen that several states are joined together in a close confederation, and make ... a system, and yet each retains the status of a perfect state" [I, 3, 7]. Classical free trade unions like NAFTA or ASEAN could easily be integrated into his picture. Demonstrating a family relationship thus

---

[9] Paradigmatically Charles Taylor, *Sources of the Self* (Cambridge, MA, 1989) and *A Secular Age* (Cambridge, MA, 2007).

[10] According to Art. 38 of its statutes, the International Court of Justice can apply "international conventions", "international custom", "general principles of law recognized by civilized nations", "judicial decisions" and "teachings". For the debate on the sources of international law, cf. Martti Koskenniemi (ed.), *Sources of International Law* (Aldershot, 2000).

proves to be easy. Grotius can be endorsed as the father of modern international law with a clear conscience. But some suspect that his son is dying.

Postmodern Global Governance

Contemporary political and legal debates erode every single element of the conception of "modern international law".

The "international" is becoming the "global". Financial transactions and virtual online communities do not recognize any national borders. States are beginning to fray. Powerful multinational enterprises, NGOs and private regulatory agencies, are creating a "new world order" of horizontal and vertical political networks.[11] Sovereignty is disintegrating.

"Law" is turning into "governance". Independent legal systems govern free trade, financial development, environmental protection, human rights and war crimes. The international legal order is fragmenting into functional regimes.

"Modern" universalism totters in the face of "postmodern" pluralism. Are terrorist attacks only the harbinger of a real "clash of civilizations"[12]? Individual human rights conflict with collectivist policies like China's one-child policy. Universal liberal values can be read as a political effort by Western societies to preserve their global power. When does economic dominance become imperial hegemony?[13] Could the subversive "multitude" fight an omnipotent global "empire"?[14] The "postmodern condition" calls any common normative or narrative ground into question.[15] Universal and homogenous international law is melting into pluralistic and heterogeneous structures of global governance. Who cares about the father of modernity in a postmodern age? Has fatherhood been established just as the son is being lost?

Liquefying Grotius

A father grows with his children. Grotius's *De iure bellis ac pacis* changes with its readers. Every interpretation of historical sources forces its ideas into present concepts. Every reading violates the author. Every reading deconstructs the past.

---

[11] Cf. the influential claim of Anne-Marie Slaughter, *A New World Order* (Princeton, 2004).

[12] Samuel P. Huntington, *The Clash of Civilization* (New York, 1996), though under permanent academic attack, continues to have a large public impact.

[13] This question seems to me a consistent result of David Saunders' reflections in this volume.

[14] Michael Hardt and Antonio Negri, *Empire* (Cambridge, MA, 2000) and *Multitude* (New York, 2004).

[15] Jean-Francois Lyotard, *La condition postmodern* (Paris, 1979).

Deconstructing the past means reconstructing the present, and restructuring the present means constructing the future.[16] Again, hopes for the future rest on the past. From a purely historical perspective, I shall violate Grotius in the following. I shall treat *De iure bellis ac pacis* as an autonomous text[17] addressing present-day readers in the current global landscape. I shall not contextualize but liquefy the text in order to consider contemporary problems of international law. How can sovereignty be restructured? How can different functional regimes be integrated? How can an expanded pluralism be stabilized? A "liquefied" Grotius suggests ways of constructing highly topical answers. A global society rests on multiple social contracts: integrated by multiple normative reasons and framed by a common promise The "performative sanctity" that emerges from this reading promises a liquefied law of nature for a global society.

Multiple Social Contracts

New Sovereignty

A mouse click in Japan can cause a financial disaster in Europe. In a truly globalised economy states are not independent but interdependent, united by shared resources, markets, information, and so on. Yet today's paradigm-shift goes further. Global trading, global communication and global norms penetrate deeply into the internal affairs of every state. Nearly every act of European national legislation is influenced by EU regulations. National sovereignty is, to understate the case, "in transition".[18] Whereas interdependence only delimits the range of

---

[16] "Deconstruction" is usually, though not exclusively, linked to the name of Jacques Derrida; cf. Jonathan Culler, *On Deconstruction* (London, 1983). Jacques Derrida, *Force de loi* (Paris 1994) pp. 44 and 46, expounds deconstruction as revealing the political contexts and structural aporiai of texts. My "liquefaction" focuses on structure but neglects context. I reconstruct the Grotian text in the world of today, drawing on the "interpretive community" (Stanley Fish, *Is there a text in these class? The Authority of Interpretive Communities* [Cambridge, MA, 1980]) of legal and political thinkers. Thus, contrary to at least the self-description of practitioners of "deconstruction", my method of "liquefaction" rests on a strong constructivist underpinning.

[17] Contrary to readings of *De jure bellis ac pacis* in the light of earlier manuscripts like *De indis*, published in the nineteenth century as *De iure praedae* (The Hague, 1868). Cf. Tuck, *The Rights of War and Peace*, p. 79 et seq.

[18] Neil Walker (ed.), *Sovereignty in Transition* (Oxford, 2003). In particular on the European Union, see Neil MacCormick, "Beyond the Sovereign State", *Modern Law Review*, 56 (1993): 1, and Robert O. Keohane, "Ironies of Sovereignty: The European Union and the United States", *Journal of Common Market Studies*, 40 (2002): 743. For a more cosmopolitan vision of European citizenship, see Jürgen Habermas, "The European

Summa Potestatis

For Grotius, that "power is called sovereign (*summa*) whose acts are not subject to the legal control of anyone else" [I, 3, 7]. Only if the actor is autonomous – that is, can make his own laws – is he sovereign.[20] Grotius leaves little doubt that the "common subject of sovereignty (*summa potestatis*) is the state (*civitas*)" [I, 3, 7]. With reference to the Roman and Jewish tradition of "private slavery" [I, 3, 8], he justifies the absolutist state of his time. How could a rigorous defender of the almighty state help us understand fraying sovereignties? To circumvent these problems, one could argue for a global super-state.[21] As attractive as cosmopolitan visions may be, they are not plausible within the foreseeable future. Grotius traces a much sounder route to global governance. Even the *summa potestatis* or *summum imperium* [II, 14] of an absolute sovereign is restricted, since "contracts which a king enters into with his subjects are binding on him" [II, 14, 6]. Contracts may delimit or transfer sovereign power. The *summum imperium* might be read as the political placeholder for an empowered institution representing the community. "For whatever a king does in his acts as king (*in regiis actibus*) must be considered as if done by the community (*quasi communitas*)" [II, 14, 1]. The international succession of sovereign rights is an application of this construction that is still topical today. Grotius ties the obligation of a succeeding sovereign to the community within a state. "A community (*coetus*), no less than a single individual (*persones singulares*), has the right to bind itself by its own act ... It can transfer this right, both explicitly and as a necessary consequence of other acts" [II, 14, 11]. Sovereignty is based on the right of the community to bind itself and to transfer this right. Two fundamental questions remain: how does one bind oneself? And

---

Nation State. Its Achievements and Its Limitations. On the Past and Future of Sovereignty and Citizenship", *Ratio Juris*, 9 (1996): 125.

[19] Abram Chayes and Antonia Handler Chayes, *The New Sovereignty* (Cambridge, MA, 1995), p. 27, define their "new sovereignty" as "status" in global governance systems, that is, "the connection to the rest of the world and the political ability to be an actor within it".

[20] Considering the underlying question of war, such a rigorous and reduced idea of sovereignty would suggest a decisionist account. In his *Politische Theologie* (Berlin, 1922), for instance, Carl Schmitt defines sovereignty as power to decide on a state of emergency: *Souverän ist, wer über den Ausnahmezustand entscheidet* (p. 1). Such an interpretation of Grotius would resemble Schmitt's reading of Hobbes, which Luc Foisneau persuasively argues against in his contribution to this volume.

[21] In the Kantian tradition of perpetual peace: James Bohman (ed.), *Perpetual Peace: Essays on Kant's Cosmopolitan Ideal* (Cambridge, MA, 1997).

how is this right transferred? Grotius offers a single answer: the ability to bind oneself and the transfer of right both result from contracts.

Multiple Social Contracts

If its contractual basis makes the Grotian approach attractive today, why not take another "social contractarian" of Grotius? Grotius's construction differs from its prominent successors. Thomas Hobbes requires a "common-wealth" united by the explicit "covenant of every man with every man".[22] Quite similar in form is Jean-Jacques Rousseau's construction of the unification of individual lives and wills into one *volonté générale* through an explicit *pacte social*.[23] Of course Hobbes's *Leviathan* justifies an omnipotent sovereign, whereas Rousseau's *pacte social* creates a republican popular sovereignty. Yet both lay out a clear state of nature to be overcome by a single social contract. Grotius drew his own picture of human nature, but he did not set up an explicit state of nature. One might say that he lacked a fully developed method of social contracting. Instead, he mentions explicit or tacit agreements in different social contexts: property, transfer of property, personal status, punishment, and political decisions. Even if Grotius too conceived of a single, all-embracing sovereign state, his theoretical construction of society does not necessarily depend on it. His account can be read as legitimising distinct social rights (property rights, personal rights, rights to punish and political rights) through multiple social contracts. Grotius's "underdeveloped" method of social contracting proves to be remarkably well adapted to today's global order. Multiple social contracts could constitute a web of overlapping societies without a supervening state.

Property Rights

In considering property rights, Grotius starts with the fiction that all things once belonged to mankind in common [II, 2]. This starting point accords with the current renaissance of a "commons" of shared cultural and natural resources.[24] Then "things passed from common to private ownership (*proprietatem*) not alone by an act of deliberate planning (*non animi actu solo*). ... But there must have been either some express agreement (*pacto*), as for a division, or a tacit understanding,

---

[22] Thomas Hobbes, *Leviathan*, ed. R. Tuck (Cambridge, 1996), Chapter 17.
[23] Jean-Jacques Rousseau, *Du Contrat Social*, ed. P. Burgelin (Paris, 1992), I, 6.
[24] Two paradigmatic expositions of the debate are Garret Hardin, "The Tragedy of the Commons", *Science*, 162 (1968): 1243, on natural "commons", and Lawrence Lessig, *The Future of Ideas* (New York, 2002) on cultural "commons". Dan Wielsch has proposed a corresponding transformation of the intellectual property regime, *Zugangsregeln* (Tübingen, 2008).

as for simple occupation" [II, 2, 2]. Property rights originate in a social agreement among all those concerned. In contrast to Locke, for whom labour creates property,[25] this contractual origin of property rights allows for public goods. Intellectual property and natural resources are both real global goods insofar as they are bound by few geographic restrictions. The internet, the atmosphere and the climate transcend national boundaries. In the domain of intellectual property rights, the TRIPS Agreement under the World Trade Organization could be read as a specific functional social contract. When it comes to natural resources, the re-nationalization of oil extraction in the Middle East overthrew all existing property rights. The founding of OPEC might be seen as a social contract among mainly Arab nations governing the reallocation of oil for the entire world. Similarly, the pollution of the atmosphere and the oceans concerns the whole world. Even so, there are no exclusive rights to the air, while the sea is free (*mare liberum*)[26] and its sustainable usage could thus be part of a global agreement like the Kyoto Protocol. The shared usage of a small river, by contrast, may only concern two states or even two farmers in the middle of Wales. Not every social contract assigning property rights has to be thought on a global scale. Property might be rethought in terms of multiple social contracts on different levels.

Personal Rights

"A right may be acquired not only over things but over persons" [II, 5, 1].[27] "Rights over persons (*ius in personas*) based on consent, come either from association (*consociatione*) or from subjection (*subiectione*)" [II, 5, 8]. As cases of consensual subjection, Grotius mentions adoption and voluntary slavery.[28] Marriage is his main example of consensual associations. Presupposing male superiority, Grotius portrays marriage as "pledge by which the woman binds herself to the man" [II, 5, 8]. Unburdened of its historical gender bias, this passage might be understood as asserting that man and woman bind themselves in the contract of marriage, thereby founding the "most natural association". The more interesting association

---

[25] John Locke, *The Second Treatise of Government*, ed. D. Wotton (London, 1993), Chapter 5.

[26] A claim Grotius defended rigorously. Cf. *Mare Liberum* and *De jure bellis ac pacis*, II, 2, 3.

[27] A personal right "has its source in either procreation, consent or crime" [II, 5, 1]. By procreation, parents acquire rights over children, which diminish with their coming to maturity. Crime is considered under the right to punish.

[28] Reading Grotius' passage on the relation between master and slave in parallel to Hegel's famous reflections (Georg Wilhelm Friedrich Hegel, *Phänomenologie des Geistes*, Akademie Ausgabe, vol. 9 (Hamburg, 1980), pp. 114–28) would be a tempting but distracting endeavour.

for today's reader is the one for "transacting business (*expediendi negotia*)" [II, 5, 17]. Grotius's account of corporate law is far less developed than its Roman model, but he takes the important step of integrating it into social contract theory.[29] Although he separates private and public associations, "they all have this trait in common, that when dealing with matters for which the association was formed, the whole body, or a majority, acting in the name of the whole, may bind every individual in the association" [II, 5, 17]. His examples demonstrate a fluid transition from private associations to the public, "most perfect association", the state. Indeed, the relation between the powerful East India Company and the precarious United Provinces in the seventeenth century resembles the current global situation more than the integrated national economies of the nineteenth and early twentieth century. Multinational enterprises are often far more sovereign actors than the poor African states they contract with. By privatising pensions and childcare, large companies break down any private-public partition. Yet international law continues to lack consistent integration.[30] Business associations are built on a corporate contract, acquire investments by contract, employ their workers by contract, outsource production by contract and of course do business by contract. Economic dependence results in rights over persons much like those Grotius described in the case of private slavery: "For in compensation for the perpetual servitude is the perpetual assurance of maintenance, which often those who work for daily hire do not have" [II, 5, 27]. Not only states but also more and more global enterprises acquire multiple rights over persons by a complex net of functional contracts.

The Right to Punish

One particular right over a person is the right to punish. For Grotius punishment too approaches "the nature of contracts. For just as a seller, even though he makes no special statement to the effect, is understood to have bound himself to perform all the acts natural to a sale, so, punishment being a consequence of serious crime, the criminal seems to have voluntarily subjected himself to punishing" [II, 20, 2]. Punishment makes up part of Aristotelian commutative or contractual justice,

---

[29] Gierke, *Natural Law*, p. 77, remarks that for Grotius an association within civil society and the government have the same contractual foundations. Thus Grotius's theory of society resembles Gierke's own "general theory of the group" (*Verbandstheorie*).

[30] Structural transitions could include international legislation like the ICSID Convention of 1965, mediating investment disputes between states and private investors. An example of national legislation is section 302 US Trade Act 1974, which entitles private companies to request governmental action against foreign states if its trading interests are concerned. On interrelations and compatibility with the WTO regime, cf. WTO Panel decision WT/DS152/R of 22 December 1999.

which Grotius calls "expletive justice" (*expletiem iustitiam*) [II, 20, 2].[31] From this perspective, punishment is like "a business transaction, as if offenders were being paid something, as they are in contracts" [II, 20, 2]. In Grotius's day as in our own the two fundamental questions of a contractual construction of punishment remain identical: "[W]ho is the possessor of the right to punish" [II, 20, 3]? And what are "the ends proposed by punishment": to "undo a wrong" or to "protect the time to come" [II, 20, 4]? A contractual account allows for distinct institutions of punishment. The Yugoslavia Tribunal and the International Criminal Court (ICC) try to accuse high military commanders or even heads of states of serious war crimes or genocide. The Truth Commissions in South Africa focused more on the local political, ordinary and personal underpinnings of apartheid. Different types of crime call for different social responses.

The Right to Govern

Finally, an independent people may "submit itself to one or more persons, completely transferring to them its right to govern itself" [I, 3, 8]. Does this right to govern not embrace all other rights in one political community and override the multiple social contract thesis? Indeed, Grotius could be and generally is read along these lines of classical social contract theory as justifying one unified state. Yet Grotius compares the acquisition of governmental rights to property rights [I, 3, 8], thereby structurally distinguishing the two spheres. And he does not restrict the transfer of political rights to states. *Populus eligere potest qualem vult gubernationis formam* [I, 3, 8] – a people may choose whatever form of "governance" it pleases. *Gubernationis* is neither *regnum* nor *imperium*. A *gubernator* steers the boat, but does not have to be its sole commander. To "steer" (*gubernare*) resembles technical control more than imperial reign. Whereas government is normally tied to an all-embracing state, governance signifies a functional regime that may cover distinct parts of social life. Cultural identity need not follow the structure of ownership, nor do the two statuses necessarily originate in the same community. Governance allows for the overlapping of multiple identities as well as different forms of political rights. One could be a citizen of Berlin, Germany, the EU and the UN. Each level may grant civil rights and demand specific duties. Global governance opens multiple political levels and distinct functional spheres.

---

[31] Grotius discusses the Aristotelian distinction in more detail in [I, 1, 8].

Contracting Societies

Governance breaks established frames.[32] Traditional components of national affairs become global. Labour markets, for instance, increasingly ignore state boundaries. Firms act globally. Without national control, international regulation is useless. Global structures undermine autonomous sovereignty. Consumer protection follows transnational patterns.[33] Internet communities elect their own governments and set internal codes of conduct. Global societies will divide less into nation-states than into separate functional spheres. These normative systems are organized by means of contracts. Functional regimes are self-stabilizing social contracts. Contrary to most constructions in recent social contract theory, these contracts have to establish real contractual regimes, not only fictive understandings. These institutions create new social life-worlds. One person can belong to different functional communities, living simultaneously in different societies. Individuals have and will have increasingly multi-layered identities. Multiple social contracts form multiple "contracting societies".

Functional Wars

Sovereignty means being an actor within a particular contractual regime. Actors include individuals as well as local, regional, national and global communities. Sovereignty is being disaggregated into different levels and spheres within multiple contracting societies. The internal structure of every contracting society is determined and justified by the contracting agents who participate in it. But how can different regimes be integrated in complex life-worlds? What happens when regimes collide?[34] Collisions between regimes provoke new "functional wars". Open access to net communities struggles with exclusive codes. Intellectual property conflicts with health and environmental regimes. Social or human rights might endanger bio-diversity. Wars are always in one way or another struggles over sovereignty. The character of war changes with sovereignty. "9/11" was not an attack by Iraq, Afghanistan or another nation-state. A religious community struck an economic community. Assuming closed functional systems with incompatible vocabularies makes war the only possible solution. Yet all communities could be

---

[32] Gunther Teubner, "Breaking Frames: Economic Globalisation and the Emergence of *lex mercatoria*", *European Journal of Social Theory*, 5 (2002): 199.

[33] Gralf-Peter Callies, "Transnational Consumer Law", in Olaf Dilling, Martin Herberg and Gerd Winter (eds), *Responsible Business: Self-governance in transnational economic transactions* (Oxford, 2008), p. 225.

[34] Andreas Fischer-Lescano and Gunther Teubner, "Regime-Collisions: The Vain Search for Legal Unity in the Fragmentation of Global Law", *Michigan Journal of International Law*, 25 (2004): 999.

reconstructed as contracting societies. The tool of contract itself might provide a common ground for alternative dispute resolution. How could contracts serve this demanding purpose? How can such a contractual myth be founded?

Multiple Contractual Reasons

Stare Pactis

Peace and pacts are true friends.[35] Regardless whether one follows the idea of multiple social contracts or simply considers the fundamental role of treaties between states in modern international law, contracts are the essential building block of a peaceful global order. Thus global order is focused on one question: why should we observe contracts? For Grotius *stare pactis* was a natural demand, "since it was necessary that men should have some way of binding themselves to one another" [Prol, 15]. Hobbes, on the other hand, pointed out that "Covenants, without the Sword, are but Words, and of no strength to secure a man at all".[36] The standard answer of a lawyer would be that contracts are binding because the law enforces promises.[37] But on the global level there is no law preceding the contract. International treaties establish the rules for the parties to them. The contract creates the law. That is precisely the idea of every social contract: people come together in a state of nature and agree on an institutional frame.

The Founding Paradox

Here we face the founding theoretical paradox of every contract theory.[38] A contract, be it explicit or tacit, establishes the social foundation of legal rules, while enforcement of the contract demands that some rules already be in place. Founding the contract itself in law leads to a vicious circle. Wittgenstein and a whole tradition of analytical philosophers addressed a corresponding problem

---

[35] Ulpian already stressed the conceptual relation between *pactum* and *pax* in Digests 2.14.1.1 (*De pactis*).

[36] Hobbes, *Leviathan*, Chapter 17.

[37] Cf. §1 US Restatement (Second) of Contracts: "A contract is a promise or set of promises for the breach of which the law gives a remedy, or the performance of which the law in some way recognizes as a duty".

[38] Gunther Teubner, "In the Blind Spot: The Hybridization of Contract", *Theoretical Inquiries in Law*, 7 (2006), describes this paradox as the blind spot of contract theory. The resulting "latency" is the never-ending process of creating differences and compensation by inventing a false unity.

in the paradox or regress of rule following:[39] to know how to follow a rule requires a new rule that sets out standards for the application of the previous one. This application-rule itself needs to be applied, *ad infinitum*. This paradox is implicit in our daily use of language as dynamic process between meaning and interpretation. And every normative order faces an equivalent paradox, at least when its deep justification – its "founding" – is addressed.[40] The circular relation between law and contract is the founding paradox of global order. Social contract theory dissolves the foundation of a global order with the question why we observe contracts.

Individual versus Social

From today's perspective, Kant offered a straightforward answer to that question: a subjective will is free only if it can bind itself autonomously (*autós nómos*).[41] The scholastic tradition had already developed such a will-based model of self-legislation. Contracts are two promises. Each promise commits the promisor because he intends to be bound. Many scholars read Grotius in this line, as a key figure of modern will theory.[42] And indeed he states that "[T]he man who has made a promise … is bound of this own will to fulfil what he chose to make his obligation (*obligatur in quod obligari voluit*)" [II, 16, 1]. But Grotius is not a liberal before liberalism. All attempts to portray him as a proto-Kantian break down with his famous *appetitus societatis* – that "peculiar to man is his social desire, that is, for life in a community" [Prol, 6]. Here Grotius seems to emphasize the Aristotelian *zoon politicon*, that is, that man is by nature a social animal. The "care to preserve society (*societatis custodia*) … which is characteristic of human intelligence, is the source of all law … From it come the rules that we … must keep our promises" [Prol, 8]. Social stability counts. The promisee's reliance commits

---

[39] Ludwig Wittgenstein, *Philosophische Untersuchungen*, ed. J. Schulte (Frankfurt, 2003), §§ 201, 202; Saul A. Kripke, *Wittgenstein on Rules and Private Language* (London, 1982), Chapter 2; John McDowell, "Wittgenstein on Following a Rule", in John McDowell (ed.), *Mind, Value, and Reality* (Cambridge, MA, 1998), p. 221; Robert Brandom, *Making It Explicit* (Cambridge, MA, 1994), 1. 3.

[40] This is a dominant theme for both Luhmann and Derrida. Cf. Gunther Teubner, "Dealing with Paradoxes of Law: Derrida, Luhmann, Wiethölter", in Oren Perez and Gunther Teubner (eds), *On Paradoxes and Inconsistencies in Law* (Oxford, 2006), p. 41.

[41] Immanuel Kant, *Kritik der reinen Vernunft*, ed. W. Weischedel (Darmstadt, 1956), Third antinomy (p. 444); Immanuel Kant, *Kritik der praktischen Vernunft*, ed. W. Weischedel (Darmstadt, 1956), §6 (p. 52).

[42] This is Malte Diesselhorst's reading, *Die Lehre des Hugo Grotius vom Versprechen* (Köln, 1959). Diesselhorst even uses the Kantian term "autonomy" (p. 34), which never appears in Grotius. Yet Diesselhorst's alternative principle of reliance (pp. 69 and 75) works only as countermove to a definite will.

the promisor. Contracts and promises oblige as social expectations. Did Grotius anticipate communitarianism?[43] Does the republican spirit bear the obligation? Wrong again.

Utility versus Justice

Instead, individual utility prevails.[44] "Man ... possesses not only the strong social faculty ... but also the judgement to weigh his joys and pains. ... Whatever we do that is plainly contrary to good judgement is contrary also to the law of nature, that is to say, of the nature of men" [Prol, 9]. One immediately feels a Machiavellian breath on one's neck: "a prudent ruler cannot keep his word, nor should he, where such fidelity would damage him, and when the reasons that made him promise are no longer relevant".[45] Today rational choice theory would insist that a promissory strategy will be stable only as long as the promisor maximizes his utility. A classical point of reference is Cicero, who stated that promises that are useless need not be kept.[46] Grotius explicitly refutes this expedient account with counter-reference to Cicero, Horace and two Platonists. Keeping one's word should be considered a matter of "justice" [II, 11, 1]. At the beginning of his book, Grotius already contrasts Carneades' sceptical claim for utility with a harsh plea for justice [Prol, 5]. Justice for Grotius requires "equality" in contracts [II, 12, 8] and "in power of free choice" [II, 12, 10]. Justice means formal and material equality.

Reasoned Pluralism

Free will, social desire, utility, justice – there are multiple reasons to honour a contract. Grotius is by no means inconsistent; rather he is a genuine pluralist. "[T]here are many ways of living (*multa sunt vivendi genera*), one being better than another, and every individual is free to chose from the many kinds what he likes best" [I, 3, 8]. Why we keep contracts influences how we keep them. The reasons for contractual obligation determine its range. Justice demands equality. A utilitarian account focusing on the "own well-being (*suum statum*)" [I, 2, 1] might lead to opposite results. The reasons thought to underlie a contract influence the contractual obligation. Reasons are decisive for practical outcomes. Different reasons represent different contractual rationalities. Reasons play different roles

---

[43] Overview in Daniel Bell, *Communitarianism and its Critics* (Oxford, 1993); historical roots in Alasdair MacIntyre, *After Virtue* (Notre Dame, 1981).

[44] This is the reading of Tuck, *The Rights of War and Peace*, pp. 78–108. Along the same lines, Haakonsen, "Hugo Grotius" links Grotius to Adam Smith.

[45] Niccolò Machiavelli, *The Prince*, trans. and ed. Q. Skinner and R. Price (Cambridge, 1988).

[46] Cicero, *De officiis*, ed. H. Gunermann (Stuttgart, 1976), I, 10, 32.

in different functional contexts. Whereas trading regimes foster free will and utility, environmental and social conventions focus on justice and social stability. Conflicts between regimes are clashes of reasons. The pluralism of contracting societies is represented by a pluralism of contractual reasons. As different as reasons may be, they are all based on the common human faculty of reason. Is that the "law of nature"?

Positive and Natural Law

Law (*ius*) might signify "nothing but what is just (*iustum*)" [I, 1, 3]. Justice is used here in a broader sense than mere equality. "Anything is unjust which is opposed to the nature of a rational society (*naturae societatis ratione*)" [I, 1, 3]. Yet "the law obliges us to do what is good (*rectum*), not simply what is just (*ad iustum*), because law in this sense has to do with matters not only of justice (*iustitiae*) ... but of all other virtues (*aliarum virtutum*)" [I, 1, 9]. Whereas natural law refers to justice, positive law is based on human or divine virtues of the good. This division resembles the distinction in moral philosophy between the right or just and the good.[47] Positive law means voluntary law made by human or divine will. Positive law follows the legislator's particular conception of the good life. Positive law reflects legislative reasons. "Natural law is a dictate of right reason (*dictatum rectae rationis*), showing the moral necessity or moral baseness of any act according to its agreement (*convenientia*) or disagreement with rational nature (*natura rationali*)" [I, 1, 10]. The plurality of legal reasons is based on a common law of reasoning.

Contract and Promise

The division between positive and natural law reflects the relation between contract and promise. Contracts are voluntarily established by the contracting parties. Indeed, every contract is a voluntary law between the parties. The more complex contracts are, the more obvious their abstract legislative quality. On the other hand, every positive law could be reconstructed as social contract between the affected legal subjects. As voluntary or positive law, contracts are based on a variety of reasons. How can this plurality be integrated? Given the plurality of underlying reasons and the many faces of contract, the rule of *stare pactis* in itself seems useless. Once we have a contractual frame, the interplay of reasons may begin. But what justifies the initial assumption of cooperation? Here we find ourselves back again at another version of the founding paradox. Will different functional gods fight each other until one surrenders? Grotius himself seemed not to be satisfied with his pragmatic *stare pactis* formula, concealing the problem

---

[47] John Rawls, *A Theory of Justice* (Oxford, 1972), §68; Rainer Forst, *Contexts of Justice* (Berkley, 2002), Chapter V.

behind a veil of natural law. At any rate, he founded his contract theory on an elaborate account of promising.

Common Promises

Transfer of Right

Promises commit without a particular *causa* [II, 11, 10]. Promises do not need further underlying reasons to form the basis of an obligation. Grotius elevated the form that Roman law considered its weakest, the *nuda pacta*, to the heart of his contract theory.[48] A mere promise "conveys a special right to another (*ius proprium alteri conferre*)" [II, 11, 4]. This transfer of right is read as a "moral power" creating an inner necessity in the other party.[49] In his definition of law, Grotius already stresses the subjective moral dimension of *ius*, that is, a "right". "There is another meaning of the word law (*iuris significatione*), different from this, but yet arising out of it, which has reference to persons. In this sense, a right (*ius*) is a moral quality (*qualitas moralis*) annexed to a person ... This moral quality, when perfect, we call a faculty (*facultas*)" [I, 1, 4]. A promise carries a moral faculty capable of fulfilling the promised contract. Grotius compares the process to the alienation of ownership. We alienate certain parts of our liberty – *Est ... alienatio particulae cuiusdam nostrae libertatis* [II, 11, 4]. There is a certain circularity in Grotius's argument.[50] A promise is a transfer of right, like the alienation of ownership. Yet the right of property or any other particular right itself rests on an agreement. Are we caught again in the founding paradox? Is there no way out of circularity?

Linguistic Contract

But we should not give up on a "promising solution" so quickly. Grotius's theory of promising is best understood as a procedural account. Promising is the linguistic medium through which multiple reasons are transmitted. Man "has the special instrument of speech (*sermonem*), and the faculty of understanding and conducting himself in accordance with general rules" [P, 7]. Language makes us human. "[I]t is the peculiar nature of man above other animals that he can express his thoughts to his fellows and for that purpose has invented words" [III, 1, 8]. Grotius builds on a conventional account of language, as he expressly states with reference to Aristotle. For him language itself entails certain obligations.

---

[48] Diesselhorst, *Versprechen*, p. 55.
[49] Karl Olivecrona, "The Concept of a Right According to Grotius and Pufendorf", in Karl Olivecrona (ed.), *Law as Fact* (London, 1971), pp. 275 and 286.
[50] Olivecrona, "The Concept of a Right According to Grotius and Pufendorf", p. 291.

"It is merely the mutual obligation which men intended to introduce at the time they began to use speech and signs of a similar sort. For without such an obligation their invention would have been valueless. We require too that at the time a statement is made this right should exist and continue to be valid" [III, 1, 11]. Linguistic conventions establish communicative rights and obligations. A "linguistic contract" precedes all other contracts.[51]

The Performative Force of Promising

The normative force of promising derives from the normative obligation of language. Linguistic obligations enable the existence of language. Language is what constitutes human rationality. Grotius illustrates this relation with his strong insistence on good faith between enemies: "Certainly those who are enemies do not cease to be men. And all men who have arrived at the use of reason are capable of acquiring rights from a promise. ... On this connection between reason and the spoken word is based the binding force of a promise ... For the obligation to tell the truth comes from a reason that existed before the war and may, to some extent, possibly, be removed by war, but the promise itself establishes a new right" [III, 19, 1]. How exactly does the promise create this right? Given his conventional account of language and the normative force Grotius attaches to the spoken word and its consequences in the real world, it is tempting to compare his account to recent speech act theory.[52] For this purpose I turn to John Searle[53] and particularly to Jürgen Habermas' version of speech act theory, which underlies his "theory of communicative action".[54] The structural parallels could not be more remarkable.

---

[51] Victoria Kahn, *Wayward Contracts* (Princeton, NJ, 2004), p. 33.

[52] Peter Friedrich addresses this relation in "Rechtsakt/Sprechakt – Die Stellung des 'Performativen' in der Versprechenslehre des Hugo Grotius", in Dieter Hüning (ed.), *Die Naturrechtslehre des Hugo Grotius* (forthcoming). The contributions in Manfred Schneider (ed.), *Die Ordnung des Versprechens* (München, 2005) also analyse the linguistic dimensions of natural law theory.

[53] John Searle, *Speech Acts* (Cambridge, MA, 1969), especially Chapter 3. Searle's theory offered the first systematic application of Austin's ideas, but his purely intentional reading of speech acts undermines their decisive communicative nature.

[54] Jürgen Habermas, "Was heißt Universalpragmatik?", in Jürgen Habermas (ed.), *Sprachpragmatik und Philosophie* (Frankfurt, 1976), p. 174; also Jürgen Habermas, *Theorie des kommunikativen Handelns*, 2 vols (Frankfurt, 1981), II, p. 97 seq. The central issues of Habermas' speech act theory already appear in his Gauss Lectures (Princeton, 1971), reprinted in Jürgen Habermas, *On the Pragmatics of Social Interaction* (Cambridge, 2001).

Grotian Speech Acts

Grotius distinguishes "three different ways of speaking of things to come (*gradus loquendi de rebus futuris*)" [II, 11, 1]: *assertio*, *pollicitatio* and *perfecta promissio*. Habermas also uses a three-fold structure, distinguishing between cognitive, expressive and interactive modes of communication. Grotius's *assertio* sets forth "our present intention regarding something in the future" [II, 11, 2]. Habermas and Searle identify a cognitive proposition in every promise, that is, an assertion of its intended content. Every mode of communication for Habermas carries a different normative validity claim (*Geltungsanspruch*). The cognitive proposition claims the truth of the assertion. With Grotius's second way of speaking, the *pollicitatio*, "the will declares its course in the future by an outward sign, sufficient to indicate a sense of obligation to abide by its intention" [II, 11, 3]. Grotius requires internal "constancy or faithfulness (*constantiae sive fidelitatis*)" [II, 11, 3]. Correspondingly, Searle demands "sincerity" and Habermas truthfulness (*Wahrhaftigkeit*) of the speakers' expression of intention. Finally, Grotius's *perfecta promissio* requires that "to the original declaration of purpose is added a sign of an intention to convey a special right to another" [II, 11, 4]. Transferring a right illustrates the external effect of the linguistic action. Since John L. Austin, this performative effect has been called the "illocutionary force" of a speech act.[55] Searle stresses the assuming of an obligation in his "essential rule" of speech acts, while Habermas defines his third interactive or regulative mode as an interpersonal relation, claiming moral rightness (*Richtigkeit*).

GROTIUS'S gradus loquendi de rebus futuris	SEARLE'S rules for illocutionary forces	HABERMAS'S modes of communication
assertio = setting forth our present intention regarding something in the future	propositional content rule = speaker expresses the plan of his future act	cognitive mode = propositional content (truth)
pollicitatio = outward sign to indicate a sense of obligation to abide by the intention	sincerity rule = speaker really intents act	expressive mode = speaker's intention (truthfulness)
perfecta promissio = conveys a special right to another	essential rule = speaker assumes the obligation to fulfil the act	interactive mode = interpersonal relation (rightness)

---

[55] John L. Austin, *How to Do Things with Words* (Oxford, 1962), Lecture 8.

Dialogical Nature of Promising

The crucial third step, the Grotian *perfecta promissio*, produces a normative effect that transcends the promisor. A promise has an explicit dialogical nature. It is addressed to the promisee, carrying a normative validity claim (*Geltungsanspruch*) that only the promisee can claim from the promisor. Grotius illustrates the interpersonal orientation of promising in his treatment of lies: "when a statement (*sermo*) is made to one who is not thereby deceived, if a third person draws a false conclusion from it there is no lying in the case. No lie has been told to the person addressed ... Nor has a lie been told to the person who accidentally heard the statement, since it was not addressed to him (*eo non agitur*), and consequently there was no obligation to him" [III, 1, 13]. Promises have normative force when used as performatives in a process of communication. A promise is the prototype of pure communicative action. Or, in Grotius's words, *ac de verbis quidem expedita res* [II, 4, 3] – one can infer the facts directly from the words.

Prima Facie *Obligation*

Promises create a legal obligation out of the much lower conventional obligation of language. The promise establishes a *prima facie* obligation, which, if disputed, may be justified with reasons like free will, social security, utility or justice. With the speech act of promising, the promisor transfers to the promisee a right to demand reasons for future actions covered by the promise. The performative force of promising opens the inter-subjective game of giving and taking reasons.[56] With the use of language, all human beings rely on a common normative structure. Of course linguistic and cultural differences are massive. But all men and women are rational animals, and reason implies the use of reasons. A promise creates a normative claim that initiates a game of reasons in the communicative frame of a contract. If this frame of reasoning becomes more institutionalised, for instance with external arbitrators, it can already be called law. Common promises enable legal foundations.

---

[56] Wilfrid Sellars, *Empiricism and the Philosophy of Mind* (Minneapolis, 1956), §36, brought up the idea of a "space of reasons", which was developed into an elaborated "game of giving and taking reasons" in Brandom, *Making It Explicit*, 3.3, and John McDowell, *Mind and World* (Cambridge, MA, 1994).

Epilogue – Etiamsi Daremus non esse Nationes

God's Nature

Does a promise really escape the founding paradox? Of course not. But it establishes an ideal potency (*ideelle Macht*) of beginning.[57] That is what the idea of natural law is all about. Natural law provides a fictive founding scenario, stabilizing the first entry into the circle of justification. Once reasoning has started, the normative game stabilizes itself. With his theory of promising, Grotius outlines a communicative law of nature. One might object that in his time not reason but God was still the real source of obligation.[58] But God doesn't help either. God is just another groundless entry point into normative reasoning. Grotius's famous dictum that "God himself … would act contrary to his own nature if he did not fulfil his promises" [II, 11, 4] points to this methodological dilemma. Though harshly criticized by Pufendorf,[59] this brilliant metaphor was not cheap talk, but consistent logic. When Grotius writes that "men at first, not by any precepts of God, but by their own accord … did meet together in civil society, from whence civil power took beginning" [I, 4, 7], he situates the normative power of obligation directly in human society. Grotius's "nature" is "rational and social" [II, 20, 5]. Nature means logical reasoning. This "law of nature also is so unalterable that it cannot be changed even by God himself … even God cannot cause twice two not to make four" [I, 1, 10]. Grotius did not take his line of argument to its end: given a conventional account of signs, God too is bound by a human convention. Though perhaps the most fundamental and most brilliant, God is still a human construction. God itself remains an eternal promise.

Performative Sanctity

Grotius initiated what Habermas would much later call the linguistic transformation of the sacred (*Versprachlichung des Sakralen*).[60] The source of obligation moved from religion to communication. This secularisation did not kill God, but replaced one mythological source by another.[61] This transformation might better be called the canonization of language. The performative act becomes sort of a

---

[57] Hägerström, *Recht, Pflicht und bindende Kraft des Vertrages*, p. 64.

[58] In his contribution to this volume, David Boucher claims that for seventeenth-century natural law theories the source of obligation remained God, while reason was only the method of elaborating its content.

[59] Samuel Pufendorf, *De jure naturae et gentium* (Frankfurt, 1684), III, 5, 7 und II, 1, 3; Olivecrona, "The Concept of a Right According to Grotius and Pufendorf", p. 290.

[60] Habermas, *Theorie des kommunikativen Handelns*, vol. II, p. 118 seq.

[61] Ludwig Wittgenstein, *On Certainty*, trans. and ed. D. Paul, G.E.M. Anscombe and G.H. von Wright (Oxford, 1969): "The mythology may change back into a state

sacred rite, the founding of a normative order. But this performative sanctity is no more justified than was God. *Etiamsi daremus* is the natural underpinning of every normative order. Given the contractual reconstruction of legal systems, promising could be described as the founding rite of law. Jacques Derrida called this performative force of law the mystical foundation of authority (*Fondement mystique de l'autorité*).[62] Law never reaches, but still strives for justice. Because of its conceptual structure, justice is a justice to come. Justice, like God, is a promise. The figure of promising embodies the performative sanctity of human communicative nature. In order to stabilize a normative order, uncovered promises have to be validated by substantial reasons. But the paradoxical entry into the world of reasoning has been accomplished. Performative sanctity indicates a common faith in cooperative human communication.

Reasoned Sovereignty

Promises initiate cooperative reasoning by transferring a right to demand justification. Such a basic "right to justification" could form the core of a deliberative conception of global justice.[63] Given the plurality of functional vocabularies, reasons are a common grammar. They integrate single actors within a system and enable normative representation. But even more, reasons form a common ground between distinct functional systems. Of course the underlying rationales may be quite different, but all share the normative ground that each legal system balances multiple reasons. Justification is a relation between different vocabularies within or beyond one functional system. On this interpretation, sovereignty assumes another form. Acting in a legal system requires the ability to reason. Sovereignty entails the possibility of giving and receiving reasons. Within the global sphere, an actor that can reason its case might be called sovereign. To achieve new forms of sovereignty, we need new communicative institutions, enlarging the spectrum of "reasoners".

Global Promises

And what we have just said would hold even if we granted that there are no nations. The faith in communication transcends national boundaries. Looking back on thousands of years of global trade, different cultures and languages have not posed insuperable barriers. Yet faith is not enough. Contracts bear the

---

of flux, the river-bed of thoughts may shift" (§97) and "The difficulty is to realise the groundlessness of our believing" (§166).

[62] Subtitle of Derrida, *Force de loi*.
[63] Rainer Forst, "The Basic Right to Justification", *Constellations*, 6 (1999): 35; Rainer Forst, *Das Recht auf Rechtfertigung* (Frankfurt, 2007).

concrete task of mediating, translating and proceduralising plural normative orders. Contracts constitutionalise reasons. The institutional design of complex contractual regimes will decide the global future.[64] The question of war and peace depends on mechanisms for channelling reasons from one functional system to another. Only if adequate balancing procedures can be established within and between the different systems is there a chance of achieving global peace. Multiple social contracts integrated by multiple reasons on the basis of common promises offer a promising theoretical basis for pluralistic global governance structures. On this liquefied reading, then, Grotius is neither the sorry comforter Kant pronounced him to be nor a conservative restorer of religious values, but rather the "Grandfather of Global Law".

---

[64] Gunther Teubner, "Societal Constitutionalism: Alternatives to State-centred Constitutional theory?", in Christian Joerges, Inger-Johanne Sand and Gunther Teubner (eds), *Constitutionalism and Transnational Governance* (Oxford, 2004), p. 3, sets out the essential tasks of such a private constitutionalism.

PART IV
State and International Relations – from Machiavelli to Hobbes

Chapter 8
The Anatomy of Power in International Relations: The Doctrine of Reason of State as a "Realistic" Impact

Peter Nitschke

International Relations in the Seventeenth Century

Did International Relations exist in a premodern world? Such a perspective may appear to be the wrong way to deal with the topic of reason of state. It is problematic in more than one respect to adapt a modern understanding for the analysis of historical structures in the Renaissance and Enlightenment.

There are no special relations that can be strictly said to lie within the international sphere in the seventeenth century because there was no understanding of "international" in our present sense. Everything that can be discussed in this sense is, after all, fixed in the phenomenon of *international politics*. And yet this assumes a very traditional understanding of politics that relates to the special sphere of the state.

This special sphere of an entity called the *state* reflects a relatively new understanding of how to treat questions of power and justice with respect to all such entities that are organised in relation to each other in different ways. Seen from this perspective, we may be allowed to use the term *international relations* to refer to the seventeenth century because politics was then structured by families and their clan networking and mixed with elements of monarchy and aristocracy in every territory of Europe. So applied, "international relations" does not mean the same thing as it does today, but it has a similar meaning in more than one respect.

As the conclusion reached in these two remarks reveals, the concept of the state was, at the time of the seventeenth century, a new topic in the understanding of politics in an international context. The key issue regarding this new understanding is the doctrine of *reason of state*, which is finally an instrumental synthesis of Machiavelli's theory of power and virtue in the pivotal field of politics.

The Doctrine

Machiavelli's whole theory can be seen as an instruction manual for political practise. And at the centre of this instruction manual stands the doctrine of reasons of state. This doctrine offers an innovative programme for the understanding of politics in an international sphere, which goes far beyond the level of traditional genealogical bonds and relations of monarchies and aristocracies. It argues for setting up new rules of law and power – with power of course at the forefront. Even Machiavelli's proclamation of the *new prince* follows this line; it has to be founded in a classical (Aristotelian) topos to understand hierarchy and political order without any special orientation towards a concrete national dimension. Consequently, the new prince or the new state can be founded anywhere in political life. It makes no difference whether the state be a republic, a monarchy or an aristocracy: "Rather, there are as many *stati* as there are princes".[1] The concept of reasons of state represents a sort of transformation from a personal understanding of political order to an institutional approach. It is not the prince alone who is responsible for politics; it is more a question of the self-understanding of the state. In this sense, we can detect a hermeneutical transformation in the debates of the seventeenth or eighteenth centuries away from Machiavelli; the personal attributes of the political leader as virtuous, energetic, courageous, decisive, prudent, and so on,[2] are now fixed upon the state itself. It now became a question of cleverness for the state to find ways of interacting with similar institutions and their different capacities. The doctrine of reason of state indicates that there must be something like a specific knowledge for each state about how to establish its own ambitions in an inter-territorial arena of different opinions and ideas. Thus the quest for victory in conflicts and wars, which is the essential dimension in which the classical prince as well as the (new) state moves, has to become more rational and, in a special sense, even more scientific. Pursuing real politics means to have the ability to set new standards in political action: instrumentally, methodically and, of course, successfully.

Related to this aim of setting new standards, reason of state presents the same hermeneutical problem as does the prince in Machiavelli's analysis: how can the state establish its "own" understanding of rule as a concentration of power for its own sake? This is a question that has to be answered by an internal strategy of state and that can be solved in the manner exemplified by Thomas Hobbes in his *Leviathan*. Yet that cannot be a sufficient answer within the inter-territorial context, where the question is how to act amidst the different desires of numerous states?

---

[1] Peter Breiner, "Machiavelli's 'New Prince' and the Primordial Moment of Acquisition", in *Political Theory* 36/1 (2008): 67.

[2] See Breiner, "Machiavelli's 'New Prince'": 68.

Machiavelli's Rationalism

In this perspective, Machiavelli's theory affords the first hints towards an understanding of politics in an international field of action. The topic of *international politics* is in fact central to Machiavelli's theory because the historical framework that he describes in the *Principe* and in the *Discorsi* refers to the international dimension of politics. Foreign policy is, on this understanding, a question of power, perhaps even more so than internal policy. In this sense, *power* describes the ability to concentrate behaviour and desire on specific aims. An agenda is therefore needed for carrying things out in the right manner and, above all, for success in reaching the goal.

It is well known that in the Machiavellian analysis the main topos refers to a sort of behaviour that is described as *rational*. "Rationality" means here the way in which an individual can act successfully in a specific situation in far from harmonious circumstances. In the world described by Machiavelli, confrontations are normal. To act rationally requires the abilities that can be designated as *prudence, virtue* and (of course) *fortune*. A rational way of behaving is based upon the analytical competence to make the right decision according to time and place, wherever that might be.

The key to this, as mentioned in Machiavelli's theory, is expressed by the term *necessity*. Doing things rationally means to act in the knowledge of the real necessity present in every historical situation. A man cannot be successful in his actions as long as he does not realise the hidden necessity for behind his specific behaviour. Power in political questions is based on this relation: to find the right combination of prudence and of necessity for the specific action. In this sense, Machiavelli is the first author since the Greeks and Romans to reveal a concrete theory of the understanding of power. As Friedrich Nietzsche was later to remark, it is the "absolute will not to delude oneself and to see reason in reality – not in 'reason', still less in 'morality'".[3] This is the starting point for the doctrine of *reason of state*.

Doing Things Reasonably

Machiavelli's theory presents an understanding of individual capacities for a *personal regime*. But during the transformation of the debates that took place in

---

[3] "Thukydides und, vielleicht, der Principe Machiavellis, sind mir selber am meisten verwandt, durch den unbedingten Willen, sich nichts vorzumachen und die Vernunft in der Realität zu sehen, – nicht in der 'Vernunft', noch weniger in der 'Moral'" (Friedrich Wilhelm Nietzsche), "Nachgelassene Fragmente 1887–1889", in Friedrich Nietzsche, *Sämtliche Werke. Kritische Studienausgabe*, vol. 13. ed. G. Colli and M. Montinari (München, 1980), p. 625).

the second half of the sixteenth century, this personal understanding changed into an institutional approach to the practice of politics. Power is now not so much a question of the personal behaviour of the prince as a question of how the state should act within the institutional structure for its own reasons. In this sense, the doctrine is the starting point for *neo-realism* in International Relations, whose repercussions continue to this day. Questions about sovereignty or territoriality that have been central since the seventeenth century[4] cannot be discussed without taking into account the doctrine of reason of state, because it is the state that has to organise the motives of the people, these being their desires and their necessities. The Hobbesian question *quis iudicat* gives the central indication of what the problem of the state might be regarding its own organisation.[5] An answer to this question requires considering the people who are in the position to make the decisions on what is right and wrong within the state. These are the *politici*, and this group of persons operates under special obligations and conditions in the field of state affairs. During the seventeenth century, it became a topos that a politician had to do his "job" in accord with certain attitudes that conflict with a Christian life. As one writer in 1674 put it: "A Politicus that is a Statist, that is a Machiavellist, that is an Atheist, that is not a Christian"[6] (cf. Stolleis 1980: 61). The techniques of power differ considerably from the mainstream interpretations of how to organise social life. On this understanding, the doctrine of reason of state reveals the most useful behaviour in politics. Anything can be *reasonable* if it is for the benefit of the state. There are no limits or taboos restraining ministers, politicians and princes as to how to think and act in protecting the state. Their specific obligation follows from the necessity of preventing anything that might be detrimental to the people living in the state.[7] Meinecke may be consulted on this point; he indicated that the

---

[4] Jens Siegelberg, "Staat und internationales System – ein strukturgeschichtlicher Überblick", in Jens Siegelberg, Klaus Schlichte (eds), *Strukturwandel internationaler Beziehungen. Zum Verhältnis von Staat und internationalem System seit dem Westfälischen Frieden* (Wiesbaden, 2000), p. 18.

[5] Cf. also Peter Nitschke, "Grundlagen des staatspolitischen Denkens der Neuzeit – Souveränität, Territorialität und Staatsräson", in Jens Siegelberg, Klaus Schlichte (eds), *Strukturwandel internationaler Beziehungen. Zum Verhältnis von Staat und internationalem System seit dem Westfälischen Frieden* (Wiesbaden, 2000), p. 95.

[6] Michael Stolleis, "Arcana Imperii und Ratio Status. Bemerkungen zur politischen Theorie des frühen 17. Jahrhunderts", in Michael Stolleis, *Staat und Staatsräson in der frühen Neuzeit. Studien zur Geschichte des öffentlichen Rechts* (Frankfurt am Main, 1990), p. 61 (transl. by P.N.).

[7] Cf. also Peter Nitschke, *Staatsräson kontra Utopie? Von Thomas Müntzer bis zu Friedrich II. von Preußen* (Stuttgart and Weimar, 1995), p. 54.

doctrine of reason of state contains the whole complex of autonomy, liberty and sovereignty that goes to make up the modern state.[8]

The (new) Method

The questions about the institutional understanding of the state are by no means the only one. Even more relevant is the change in the methodological approach, the realisation of what happens and what is really important for benefit of the state. The *discorso* method, which was quite successful in the second half of the sixteenth century,[9] favours questions both about reality and about formal prudence. In Machiavelli, it is a kind of mechanical understanding of dialectical reasoning, a sort of *contrary dialectics* as René König has described it.[10] With this method, antithetical sentences can be formulated and given such a strong spin that there will be only one solution at the end. Each problem in political life can be constructed to a point where only two possibilities remain – and only one will be the *right one*.

On this understanding, there is no place for any relative propositions and decisions; the prince and the ministers of state have to choose the very best possibility. *Necessity* shows its face in the form of a logical rigorism that resembles a hermeneutical existentialism. Each problem can be discussed from the perspective of neither and nor, and a political action is always a physical one. There is no virtuality in analysing politics because the *body politic* is a real physical body that undergoes pain, desires and fears. The field in which the physical understanding of politics reveals its inner logical structure is *war*, because in war the physical action of all bodies (men and states) reach their final conclusion: who will keep and who will lose his body. The state (and the prince) that is better able to coordinate its will in terms of reason, rather than in terms of desire, will derive greater benefit from its actions. Thus *reasonable action* means utility in practise.[11]

---

[8] Friedrich Meinecke, *Die Idee der Staatsräson in der neueren Geschichte* [1929], ed. W. Hofer (München, 1957).

[9] Cf. Cornel Zwierlein, *Discorso und Lex Dei. Die Entstehung neuer Denkrahmen im 16. Jahrhundert und die Wahrnehmung der französischen Religionskriege in Italien und Deutschland* (Göttingen, 2006).

[10] Cf. René König, *Niccolò Machiavelli. Zur Krisenanalyse einer Zeitenwende* (München, 1979), p. 267.

[11] Cf. also Frank Grunert, *Normbegründung und politische Legitimität. Zur Rechts- und Staatsphilosophie der deutschen Frühaufklärung* (Tübingen, 2000), p. 279.

A World of Concurrence

The orientation towards utility for the sake of state benefit underlines the strategic impulse contained in the doctrine of reason of state that produces a different view for each state. There is no universal approach possible according to this concept. The sceptical tradition in western political philosophy, which does not expect peace and justice from a super-territorial or super-national institutional structure,[12] is a legacy from Machiavelli. Each state is responsible for its own territory and affairs: this is the classical topos of the contemporary neo-realistic school in international relations, corresponding to the understanding of reasons of state in the debates of the premodern world. In this hermeneutical context the whole structure of states is an anarchistic setting. Statesmen (and kings) who act within this structure must be bound primarily to their national interests. To operate successfully in the field of international politics means that the primary concern of each state must be to organise its military power.[13] Acting according to *reason of state* means to do practical things in politics, without esotericism, without metaphysical symbolism. This doctrine focuses on the constitutional facts of the body politic called state. The aim is to prevent all dangerous effects upon the specific body politic. The most important threat of course is *anarchy*,[14] because it leads to civil war, which is always a disaster for people and state.

In this connection, the doctrine of reason of state has not only a realistic impact but also an ethical sense. Searching for *good* reasons of state means to examine how the institutions of a particular state (and its people) can organise their own benefits into special topics. In the area of international affairs, this understanding gives a strategic value to politicians and statesmen: desires, culture, history and state are all structured in a specific (that is, a national) sense. Each state has its own history that has to be consulted in determining its own specific interests.

These specific national interests often occur in an antagonistic constellation; therefore the situation of the states among themselves may be seen paradigmatically as being a state of war. Thus the topos of the reason for war is the hidden centre of all politics and is basically the reason for the hermeneutical behaviour of politicians who argue using reasons of state and the basic tenets of contemporary neo-realists. Each government (and especially the governments of republics),

---

[12] Cf. Herfried Münkler, "Niccolò Machiavelli – Gedanken zu den zwischenstaatlichen Beziehungen", in Jürgen Bellers (ed.): *Klassische Staatsentwürfe. Außenpolitisches Denken von Aristoteles bis heute* (Darmstadt, 1996), p. 47.

[13] Cf. also Daniel S. Geller and J. David Singer, *Nations at War. A Scientific Study of International Conflict* (Cambridge, 2000), p. 6.

[14] See also Rüdiger Voigt, "Im Zeichen des Staates. Niccolò Machiavelli und die Staatsräson", in Herfried Münkler, Ralf Walkenhaus, Rüdiger Voigt (eds), *Demaskierung der Macht. Niccolò Machiavellis Staats- und Politikverständnis* (Baden-Baden, 2004), p. 43.

therefore, must organise its politics in such a way as "to love peace and to know how to fight a war".[15]

---

[15] Machiavelli, cit. by Maurizio Viroli, *Das Lächeln des Niccolò. Machiavelli und seine Zeit* (Reinbek, 2001), p. 277.

Chapter 9

Security as A Norm in Hobbes's Theory of War: A Critique of Schmitt's Interpretation of Hobbes's Approach to International Relations

Luc Foisneau

It is well known that security is a central concern of Hobbes's theory of the state and international relations. Indeed, the end for which men agree to submit themselves to the common power of a sovereign is "to live peacefully among themselves, and be protected against other men".[1] It is also well known that Hobbes wrote very little on security and war in international relations proper. No long and technical treatise such as Grotius's *De jure belli ac pacis*, not even a separate chapter in one of his three major political treatises. Despite this rather thin production on the subject, coming to no more than a few paragraphs and remarks here and there, Hobbes's name appears to be very familiar to contemporary specialists in international relations, who tend to consider him the original proponent, alongside Thucydides and Machiavelli, of the realist view that there can be no morality in the way states deal with one another.

Even though international life is not only a battlefield, it seems possible to describe it in Hobbesian words as a permanent war, consisting "not in the act of fighting, but in a tract of time wherein the will to contend by battle is sufficiently known".[2] Contemporary references to Hobbes's views on power politics,[3] or the anarchical society,[4] can be considered either as a symptom of the historical ignorance of specialists in international relations,[5] or as testimony to the

---

[1] Thomas Hobbes, *Leviathan*, XVIII, 1, ed. Edwin Curley (Indianapolis and Cambridge, 1994), p. 110. When possible, I give references to Hobbes's works in the form of the chapter and paragraph number. For *Leviathan*, I do the same, although the paragraph number does not appear in the original version.

[2] Hobbes, *Leviathan*, XII, 8, p. 76.

[3] Hans J. Morgenthau, *American Foreign Policy: A Critical Examination* (London, 1952), p. 34.

[4] Hedley Bull, *The Anarchical Society: A Study of Order in World Politics* (London, 1977).

[5] Noel Malcolm's frontal attack against international relations theorists illustrates this position: "And the interpretation of Hobbes put forward by modern international

productivity of Hobbes's theory beyond its historical context. Noel Malcolm has followed the first line of interpretation, showing that the standard portrayal of Hobbes's theory of international relations "appears to be based, for the most part, on a handful of passages in one or two of his works (ignoring many comments on international affairs elsewhere in his writings); and even those few passages have been misunderstood".[6] This critical textual approach is a helpful reminder that what Hobbes actually says about relations between states is very far from the caricature which often circulates under his name in the field of international relations theory.

Contrary to that view, I would like to consider here Hobbes's approach to security in international relations as a normative one, and in order to do so I shall contrast it with the reading of the most radical form of realism in this field, that of Carl Schmitt and his views on the formation of European international law. This comparison is all the more interesting because the idea that security could be a Hobbesian norm clashes from the start with Schmitt's decisionist interpretation of Hobbes. My approach, however, will not be to discuss Schmitt's interpretation of the Hobbesian sovereign as the typical decision-maker,[7] but rather to examine how Hobbes fits into, or rather does not fit into, the Schmittian interpretation of the seventeenth-century international world order.

Despite its political origins in Nazi Germany,[8] Carl Schmitt's approach to international relations still exerts a fascination and claims a right to impose its mark on the reading of Hobbes's place in the history of war and state. One explanation for this fascination is that Schmitt's theory is supposed to help us consider the double aspect of a classical sovereign state: as a means, on the one

---

relations theorists, meanwhile, has become fixed and ossified, functioning at best as an 'ideal type' and at worst as a caricature." "Hobbes's Theory of International Relations", in Noel Malcolm, *Aspects of Hobbes* (Oxford, 2002), p. 433.

[6] Malcolm, "Hobbes's Theory of International Relations", p. 435.

[7] For a definition of Hobbes as the characteristic decisionist thinker, see Carl Schmitt, *Über die drei Arten des rechtswissenschaftlichen Denkens* (Hamburg, 1934), chap. 1.2; *On the Three Types of Juristic Thought*, transl. by J.W. Bendersky (Westport, Conn. and London, 2004), p. 61: "The classic case of decisionist thinking first appears in the seventeenth century with Hobbes. All *Recht*, all norms and statutes, all interpretations of laws, and all orders are for him essentially decisions of the sovereign, and the sovereign is not a legitimate monarch or established authority, but merely the one who decides in a sovereign manner."

[8] For a clear presentation of the origins of the book and interesting remarks on the link with the *Glossarium*, see Peter Haggenmacher, "Présentation. L'itinéraire internationaliste de Carl Schmitt", in Carl Schmitt, *Le Nomos de la terre*, trad. L. Deroche-Gurcel (Paris, 2001), pp. 1–46. On the various facets of Schmitt's anti-Semitism and in particular on the origins of the notion of nomos in the Protestant theology of nomos, see Raphael Gross, *Carl Schmitt and the Jews: the "Jewish Question", the Holocaust, and German Legal Theory*, transl. by J. Golb (Madison, 2007).

hand, of limiting the intensity of war within the frontiers of Europe, and on the other hand, as an instrument for waging wars of destruction beyond the borders of Europe.[9] Being as it is a geopolitical approach to law and politics, Schmitt's analysis has been claimed to help us understand Hobbes's philosophy in what would be its real, that is, geographical, international context.[10]

In order to break the Schmittian spell, it is necessary to stress first, as I shall try to do in the first part of this chapter, that the aspect of Hobbes's foreign politics which is stressed in *The Nomos of the Earth* (a book published in 1950, but whose material is already present in articles and essays of the war period)[11] is part of a broader interpretation of international relations based on sovereign territorial states at war with one another. This international theory, which was to govern the life of European states from the sixteenth to the nineteenth century, is based at the same time on the assumption of territorial sovereignty as the ultimate definition of politics, and on the paradoxical hypothesis that a plurality of sovereign states is less dangerous for peace than the spiritual competition between various Christian faiths, since it allows for a moderate state of war within the frontiers of Europe. We shall see whether Hobbes fits into this Schmittian interpretation of the history of law and politics.

In the second part, I turn to what Schmitt says about Hobbes's international relations theory in the context of the division of the earth according to what Schmitt called "global lines". Global lines theory is used to explain how the Hobbesian state of nature could also apply to the terrible war of all against all supposed to be raging beyond certain geographical lines secretly agreed upon by the European powers.

In a last part of this chapter, I offer evidence for the contradiction between this interpretation and the actual Hobbesian approach to international relations.

---

[9] Cf. Carlo Galli, *Spazi politici. L'età moderna e l'età globale* (Bologna, 2001) and also the quotations from this book in Etienne Balibar, *Europe Constitution Frontières* (Bègles, 2005), p. 96, note 2: "Parmi ses nombreuses publications [which is Galli's] figure le travail de référence sur la pensée de Carl Schmitt: *Genealogia della politica: Carl Schmitt e la crisi del pensiero moderno*, Il Mulino, Bologna, 1996, dont une grande partie est consacrée à la discussion de la théorie du 'Nomos de la terre' (au double sens de distribution et de loi). A beaucoup d'égards le dernier livre de Galli relève du débat international très animé qui tend à rechercher des *alternatives non schmittiennes au problème géo-politique posé par Schmitt*, et à la philosophie de l'histoire qui le sous-tend" (my italics).

[10] In his interpretation of Hobbes, Carlo Galli stresses the "spatial" characteristics of the state of nature and of the civil state in a way that blurs the ideological dimension of Schmitt's argument, notably in the case of the non-discriminating concept of war: "… data la parità ontologica dei contendenti, la guerra *risulta* limitata e non 'giusta', ovvero non assoluta né discriminatoria." (Carlo Galli, *Spazi politici*, p. 47; my italics).

[11] For some of those articles, see Carl Schmitt, *Staat, Grossraum, Nomos. Arbeiten aus den Jahren, 1916–1969*, ed. Günter Maschke (Berlin, 1991).

The Hobbesian State of Nature and the Schmittian *jus Publicum Europaeum*

Let us begin with the analysis of Hobbes as a good representative of the European law of nations. The first characteristic of this law, referred to by Schmitt as *jus publicum Europaeum*, is that it is based on the concrete principle of territorial sovereignty, or more exactly on a division of the territory of Europe amongst separate sovereign entities.[12] In contrast with the legal organisation of empires, either spiritual (papacy) or temporal (the medieval Holy Roman Empire), and with the feudal organisation of medieval kingdoms, this new legal set of principles can be called truly international, or interstatal, as it aims at organising the relations between states, soon to become nation-states, on the basis of the occupation of a well-defined territory. This territorial division of Europe into different states with borders to defend presupposes the occupation of a geographical space that is not limited to the borders of Europe but extends to territories in the New World.[13] The classical international order is thus based on discovery as a legitimate title to occupying newly found lands.[14] Seventeenth-century European states do not therefore proceed from an abstract model, which we might call the universal state-form, but from a European way of organising the world order by means of discovery and conquest: this is precisely what the Greek term *nomos* is here taken to mean, that is, a juridical world-ordering based on the occupation of the earth. Schmitt's understanding of the world order as a "nomos of the earth" thus explains his refusal to consider the state as a universal political category.[15] The state-form is linked to the geopolitical development of Europe, to a certain

---

[12] "Continental European international law since the 16th century, the *jus publicum Europaeum*, originally and essentially was a law among *states*, among European sovereigns. This European core determined the *nomos* of the rest of the earth." (Carl Schmitt, *Der Nomos der Erde im Völkerrecht des Jus Publicum Europaeum* (4th edn, Berlin, 1997; [1st edn, 1950]), p. 97; *The Nomos of the Earth in the International Law of the Jus Publicum Europaeum*, transl. by G.L. Ulmen (New York, 2003), pp. 126–7; Abrev.: *The Nomos of the Earth*, page in the German edition/page in the English translation.

[13] On the fact that the enclosed European territorial order is linked to the opening of a maritime space, see Jean-François Kervégan, "Carl Schmitt and 'World Unit'", in Chantal Mouffe (ed.), *The Challenge of Carl Schmitt* (London, 1999), pp. 65–6. See also Schmitt, *The Nomos of the Earth*, p. 112/140: "The concrete spatial order of these territorial states gave European soil a specific status in international law, not only within Europe, but in relation to both the free space of the open sea and to all non-European soil overseas."

[14] Cf. Schmitt, *The Nomos of the Earth*, pp. 100–104/130–33: "Occupation and Discovery as Legal Title to Land-Appropriation".

[15] "'Statehood' is not a universal concept, valid for all times and all peoples. Both in time and space, the term described a concrete fact." (Schmitt, *The Nomos of the Earth*, p. 97/127).

relationship between Europe and the rest of the world, and therefore cannot be considered as the universally valid result of a logical deduction.

This statement constitutes a first difference between Schmitt's and Hobbes's approaches to the state. Hobbes considered his demonstration to have a universal scope: "The final cause, end, or design of men (who naturally love liberty and dominion over others) in the introduction of that restraint upon themselves in which we see them live in commonwealths is the foresight of their own preservation, and of a more contented life thereby".[16] This quotation clearly shows that *Leviathan* was not written for the citizens of Europe only, let alone for the citizens of Great Britain, but for any man willing to live a peaceful life under the protection of a state. There is no reference here to the well-delineated territory of a particular state, but the general formula of the solution to a universal problem: if the timber of human nature is crooked, as indicated by the fact that most human passions are contrary to morality, then there is only one solution to the problem of having men act morally, that is, to establish a "visible power to keep them in awe, and tie them by fear of punishment to the performance of their covenants".[17] Since the "visible power" is a general solution to a universal problem, it is of no importance who invented the solution and where on earth it was invented.

The emergence of several states, instead of a single empire, was of course a new source of contention in seventeenth-century Europe, as the Thirty Years War was notably to demonstrate; since those states exerted their power over a determined territory, the defence of territorial borders was likely to lead to war. However, this obvious feature of the interstatal organization of classical Europe has – and this is a second aspect of Schmitt's analysis – concealed the fact that those interstate wars were far less dangerous for the stability of the continent than had been the previous wars of religion. The reason for this difference in the intensity of war is that the state operates a *de-theologisation* of public life, in both domestic and foreign affairs.[18] Thus the new interstate wars no longer split society into opposed factions, each fighting for transnational religious truths, such as sixteenth-century wars between French Protestants and Catholics had done. No longer a war for eternal salvation, that is, a theologically justified war, interstate war is supposed to be less violent because the enemy's cause is not *ipso facto* considered unjust and the enemy himself wicked. Playing its part in *Der Nomos der Erde*, this conceptual distinction between two kinds of war is already

---

[16] Hobbes, *Leviathan*, XVII, 1, p. 106.

[17] *Ibid.*

[18] "The first effective rationalization of the 'state' as a spatial form, in terms of both domestic and foreign policy, was achieved by the detheologization of public life and the neutralization of the antitheses of creedal civil wars." (Schmitt, *The Nomos of the Earth*, p. 112/140; modified translation).

central to Schmitt's 1938 book on the concept of discriminating war;[19] in both cases, the idea is that the violence of a war is due not only to the techniques and technologies of war, but also to the claim that the war being fought is a just war. Schmitt refers to the just war theories of the Middle Ages, notably to the one developed by Francisco de Vitoria, but he also has in mind the military intervention of the United States in 1917 and the spirit of the Treaty of Versailles. The idyllic picture he draws of seventeenth-century interstate wars is the exact, and perhaps all-too-clear-cut, opposite both of sixteenth-century religious wars and twentieth-century ideological wars of destruction. When compared with wars of annihilation, fighting for limited goals, such as a modification to a border or a claim to dynastic heritage, can appear as relatively benign.

How does this historically far-reaching Schmittian analysis apply to Hobbes's conception of interstate relations? Let us turn first to the famous passage about states' relations in the description of the state of nature in chapter XIII of *Leviathan*:

> But though there had never been any time wherein particular men were in a condition of war one against another, yet in all times kings and persons of sovereign authority, because of their independency, are in continual jealousies, and in the state and posture of gladiators, having their weapons pointing, and their eyes fixed on one another; that is, their forts, garrisons, and guns upon the frontiers of their kingdoms, and continual spies upon their neighbours, which is a posture of war. But because they uphold thereby the industry of their subjects, there does not follow from it that misery which accompanies the liberty of particular men.[20]

Two things, at least, are clear in this text: first, Hobbes recognises that states have always been in a condition of war with one another; second, that the interstate condition of war is not as bad as the inter-individual state of hostility, since the former, and not the latter, allows for peace, that is, for economic exchanges and industry at home. Whereas commentators have often read this text as if it described relations between states as anarchical, stressing the less than friendly description of "their weapons pointing, and their eyes fixed on one another", they have hardly noticed that the whole description relies on a comparison of states with gladiators, which could allow for a very different interpretation. And this is precisely what Schmitt puts forward. If states can be legitimately compared to duellists, there is certainly a good reason for considering their conflicts in the Hobbesian state of nature in a different perspective. Although duels can be fatal to

---

[19] Carl Schmitt, *Die Wendung zum diskriminierenden Kriegsbegriff* (Munich, 1938).
[20] Hobbes, *Leviathan*, XIII, 12, p. 78.

the life of those actually engaged in them, Schmitt stresses the fact that this danger is less threatening than in private wars waged in the name of God or of justice. If justice matters, it is not because the just cause should always triumph, but because there are juridical forms that have to be respected.[21] The duellists must be men of honour, they must keep to the rules established in such circumstances, and they must abide by the decisions of a referee.

Just as in duels fighting is limited by respect for strict juridical rules, so the effects of war between states in the classical period are considered by Schmitt to have been limited by respect for juridical laws defining the *casus belli*, the juridical conditions of warfare, and the obtaining of peace. Just as in duels there are witnesses who attest to the proper course of the fight, so in the classical European law of nations there are neutral states capable of playing the part of mediators between conflicting parties. The plausibility of this analogy rests on one central element, namely the definition of the state, but this definition itself varies somewhat in the two texts where the analogy is introduced. In Schmitt's *The Leviathan in the State Theory of Thomas Hobbes*, the state is featured as a juridical mechanism, allowing for both technical efficiency in the transmission of orders and for a strictly positivistic respect of the law, excluding by definition all kind of resistance;[22] in *The Nomos of the Earth*, a new dimension comes to the fore, that is, the territory occupied by the state, which is the spatial subject represented as a person.[23] This does not mean that the two other aspects have been denied, but rather that the geopolitical dimension is now the crucial dimension. There has been an evident change in the presentation, but the core thesis remains unchanged by the transformed historical context: the modern state has modified the nature of the relations between justice and war, since justice in war is no longer of a substantial theological nature, but

---

[21] "In other words, a duel is not 'just' because the just cause always wins, but because there are certain guarantees in the preservation of the form – in the quality of the parties to the conflict as agents, in the adherence to a specific procedure (effected by bracketing the struggle), and, especially, in the inclusion of witnesses on an equal footing. Here, law has become a completely institutionalized form; here, men of honor have found a satisfactory means of dealing with a matter of honor in a prescribed form and before impartial witnesses." (Schmitt, *The Nomos of the Earth*, p. 115/143; modified translation).

[22] On the mechanistic and neutral dimensions of the modern state illustrated by Hobbes, see Carl Schmidt, *Der Leviathan in der Staatslehre des Thomas Hobbes. Sinn und Fehlschlag einer politischen Symbols* (Hamburg, 1938), transl. in English by G. Schwabe and E. Hilfstein as *The Leviathan in the State Theory of Thomas Hobbes: Meaning and Failure of a Political Symbol* (Westport, Connecticut and London, 1996), chap. 4.

[23] "Now the state was conceived of juridically as a measure relative to a new spatial order, as the new legal subject of a new international law; as a juridical concept, it had become irresistible. However, essentially this state was a unified, self-contained area of European soil that was at the same time represented in the guise of a *magnum homo* [great man]." (Schmitt, *The Nomos of the Earth*, p. 117/145; modified translation).

of a procedural juridical nature, which can be addressed in front of a tribunal – precisely the tribunal of war. To the main features Schmitt has added a new one, space and its importance for the state, but the central thesis is still the same: reintroducing a discriminating concept of war in the twentieth century, as was done according to Schmitt by the Treaty of Versailles, was an enormous juridical and political mistake. In a way, the violence of European conflicts after World War I is a direct consequence of this mistake. This remark shows the Schmittian thesis on discriminating war to be more relevant to the situation of the early twentieth century than to seventeenth-century Europe.[24] The question now is to determine how this twentieth-century context affects Schmitt's interpretation of Hobbes, and, in particular, the description of interstate relations as a "state of nature". Is this not in contradiction with what Schmitt suggests, that is, that a state of war between two states should be less opposed to a rapid return to peace than a Hobbesian state of nature is usually considered to be?

One way of dealing with this embarrassing question is to say, as Schmitt does, that the important point is not the nature of the state of nature, but the nature of the state. As a matter of fact, the state of nature is only a type of relation existing outside the state-order. Whether the new European international order is to be considered "an antisocial struggle between Leviathans (according to Hobbes) or (with Locke) as an already sociable community of gentlemen" is a "secondary question"[25] for the historian of political thought, but not for the legal philosopher. What really matters is the *"international personal analogy"*[26] at the basis of the new international order, in as much as it allows the *jus gentium* to be considered as the right existing between persons who are the representatives of states equally entitled to wage war.

---

[24] But the main reference here is the essay on the transformations of the concept of war after World War I and the Treaty of Versailles: Carl Schmidt, *Die Wendung zum diskriminierenden Kriegsbegriff* (Munich, 1938), and also "Über das Verhältnis der Begriffe Krieg und Feind" (1938), in Carl Schmitt, *Positionen und Begriffe im Kampf mit Weimar-Genf-Versailles, 1923–1939* (Hamburg, 1940).

[25] Schmitt, *The Nomos of the Earth*, p. 118/146 (modified translation): "For example, one such secondary question is the dispute about whether one should think of these 'great men' as existing in a 'state of nature' beyond an amity line and, in turn, whether one should consider this state of nature (in the sense of Hobbes) to be an asocial struggle of leviathans, or (in the sense of Locke) already to be a social community of thoroughly proper gentlemen".

[26] *Ibid.* This passage is quoted in English in the text. When first using this expression, Schmitt (*The Nomos of the Earth*, p. 119, note 1/147, note 7) refers to "the extraordinarily important article by Edwin de Witt Dickinson, 'International Personal Analogy', in the *Yale Law Journal*, vol. XXII (1916–17), pp. 564–89", which does not support his thesis and was published under a different title: "The Analogy between Natural Persons and International Persons in the Law of Nations".

Hobbes is important for Schmitt not so much for his characterisation of the state of nature as for his definition of the international personal analogy.[27] The comparison between states and persons must nevertheless be correctly interpreted, that is, on the basis not of a psychological analogy, but of a juridical definition.[28] When the gigantic persons – states – are compared to gladiators in a posture of war, it does not necessarily mean that they do not belong to the same society. All the more so as those gigantic persons are linked not only by treaties and international contracts, but also by more traditional bonds such as religion and economy,[29] not to mention the blood ties of most the sovereigns of seventeenth-century Europe. Seen in the perspective of this new concept of state personality, it is clear that Hobbes's contribution to the definition of a new European international order has been quite central. Although the representation of states as *magni homines*, or "big men", can be traced to its use in allegory and so was not invented by Hobbes, it remains true that Hobbes contributed greatly to the juridical clarification of the notion itself, notably in chapter XVI of *Leviathan*. It is therefore no less true to say that the rules which apply to seventeenth-century Europe are not those of an anarchical society, but rather those of a relatively polite, if undisciplined, society of states. After all, duels take place only between people belonging to the same aristocratic milieu.

The famous Hobbesian observation in the preface to *De Cive* – *homo homini lupus* – may be interpreted within the same perspective: not only does it not mean that men behave as ferocious beasts to one another; it also does not imply that some states are ewes. Since every one of those public persons has an equal *jus ad bellum*, there is no single wolf among the European flock. If Hobbes is right to consider these big individuals as wolves to one another, it is because all share this quality. Schmitt's fixed idea is that no one can deprive the others of their *jus ad bellum*; no one can declare that he is a ewe, while only the others are wolves.[30]

---

[27] Schmitt, *The Nomos of the Earth*, pp. 118–19/p. 146 (modified translation): "Moreover, Hobbes's theory of *magni homines* in the [international] state of nature was accepted as true and exercised the strongest intellectual influence."

[28] Noel Malcolm gives a clear formulation of the difference between the psychological and the juridical concepts of persons: "As the famous engraved title page of *Leviathan* reminds us, Hobbes does indeed have a theory of the collective person-hood of the commonwealth. But his use of the concept of a 'person' here is not a matter of some generalized psychological comparison between individual and collective behaviour". (Malcolm, "Hobbes's Theory of International Relations", p. 443).

[29] Schmitt, *The Nomos of the Earth*, p. 120/148: "But, in reality, strong traditional ties – religious, social, and economic – endure longer."

[30] Schmitt, *The Nomos of the Earth*, p. 119/147: "Even if one accepts that 'man is a wolf among other men' in the *bellum omnium contra omnes* [war of everyone against everyone] of the state of nature, this has no discriminatory meaning, because also in a state

Here, again, the same obsession comes to the fore, that is, that the classical right of war is right because it does not recognise a discriminating concept of (just) war.

If this duel-like attitude of person-like states towards one another were the whole story, however, there would be no reason to discuss Schmitt's interpretation any further, since there is no such a contradiction between the latter and a normative approach to Hobbes's state of nature. Indeed, duels would not exist were there no established rules to organise them. Similarly, the wars between classical European states would not have arisen without a certain amount of regulation,[31] to which each state agreed to submit. But whereas recent commentators have tended to consider this moderate view on the international state of nature as the whole Hobbesian story, Schmitt adds a few features in relation to his conception of the spatial dimension of politics, and those features completely change the nature of the picture.

The Hobbesian State of Nature and the Space Beyond the Lines

One characteristic feature of Schmitt's reflection in *The Nomos of the Earth* is its interest in the process that establishes a new international juridical order: not only constituted power matters, that is, the state system and its bureaucracy, but also constituting power, that is, the original violence behind institutions. In world history, this phenomenon is described by Schmitt as a phenomenon of conquest, what he calls *Landnahme*, the taking of land, which he says is more fundamental than *Landteilung*, the division of conquered territory.[32] Since not all kinds of conquests are the beginning of a new juridical order, what is of interest to Schmitt is how Europe juridically organised its conquest of the new world, and what consequences this way of conquering the world had on the organisation of a European law of nations.

This historical approach to the formation of the European state system constitutes a second major difference between Schmitt and Hobbes, since Hobbes says extremely clearly that the question of the origins of commonwealths is of no consequence as far as the obligation to obey them is concerned. Although the English philosopher

---

of nature none of the combatants has the right to suspend equality or to claim that only he is human and that his opponent is nothing but a wolf."

[31] N. Malcolm provides evidence that this regulation finds its expression in the laws of nature: "Indeed, there is something very implausible about the claim that Hobbes's laws of nature cannot apply at the international level, given that one of them relates directly to diplomatic practice". ("Hobbes's Theory of International Relations", p. 439).

[32] Schmitt, *The Nomos of the Earth*, p. 49/81 (modified translation): "For our purposes, the term land-appropriation is better than land-division, because land-appropriation, both externally and internally, points clearly to the constitution of a *radical title*."

acknowledges that some commonwealths are such by acquisition,[33] he stresses the fact that the latter's violent origins are not relevant as far as rights of sovereignty are concerned: "… the rights and consequences of sovereignty are the same in both [therefore in the commonwealth by institution and in the commonwealth by acquisition]".[34] Schmitt maintains exactly the contrary: the way a piece of land (or of sea) is conquered determines the kind of law that will apply to it and also the relations between the conquering powers. When considering the interpretation Schmitt gives of Hobbes's state of nature in relation to the discovery of America, this important difference should be borne in mind.

The latter interpretation of the Hobbesian international state of nature depends on the idea that, once European powers took possession of the New World, they established their respective properties on it by means of global divisions of the earth, which established very different regimes of law and of war according to where one lived or waged war. The peace treaties signed by the powerful kingdoms of Europe throughout the classical period would not be complete, insists Schmitt,[35] if one were to ignore a few secret clauses which were attached to them. Those secret clauses, based on the global division of the earth amongst the European powers, describe a very different picture of international relations than the peaceful one that we have previously envisaged. Before turning again to Hobbes's state of nature, it is therefore necessary to say a few words about the idea of global lines dividing the earth, since they play a significant role in Schmitt's interpretation of Hobbes.

The first thing to be noted is that those lines have had a global character from the start, that is, since the discovery of the New World by Spain and Portugal. Those lines are therefore, according to Schmitt, the expression of a Eurocentric approach to world politics. The second thing to be noted is that, although the geographical situation of those lines have greatly varied from the time of the first discoveries and the intervention of the papacy to the end of nineteenth century, the Monroe doctrine and the intervention of the United States, they have been, from the start, not merely geographical but also geopolitical and, if it may be put this way, geojuridical[36] divisions, based on a global view of the domination of the earth. In this perspective, globalisation, or global thinking, is not at all a new

---

[33] Hobbes, *Leviathan*, chap. XX, "Of Dominion Paternal and Despotical".
[34] Hobbes, *Leviathan*, XX, 3, p. 128.
[35] Schmitt, *The Nomos of the Earth*, p. 60/92: "Although the historical type of so-called *amity lines* was related to European land- and sea-appropriations of the New World, it was based on completely different premises. Amity lines first appeared (and were agreed upon only verbally) in a secret clause in the Treaty of Cateau-Cambrésis (1559)."
[36] Friedrich August von der Heydte described Schmitt's approach as constituting some kind of "Geojurisprudence". Cf. Haggenmacher, "Présentation", in Carl Schmitt, *Le Nomos de la terre*, p. 41, note 2.

concept, for it dates back to the first treaties between Portugal and Spain at the end of fifteenth century. But the characteristic feature of this Schmittian approach to globalisation is that it is an anti-universalistic one: global lines are there to delineate different kinds of juridical regimes according to the powers that have command over a land; they are the expression of a geographical way of thinking about international matters, where the central question is not so much the validity of the norms *per se* as of the imperial powers behind the norms. A major aspect of this global line of thinking is, indeed, that it rests on the idea of empire more than on the idea of state. This, of course, raises the essential question (to which I shall return in my conclusion) whether or not Hobbes's vision of politics is sympathetic to an imperial approach to international relations.

But before treating that point, it is necessary to consider what Schmitt's global lines were, and in particular what they were at the time of Hobbes. Among the three main divisions considered by Schmitt, the first type – the *raya* – was clearly linked to the hegemony of the papacy in European politics, since the first global line was defined in the papal bull *Inter caetera divinae*, issued by Pope Alexander VI (4 May 1494 [in fact 1493]), and was followed not long after by the famous Treaty of Tordesillas (7 June 1494), which divided the Atlantic Ocean between Portugal and Spain.[37] But what is of more interest for our seventeenth-century perspective is Schmitt's comment on the second type of global lines. Also called "Amity" lines, since they express some kind of "friendship" between the contracting European powers, those lines established new rules for dividing newly discovered territories among European powers. But contrary to what was the case with the *raya*, the agreement was now based on the absence of a common referee, since the Pope could no longer play such a part in mediations between Protestant and Catholic powers. In the absence of a common judge capable of deciding conflicting claims, the powers agree that force will be the judge beyond certain lines. For the study of the treaties, including clauses on Amity lines, Schmitt relies mainly on F.G. Davenport's *European Treaties bearing on the History of the United States* (Washington, 1917), but historical evidence is scarce: Schmitt refers, for example, to a declaration of the King of France, Louis XIII, on 1 July 1634, forbidding French sailors to attack Portuguese and Spanish boats on the European side of the Tropic of Cancer, but allowing them to do so beyond that line.[38]

---

[37] Schmitt, *The Nomos of the Earth*, p. 57/89: "Pope Alexander VI's global line was consistent with the one drawn somewhat to the west of it, approximately through the middle of the Atlantic Ocean (370 miles west of Cape Verde), by the Spanish-Portuguese Treaty of Tordesillas (June 7, 1494), in which the two Catholic powers agreed that all newly discovered territories west of the line would belong to Spain and those east of the line to Portugal. This line was called a *partition del mar océano*, and was sanctioned by Pope Julius II."

[38] Schmitt, *The Nomos of the Earth*, p. 61/93: "Thus, Cardinal Richelieu made a declaration in the name of the French king on July 1, 1634, according to which French

On the European side of those lines, peace was more or less preserved thanks to a law of nations allowing war only between states;[39] but beyond those lines the limits on war no longer existed, and privateers were allowed to ransom or destroy foreign ships and wage what might be called total war. Incapable of agreeing on a fair distribution of lands and seas in the New World, the European powers could only agree on the fact that the new spaces were free, which means, according to Schmitt, that the distribution of lands and seas could only be decided by force. Of course, the other implicit point of agreement was that the New World could only be divided between the European powers. What was then the juridical consequence of those Amity lines? That what happened "beyond the line" was not submitted to the moral, juridical and political limitations imposed on European states by the *jus publicum europaeum*, that is, the law of supposedly civilized nations. The new space of liberty thus opened both on land and sea was indeed a space in which international laws limiting the violence of interstate conflicts would no longer apply. Properly speaking, the space beyond the Amity lines was anything but a friendly one; rather something like the wild west of Europe.[40]

The few elements that I have just mentioned will help us to understand the second dimension of Schmitt's interpretation of Hobbes's international relations theory. If we allow this global division of the earth in seventeenth-century Europe (a point I shall discuss in the final section), we can clearly see that there is room for a completely different approach to the Hobbesian notion of an international state of nature.

On the one hand, as we have already seen, the relations between states can be interpreted on the model of a duel between public persons, and the state of nature as a juridical concept liable to impose limits on the effects of war within Europe; but, on the other hand, there is also room – and quite a lot, it could be said – for a more radical interpretation in which the state of nature would be considered a radical state of war among pirates, with no juridical limits imposed on violence. The idea of global lines thus allows us to conciliate two apparently contradictory readings of Hobbes, one which insists on the absence of laws in the international state of nature

---

seafarers were forbidden to attack Spanish and Portuguese ships on this side of the Tropic of Cancer, but were given liberty to do so beyond this line, if the Spanish and Portuguese refused them free access to their Indian and American possessions on land and sea." For a convincing critique of the historical evidence, see Haggenmacher, "Présentation", in Carl Schmitt, *Le Nomos de la terre*, p. 41.

[39] On this aspect, see Schmitt's comments (*The Nomos of the Earth*, p. 122/149) on Rousseau's statement in *On the Social Contract* (Book I, chap. IV, ed. by Donald A. Cress, Indianapolis, 1987, p. 21): "War is a relation between one state and another." Schmitt quotes Rousseau in French: "La guerre est une relation d'Etat à Etat."

[40] Schmitt, *The Nomos of the Earth*, p. 62/pp. 93–4: "Beyond the line was an 'overseas' zone in which, for want of any legal limits to war, only the law of the stronger applied."

(the anarchical society reading) and the other which presses the existence of the natural law as the law of nations (the society of states reading). But before assessing the validity of this possible conciliation, let us consider the interpretation given by Schmitt of the state of nature in the light of the Amity lines.

The reference to Hobbes is one among three, the two others drawing on Pascalian and Lockean arguments, but it may be considered the most important one. Schmitt declares here that the Hobbesian idea of a state of nature is the "effect of the Amity lines"[41] and that the general, quasi neo-Kantian, interpretation of it must be rejected on the basis of this historical evidence. Although he does not deny that this idea may have had other historical origins (following here Leo Strauss and Franz Borkenau),[42] and that it might have gained in generality in the later works (agreeing here with Ferdinand Tönnies),[43] he stresses the fact that the real and most concrete origin of Hobbes's idea is to be found in the transformation of international relations and the institution of Amity lines. The state of nature is not a general idea, but rather a concrete idea that can be ascribed a local origin in the space beyond the line. A first argument is taken from the revival in Hobbes's work of the famous Latin formula, *homo homini lupus*. Whereas Vitoria rejected this formulation, for which he substituted the humanistic formulation *homo homini homo*, Hobbes was to recast the idea under the impact of the absence of common power in the New World. But the geographical dimension of the state of nature only appears when Hobbes comes to concrete examples.

When Hobbes declares in chapter XIII of *Leviathan* that "It may peradventure be thought, there was never such a time nor condition of war as this; I believe it was never generally so, *over all the world*",[44] Schmitt would underline the last part of the sentence. If the state of nature, in its more radical form, was not generally so all over the world, it may well be because of the division of the earth between Europe and the spaces beyond the line. If we understand it in this way, we can also better understand the meaning of the example given by Hobbes in support of his thesis:

---

[41] Schmitt, *The Nomos of the Earth*, p. 64/95: "The second [example] is Thomas Hobbes's doctrine of the state of nature contained in his construction of the state."

[42] He refers here to the historical interpretation of the state of nature as the anarchy of feudal organisation; Leo Strauss, *Archiv für Sozialwissenschaft und Sozialpolitik*, 67 (1932), pp. 738–9; Franz Borkenau, *Der Übergang vom feudalen zum bürgerlichen Weltbild* (Paris, 1934), p. 458.

[43] Ferdinand Tönnies, "Hobbes und das Zoon Politikon", *Zeitschrift für Völkerrecht*, 12 (1923): 471–2. While praising Tönnies as the best specialist of Hobbes and acknowledging the relevance of his interpretation of the development of the idea of the state of nature in terms of interiorisation, Schmitt insists on the fact that Tönnies is not a neo-Kantian philosopher and that he does not content himself with general distinctions.

[44] Hobbes, *Leviathan*, XIII, 11, p. 77 (my italics).

> For the savage people in many places of America, except the government of small Families, the concord whereof dependeth on natural lust, have no government at all; and live at this day in that brutish manner, as I said before. Howsoever, it may be perceived what manner of life there would be, where there were no common power to fear; by the manner of life which men that have formerly lived under a peaceful government use to degenerate into a civil war.[45]

The surprising comparison of the life of the savage people of America to the condition of life during civil wars can thus be read as the effect of the absence of limits on the use of violence on the part of the European colonising powers. Schmitt concludes his analysis by saying that if Hobbes's state of nature is a *no man's land*, as there clearly exists no ownership in it, "it is not therefore a nowhere", for "it is situated by Hobbes in, among other places, the New World".[46] Here again, Schmitt stresses the fact that Hobbes's thought must be geographically situated. Before turning to my critique, I should like to add three additional remarks.

First, this interpretation is a new *historical* interpretation. There are other historical interpretations of the Hobbesian state of nature of which Schmitt is aware (for example, those of Leo Strauss and Frank Borkenau that have already been mentioned), but the originality of his own is due to the fact that it is both historical and geographical. This interpretation is also new when compared with the previous Schmittian interpretations. Thus Schmitt writes in a note of *The Nomos of the Earth* that, in his *The Leviathan in the doctrine of the state of Thomas Hobbes* (Hamburg, 1938), he had not "yet taken into consideration, in presenting the theory of the state of nature, the historical relevance of the Amity lines".[47] Second, the evidence presented by Schmitt in favour of the Amity lines is scanty, and he acknowledges this. He says in particular that the references to those secret clauses are rare in the juridical literature of the time. In Pufendorf's *Jus naturae et gentium*, for example, there are only a few remarks on the notion of armistice (book VIII, c. 7), but nothing directly on secret clauses appended to treaties.[48] Third, Schmitt is hostile to the interpretation of the state of nature as a sceptical hypothesis. This sceptical interpretation of Hobbes, initiated by Barbeyrac and of which we find a contemporary version in Richard Tuck[49] and in Michael Williams's

---

[45] Ibid.

[46] Schmitt, *The Nomos of the Earth*, p. 64/96 (modified translation): "Thomas Hobbes's state of nature is a *no man's land*, but this does not mean it exists *nowhere*."

[47] Schmitt, *The Nomos of the Earth*, p. 65, note 1/96, note 20. Cf. Schmitt, *The Leviathan in the State Theory of Thomas Hobbes*.

[48] Schmitt, *The Nomos of the Earth*, p. 60/92: "… jurists hardly knew what to make of them and treated them perfunctorily under the category of 'truce'."

[49] Richard Tuck, "Hobbes and Descartes", in G.A.J. Rogers and Alan Ryan (eds), *Perspectives on Thomas Hobbes* (Oxford, 1988), pp. 11–41.

reconsideration of Hobbes's international relations theory,[50] is considered by Schmitt as being too abstract; that is, failing to capture the impact of the existence of free spaces on seventeenth-century ways of thinking. In order to support a non-sceptical interpretation when the reference to scepticism seems most obvious, Schmitt cites Pascal on a meridian that decides truth,[51] but Hobbes too, as we have seen, plays a central part in the whole anti-sceptical demonstration.

In the final section, which will add a fourth remark to the three previous ones, I shall suggest a way of assessing the Schmittian interpretation of Hobbes and the situation of international law in the historical perspective of the idea of a global line.

Reconsidering Schmitt's Reading of Hobbesian International Theory and the Question of Empire

The link between politics and space is clearly central to Schmitt's whole interpretation of Hobbes in *The Nomos of the Earth*. The first question is therefore to determine whether this interpretation is true to Hobbes's approach to international relations. How much is there in Hobbes about the territory of the states and the conquest of new territories? As we have already seen, Hobbes certainly presupposes the existence of state territory, but it is not a major topic in *Leviathan*. Moreover, the notion of a state of nature is not considered spatially, but as a state of relation between individuals or groups. If the introduction of geography into the picture (as in Abraham Bosse's frontispiece of *Leviathan*)[52]

---

[50] Michael C. Williams, "Hobbes and International Relations: a Reconsideration", *International Organization*, 50–52 (1996): 213–36.

[51] Schmitt gives the following quote in French: "Trois degrés d'élévation du Pôle renversent toute la Jurisprudence. Un Méridien décide de la vérité, ou peu d'années de possession. Les lois fondamentales changent. Le droit a ses époques. Plaisante justice qu'une rivière ou une montagne borne! Vérité en deçà des Pyrenées, erreur au delà." ["A three-degree rise of the Pole would ruin the whole jurisprudence. A meridian decides the truth or at least the years of possession. Fundamental laws change. Law has its own epochs. This is a strange justice that is defined by a river or a mountain. Truth on this side of the Pyrenees is error on the other."] (*The Nomos of the Earth*, p. 63/95). For a more accurate quote, see Blaise Pascal, *Pensées*, ed. Louis Lafuma, no. 60. Schmitt makes the following comment: "Pascal's Meridian is nothing other than the amity lines of his time, which had created an abyss between freedom (the lawlessness of the state of nature) and an orderly 'civil' mode of existence." (Schmitt, *The Nomos of the Earth*, p. 64/95).

[52] On the authorship of Abraham Bosse, see Horst Bredekamp, *Thomas Hobbes' visuelle Strategien* (Berlin, 1999), I.2.c; see also Jean-Claude Vuillemin, "Bosse, Abraham (1602–76)", in Luc Foisneau (ed.), *The Dictionary of Seventeenth-Century French Philosophers*, London and New York, 2008, vol. 1, pp. 176–9.

no doubt adds a new dimension, it is not a dimension that is central to Hobbes's preoccupation.

Although Schmitt never says it so clearly, his interpretation of Hobbes's international relations theory presupposes that almost all European states were empires, since their relations beyond the lines are based on the will to create, maintain or extend their territorial possessions in the New World. This kind of analysis is certainly consonant with the new additions to the third and fourth editions of *Völkerrechtliche Grossraumordnung*, whose chapters' titles (for example, "Empire and Space") insist on the fact that colonialism has been the main vector of the international law of peoples, allowing almost every state, with the notable exception of Prussia, to enlarge their empires beyond the line. But Schmitt's preoccupation of the 1940s cannot be attributed to Hobbes in the 1640s and 50s, for there is no evidence that Hobbes supported the imperialist ventures of his time,[53] still less that he based his political theory on the necessity of building empires. In *De Cive*, commenting on the fact that Rome and Athens sometimes enriched themselves by conquest and in accord with a recurrent critique of Machiavelli,[54] Hobbes says that no state can count on such a means, since it seldom succeeds.[55]

Amity lines are central to the Schmittian construction, since they are an open critique of the formalism of a normativist, not to say Kantian, approach to international order. But is Hobbes – and this is a third question – so far from the normativist approach when he stresses the link between security and laws of nature, both at the state and at the interstate level? His doubts about the force of positive norms in the international realm do not mean that he does not believe in the existence of organising rules: the point is that he considers the determining factors not to be the positive treaties, but the natural laws, which, whenever it is possible and useful to the international stability and not contrary to the security of a state, must be obeyed. In the seventeenth-century debate on whether the international order was based on positive or natural laws, Hobbes clearly answered that it was based on the second category of laws.[56] In that category, he could be portrayed as a representative of security as a norm option, that is, a proponent of

---

[53] On Hobbes's participation in the Sandys and Virginia company and his opinion on imperialism, see Noel Malcolm, "Hobbes, Sandys, and the Virginia Company", in Id., *Aspects of Hobbes*, pp. 53–79.

[54] Cf. Luc Foisneau, "Hobbes et la théorie machiavélienne de la virtù", *Archives de philosophie*, 60-3 (1997): 371–91.

[55] Hobbes, *De Cive*, XIII, 14, English transl., p. 150.

[56] Cf. Malcolm, "Hobbes's Theory of International Relations", p. 439: "The debate was a real one, and even those contemporary writers who strongly rejected Hobbes's viewpoint treated it as a serious argument about how to classify international law, not as a rejection of international law as such". For a more thorough presentation of the debate,

applying the law of nature to the context of security. But Hobbes' bias in favour of natural law did not particularly make him a partisan of international treaties, and still less of the secret clauses appended to those treaties. One may fear that, in a strictly historical perspective, Schmitt got this the wrong way round.

To conclude, I would say that there is more in the Schmittian interpretation of Hobbes's state of nature than is generally found in the latter by scholars of Hobbes. Schmitt does not maintain that the state of nature that existed among European states in the seventeenth century was as anarchical as has been claimed, but rather that this state of nature was twofold: a relative state of peace within the borders of Europe, and a terrible space of liberty, that is, of open violence, beyond those frontiers. If there is war in both cases, this war does not have the same intensity. In the one case, it is war between civilized states, a war therefore to be waged according to certain rules; in the other case, it is a terrible warfare, in which all means are used to achieve conquest.

This Schmittian contrast is fascinating for whoever wants to understand the violence that began with the development of a new phase of imperialism at the end of the nineteenth century, and which eventually turned itself against the relatively protected states of Europe during the two World Wars. Nothing compared in intensity to the killing of Atabalipa, the King of Peru, by the Spanish soldiers, recalled by Hobbes in *Behemoth*,[57] but the connection between the two events has been judged enlightening, even in the present post-colonial situation.

The difficulty, however, rests with the fact that this geopolitical interpretation of Hobbes's state and Hobbes's state of nature decidedly ignores the fact that Hobbes is not an imperialist thinker and that his vision of international relations rests on a universalistic theory of the laws of nature. Just as Schmitt turned *Leviathan* upside down in reading it from a decisionist perspective, so too he turned Hobbes's worldview upside down in reading it as the vademecum of an imperialistic Europe. Setting things upright again is all the more important for us today in view of the still open political debate regarding the interpretation of Europe's borders and of Europe's relations to the rest of the world.

Malcolm refers to P.E. Corbett, *Law and Society in the Relations of States* (New York, 1951), pp. 21–6.

[57] Hobbes, *Behemoth*, ed. F. Tönnies, 2nd edn, London, Frank Cass, 1969, p. 11.

Chapter 10
Hobbes on the Concepts of the State and Political Sovereignty

Christine Chwaszcza

In his introduction to *Leviathan*, Hobbes invokes God's creation of man as the model by which the creation of a commonwealth can be understood. Similarly, in the introduction to the first part of the *Elements of Philosophy* (*De Corpore*, or "*Concerning Body*"), Hobbes presents the "new" philosophy, that is, philosophy based on natural reason, as an imitation of the order of creation. Where creation started with "light" and the "distinction of day and night", *De Corpore* starts with "reason" and "definition" and straightaway a definition of philosophy itself: "Philosophy", according to Hobbes, "is such knowledge of effects or appearances, as we require by true ratiocinatio from the knowledge we have first of their causes or generation: And again of such causes and generations as might be known from their effects".[1]

The paradigm of philosophical knowledge for Hobbes is, notoriously, the mode of demonstration in Euclid's geometry (*mos geometricus*), and his paradigm of giving a philosophical definition is the instruction for how to generate a perfect circle, assuming that we can infer all (geometrical) properties of the figure from the knowledge of its generation, even if none of our actual drawings ever comes close to resembling the conceptual "ideal" of a perfect circle.

The following reconstruction of Hobbes's analysis of sovereignty and the generation of the state will read chapters 16 and 17 of the English version of *Leviathan* from 1651[2] as an analysis of the concepts of "commonwealth" and "sovereignty."[3] Chapter 16 plays a crucial role in Hobbes's analysis of the concepts of state and sovereignty, but is notoriously difficult to interpret.[4] I shall argue

---

[1] Thomas Hobbes, *Metaphysical Writings*, ed. Mary Whiton Calkins (La Salle, Ill., 1989), p. 6.

[2] Thomas Hobbes, *Leviathan*, ed. Edwin Curley (Indianapolis, 1994). The chapters have the titles "Of Persons, Authors, and Things Personated" and "Of the Causes, Generation and Definition of a Commonwealth".

[3] See Bernd Ludwig, *Die Wiederentdeckung des epikureischen Naturrechts: Zu Thomas Hobbes's philosophischer Entwicklung von De Cive zum Leviathan im Pariser Exil 1640–1651* (Frankfurt am Main, 1998), for the systematic differences of Hobbes's version of the social contract in *Leviathan* and in *De Cive*.

[4] Chapter 16 has recently been discussed more carefully in David Runciman, *Pluralism and the Personality of the State* (Cambridge, 1997), pp. 6–33; Quentin Skinner,

that, despite the analogy between the creation of man and the Leviathan, Hobbes conceptualises the state as an impersonal institution or, as one might say, a "legal fiction", that is fully defined by the *legal status* of government and subjects and the *legal relations* between them. In order to function, the state needs to be "represented" by a sovereign government; or, as Hobbes puts it, in order make Leviathan move, it must be given an artificial soul, which in the introduction is identified with the sovereign. What the metaphor suggests, as I shall argue, is that Hobbes conceives of government as an office, that is, a legal competence, which must be represented and impersonated by natural persons who receive authorisation from the social contract.

If this institutional account is correct, it follows, first, that Hobbes's use of the social contract model is not meant to inform us how to "create" the state, but rather to clarify the fact that "the state" is neither identical with the government that represents it nor with the persons who constitute the government. The contractual agreement concerns not the right of the government to exercise force over subjects, but its right to act as representer of the state. All rights and duties of the sovereign are as such functions of the state, not rights of any natural person, be it the person of the king or the persons who are the members of Parliament. Second, it follows that the legal status of the sovereign is determined by the task of the office of government and that, accordingly, sovereign power, even if supreme, is not "unlimited", but conditional. Third, although Hobbes does not say much about international law and interstate pacification, his analysis of sovereignty does not entail any systematic arguments, which would exclude the development of a system of international law for any systematic reasons, although he also does not encourage such an extension. In fact, his few fragmentary remarks suggest that he simply considers interstate war as less damaging and less important a challenge than intrastate conflict. As far as Hobbes's philosophical method is concerned, it can easily be adjusted to the analysis of international institutions and international law. If his accounts of sovereignty and the state are interpreted as clarifying their institutional structure, they in fact provide a fruitful starting point for the understanding of their international counterparts. My reconstruction will therefore end with a brief account of the differences between state and law and the law of nations for Hobbes as far as they can be reconstructed from the few fragmentary remarks that he makes about the latter, and suggest a perspective from which international peace might be promoted within a Hobbesian framework. I should like to start, however, with a brief comment on Hobbes's account of philosophical knowledge and analysis.

"Hobbes and the Purely Artificial Person of the State", *Journal of Political Philosophy*, 7/1 (1999): 1–29; David Runciman, "What Kind of Person is Hobbes's State?", *Journal of Political Philosophy*, 8/2 (2000): 268–78; Quentin Skinner, "Hobbes on Representation", *European Journal of Philosophy*, 13/2 (2005): 155–84; and Alexander von Pechmann, "Der Souverän als 'Träger der Persona'", *Zeitschrift für philosophische Forschung*, 59 (2005): 164–85.

Philosophical Knowledge and Political Philosophy According to Hobbes

Hobbes's rhetorical use of metaphor is sometimes taken at face value, and his political philosophy is accordingly understood as informing us about how to "create" a commonwealth in order to pacify interpersonal relations by agreeing to establish an authority that constitutes and enacts a legal order. In the light of such an interpretation, Hobbes appears as a "social constructivist" *avant la lettre*, or at least somebody who tells us what we have to do if we want to transform a situation of war into one of order. His political philosophy is in this sense often considered not only to be motivated by his experience of the English Civil War, but also to reflect his perception of his historical situation.

Although it would certainly be strange if a political philosopher ignored his own historical context, Hobbes's method of philosophical reasoning is as abstract and ideal as philosophy can get. He leaves no doubt that his philosophical writings, which include *Leviathan* as well as *De Cive*, are *not* derived from experience but exemplify *ratiocinatio*, that is, philosophical reasoning. "Experience", in fact, is a technical term that according to Hobbes specifies a particular form of acquiring knowledge, namely repeated observation of similar sequences of events.[5] Although experience generates expectations about future events – because the occurrence of an event that has repeatedly been observed to be followed by another will raise an expectation that an event of the other type will occur – the type of knowledge generated by experience is called by Hobbes "prudence" or "foresight" and considered to be much less reliable than true philosophical knowledge as defined in *De Corpore*. Whereas the Aristotelian tradition of political philosophy regarded prudence (*phronesis* in Greek)[6] as the intellectual virtue that characterizes the virtuous politician, the only discipline that can (and must) rely on experience, according to Hobbes, is history – and explicitly not political philosophy.[7]

What Hobbes calls "philosophical knowledge" aims at a form of epistemic insight that is primarily concerned with the attainment of clear concepts and definitions. In that sense, it resembles in a way what today would be called "conceptual analysis" in Anglo-American philosophy. Although Hobbes sometimes talks as if "analysis" concerns the resolution of complex objects into their constituent parts, the largest part of philosophical analysis in *Leviathan*

---

[5] See Hobbes, *Leviathan*, chap. 3, and chap. 46, para. 2, p. 454. For his criticism of the Aristotelian and Ciceronian tradition, and maybe even more broadly of the conception of political philosophy as a part of the ethics of virtue, see also Thomas Hobbes, *Behemoth*, ed. Ferdinand Tönnies, intro. Stephen Holmes (Chicago, 1990), pp. 43–6, 56.

[6] See Aristotle, *Ethica Nicomachea*, trans. W. D. Ross, in Richard McKeon (ed.), *The Basic Works of Aristotle* (New York, 1941), pp. 935–1126, Book. 7. See also Marcus Tullius Cicero, *De re publica*, trans. Clinton Walker Keyes (Cambridge, Mass., 1977).

[7] For Hobbes's historical account of the English Civil War, see Hobbes, *Behemoth*.

concerns *concepts*, more precisely legal (or normative) concepts such as "right" (*ius*), "sovereignty", and so forth. Concepts, of course, cannot be resolved or divided into parts. Even Hobbes's paradigm example, the analysis of the concept "man" into the components "body", "moving", and "rational", does not mention parts in any material sense, but rather characteristics that help to clarify or specify the meaning of the concept. In another sense, Hobbes's philosophical analysis differs significantly from modern accounts. First and foremost, the unit of Hobbes's analysis is concepts considered as single words, not sentences. And second, the idea that we achieve philosophical understanding of concepts by knowing the causes and generations of what those concepts are meant to signify is one that few philosophers today share. As Hobbes's paradigm definition of man shows, not all understanding of concepts is achieved in such a way, but understanding achieved by "knowledge of generation" seems obviously of major importance for concepts that either refer to complex phenomena, such as social phenomena, or are non-referential in the strict sense, as are most, if not all, legal and normative terms.

Whereas "man" can be considered a simple concept and "body", "moving", and "rational" considered as attributes or properties of man (or ideal men), Hobbes clearly regards central political concepts as complex concepts and seems to conceive of them primarily in terms of legal *relations* that hold between (natural or legal) agents or define social roles in relation to each other. Unlike attributes, the analysis of legal relations, according to Hobbes's definition of philosophy, must offer an account of how those relations can *be conceived* of being established, or, as Hobbes says, "generated". Their logical analysis must accordingly combine analysis and synthesis. The point of offering an account of how to conceive of the establishment of legal relations, however, is quite different from actually establishing them, because the aim is not practice but philosophical knowledge, that is, a better and clearer understanding of the meaning of concepts. As Hobbes's reference to the construction of geometrical figures and demonstrations clearly indicates, such generative knowledge is understood to *exemplify* an "ideal" generation in a genuinely Platonic sense: a *perfect* paradigm, which at best might be approximated by any concrete phenomenon.

Sovereignty and the Representation of the State and Unity of the Commonwealth

The most striking aspect of Hobbes's use of the social contract model is his transformation of the traditional two-step structure, *pactum unionis* followed by *pactum subjectionis*, into a single act of authorisation. Authorisation, as Hobbes understands it, is a legal relation and authority a legal status, namely "*the right* to do any act".[8] Since legal relations, according to Hobbes, are not part of the natural condition or equipment of men and have a place only within the context of political society, the constitution of society either cannot be conceived of in terms of legal relations or it must coincide with the establishment of political order. Accordingly, a logically consistent version of the social contract has to combine the horizontal and vertical legal relations that characterise political society, that is, those that hold among subjects and those that hold between subjects and government. Hobbes masters the challenge by giving the social contract the form of a mutual (conditional) agreement among disconnected individuals to authorise a third party to govern them, which *thereby* transforms the multitude into a political society. For the unity of a multitude, as Hobbes insists, lies in the person of the representer, not the persons represented. It is, however, not unambiguous who represents whom or what.

A common interpretation understands the contract as generating political order by investing the government with a monopoly of power, because whoever it is that is authorised to govern, not being party to but beneficiary of the contract, retains the rights of nature to do whatever he considers apt for his own preservation. This interpretation, however, falls short of clarifying in which way Leviathan *represents* political unity. As a matter of fact, the contract so understood fails to establish a commonwealth at all, because only natural persons hold a right of nature, and if the power of Leviathan were to rest in a man's right of nature, the commonwealth would die a natural death each time the king or members of Parliament die, which is an absurd consequence.

The picture, accordingly, must be more complex, although prima facie Hobbes's account of the generation and definition of a commonwealth in Chapter 17 seems to suggest that individuals straightforwardly authorise "a man" or "assembly of men" to represent them:

> I authorise and give up my right of governing myself to this man, or to this assembly, on this condition that thou give up thy right to him, and authorise all his actions in a like manner. This done, the multitude so united in one person is called a COMMONWEALTH, in Latin CIVITAS. This is the generation of the great LEVIATHAN, or rather (to speak more reverently) of that MORTAL GOD to which we owe, under the Immortal God, our peace and defense. For by this authority, given him by every particular man in the commonwealth, he hath the use of so much power and strength conferred on him that by terror thereof he is enabled to conform the wills of them all to peace at home and mutual aid against their enemies abroad. And in him consisteth the essence of the commonwealth, which (to define) is one person, of whose acts a great multitude, by mutual

---

[8] Hobbes, *Leviathan*, chap. 16, para. 4, p. 101.

covenants one with another, have made themselves everyone the author, to the end he may use the strength and means of them all, as he shall think expedient, for their peace and common defence.[9]

In the very next sentence, however, Hobbes continues with a further definition: "*And he that carrieth this person* is called SOVEREIGN, and said to have Sovereign Power, and every one besides, his SUBJECT".[10] If, as the first quotation suggests, the government is identical with the "person" called Leviathan who unites the multitude into one single person, it seems superfluous to refer to a further person, that is, "he that carrieth this person" (Leviathan), who is called "sovereign". In addition, in the introduction, Hobbes compared sovereignty with "an artificial soul" that moves the body and limbs of the commonwealth, and so the sovereign must be in some sense different from the commonwealth. An obvious response is that "he that carrieth this person" is not identical with the commonwealth and that Hobbes's unspecified reference to persons refers either to different persons or, as I will argue, to persons in different senses of the term.

"A person", as defined in Chapter 16, is:

> he whose words or actions are considered either as his own, or as representing the words or actions of another man, *or of any other thing to whom they are attributed, whether truly or by fiction*. When they are considered as his own, then he is called a natural person; and when they are considered as representing the words and actions of another, then he is a feigned or artificial person.[11]

As Hobbes's distinction between natural and artificial persons reveals, conceiving of the commonwealth as a person by no means implies that it resembles natural human beings in any ontological or substantive aspects whatever, because words and actions can be *attributed* to any "thing" *by fiction*. In order to conceive of the commonwealth as a person, it must be possible that it be "represented" by a person or "impersonated", whereby the representing person can be either a single natural person or an assembly of natural persons. As Hobbes unambiguously makes clear a few paragraphs later, almost everything can be represented, not only humans but also "[i]nanimate things (such as a church, a hospital, a bridge) may be impersonated by a rector, master, or overseer".[12] Whereas a bridge is a "thing" in the common sense of "medium-size solid object", a church and a hospital represented by a rector are better understood as institutions or corporations. They do not "exist" in any material sense, but only *qua* serving a specific purpose and appropriate social

---

[9] *Ibid.*, chap. 17, para. 13, p. 109.
[10] *Ibid.*, para. 14, p. 109.
[11] *Ibid.*, chap. 16, para. 1, p. 101 (emphasis added).
[12] *Ibid.*, para. 9, p. 102.

or legal conventions. Hospitals and churches in this sense resemble universities and states.[13] Since inanimate things, however, cannot themselves be *authors* and invest somebody else to act as their representative, Hobbes states that they cannot be impersonated outside "some state of civil government",[14] because their representation already presupposes the validity of legal relations.

Following Hobbes's definitions of legal personhood and representation, it makes perfectly good sense to conceive of the sovereign as either the single man (in a monarchy) or assembly of men (in a republic) who *represents* the government, whereby "government", like universities or churches, is just a legal "fiction", that is, an office or institution. Considered as an institution, the establishment of a government constitutes the commonwealth and transforms the multitude of individuals into political society by establishing legal order. Government considered as an institution can in this sense be said to "unite" the multitude of individuals and to constitute a commonwealth. But since neither the institution of government nor the commonwealth can be conceived to "exist" unless somebody is authorised to represent the office, the commonwealth cannot be alive unless those natural persons who are meant to be united by the institution of political government authorise somebody to represent the institution of government. The "person" of Leviathan in this sense is constituted by authorising a *representer* for the institution of government, that is, by appointing a sovereign. The sovereign, accordingly, has two related but formally independent *legal* personalities, insofar as he, as a natural person, represents the office of government and, at the same time, *qua* his office (that is, as an artificial person) represents the unity of the commonwealth.[15] In this sense, unification and subjection fall together into a

---

[13] I disagree here with Runciman, who considers the sovereign to be an "author", that is, of the commonwealth. According to Runciman, being a person requires the possibility of a being a subject to whom words and acts can be attributed. The state, for Runciman, is a fictitious person in the sense in which Emma Bovary is a fictitious character. See Runciman, *Pluralism and Personality*, pp. 29–31. The interpretation defended here considers the state to be a person in the sense in which a university can be considered a (legal) person, that is, by being represented by natural persons. Unlike most other things whose representation presupposes the existence of the legal context, the commonwealth, the person of the state or commonwealth itself comes into existence *by* authorising somebody to represent it. To ask "What kind of body" Leviathan (or the commonwealth) is in this sense recalls the questioner in Ryle's *Concept of Mind* who, after having been shown through colleges, libraries, and so on, asks, "But where is the university?" See Gilbert Ryle, *The Concept of Mind* (Harmondsworth, 1990), pp. 17–20. I therefore see no difficulty or paradox in Hobbes's concept of personhood and representation, as does von Pechmann, "Der Souverän als 'Träger der Persona'".

[14] Hobbes, *Leviathan*, chap. 16, para. 9, p. 109.

[15] In addition, of course, the person who is appointed as sovereign *is* also a natural person. That one and the same person can have different legal personalities and also represent

single act of authorisation that invests the sovereign with the legal *authority*, that is, the *right*, not only the power, to govern and to represent the state.

Unfortunately, the textual evidence is not entirely unambiguous and therefore does not rule out alternative interpretations. I should therefore like to support the one presented here by showing that it strengthens the systematic coherence of Hobbes's political views on the state and sovereignty.

A Few Arguments in Support of an Institutionalist Reading of Hobbes

To the extent that the above interpretation offers an appropriate reconstruction of Hobbes's version of the social contract, it sheds light on several controversial aspects concerning the concept of political sovereignty in *Leviathan*. First, it strongly supports the thesis that Hobbes's sovereign, although "above (positive) law", is not unconstrained in his power and competences. His rights and competences are restricted by the function of the office of government, as Hobbes explicitly declares in Chapter 30, wherein he discusses the duties of the *sovereign representative*:

> The office of the sovereign (be it a monarch or an assembly) consisteth in the end *for which he was trusted with the sovereign power,* namely the procuration of the safety of the people, to which he is obliged by the law of nature, and to render an account thereof to God, the author of that law, and to none but him. But by safety here is not meant a bare preservation, but also all other contentments of life, which every man by lawful industry, without danger or hurt to the commonwealth, shall acquire to himself.[16]

Although Hobbes has a very wide view of what this is supposed to imply, the sovereign is clearly obliged to respect the "rule of law" at least in the formal sense of respecting equity and having to rule (exclusively) through law (see below). Sovereign competences are in this sense regulated partly by law, but partly determined by the status of the sovereign among other sovereigns, and they will therefore be discussed in more detail in a separate subsequent section.

Second, and more precisely, sovereign rights and competences "belong" in the strict sense to the institution of government, not to the natural person who represents it. Accordingly, no *natural* person "possesses" a right to rule or govern. This excludes the invocation of dynastic privileges and a divine right of kings and

---

different persons is clearly part of the quotation from Cicero in Hobbes, *Leviathan*, chap. 16, para. 3, p. 101: "Unus sustineo tres personas: mei, adversarii, et judicis" [I bear three persons: my own, my adversary's, and the judge's].

[16] *Ibid.*, chap. 30, para. 1, p. 219 (emphasis added).

religious or other forms of personal authority, as well as claims such as a right of "the people" to participate in government. Whereas the claim that a right to rule cannot be conceived of as a property or attribute of any natural person explains itself, it might be worthwhile to remind ourselves that "the people" also does not exist outside the context of a commonwealth with a specific form of government, because the concept refers to a socio-political or legal status that is granted some individuals in accordance with certain criteria (in Hobbes's time, "the people", of course, was a rather small subgroup of the overall population). Thus conceiving of government as an institution implies that not only the appointment of a person to represent government, but also the specific structure or organization of government is a matter of mere convention – which might explain why Hobbes's analysis was attacked equally fiercely by proponents of all political parties. The question whether, for instance, republican government is to be preferred over an absolute monarchy, or vice versa, appears in the end as one that is best decided on purely pragmatic and functionalist grounds.

Third, the internal constitution of the representer of the institution of government is irrelevant for the determination of sovereign powers, which are (and must be) derived from the functional needs of government. Hobbes therefore correctly insists that sovereign powers are the same in all forms of government, regardless of whether the government is represented by a single person or an assembly or a mixture of both accompanied by some form of division or balance of powers. However powers are divided between branches of government, they must sum up to the same powers. Despite Hobbes's explicit preference for absolute monarchy, his analysis does not structurally exclude mixed or republican government, and reinforces the claim that no form of government is more natural (or less conventional) than any other.

Fourth, if the legal personality of the sovereign is understood to be that of a representer of the government, Hobbes's claim that government by usurpation is no less "artificial" than government by authorisation can be made intelligible. Although usurpation clearly differs from the ideal of authorisation, the usurper no more *deserves* the right to govern than a sovereign who has been elected or authorised in any other way – the usurper simply cannot be resisted.[17] Nevertheless, he has not gained his *legal* status by natural force, because being a representative requires being acknowledged as such by the people, if only because of their fear or resignation. The legal status of a sovereign by usurpation is thus structurally the same as that of an authorised sovereign: he represents the institution of government.

---

[17] Hobbes's discussion about at what point of events exactly Cromwell must be acknowledged to have become sovereign shows that acquisition of sovereignty can be a matter partly of power and partly of formal acknowledgement. See Hobbes, *Behemoth*, dialogues 3 and 4 (*passim*).

Finally, to conceive of "government" as an institution or office in an important sense means to conceive of it as *impersonal* or *detached* from those who happen to be in charge. Although the latter can govern well or badly, the institution of government remains the same. That explains why Hobbes criticizes the traditional classificatory scheme of governments into monarchy-tyranny, aristocracy-oligarchy, and "polity"-democracy ("anarchy" in Hobbes's terms). A tyrant might be considered simply as somebody who abuses his sovereign powers.

It seems, however, that the proposed interpretation runs into one of the well-known difficulties that trouble the interpretation of Hobbes, because Hobbes notoriously insists that the sovereign cannot commit any injustice towards the subjects (beyond infringing on entitlements and commitments that are articulated in positive law by his own legislation), even though he can violate equity.[18] Although Hobbes's formula of authorisation explicitly obliges individuals who are governed to regard all words and actions of government as their own, it seems awkward that an institution should be accepted however well or badly it serves its very purpose. Institutions, unlike "men", should be expected either to function well or to be changed. As Locke famously remarked, "This is to think that Men are so foolish that they take care to avoid what Mischiefs may be done them by *Pole-Cats*, or *Foxes*, but are content, nay think it Safety, to be devoured by *Lions*".[19]

In the light of Locke's objection, Hobbes's account of government by authorisation might be alternatively interpreted along the lines of his dictum that "authority, not truth, makes law" (*auctoritas non veritas facit legem*), and be taken to refer to a radically different interpretation of "authorisation", namely brute empowerment of or unconstrained subjection to some man (or men). The alternative interpretation, of course, does not meet the challenge raised by Locke and instead seems somewhat to soften it, because "men" can never be fully trusted.

Two considerations, however, can be invoked to show that an interpretation of government by authorisation along the lines developed in this article is not incompatible with the claim that the sovereign cannot commit injustices towards the subjects. It might first be argued that Hobbes's absolutism reflects his functional and pragmatic views about the appropriate form of government. The claim that the sovereign cannot commit any form of injustice must apply to the legal status of the office of government, however it is organised, and thus also to republican government. Second, if it is accepted that the office of government is distinct from the persons who represent it, it can be argued that, whereas the office of government stands above the law, the persons who represent it can abuse their legal powers. To the extent that such abuse constitutes a moral deficiency, it is a vice to be attributed to the representers of government considered as natural

---

[18] Hobbes, *Leviathan*, chap. 43, para. 6, p. 113.

[19] John Locke, *Second Treatise*, in *Two Treatises of Government*, ed. Peter Laslett (Cambridge, 1960), para. 93, p. 328.

persons. As long as they represent the office, they cannot be charged with abuse, because the office protects them. But neither can they be accused of abuse of sovereign powers once they leave office, because those powers were never attributed to them as natural persons. Such a conjecture still sounds unacceptable from a liberal point of view, because it concedes general immunity to officeholders. It articulates, however, a position that came very close to the established practice of international law until quite recently and can, in addition, be found also in other historical sources, such as Kant's comments on the Jacobins' decapitation of French aristocrats.[20]

Government and Legal Order

Unlike the structure and purpose of the state, the determination of the means and competences that must be granted to government in order to accomplish its task is informed by pragmatic and functional considerations that must reflect empirical constraints and challenges. At this point, *experience*, finally, must come into play and inform or enrich conceptual analysis by identifying the main *institutional* or *structural* obstacles or challenges to the stability of political order and prosperity.[21] Although Hobbes seems well aware of the fact that social and economic cleavages and motivations played a significant role in the English Revolution, he clearly regards factionalism based on pluralism of (religious) allegiance and opinions as the main source of disorder and discord[22] – if only because not *natural reason* but reference to religious arguments still constituted the major form of justification for *any* claim, and because the clergy exercised a dominating influence on public opinion and in universities, especially in the faculties of law.

Hobbes's practical remarks do not suggest that he thinks that things will change very soon, because the remedies he recommends are not all as innovative as they might seem at first sight. The claim that the sovereign must represent not only the state, but also the church, in fact merely reinforces an institutional development that can be considered to have been firmly established in England at the time

---

[20] See Immanuel Kant, "Perpetual Peace", in *Political Writings*, trans. Hans Reiss, ed. H.B. Nisbet (Cambridge, 1970), pp. 93–130; appendix I, p. 118.

[21] "Structural" here is meant to refer to causes of quarrel in political associations. Given the widespread view that Hobbes promotes a "negative" or "pessimistic anthropology", it also seems worth mentioning that the "three principal causes of quarrel" in the state of nature – "first, competition; secondly, diffidence; thirdly, glory" – are "structural" causes in the sense that they concern patterns of social interaction. See Hobbes, *Leviathan*, chap. 8, para. 6, p. 76.

[22] In *Behemoth*, the publication of the English translation of the Bible is mentioned as the crucial trigger, if not cause, for the growth of dissent and civil discord.

of Elizabeth I. The most interesting aspect of the amalgamation of political and religious sovereignty is that, insofar as political sovereignty is territorially defined, it indicates a step toward a territorial conception of sovereignty already established by the Peace of Westphalia. From the domestic perspective, Hobbes's position is in this regard clearly "conservative", although progressive with regard to the restriction of law to actions and public conduct, which leaves *legal* space for freedom of faith and conscience.[23]

The point where Hobbes more clearly breaks with the tradition of political philosophy, and probably the dominant opinion of his time, concerns his rejection of the idea that stability can be achieved through a balance of (socio-political) powers, a rejection that lies behind Hobbes's insistence that sovereignty must be undivided, unified, and supreme. Chapter 29 explicitly mentions the doctrine of mixed government as among the "things that weaken a commonwealth". Whereas the model of a balance of powers is characteristic for the Aristotelian tradition of mixed government as well as Machiavelli's interpretation of (Roman) republicanism, it is important to note that Hobbes's account of sovereignty is fully compatible not only with a system of absolute monarchy but also with aristocratic and republican government if the preceding reconstruction is correct. Hobbes, indeed, repeatedly concedes that his analysis does not exclude either republican or aristocratic government, although he is convinced that the unity of sovereignty can best be preserved if the government is represented by a single natural person who unites all the sovereign powers in one hand (or mind). The point of insisting on the supremacy of sovereignty in that case again consists in excluding foreign intervention, most notably by the Pope[24] and the exemption of the Catholic clergy from state jurisdiction by the canon laws.[25]

More difficult to answer is the question whether the supremacy of sovereignty also eliminates all normative or moral constraints and amounts to a straightforward account of legal positivism, because the question leads to a debate about how to understand the very concept of law, which is itself contested. Since Hobbes repeatedly concedes that the sovereign must respect the laws of nature listed in chapters 14 and 15, the sovereign remains at least constrained by some normative restrictions, which are far from being merely formal but include, among other things, gratitude, complaisance, blame of contempt, pride and arrogance, "equity" understood as impartiality in judgments concerning quarrels of other parties, and the principle that no man should be the judge in his own case. "Equity" is also

---

[23] For a more detailed discussion, see Peter Schröder, "Thomas Hobbes, Christian Thomasius and the Seventeenth Century Debate on the Church and State", *History of European Ideas*, 23/2–4 (1997): 59–79.

[24] See Hobbes's attack on Cardinal Bellarmine's *De Summo Pontifice* in *Leviathan*, chap. 42, para. 81–135, pp. 373–97.

[25] See Hobbes, *Leviathan*, chap. 26.

repeatedly invoked as a normative standard for conduct in interstate relations, which clearly includes some form of normative settlements even for Hobbes, who in *Behemoth* several times refers to just war theory.[26] Those references unambiguously indicate that Hobbes acknowledges the validity and practical relevance of at least some form of moral or generally non-legal normative rules or principles, but that he sharply distinguishes them from positive law.

In addition, Hobbes's sovereign is clearly obliged to respect the rule of law understood as rule through law, which excludes arbitrary and ad hoc commands and punishments, and establishes at least the framework of a legal state, but which need not, of course, be identical with a "just" state in any substantive sense. Yet a careful reading of the chapters shows that the legal constraints on government are far from unsubstantial. They include among other things the prohibition of retroactive accusation or retroactive increase of punishment for any crime; they allow for positive legal constraints on and commitments to the use of sovereign power that are de facto binding (and as such restrict the recourse to precedence); and they require that all legal regulations must be made public and that all subjects be treated equally and impartially before the law.[27] Insisting on the supremacy of the sovereign in this light again seems primarily aimed at eliminating controversial opinions, most importantly, of course, the influence of judges on the development and interpretation of law, as in the English tradition of common law. Hobbes's remarks about the structure and form of domestic law seem much closer to the Continental system of Roman law than the English common law tradition or a system of customary law.[28] The supposed advantage of the continental system, it seems, is the (rather optimistic) expectation that its practice yields incontestable *judgments* about right and wrong in the legal sense, because in case of disagreement the judgment of the sovereign decides the case.

If such an outline of the legal structure of government catches Hobbes's intention, then his argument clearly concerns not so much the transformation of the state of nature into political and legal order, but more precisely the establishment of a legal system that yields *uncontested judgments*. Such an interpretation reads Hobbes as showing not why men must have a legal order and how they can construct it "out of nothing", but rather why they should adopt a specific legal system or structure because it serves the agreed-upon purpose of legal systems (namely: peace, justice, security, and promotion of well-being) better than the alternatives. The latter argument, in fact, is less fundamental, but precisely for that reason also stronger.

---

[26] See Hobbes, *Behemoth*, dialogue 3, pp. 124, 128, and dialogue 4, pp. 176, 167 for a reference that can also be understood as a complaint about the ambiguity of just war doctrine.

[27] See Hobbes, *Leviathan*, chap. 26.

[28] *Ibid.*, chaps 25 and 26, for Hobbes's criticism of the common law tradition and the jurisdictional influence it grants to judges.

Interstate War and Peace

In light of the previous section, it is, on the one hand, obvious why Hobbes does not consider an extension of his analysis to interstate relations: the scope and purpose of the law of nations seems not to require the establishment of a global *legal state*. Most obviously, the order and situation of states does not resemble that of individuals in crucial respects: states are not equal and do not have equal power; a commonwealth can very well survive changes of the structure of government or its representers; and sovereigns themselves are threatened not so much with death but with loss of status or power. Although somehow surprising from a post-twentieth-century perspective, ample textual evidence suggests that Hobbes regards interstate war as much less damaging and devastating than intrastate war.[29]

On the other hand, nothing said so far suggests that interstate relations constitute an entirely "norm-free" sphere. The principles of equity, just war, and customary law of nations articulate a normative background structure that might very well regulate interstate conduct. Although Hobbes seems well aware of the problem that the doctrine of just war is highly ambiguous and has continually provoked competing claims and interpretations of entitlements, rights, obligations, and the assessment of justice or reparations, an ambiguous normative order nevertheless is still a *normative* order, even though it might be called imperfect or, rather, ineffectual. Hobbes's *general strategy* of improving the effectiveness of legal order, by defining legal regulations more precisely and making sure that they will be applied, can easily be extended beyond Hobbes's own philosophical interests to interstate relations. Abstracting from his personal experience and his concern with factionalism, modern history provides ample evidence to sustain the claim that legal and political order can be stable despite pluralism and decentralized organisation. The seemingly greater obstacle, from today's perspective, lies in the revival of the idea that – *pace* Hobbes – political order must be based on some form of social or national cohesion: before there can be unity of political association, there must exist a united people. Since this idea is more often simply taken for granted than systematically (or conceptually) explored, Hobbes's analysis of representation certainly deserves to be reconsidered.

---

[29] For a detailed assessment, see Tom Sorrell, "Hobbes on Trade, Consumption and International Order", *The Monist*, 89/2 (2006): 245–58.

PART V
War and State in the Expanding European State System

Chapter 11
Peace Impossible?: The Holy Roman Empire and the European State System in the Seventeenth Century

Christoph Kampmann

The Holy Roman Empire, the Thirty Years' War and the State System

The concept of a state system has been intensely and repeatedly discussed in recent years.[1] This discussion about the character of such a system has taken place mainly among philosophers, political philosophers and political scientists. Historians have often been very reluctant to participate in it. This does not mean that historians do not use the term "state system", but rather that they often do so in a rather uncritical manner. This of course is also true of early modern historians. One important exception among German historians of early modernity is Heinz Duchhardt. Some time ago he criticised the somewhat unspecific use of the concept of system in a way similar to the criticism of the use of the term "state organism" (*Organismus der Staaten*) by an earlier generation of historians. At the same time, he warned historians against introducing excessively abstract notions of "system" that are hardly applicable to their normal source-based work.[2] On this basis, he then proposed a definition of a "state system".

For Duchhardt, a "state system" is a multiplicity of states that maintains permanent relations in different fields of interaction: policy, diplomacy, culture or economy. The crucial point is the character of these relations: within a state system the final intention of these relations is *not*, according to Duchhardt, the extermination of other members and thereby the destruction of the whole system.[3] This is, so to say, a very "light" and not highly profiled definition of a state system.

---

[1] For a recent historical analysis from the viewpoint of political science, cf. Barry Buzan and Richard Little, *International Systems in World History. Remaking the Study of International Relations* (Oxford, 2000).

[2] Heinz Duchhardt, "Das Reich in der Mitte des Staatensystems. Zum Verhältnis von innerer Verfassung und internationaler Funktion in den Wandlungen des 17. und 18. Jahrhunderts", in Peter Krüger (ed.), *Das europäische Staatensystem im Wandel. Strukturelle Bedingungen und bewegende Kräfte seit der Frühen Neuzeit* (Munich, 1996), pp. 1–9.

[3] *Ibid.*, p. 2: "Staatensystem" as "eine durch zahlreiche kulturelle, ökonomische und politische Verflechtungen verbundene Vielheit von politischen Organismen verstanden,

Yet even such a careful, reluctant, rather vague definition of a state system does not make it possible to speak about a state system with regard to the Thirty Years' War, or at least not at the first glance. The Thirty Years' War was characterised by thirty years of permanent, bitter and merciless military confrontation. Even more importantly, it was a war in which the main parties and opponents were not at all interested in a peaceful settlement, and instead sought the destruction and annihilation of their enemies.

These common assumptions are based very much on the character of the war as a confessional confrontation, in which a compromise seemed to be impossible for religious reasons. In short, it is impossible to come to an agreement with Antichrist. The character of the war as a merciless confessional conflict has been underlined in recent literature by catchwords like "Holy War" (a phrase used by Robert Bireley)[4] or "confessional fundamentalism" (*Konfessioneller Fundamentalismus*, a phrase used by Heinz Schilling).[5] Both phrases refer to the more or less destructive relationship between the opponents until solutions were found at the Westphalian Peace conference. The same destructive relationship seems to have existed on the political level between the main participants, the "superpowers", of the Thirty Years' War. The catchword here is "Universal Monarchy". As long as the ultimate intention of the superpowers, especially France and Spain, was to acquire *dominatio totius mundi*, domination of the whole (Christian) world, there was evidently no place for a state system in Duchhardt's sense, so that the policy pursued could only be the destruction of the enemy, at least as an independent political entity.[6]

In recent years there has been intense research into the policy and diplomacy of the principal powers during the Thirty Years' War. This has been occasioned by a renaissance of political history in general. I should like to mention only a few more extensive works I shall rely on here. First, there are two new and very valuable *Habilitationsschriften*, one by Thomas Brockmann about Emperor Ferdinand II[7] and the other by Michael Rohrschneider on the French-Spanish relations;[8] and

---

deren mehr oder weniger ausgeprägte Interaktion auf Dauer angelegt sind und nicht in erster Linie auf die Vernichtung des Partners und damit des Systems zielen".

[4] Robert Bireley, "The Thirty Years' War as Germany's religious war", in Konrad Repgen (ed.), *Krieg und Politik 1618–1648. Europäische Probleme und Perspektiven* (Munich, 1988), pp. 85–106, here pp. 95–6.

[5] Heinz Schilling (ed.), *Konfessioneller Fundamentalismus. Religion als politischer Faktor im europäischen Mächtesystem um 1600* (Munich, 2007), Foreword, pp. VII–VIII.

[6] Johannes Burkhardt, *Der Dreißigjährige Krieg* (Frankfurt, 1992), pp. 30–63.

[7] Thomas Brockmann, *Dynastie, Kaiseramt und Konfession. Politik und Ordnungsvorstellungen Ferdinands II. im Dreißigjährigen Krieg* (Paderborn et al., 2009).

[8] Michael Rohrschneider, *Der gescheiterte Frieden von Münster. Spaniens Ringen mit Frankreich auf dem Westfälischen Friedenskongress (1643–1649)* (Münster, 2007).

then there are new studies by Randall Lesaffer[9] and Anja V. Hartmann[10] on the French-Spanish Relations and those of Erik Thomson[11] and Jenny Öhmann[12] on Sweden. Thanks to these valuable studies, we have been afforded many new insights not only into details, but also into general aspects of the Thirty Years' War. One of the most fascinating results is that the traditional picture of the conflict as a hopeless, "fundamentalist", thoroughly destructive confrontation is superficial and not really appropriate; and that it is in some sense justified to speak even here of a state *system* in the sense that Duchhardt has given the term.

I should like to illustrate this by discussing three important aspects of political history during the Thirty Years' War.

The first aspect is that of the war as a field of permanent political and diplomatic relations between the opponents. One of the most astonishing features of the war is that it was accompanied from the very beginning by almost uninterrupted political and diplomatic talks between the main parties. These diplomatic relations on different levels started as early as 1618, and the history of these talks, which continued over the whole thirty years,[13] and not only during the peace conferences, is at least as complex and complicated as the history of the military events. Even more striking is that parties which from a strict juridical point of view could not negotiate at all, negotiated with each other; to use a modern phrase, they repeatedly entered into utterly "incorrect" negotiations. It would have been easy to refuse to enter into such dealings by invoking their unlawful character. The permanent presence of these "illegal" negotiations is one of the most interesting aspects of the war. I shall give two brief examples, one from the beginning and one from the end of the conflict.

Shortly after the outbreak of the rebellion in Bohemia, which marked the beginning of the war, different princes of the Holy Roman Empire recommended the Emperor to enter into direct negotiations with the rebellious Bohemian

---

[9] Randall Lesaffer, "Defensive Warfare, Prevention and Hegemony. The Justifications of the Franco-Spanish War of 1635", Part I–II, *Journal for International Law*, 8 (2006): 91–123 and 141–79.

[10] Anja V. Hartmann, *Von Regensburg nach Hamburg. Die diplomatischen Beziehungen zwischen dem französischen König und dem Kaiser vom Regensburger Vertrag (13. Oktober 1630) bis zum Hamburger Präliminarfrieden (25. Dezember 1641)* (Münster, 1998).

[11] Erik M. Thomson, *Chancellor Oxenstierna, Cardinal Richelieu, and Commerce. The Problems and Possibilities of Governance in Early-Seventeenth Century France and Sweden* (Leiden, 2007).

[12] Jenny Öhmann, *Der Kampf um den Frieden. Schweden und der Kaiser im Dreißigjährigen Krieg* (Vienna, 2005).

[13] Christoph Kampmann, *Europa und das Reich im Dreißigjährigen Krieg. Geschichte eines europäischen Konflikts* (Stuttgart, 2008). The results of this book are important for the following considerations.

estates.[14] Theoretically, from the point of view of international law (*Ius Gentium*) and the law of the Empire (*Reichsrecht*), this would have been totally impossible. For the government in Vienna, these Bohemian estates were nothing other than criminals, guilty of *crimen laesae majestatis*, who had just tried to kill the imperial governors in Prague and notoriously made war against their lawful lord, the Emperor and King of Bohemia.[15] In theory there was nothing to negotiate about until they surrendered. In effect, exactly this strict position was adopted towards the proposed negotiations by the imperial lawyers in the *Reichshofrat*.[16] The proposal of the princes of the Empire was in this sense a provocation for the Emperor. Even worse in the eyes of the imperial jurists, it was proposed that these talks should take place under the *neutral* mediation of these princes, that is, under the mediation of vassals of the Emperor. It was altogether provocative to propose that the Emperor should negotiate with rebels and criminals, and that his own vassals, who in theory were bound by feudal duty to support their lord, should play the role of neutral mediators. But astonishingly enough, after only short hesitation, the Emperor accepted the proposal.[17] That meant he formally accepted to enter into dubious negotiations with the Bohemian rebels. Between 1619 and 1620, these talks indeed took place and for a short time were very successful. This was the first chapter in the permanent negotiations that accompanied the war.

Another example comes from the end of the war, from the Westphalian Peace conference: When the peace talks between France and Spain ran into serious difficulties, it was proposed that the official mediators should be replaced. Officially the Papal nuncio, Fabio Chigi, and the Venetian ambassador, Alvise Contarini, undertook the difficult task of mediation.[18] Then, in 1646, diplomatic circles suggested that no longer the papal and Venetian diplomats, but rather the Netherlands should undertake the neutral mediation.[19] Again, a thoroughly "incorrect" proposal: in the eyes of Spain, the Netherlands were still mere rebels,

---

[14] Frank Müller, *Kursachsen und der Böhmische Aufstand* (Münster, 1997).

[15] Christoph Kampmann, *Reichsrebellion und kaiserliche Acht. Politische Strafjustiz im Dreißigjährigen Krieg und das Verfahren gegen Wallenstein 1634* (Münster, 1993), pp. 20–22.

[16] *Ibid.*, pp. 18–46.

[17] Müller, p. 197.

[18] Konrad Repgen, "Friedensvermittlung und Friedensvermittler beim Westfälischen Frieden" in Konrad Repgen, *Dreißigjähriger Krieg und Westfälischer Friede. Studien und Quellen*, eds Franz Bosbach and Christoph Kampmann (Paderborn et al., 1998), pp. 695–719.

[19] Cf. Braun, Introduction to *Acta Pacis Westphalicae, Serie 2 [Korrespondenzen]*, B 5, pp. XCV–XCVI; Anuschka Tischer, *Französische Diplomatie und Diplomaten auf dem Westfälischen Friedenskongreß. Außenpolitik unter Richelieu und Mazarin* (Münster, 1999), pp. 83–4.

not an independent state;[20] in the eyes of France, they were close allies and could not be neutral;[21] and in the eyes of the Pope, they were heretics. Moreover, the transfer of responsibility meant no less than a severe blow to the Pope's reputation, because by transferring the mediation to the Netherlands the two leading Roman Catholic powers would be declaring papal mediation to be useless. But again and astonishingly enough, after a short time both the leading Roman Catholic powers agreed to the proposal. And for more than a year the theoretically impossible became possible: papal mediation was replaced by Dutch mediation, the Dutch being now called the "new" mediators to distinguish them from the old papal and Venetian mediators.[22]

These are only two examples of "illegal" negotiations; many more could be added to the list. The Thirty Years' War was accompanied by thirty years of permanent, flexible and sometimes absolutely incorrect diplomatic and political contacts among the main parties. The leading powers were not only prepared to negotiate, but also to adopt very innovative and flexible means of negotiations.

I turn now to the second common opinion about the war, its character as a necessarily destructive confessional confrontation, as a kind of "Holy War" (Robert Bireley) in the view of the participants, or at least of the radical confessionalist participants such as the Emperor Ferdinand II or King Gustavus Adolphus of Sweden. The result of recent research suggests a different picture. To a large extent the common view was propaganda fabricated by followers and publicists of the monarchs so as to style both as ardent religious heroes. If we look more closely, it becomes clear that the relationship between the confessional enemies was of a different character.

In general, we must distinguish between the attitude of the politically responsible elites on the one hand and theologians on the other; and even among the theologians, the extremist group, who opposed every settlement, should not to be seen as the overall majority.

I shall again offer a few examples illustrating this general thesis. The peak of confessional confrontation during the war seemed to come during the reign of Emperor Ferdinand II (1619–37), and especially during the short time of clear Roman Catholic predominance in the Empire after Wallenstein's and Tilly's victories in the Danish war of 1626–27. The older German historiography spoke

---

[20] For the best account about the Spanish-Dutch conflict, cf. Geoffrey Parker, *The Dutch Revolt*, 2nd edn (New York, 1985).

[21] Fritz Dickmann, *Der Westfälische Friede*, 5th edn (Münster, 1985), pp. 261–3; Tischer, pp. 209–11.

[22] The Netherlands were called the *nouveaux médiateurs* in contrast to the *anciens médiateurs*, the Pope and Venice (Braun, p. XCVI, fn. 137). The exchange of the mediators was formally announced, but the relationship between the old and the new mediators was uneasy.

of the imminent danger that the Emperor and his allies were about to crush all Protestantism in the Holy Roman Empire.[23] Our knowledge of imperial policy at this time is now considerably greater than before, thanks to the historical studies of Thomas Brockmann and the juridical studies of Michael Frisch.[24]

These studies show very convincingly that the party of radical theologians at the Imperial court never had the slightest chance of imposing their view on official imperial policy. The basis of all political, juridical and confessional considerations at the Viennese Court was the Augsburg Peace of 1555 (*Augsburger Religionsfriede*), which guaranteed the existence of both Roman Catholicism and Lutheran Protestantism. The leading political circles at the Hofburg, the Emperor and his main advisors, never had any intention of withdrawing from the Augsburg religious peace with this general guarantee for Protestantism. The main question under discussion at court was that of the right interpretation of the Augsburg Treaty, but there was no dispute about the Treaty's validity. In the end, the Viennese court decided to impose a relatively strict Roman Catholic interpretation on the Augsburg Peace, but not – and this is decisive in our context – to withdraw either openly or secretly.[25]

With regard to the principal decision of the Imperial Government to uphold the Augsburg Religious Settlement, Martin Heckel, a leading Protestant historian of the early modern Holy Empire, could maintain convincingly that the political and confessional policy of the Imperial court in the moment of its greatest success can be characterised as a confessional *via media* between the extremist and the pacifist solutions, and not at all as an extremist position.[26] From the traditional viewpoint, Heckel's interpretation is puzzling, but recent studies support it. Although Emperor Ferdinand II hated the "Protestant heresy", he had no intention of wiping it out within the Holy Roman Empire during his lifetime. Ferdinand's chief concern was the fate of his dynasty, the Austrian branch of the Habsburgs, and his hereditary territories.[27]

---

[23] For example Wilhelm Mommsen: "Die Ausführung des [Restitutions-]Edikts hätte die Axt an die Wurzel des deutschen Protestantismus gelegt, damit wohl überhaupt die Vernichtung des Protestantismus herbeigeführt", *Propyläen-Weltgeschichte*, vol. 5, *Reformation und Gegenreformation* (Berlin, 1930), p. 424.

[24] Michael Frisch, *Das Restitutionsedikt Kaiser Ferdinands II. vom 6. März 1629. Eine rechtsgeschichtliche Untersuchung* (Tübingen, 1993).

[25] See Brockmann's detailed investigation, chap. V, 6.

[26] On the *Restitutionsedikt* as the victory of a confessional "middle of the road" policy (*Mittellinie*) over theological extremists, cf. Martin Heckel, *Deutschland im konfessionellen Zeitalter* (Göttingen, 1983), p. 146.

[27] Brockmann, chap. VI, II.6; Friedrich Edelmayer, "Einheit der Casa de Austria? Philipp II. und Karl von Innerösterreich", in France M. Dolinat et al. (eds), *Katholische*

The same is true for Sweden at the moment of Gustavus Adolphus's greatest success in 1631–32. In contrast to his fiercely confessional propaganda (or better, the propaganda of his fiercely confessional followers), the Swedish king acted very cautiously in religious matters and made no serious effort to change the general religious situation. First and foremost, he felt obliged to uphold the Augsburg Peace.[28] He supported its Protestant interpretation, but not its destruction, in the last point very like his main opponent, the Emperor in Vienna.

None of this means that confession did not play an important role. Of course it did, and did so until at least the end of the century. But total destruction of the opposing confessional party was not part of it. It is remarkable that this was, in political terms, true even for the Pope, as Alexander Koller has recently shown in an impressive study.[29] Even papal policy distinguished very carefully between political and confessional intentions. In 1631, at the peak of Swedish-Protestant predominance in the Empire, Pope Urban VIII did what he could to bring Bavaria into an alliance with France. The Pope knew very well that this meant leading Bavaria into an indirect alliance with Sweden, which had signed the treaty of Bärwalde with France. This led to a famous confrontation in the solemn Consistorium of Cardinals when one of the Cardinals, Borghia, openly attacked the Holy Father for having the responsibility for the destruction of Roman Catholicism in the Holy Roman Empire on his hands because he supported France and Sweden.[30] In some sense, the Cardinal was right.

Again, we could add many examples. The picture of the Thirty Years' War as a Holy War between the confessions is a myth, created by clerics and pastors, and inapplicable to the politically ruling elites.

The same is true for the thesis that a "universal monarchy" was the ultimate intention of France and Spain. Again, recent research has changed and added

---

Reform und Gegenreformation in Innerösterreich, 1544–1628 (Klagenfurt et al., 1994), pp. 373–86, here p. 386.

[28] For the change in historiographic views of Gustavus Adolphus's German war aims, cf. Öhmann, pp. 23–4. The older historiography generally preferred a more defensive interpretation of Gustavus Adolphus's political aims. Recently Gustavus Adolphus has been seen as a more aggressive leader with imperialistic aims, but even recent historiography regards Sweden's religious aims in Germany as relatively unimportant. A general religious transformation of the Holy Roman Empire does not seem to have been on the Swedish agenda.

[29] Alexander Koller, "War der Papst ein militanter, kriegstreibender katholischer Monarch? Der Hl. Stuhl und die protestantischen Häresien um 1600", in Schilling (ed.), pp. 67–82.

[30] Ludwig von Pastor, *Geschichte der Päpste*, vol. XIII/1 (Freiburg, Br., 1928), pp. 431–41.

to our knowledge on this point.[31] It has become clear that although the idea of universal monarchy played of course an important role for both powers, it was never in the form of an open or silent aim. Instead both sides suspected the other side of striving to attain universal monarchy.[32] The policy of Spain and France was based very much on the feeling of their own weakness and the fear that the other side would exploit their weakness to advance its hegemonic plans. In a remarkably parallel manner, both saw the danger of being overwhelmed by the universalistic ambitions of the other. Olivares and Richelieu therefore struggled to achieve one central aim, namely, not to stand alone against the rival.[33]

In this respect, it is very revealing to look to the relationship between Spain and the Northern Netherlands during the Thirty Years' War. After the turn of the century, Spanish policy was never directed to reoccupying the whole Netherlands in the manner of a *Monarchia Universalis* and abolishing the independent Dutch State. Madrid knew very well that this aim was impossible to achieve. The whole question rather turned on what conditions Madrid would offer for the formal recognition of Dutch independence.[34]

To sum up, it is possible to speak of a state system during the Thirty Years' War in the sense of Heinz Duchhardt's definition. The ongoing war was accompanied by permanent negotiations and the opponents never totally broke off political contact. Even more importantly, ideas of mutual destruction did not exercise a decisive influence over the political elites. And this is true even of the confessional conflict. The war aim was to weaken the confessional enemy, not to destroy him. In theological circles there existed the idea of a completely Roman Catholic or a completely Protestant Holy Roman Empire, but political leaders did not share this view.

These results have consequences for the concept of peace and its real importance for the political agents during the Thirty Years' War. All political parties and

---

[31] Hartmann, *Von Regensburg nach Hamburg. Die diplomatischen Beziehungen zwischen dem französischen König und dem Kaiser vom Regensburger Vertrag (13. Oktober 1630) bis zum Hamburger Präliminarfrieden (25. Dezember 1641)*; Rohrschneider, *Der gescheiterte Frieden von Münster. Spaniens Ringen mit Frankreich auf dem Westfälischen Friedenskongress (1643–1649)*.

[32] For France and Spain, cf. Rohrschneider, pp. 289–93. Kampmann, *Europa und das Reich im Dreißigjährigen Krieg*, pp. 103–9.

[33] Olivares always tried to bring the Austrian relatives of his king into a close alliance with Spain – an aim that he never really achieved during the whole war. Richelieu's whole policy was directed to forming solid alliances with the Netherlands and Sweden; and though initially both were reluctant to accept the French offer, in the end they had to conclude an alliance with France for military reasons.

[34] Jonathan Israel, *The Dutch Republic and the Hispanic World, 1606–1661* (Oxford 1982), p. XIV.

all princes solemnly declared that their war aim was peace. In all declarations, manifestos, pamphlets and the like, their repeated credo was *finis belli pax esto*, that is, the aim of all war must be the achievement of peace.

For a long time historians have regarded these declarations as empty phrases that had no influence on the actual policy of the warring powers. In view of the recent historical research, we should be very careful in making such quick judgements. The politically responsible elites genuinely desired the peace. Their profession of this desire was not mere propaganda intended to conceal their real intentions.

Pax honesta and Ongoing War

These results raise another important question. If there was a sort of state system (in Duchhardt's sense), if the warring powers were not seeking to destroy their enemies, and if peace did in fact play a role for them, why then did the war go on for thirty years? Why had Germany to experience such a long war? I shall now turn to this question in the second part of this article.

There were of course many reasons, but I shall concentrate on only one here. This is the special concept of peace that was shared by the main political agents and that exercised great influence on their political behaviour and the formulation of their political aims and intentions. As I have already mentioned, there is no doubt that the different parties genuinely tried to achieve peace. But the peace they wanted to achieve meant more than the mere absence of war, more than what political science calls "negative peace".[35] The peace sought by the opposing parties was a very special peace, a peace that corresponded to their own often different and sometimes incompatible ideas of security and justice. The crucial point is that the attainment of these very special concepts of peace was more important than a swift end to the military confrontation. This position can be summarised in the statement that war seemed to be better than the wrong peace. In other words, because the main parties had highly elaborate, complicated ideas of what a peaceful order should look like, the war went on and on. In this respect there are striking similarities among the various warring parties, even in the definition of the right peace. Usually the right peace was called the "honourable peace" (*Pax honesta, paix honnête, der Ehrenvolle Friede*). In order to achieve the *Pax honesta*, the different parties were prepared to continue the war, even in very difficult circumstances.

---

[35] For the concept of "negative" peace in the political science, cf. Ernst-Otto Czempiel, *Friedensstrategien. Eine systematische Darstellung außenpolitischer Theorien von Machiavelli bis Madariaga*, 2nd edn (Opladen, 1998), pp. 45–52.

It is very important to understand what honour (*honneur*) meant in this context. Honour should not be confused with glory (*gloire*). In fact, the early modern concepts of honour and of glory meant totally different things. Of course glory, especially the glory of war, was important for the princely rulers. They all belonged to the high aristocracy and glory was traditionally of central importance to them.[36] Nevertheless, glory was *not* indispensable. In severe circumstances it was possible to relinquish the prospect of glory. And the rulers in the Thirty Years' War were prepared to do exactly that. We have many examples of this willingness. For example, the occasions when princes intended personally to lead troops into battle because they thought this was required for their glory, but were persuaded by their counsellors not to do so, or to postpone the campaign, despite the loss of *gloire*. A good example of this is Cardinal Richelieu's constant advice to his monarch to use *juste modération*, that is, not to strive for superfluous glory. This was in accord with the common prudential *gubernatoria*, which told the princes that glory is important, but that it is also sometimes important to dispense with glory.[37]

Honour was a completely different matter. Honour was an indispensable condition for a prince to be taken seriously by the other princes and states, to be accepted as an important player in the political game, and to play a political role at all.[38]

This is crucial for the understanding of *Pax honesta*. *Pax honesta* was more than a mere addition to each party's most important peace conditions. It meant a peace settlement that guaranteed the fundamental reputation and the rank of the monarchy. This guarantee depended upon certain political questions and peace settlements – settlements that in retrospective sometimes seem not to be so important, but were extremely important from the point of view of the political elites. The various warring parties continued the war in order to accomplish these

---

[36] On glory as important aristocratic value, cf. Johannes Kunisch, *Fürst – Gesellschaft – Krieg. Studien zur bellizistischen Disposition des absoluten Fürstenstaats* (Cologne et al., 1992).

[37] On *juste modération*, just moderation, in the thought of Cardinal Richelieu, cf. Fritz Dickmann, "Rechtsgedanke und Machtpolitik bei Richelieu. Studien an neu entdeckten Quellen", in Fritz Dickmann, *Friedensrecht und Friedenssicherung. Studien zum Friedensproblem in der neueren Geschichte* (Göttingen, 1971), pp. 36–78, here pp. 64–5.

[38] For the understanding of honour (*Ehre*), see Sibylle Hofer, "Ehrverlust", in *Enzyklopädie der Neuzeit*, vol. 3 (Stuttgart, 2006), pp. 88–90; François Billacois, "Honneur", in François Bluche (ed.), *Dictionnaire du Grand Siècle* (Paris, 1990), pp. 729–30; and Klaus Graf, "Adelsehre", in *Enzyklopädie der Neuzeit*, vol. 1 (Stuttgart, 2005), pp. 54–6, here p. 56. For the difference between honour and glory, see the article "Ruhm, öffentlich", in Johann H. Zedler, *Großes vollständiges Universal-Lexikon*, vol. 32 (Halle, Leipzig, 1740) column 1596. A detailed investigation of the political concept of honour is still lacking.

goals, even in extremely unfavourable circumstances. The prolongation of the war was then inevitable, especially when one party declared something to be a crucial and indispensable condition for a *Pax honesta* that another party rejected for exactly the same reason.

I should like to clarify and illustrate these rather abstract explanations by giving one example. It refers to one of the crucial conflicts within the Thirty Years' War, the Franco-Imperial confrontation over the means to a universal peace.

The historical picture of the French Prime Minister, Cardinal Richelieu, and his attitude towards peace, has undergone a total transformation. The older literature, especially the older German historiography, regarded Richelieu as a "Machiavellian in red robe", who was not really interested in peace but only in the extension of his power and the power of his monarch. Intense research in recent decades has convincingly shown that this picture is utterly misleading. Historians such as Fritz Dickmann, Hermann Weber and more recently Klaus Malettke have made very important contributions to this revision.[39] Today it may be taken for granted that Richelieu was in fact interested in peace and the construction of a peaceful and stable Christian order. Yet at the same time the extensive research has also made it clear that the Cardinal had a very special idea of peace: it had to be a peace in accordance with the honour of the French monarchy, a sort of *Pax honesta gallica*, which was regularly called the *paix universel*, the universal peace of Christendom.[40] In other words, Richelieu and his monarch, Louis XIII, would agree only to a peace settlement that would solve all controversial questions of French foreign policy and would abolish all the French monarchy's problems with its neighbours and rivals. Richelieu therefore constantly demanded that all his allies had to be included in the peace talks and consequently in the final settlement. Exactly this last condition proved to be extremely difficult and problematic for concluding a peace. Moreover, Richelieu demanded that the estates of the Empire (*Reichsstände*), or at least those allied with France, should also participate in the peace congress and in the peace treaty.[41] This condition was extremely difficult to accept for the Emperor because he regarded the estates as vassals and not independent foreign powers, and because he was not willing to

---

[39] Klaus Malettke, *Frankreich, Deutschland und Europa im 17. und 18. Jahrhundert. Beiträge zum Einfluß französischer politischer Theorie, Verfassung und Außenpolitik in der Frühen Neuzeit* (Marburg, 1994), pp. 286–302; Dickmann, "Rechtsgedanke und Machtpolitik bei Richelieu. Studien an neu entdeckten Quellen", pp. 36–78.

[40] Cf. Hermann Weber, "Vom verdeckten zum offenen Krieg. Richelieus Kriegsgründe und Kriegsziele 1634/35", in Konrad Repgen (ed.), *Krieg und Politik 1618–1648. Europäische Probleme und Perspektiven* (Munich, 1988), pp. 203–17; Klaus Malettke, pp. 286–302.

[41] Kampmann, *Europa und das Reich im Dreißigjährigen Krieg*, p. 133.

accept that a foreign power should intervene in the question of the future order of the Holy Roman Empire.

The French demand had much to do with honour and reputation. This becomes clear from the fact that Richelieu demanded the participation of his allies within the Empire only from France's entry into the war in 1635 onwards. It should be noted that in 1635–36 France had only very few allies within the Holy Roman Empire – in fact only two of any importance, the elector of Trier and the Landgrave of Hessen-Kassel. And both these allies were driven out of their territory and were of no great real military use for France. But their "real" use was not a matter of great import for Richelieu. For him the whole question of the participation of France's allies was a question of honour; what was really important for the First Minister was to demonstrate that France would not agree to any peace which was incompatible with its honour.

One year after France's entry into the war, it became clear how important the *Pax honesta* or *pax universalis* was for Richelieu. In 1636 France fell into serious military troubles and was at the brink of defeat. After successful attacks of the Spanish and Imperial armies, the way to Paris seemed to be open and this led to a general panic in the French capital. Richelieu's war policy was totally discredited and his political enemies within and outside France triumphant. The Emperor tried to exploit this situation by offering a separate peace to France, accompanied by very friendly gestures.[42]

But the Emperor's gestures were fruitless; Richelieu stood firm. He was convinced that even amidst such serious and dangerous circumstances nothing but a *Pax honesta* was tolerable for France. And one of the most important conditions of this *Pax honesta* was not to conclude a peace treaty without his allies in the Empire. Richelieu held out for this peace condition even in a situation in which France seemed unable to help itself, much less its helpless allies.

Even those historians who take a very sympathetic view of Cardinal Richelieu could not deny that his demand for a *paix universel*, a universal peace, contributed much to the prolongation of the war, although his quest for peace was honest.[43] Richelieu's fight for the *Pax honesta* as *pax universalis* became a great obstacle to peace because it collided with the Emperor's idea of a *Pax honesta*. The Emperor was not interested in a long war with France, as we have already seen. But he was not at all

---

[42] For example, Ferdinand II forbade his son, Ferdinand III, commander-in-chief of the intervening imperial army, to publish a declaration of war against France. We should imagine the rather odd situation: imperial troops, moving against Paris although no state of war existed between the opponents, offered Richelieu a swift withdrawal of all troops and the return to the status quo ante if France agreed to a separate peace; Hartmann, pp. 258–62.

[43] Hermann Weber, "Une Paix sûre et prompte. Die Friedenspolitik Richelieus", in Heinz Duchhardt (ed.), *Zwischenstaatliche Friedenswahrung in Mittelalter und Früher Neuzeit* (Cologne and Vienna, 1991), pp. 111–29, here pp. 128–9.

prepared to admit the estates of the Empire to peace talks with France. In special circumstances, he was willing to accept the participation of other foreign powers and the electors who were seen as sort of co-sovereigns in the Empire. But the demand that he should allow the participation of his vassals was seen as a major insult to the honour of the Emperor, incompatible with a *Pax honesta* and altogether intolerable.

In the last years of the war, the imperial government took the same firm stand in this respect as had the French Government before. Even in extremely complicated and dangerous circumstances, Vienna rejected any proposal to sign a peace treaty without honour. With astonishing persistence and obstinacy, the Emperor and his Privy Council rejected any idea of participating in the Westphalian Peace conference, because they were not willing to accept the participation of the imperial estates. As this was not in accord with their idea of *Pax honesta*, the government decided that it would be better to fight even in difficult circumstances against an obviously more powerful enemy than to agree to a peace without honour.[44] Three times, in 1642, 1644 and 1645, the imperial army was badly defeated. After the disastrous campaign of 1644, which led to the loss of a whole army without a battle and revealed the weakness of the Emperor, one could have expected a changed attitude in Vienna. But the opposite was the case: at the end of 1644, Emperor and Privy Council unanimously agreed that it would be better to fight even in desperate circumstances than to forfeit imperial honour in a peace conference with participants from the Empire. It was therefore decided to raise another army again – for the third time within three years. The raising of this army represented an extreme and devastating effort on the part of the already heavily exploited Habsburg hereditary lands (*Erblande*). In spring 1645 this army was sent on campaign, now under the symbolic command of the Emperor himself. The predictable happened: this army, which was to turn the imperial military fortune and save the Emperor's honour, was again beaten and virtually destroyed in March 1645. Now the military and moral catastrophe was complete. The victorious Swedish Army advanced swiftly into the hereditary lands, appearing on the Danube and threatening Vienna and Lower Austria. At the same time, from the south-east the Swedish ally, the Prince of Transylvania, appeared. The Emperor was faced with the loss of his central territories. Moreover, his closest allies, Bavaria and Saxony, deserted him. And only now, at the brink of utter defeat and given the choice between dishonourable defeat and dishonourable peace, did the government accept the universal peace conference at Münster.[45]

Again, many other examples could be adduced. A very impressive one is the Swedish policy during the Thirty Years' War, which was shaped by the fight

---

[44] Karsten Ruppert, *Die kaiserliche Politik auf dem Westfälischen Friedenskongreß* (Münster, 1979), pp. 75–9; Kampmann, *Europa und das Reich im Dreißigjährigen Krieg*, pp. 148–9.

[45] Kampmann, *Europa und das Reich im Dreißigjährigen Krieg*, pp. 148–50.

for a *Pax honesta*. After the death of Gustavus Adolphus, the Swedish policy in Germany became highly flexible. But there remained several political goals that were essential for Swedish "honour": *Satisfactio*, territorial compensation for the Swedish war effort; *Contentament*, financial compensation for the Swedish war effort; and *Amnestia*, the return to the political and confessional *status quo ante* in Germany. Even in most dire military circumstances, when the Swedish army seemed to be on the verge of surrender, the Swedish government refused to withdraw from Germany without having achieved *Satisfactio*, *Contentament* and at least partial *Amnestia*, that is, without having achieved an honourable peace.[46] Recently Jenny Öhmann has published a book on Swedish policy during the Thirty Years' War with the eminently appropriate title *Der Kampf um den Frieden* (*The Fight for Peace*). But it was not peace as such that Sweden was fighting for, but its very special idea of honourable peace – a term which appears frequently in the Swedish records and political correspondence. Öhmann might also have called her book "The Fight for Honourable Peace", and this would be a fitting description for the policy of all the important powers in the Thirty Years' War.

Conclusion

At the time of the Thirty Years' War there indeed existed a system of states: there was permanent and uninterrupted communication among the warring parties and a readiness to use flexible means of negotiations. And among the political elites there was no predominant intention of mutual destruction.

But all this could not prevent the military catastrophe. One main reason for this was the universal insistence on a *Pax honesta*. All important participants agreed that a peace settlement was only possible on the basis of their own understanding of an honourable peace. It was this special idea of honour and peace that led to the military catastrophe within the European state system.

---

[46] Sigmund Goetze, *Die Politik des schwedischen Reichskanzlers Axel Oxenstierna gegenüber Kaiser und Reich* (Kiel, 1971).

Chapter 12
Hegemon History: Pufendorf's Shifting Perspectives on France and French Power

David Saunders

Introduction

As a political phenomenon, "hegemony" merits attention.[1] It raises the question of enforcement, that is, of implementation and execution of norms, as distinct from their conception. Conceiving a norm – for instance that of a just peace (*une bonne paix*) – is one thing. Enforcing the norm is another. The actual enforcement of international pacts, and sometimes their design and fashioning, might rest more on the political intervention of a hegemonic super-state or states as arbiter-broker than on cosmopolitan imperatives or transcendental values. In the international as in the domestic sphere, "Covenants, without the Sword, are but Words".[2]

At issue is France's (along with Sweden's) role as hegemon in the Westphalian settlement of 1648. Given our German context, it is fitting to review this French action through the Brandenburg-Protestant perspectives of Samuel Pufendorf. These are two sharply divergent perspectives, the one post-dating the revocation of the Edict of Nantes in 1685, the other pre-dating what European Protestants (including Pufendorf as exemplar) perceived as that seismic event. At mid-century French hegemony could serve to guarantee a general peace and allow religious pluralism. After 1685, Pufendorf saw French domination not as a positive relation of force, but as threatening an antipluralist re-Catholicisation of Europe by a would-be "universal monarchy".

How should we characterise this mutation? Does it signify a more intense exercise of hegemony, a difference of degree? Or does it signify a difference of kind, a different mode of domination exercised by a greater power upon lesser

---

[1] On hegemony, see Randall Lesaffer, "Defensive warfare, prevention and hegemony. The justifications of the Franco-Spanish War of 1635", *Journal of the History of International Law* 8/1 (2006): 91–123 (especially on "hegemonic defence" in the context of the Franco-Spanish war of 1635 and the rise of France as a "power-broker" on the seventeenth-century scene. See also Gerry Simpson, *Great Powers and Outlaw States: Unequal Sovereigns in the International Legal Order* (Cambridge, 2004) on "legalised hegemony" as the condition of "great powers" exercising domination over lesser states from the time of the Congress of Vienna in 1815.

[2] Thomas Hobbes, *Leviathan* (Cambridge, 1991), p. 117.

states? The fact of raising these conceptual questions is motivated, in part, by an overriding political feature of our own times: the shift in American "hegemony" from World War II to the recent US administration. I return to this comparison briefly in a concluding reflection.

But first I shall provide a background note on Pufendorf as natural law theorist on public law and religious peace. Then I present his perspectives on the uses and abuses of French power as formulated in two quite different genres of writing: religious polemic and political history. To establish the sense of a perceived mutation in French power, I take the post-1685 negative perspective first, as formulated in Pufendorf's 1687 *De habitu religionis christianae ad vitam civilem* (*Of the Nature and Qualification of Religion in Reference to Civil Society*). By way of underscoring the contrast and to outline a positive pre-1685 "Westphalian" perspective on France as hegemon, I proceed to consider his 1682–85 *Einleitung zu der Historie der vornehmsten Reiche und Staaten so itziger Zeit in Europa sich befinden* (*Introduction to the History of the Principal Kingdoms and States of Europe*). In the *History*, the fact of French power is recognised – "there is not any State in Christendom which *France* does not equal, if not exceed, in Power" – but in no way condemned as a general threat to peace and Protestantism in Europe.

Pufendorf, Public Law and Religious Peace

With the rupture of the universal Christian church, triple waves of Lutheran, Calvinist and Catholic confessionalising had been rolling across northwestern Europe since the mid-1500s. These sectarian confessionalisations converged with forces of territorial state-formation, propelling a new political entity onto the European scene: the confessional territorial state. This was an "organic" state, its political legitimacy founded in its spiritual mission to save the souls of all who lived within its borders. The modern French term, *intégrisme*, well captures the nature of these confessional programs, each aimed at incorporating whole populations within one of the exclusive Christian truths. With this mission came a dynamism of faith, but also a deadly rivalry of faiths. Where once there had been the unity of the *Respublica christiana*, now there was inter-confessional religious war. And once there was war, who could doubt that the absolute precondition for survival of the state remained a unity of religion, imposed as common cause by both prince and bishop?

Samuel Pufendorf was one who doubted. This doubt was elaborated in his *De jure naturae et gentium* (1672).[3] As an exit from intractable confessional conflict,

---

[3] For recent Anglophone discussion of Pufendorf's natural jurisprudence as a "civil philosophy", see Ian Hunter, *Rival Enlightenments. Civil and Metaphysical Philosophy in Early Modern Germany* (Cambridge, 2001).

a peace relay had emerged in the form of an imperial public law (*ius publicum*) aimed at containing the violence between rival confessional parties. Through an extraordinary process of juridification, the conflict was thus in some measure addressed in legal terms. The settlements of Augsburg (1555) and Westphalia (1648), legal solutions to religious conflict, carried the force of imperial law. The Imperial jurists' creation was a "non-confessional or supra-confessional order of coexistence between the two great confessional blocs".[4] This unprecedented "order of coexistence" signalled a novel political-legal conception of civil peace that was not contingent on settling the question of religious truth (or error). True, the rival confessions themselves could (and of course did) treat the historic legal settlements as merely provisional, pending their own future return to the scene as the one "true" and universal church for all of a reunited Christendom.

Prepared to learn from history, Pufendorf recognised what had ensued when confessionalising princes deployed their civil powers to render the citizenry theologically virtuous by means of an imposed conformity. With *De jure*, he mounted a massive post-Westphalian program to wrest the law of nations, positive law and worldly politics away from the grasp of theology, thereby separating what the confessional state had conjoined. In the Pufendorfian mode of modern natural law, civil peace under sovereign rule was to be the overriding norm of positive law and political order. This suggests something of the complex religious, political and legal backdrop to Pufendorf's shifting perspectives on the hegemonic role of France.

The Hobbesian Pufendorf of *De jure* took no particular issue with absolutist rule in France.[5] Symptomatic of this disposition is the fact that his translator and glossator, Jean Barbeyrac, would find occasion to "adjust" what he clearly regarded as Pufendorf's understating the negative dimension of sovereign power.[6] At one point in his 1706 French edition of *De jure*, *Le droit de la nature et des gens*, Barbeyrac concludes a sequence of ten footnotes with what is clearly an implied critical reflection on French historical practice:

> Civil Government being a proper Means to restrain the Malice of Men, the *Civil State*, without Contradiction, may be more sociable and happy than the

---

[4] Martin Heckel, "Das Säkularisierungsproblem in der Entwicklung des deutschen Staatskirchenrechts", in Gerhard Dilcher and Ilse Staff (eds), *Christentum und modernes Recht. Beiträge zum Problem des Säkularisation* (Frankfurt am Main, 1984), p. 50.

[5] The case for Pufendorf as "the only great juristic exponent of Hobbes" is powerfully made by Fiammetta Palladini, *Samuel Pufendorf discepolo di Hobbes. Per una reinterpretazione del giusnaturalismo moderno* (Bologna, 1990).

[6] On Barbeyrac as translator and editor of Pufendorf, see David Saunders, "The natural jurisprudence of Jean Barbeyrac: translation as an art of political adjustment", *Eighteenth-Century Studies* 36/4 (2003): 473–90.

> *State of Nature*; but then we must suppose the *Civil Society* to be well governed, otherwise, if a King abuses his Power, or devolves the Management of civil Affairs to Ministers both ignorant and vicious, as it often happens, a *Civil State* is then more unhappy than the *State of Nature*; which appears by the Wars, Calamities and Vices which spring up from such Abuses, and from which the *State of Nature* would be free.[7]

Two decades after Louis XIV's revocation of the Edict of Nantes (for Protestants the most egregious of "Abuses"), Barbeyrac thus darkened the roseate image of the civil state that Pufendorf had drawn in 1672. In fact, in 1687, with *De habitu*, Pufendorf was himself already writing in a genre quite different from that of the natural law treatise *De jure*.

Before considering the purpose and polemic of *De habitu*, however, it is worthwhile re-stating what Westphalia achieved. For the first time, legal standing was extended to the Reformed Protestant Church, Calvinism having been excluded from the 1555 settlement. Now princely and imperial signatories to the 1648 settlement would have to tolerate freedom of worship for three confessions within their territorial jurisdictions. In principle, there would be no return to enforced religious unity given this constraint upon a territorial prince's capacity to exercise the *jus reformandi*. Importantly, if the *Respublica christiana* no longer ruled, treaties such as Westphalia became the very foundation of a law of nations conceived in Pufendorfian style.

Yet if the terms of the Westphalian treaty were to be binding, it would have to be by virtue of the guarantee provided by French power. This was of course an act of national interest quite in keeping with France's longstanding anti-imperial aims: resisting the Habsburgs' Madrid-Vienna axis and neutralising the Catholic co-ordinates of the German Holy Roman Empire. Though anti-imperialism sat awkwardly with Pufendorf's respect for the imperial public law, as a juristically-minded "Westphalian" he could nonetheless approve mid-century French power as a contribution to religious peace in Europe.

Pufendorf's Post-1685 Perspective on France

The situation was different after 1685. As the instrument of Catholic Bourbon power, France now posed the danger. Within two years of the revocation of the Edict of Nantes, Pufendorf published *De habitu religionis christianae ad vitam civilem* (*Of the Nature and Qualification of Religion in Reference to Civil Society*).

---

[7] Barbeyrac, in Samuel Pufendorf, *Le droit de la nature et des gens, ou Système général des principes les plus importants de la morale, de la jurisprudence, et de la politique*, trans. J. Barbeyrac (Amsterdam, 1706), p. 102.

De habitu is a resolutely anti-Catholic and anti-Louis XIV polemic dedicated to Friedrich-Wilhelm, Prince Elector of Brandenburg. The one sovereign was the current aggressor against Christ's church, the other its potential defender. The hegemon-protector remained in place, but now in a different guise, threatening Protestants with the ancient "Yoke of Popish Slavery".

Speaking with the voice of history, Pufendorf ends *De habitu* with an appeal to princes and states that have not endured such slavery: "if they seriously reflect, how their fellow-Protestants are persecuted, and in what barbarous manner they are treated, [they] will, questionless without my Advice, take such measures, as may be most convenient to secure themselves from so imminent a Danger".[8]

The point is to cement the Protestant case as just and the Catholic as unjust, first in general terms and then in the concrete terms of contemporary circumstances. The method is to deconstruct once and for all – in the eyes of God, the Great Elector and the law – any residual justification for enforcement of religion by a civil state. *De habitu* confronts its readers with a normative pedagogy sustained by Scriptural referencing, the lesson of which is that state and church constitute irreducibly separate "Kingdoms":

> The Kingdom of Christ therefore, is a Kingdom of Truth, where he, by the force of Truth, brings over our Souls to his Obedience; and this Truth has such powerful Charms, that the Kingdom of Christ needs not to be maintained by the same forcible means and Rules, by which Subjects must be kept in Obedience to the Civil Powers. (35)

This fundamental distinction between different spheres of human duty is confirmed by the Scriptural evidence that Christ's kingdom established no civil state and founded no temporal court (48). Thus the "Civil Power does not reach this Kingdom; true Piety being not implanted by Human Force, which is insufficient to procure God's Grace, or raise those inward Motions which are chiefly acceptable to God Almighty; and without which, all our exterior Actions, that may be enforced by a Civil Authority, are to be deem'd vain and fruitless" (57). Pufendorf allows his readers no choice but to agree: "Who is so ignorant as not to know, that for obtaining the Ends of Civil Societies, it was requisite to constitute various Degrees of Dignities appertaining to the Managers of the State; whereas the most plain and natural Distinction betwixt Christians in reference to the Church, is only that of Teachers and Auditors" (68–9).

---

[8] Samuel Pufendorf, *De habitu religionis christianae ad vitam civilem/ Of the Nature and Qualification of Religion in Reference to Civil Society*, trans. J. Crull, ed. Simone Zurbuchen (Indianapolis, 2002), p. 121. In this section, further references to this work of Pufendorf give page numbers only.

The demarcation is drawn and redrawn, but never to the simple disadvantage of the civil state (or Friedrich-Wilhelm). Thus, on the one hand, "Sovereigns are always invested with a full Power to force their Subjects to a compliance with their Commands, by inflicting Punishments upon them". On the other hand:

> But how is it possible to imagine that any Church or Congregation of the Believers should ever, or ought to subject themselves so entirely to the Pleasure and Disposal of their Teachers; as to oblige themselves to acquiesce barely in, and to follow blindly, whatever shall be proposed to them, as conducing and leading to the way of Salvation. (69)

By 1687, Pufendorf had been around long enough to know his adversaries' moves. For instance, the latter would argue that if church and state are such different entities, then why could not each exercise coterminous sovereign power? Pufendorf's counter argument is immediate: "It is a frivolous Objection, that the Church and civil Government have different Ends and Objects, not repugnant to one another; For, from thence is not to be inferred, that the Church must be a State, or that the Christian Religion cannot be propagated, maintained or exercised, without the Church assume the same Power that belongs to the civil Government" (93).

These were not messages for a tranquil, normal time. *De habitu* is not an exercise in metaphysical abstraction, an architectonic for a world defined by the ideal relation between religion and the civil state. It is not a speculative discourse on toleration, but a campaign text, a call to arms. At stake was an emergency: the very survival of European Protestants now confronted by a perceived Franco-Catholic claim to supra-sovereignty. Responding to Louis XIV's revocation of what remained of state protection for Huguenots' security in France, Pufendorf is perfectly concrete in his political aim: to cut the ground from under advancing Catholic forces.

The anti-Catholicism of these pages is multiform and unrelenting. Depicted as indelibly temporal in its interests and thus less church than state, the Roman Church's claim to apostolic status is placed in doubt:

> That the Church, according to the intention of Christ and his Apostles, neither was, nor could be a State, it may from thence be concluded, whether that Church which pretends to a Sovereignty, considered as such, be Christ's Church? (59)

Yet Rome's claim to legitimacy as a state is dismissed, regardless of its alleged antiquity: "For it is a very insignificant Proof, to allege in a case of such Moment Tradition, and a long continued Usurpation, which adds nothing to the right of a long continued illegal Possession" (77). To make the point crystal clear, we are then reminded that no matter what might have been the case in "in primitive times", the ancient claim "in process of Time, has been abused, and consequently degenerated into an insufferable Tyranny" (77).

As to the Papal office in the role of "Judge General of Controversies in the Church", the attack is withering. Far from settling such controversies either by oblivion or by a measure of flexibility, the "Popish Monarchy" has only increasingly hardened its doctrinal posturing. Thus "it is impossible for the *Roman Catholicks* to recede an Inch from the point of the controverted Articles, without diminution of their Authority, and endangering their great Revenues" (80). Consensus between Catholics and Protestants is impossible, since the Catholics always "attribute only to themselves the glorious Name of the *True Church*, excluding all other Christians from it, but such as are of the same Communion with them" (81). Rather than the deliberation that Pufendorf regularly recommends to settle differences, the Catholic practice is "to endeavour to establish their Authority by all manner of violence against those, that dare to maintain Truth in opposition to their Doctrine. For which reason God has threatened in a most peculiar manner to destroy this Monster of a State" (81).

Should any Christian "prince" still hesitate as to the most just and politic choice between Protestant and Catholic ways, Pufendorfian counsel is forthcoming. The Protestants allow the laity to read the Bible for themselves so as to "make the Scriptures the Touchstone of their Doctrine, and the true Judge of their Controversies". By contrast:

> [I]n the Church of *Rome*, the Laity is not allowed the reading of the holy Scripture, nay, that they leave no stone unturn'd, to suppress the Validity of the holy Scripture; so, that in those places where the Inquisition is in vogue, a Man may with less danger be guilty of Blasphemy, Perjury, and the other most enormous crimes, than to read and examine the Mysteries of the holy Scripture. (110)

This devotional note is supplemented with a predictable reminder to the prince. Protestant clergy are "stinted in their Revenues" such that "their Persons and Estates depend from the Authority of their Sovereigns, neither have they anywhere else to seek for Protection". Conversely, "in what Pomp and affluence of Fortune does the *Popish* clergy live! Unto what height have they not exalted their Power in *Europe*! Have they not so ordered their Matters, as to be almost independent from the Civil Magistrates?" (111).

The political register intensifies with a warning against Catholic encroachments on the territorial sovereign's authority. The Roman Catholic clergy "by various Artifices and Intrigues … have at last patch'd up a Potent State of their own", with the Pope as their "Supream Head", exercising "an Absolute Authority of determining all Matters of Faith, by which means he is sure to guide the Minds of the People where ever he pleases" (113). The danger to civil order could not be greater:

> If any thing in the World is destructive to the Civil Powers, it must of necessity be this, when a Party inhabiting their Territories, disown their Jurisdiction and depending from a Foreign Power; deny the Authority of their Natural Prince over them, or at least acknowledge it no longer than they think it convenient. If Neighbouring States are commonly the most jealous of one another, must it not be look'd upon as a great Solecism of State, to permit such as depend from a Foreign Jurisdiction to abide in the Commonwealth. (113)

Adding that this is "next door to taking Foreign Garisons into our forts", Pufendorf reminds his readers that the Roman "Ecclesiastical State" drains away the material wealth of the princely territory. What is more, it claims legal authority to "inflict Punishments upon the Subjects, and to absolve them from their Allegiance due to their Sovereign" (113).

Alongside this sustained polemic against Catholic ambition in general, *De habitu* targets the specific case of France. In fact, Pufendorf offers more than denigration. Mindful of the French state's many historical clashes with Rome, he verges on complimenting a Gallican church's efforts at independence from the "Popish Monarch". Discussing the advisory role of expert councils in resolving doctrinal controversies, Pufendorf cannot resist the classic Gallican theme of "*The Council is above the Pope*", a theme that allows him to signal "somewhat of a Contradiction, that this Point is asserted by the self-same People, who make the Papal Chair the Center of the Church, and the Pope the Oecumenick Bishop" (84). This contradiction noted, an opportunistic French clergy gains only backhanded praise for their historical stance towards the ultramontane power:

> The *French* clergy allows the Pope to be the Supream Head of the Church, as far as they find it suitable with their Interest. But whenever he attempts anything against them, or the States Policy of that Kingdom, the old Song of the Liberty of the *Gallican* Church, and the antient Doctrine of the *Sorbone* is revived, which serves the *French* Clergy now and then for a Pretext, to persuade the vulgar sort of People, that the *Gallican* Church has not been polluted with those gross and abominable Errours as are introduced in the Church of *Rome*. (85)

This almost irenic tone is, however, the exception rather than the rule in *De habitu*.

The attack on France begins with generalities. Thus discussion of religion in the state of nature recognises that "as to the Mysteries of the Christian Religion ...

these must be acquired by the assistance of Divine Grace, which is contrary to all Violence". Then comes the political point:

> 'Tis true, a Prince may force a Subject to make an outward Confession by way of Mouth, to comply in his Behaviour, with his Commands, and to dissemble his Thoughts or to speak contrary to his Belief; but he can force no body to believe contrary to his own Opinion. (15)

The Louis of the mid-1680s – *rex christianissimus* – fitted this mould of a violent confessionalising prince, a tyrannical abuser of the sovereign office. Civil power is abused when used to enforce religion. Thus "whenever Sovereigns pretend to extend thus far their Authority, they transgress their Bounds; and if they inflict any Punishment on their Subjects, for refusing to be obedient to their Commands, on this Account; such an Act ought to be look'd upon as illegal, unjust, and tyrannical" (18).

Reference to French abuse can be more explicit. *De habitu* opens with a statement of its occasional (in the serious sense) nature, being undertaken "at this juncture of Time, when not only the *Romish Priests* apply all their Cunning for the rooting out of the *Protestants*, but also some of the greatest Princes in Christendom (setting aside the Antient way of Converting People by Reason and force of Arguments) have now recourse to open Violence; and by Dragooning, force their miserable Subjects to a religion, which always appear'd abominable to them" (12). Having observed that Christ the teacher used no external coercion, Pufendorf writes: "It was not God Almighty's pleasure to pull People head-long into Heaven, or to make use of the new French way of Converting them by Dragoons" (33). Louis XIV's deployment of *dragonnades* against the Huguenots (the billeting of soldiers in Protestant households in the Midi, Languedoc and Béarn since the early 1680s, these "dragoons" having full freedom to "convert" by any means that came to hand) provides the occasion for a leading question:

> How can a Prince be esteemed to follow the Foot-steps of Christ, who makes such profligate Wretches as the Dragoons his Apostles, for the Conversion of his Subjects? That Pretence of the Love of Sovereigns toward their Subjects, let it be never so specious, he ought not under that colour endeavour to subvert or alter the Method of propagating the Christian Doctrine, according to the true Genius of the Christian Religion. (105)

No less contrary to this "true Genius" is the stretching of "the Power of Sovereigns to such a pitch, as to make them the absolute Judges of the Christian Religion … and to force upon their Subjects a certain Religion, under severe Penalties, or oblige them either to profess or deny certain Points of Doctrine, which are controverted amongst Christians" (103).

For all their traditional loyalty to the monarch, the Huguenots of France were now victims of forced expulsion. "What Prince", Pufendorf asks rhetorically, "can be so unreasonable, as to expect that his Subjects should Sacrifice their Souls to the Devil for his sake" (119). The answer follows: "That Prince therefore who does trouble to his faithful Subjects for no other reason, but because they cannot conform to his Opinion (especially if they can maintain theirs out of the Holy Scripture) commits an Act of Injustice; Nay, I cannot see how he can with Justice force them out of his Territories" (119). Forced expulsion of "an in-born Natural Subject" is termed "the greatest Injustice in the World" (120). The hyperbole rests on dual ground. Not only is divine justice violated, but so too are the civil laws:

> A much greater Obligation lies upon Sovereigns to tolerate Dissenters, if they, when they first submitted to the Government, had their Liberty of Conscience granted them by Contract; or have obtain'd it afterwards by certain Capitulations, any following Statutes, or by the fundamental Laws of the Land. (108)

All such positive laws, Pufendorf adds, ought to be "sacred" to the prince, to be observed by him with no less care than he demands from an obedient citizen. The Huguenots were precisely the beneficiaries of such a contract: the Edict of Nantes that had survived various rescissions – until 1685.

A final point about *De habitu*. Dedicated to Prince-Elector Friedrich-Wilhelm as the presumptive leading defender of European Protestantism in the face of an advancing Franco-Catholic enemy, Pufendorf could not deny a substantial role for the sovereign regarding religion – and this despite his radical "separationist" thesis on the relation of state and church. In becoming a Christian, the sovereign bears "certain Obligations, which owe their off-spring to the union of that Duty, which is incumbent to every Christian, with that of the Royal Office" (94). The principal obligation is to be "Defenders of the Church", an obligation exercised in matters such as determining which wrongs are justiciable under civil laws, and which pass to the jurisdiction of ecclesiastical courts. Policing the boundary line becomes critical if ever the sovereign uses force (in the manner of Louis XIV's dragooning) to achieve religious ends. The sovereign may not enforce religion. Yet use of force to protect public tranquillity – and to protect those of the "true" religion – is justified.

How does Pufendorf cut this knot for the benefit of Friedrich-Wilhelm? One move is to envisage a basic form of Christian faith known through natural reason, an as yet undenominated "Natural Religion" to which all can adhere, and in defence of which the sovereign can deploy worldly power, including banishment:

> Neither can it be called in question, but that Christian Sovereigns have a Right to inflict Civil Punishments upon such as revile the whole System of the Christian Religion, and ridicule the Mysteries of the Christian Faith, at least, they may Banish them the Country. (103)

We are thus to distinguish between Louis expelling Huguenots (an action backed by sheer violence) and "Christian Sovereigns" banishing those who have engaged in "Idolatry, Blasphemy, Profanation of the Sabbath" (103). Small wonder, as Pufendorf then warns, that "nevertheless great care is to be taken" in such actions against those who thus "strike at the very Foundation of Civil Societies".

At stake is peaceful coexistence in multi-confessional settings. Facing the fact of Christian division, Pufendorf contemplates a desire for religious unity. Cautiously, he envisages a non-controversial "minimalist" creed. He takes steps to de-dramatise the religious question, suggesting that princes confronted by diversity of confessions should cool their fears:

> [I]t is not absolutely necessary to maintain the Publick Tranquillity, that all the Subjects in general should be of one Religion, or, which is the same in effect, the differences about some Points in Religion, considered barely as such, are not the true causes of Disturbances in a State. (105)

Rather, what causes real civil disturbance is the "perverted Zeal of some, who make these Differences their Tools". Thus "what should move a Prince to disturb his good Subjects upon the score of Differences in Opinion, as long as they live quietly under his Government? For, supposing their Opinion to be erroneous, it is not at his, but their own Peril, and they alone must be answerable for it" (106).

A like appeal for some princely indifference to religious difference had been made earlier in *De habitu*, to the effect that the state need concern itself only with the "outward" conduct of citizens. If anyone "should attempt to deny publickly the Existence of a God" or to "set up plurality of Gods", the civil sovereign must sanction them. Yet "if these [actions] are kept within the compass of Peoples Thoughts, without breaking out into publick or outward Actions, they are not punishable by the Law" (20). Thus, while uniformity of religion could remain desirable, "Sovereigns need not be so very anxious on this Account, because these Differences do not Overturn religion it self ... Neither can Sovereigns be any great Loosers by the Bargain, if their Subjects differ in some Ceremonies" (20–21). Under this calming shield Pufendorf places not only atheism and polytheism, but also idolatry, blaspheming and devil-worship, as long as these remain harmless private acts.

Yet the very fact that the civil sovereign must protect the public peace has furnished certain persons with a "specious Pretence", namely to claim that religious conformity may be justifiably enforced so as "to extirpate these Differences in Religion" by any means, "tho' never so violent":

> They alledge, that as much more precious our Souls are before our Bodies, the more Sovereigns are obliged to be watchful over them; and, that the true Love which a Sovereign bears to his Subjects, can never be more conspicuous, than when he takes effectual care of their Salvation. (104–5)

If certain princes have accepted "these plausible Arguments", it was because they have been "prevailed upon to assist with their Authority the cruel Designs of Priests". If this Pufendorfian statist and therefore secularising account affords an alibi for a territorial prince as dangerous to Protestant Europe as Louis XIV appeared to be in 1685, it lay in his royal office having fallen into the hands of evil clerical counsellors

The final section of *De habitu* explains that the "certain Proverb among the *Germans*, viz. *He that Commands the Country, Commands Religion* … cannot be applied to the Princes of the *Roman Catholick Religion*, who cannot lay any Claim to it, it being evident that the Popish Clergy do not allow any such thing to these Princes" (120). By contrast, when the "Protestant Estates of *Germany*" cited the principle of *cuius regio eius religio*, they did so for a quite different, praiseworthy and non-French reason:

> That they denied the Emperor to have any Power of intermeddling in the Affairs of their own Dominions, not, that only they claim'd it as belonging to the Rights of Sovereignty to impose any Religion, tho' never so false, upon their Subjects. (120)

We must imagine Friedrich-Wilhelm – a Calvinist territorial prince confronting the resistance of noble estates that were predominantly Lutheran – reading this happily.

The strategic issue of Protestant defence continued to focus Pufendorf's attention beyond the immediate response in *De habitu* to the revocation of the Edict of Nantes. Published in 1695, one year after his death, *Jus feciale divinum sive de consensu et dissensu protestantium exercitatio posthuma* (*The Divine Feudal Law; or, Covenants With Mankind, Represented Together With the Means for the Uniting of Protestants*) proposed grounds for Calvinists and Lutherans to set aside their history of mutual antipathy so as to protect a common Protestant interest against the uneliminated Catholic threat. Catholics remained beyond the civil pale, being judged incapable of loyal obedience to the civil sovereign and therefore incapable of peaceful coexistence. In *Jus feciale*, once more against the historical backdrop of confessional conflict, Pufendorf advocated the supreme civil norm of "Publick Peace":

The Lutheran Princes urged, that although it was not to be denied but these [Reformed] Men dissented from them in some Things, yet they should not be excluded from the Publick Peace, especially since there might be some Hope that they might forsake their Errors, and return to their former Communion.[9]

But encouraged by the Papists, the Lutherans proceeded to oppress the Calvinists, who formed themselves into fighting leagues such that this "gave Matter for a horrid Civil War". Only the Osnabrück treaty afforded a measure of peace. Yet Pufendorf remained concerned with the civil order confronted by religious differences to the end. Thus, in *Jus feciale*, to better ensure the well-being of the state, he accords civil standing only to those who have "no Principles of Religion, which are contrary to the Peace and Safety of the State, nor such as are apt and tending in their own Nature to create Troubles and Commotions in the Commonwealth".[10]

Pufendorf's Pre-1685 Perspective on France

Viewing post-1685 Catholic France through the alienated German Protestant eyes of the Pufendorf of *De habitu*, might offer the advantage of what Bertolt Brecht would term a "distancing effect". But it also has a disadvantage: it risks flattering the Anglophone disposition – a residual Protestant empathy with oppressed Huguenots – to reduce the political-legal history of pre-Revolution France to the brutalism of an absolutist Louis XIV.

In 1682–85, however, this was not at all the picture painted by Pufendorf in his role as a political historian. His *Einleitung* or *Introduction to the History of the Principal Kingdoms and States of Europe* treats the religious civil wars that had torn France, recognising how under François II "the French Divisions began to break out with Fury in their own Bowels, which continued near 40 Years".[11] The Huguenots, he records, "laboured then under a severe Persecution, and wanted a Head, under whose Conduct they might obtain the free Exercise of their Religion" (187). Principal events of the French wars of religion are cited: the 1561 Colloque

---

[9] Samuel Pufendorf, *Jus feciale divinum sive de consensu et dissensu protestantium exercitatio posthuma /The Divine Feudal Law: Or, Covenants with Mankind, Represented Together with the Means for the Uniting of Protestants*, trans. T. Dorrington (London, 1703), p. 198.

[10] Pufendorf, *Jus feciale divinum /The Divine Feudal Law*, p. 15.

[11] Samuel Pufendorf, *Einleitung zu der Historie der vornehmsten Reiche und Staaten so itziger Zeit in Europa sich befinden/An Introduction to the History of the Principal Kingdoms and States of Europe*, trans. J. Crull, 8th edn (London, 1719), p. 185. In this section, further references to this work of Pufendorf give page numbers only.

de Poissy, the Edict of January 1562, the Guise massacre of Huguenots at Vassy as "the first Blood shed in this civil War" (188), and the St Bartholomew's Day Massacre.

Pufendorf's characterisation of the *politiques* is interesting as a political reflection on the question of religion: from 1573 "a third Faction arose in France, which was call'd, *That of the Politicians*; they pretended, without having any regard to the Religious Differences, to seek the Public Welfare" and "were afterwards very instrumental in helping Henri IV to the Crown" (190). This is scarcely Protestant propaganda directed against France. Indeed, we note the comment on the "famous Edict of Nantes, as it is called, by virtue of which [the Huguenots] have hitherto enjoyed the free Exercise of Religion" (198). "Hitherto" must mean until 1682–85. Confirmation follows with a description of the Huguenots' then contemporary situation under Louis XIV: "And tho' the King hitherto does not force their Consciences, yet he draws off a great many from that Party, by hopes of his Royal Favours and Preferments" (214). Here Pufendorf is not yet the future partisan Protestant of *De habitu*. Indeed, he writes that under Louis XIII it was the Huguenots who "grew stiffer and more violent" (199), leaving the task of "extirpating the intestine Evils of France" to the statecraft of Richelieu:

> He laid this down as a Fundamental Principle, that he should take from the *Huguenots* the Power of doing any Mischief, considering that such as were dissatisfied at any time, or were of a Turbulent Spirit took always refuge, and were afflicted by them. (200)

Pufendorf's own "princely absolutist" tendency allows him to recognise that, in France, thanks to Richelieu, the nobles "now ... dare not utter a Word against the King" (213). French strength is recognised but not condemned: "it is easily perceiv'd that there is not any State in Christendom which *France* does not equal, if not exceed, in Power" (214).

In the Preface to his *History*, Pufendorf advised that "What I have related concerning the Interest of each State, is to be consider'd as relating chiefly to the Time when I compos'd this Work" (np). Perhaps this disclaimer provides some dispensation for his pre-1685 perspective on a France whose exercise of hegemonic power, as the super-state of the Westphalian settlement, he appears fully to have accepted. Yet compared to the virulent anti-French polemic of *De habitu*, this earlier account of France as the dominant power is benign, even shockingly so. That there was a swing from positive to negative perspectives on French hegemony after the revocation of the Edict of Nantes is beyond question.

De habitu exemplifies the panic-polemic publications that swept through the Protestant media after 1685. Rather than retelling that familiar story, however, can we instead construct the political rationality of Pufendorf's previously positive perspective on France, in relation to a French capacity for hegemonic intervention at Westphalia? As noted, he credits Richelieu with "extirpating the intestine Evils of France", that is, with confronting the horrors of religious civil war, establishing stable government and providing a unifying measure of civil peace. These are in fact crucial norms for Pufendorf's own 1670s re-thinking of the natural law tradition.

In Hermann Weber's once revisionist but now acceptable account, Richelieu gained recognition as a key peace-making figure in seventeenth-century Europe.[12] For Weber, the Cardinal's enduring goal was to secure "une bonne paix en toute la Chréstienté", that is, a "framework ... and yardstick for all practical peace policies" as formulated in the general directive for the Westphalian negotiations.[13] Implementation of such policies as credible rules of settlement would rest on "a group of forces with France at its centre [that] would serve as a counterweight to Habsburg predominance".[14] That the protective framework for an "ordered peace" under French hegemony had to be political and legal in character, not confessional, would have proved most amenable to the Pufendorf of *De jure*.

It is true that in Weber's assessment Richelieu's peace policy of the 1620s "fitted perfectly into a theocentric world-view and was in accord with the will of God for order". An "ultimate re-establishment of the confessional unity of Christendom" was deferred, but not abandoned.[15] For Richelieu, "*homo politicus* never excluded *homo religiosus*", such that "in his theologically oriented view of the temporal world's duty to create order, the dimensions of peace extended well beyond the merely political".[16] In Pufendorf's normative schema, too, divine sovereignty was indeed a given.

---

[12] While Hermann Weber made the case for granting a serious measure of respectability to Richelieu's imaginative diplomacy for peace in Europe, there is now less need to whitewash the Cardinal as precursor of a "balance of powers" solution for the European states system. For a current assessment of Richelieu as agent of a *pax honesta*, see Christoph Kampmann's "Peace impossible? The Holy Roman Empire and the European state system in the seventeenth century" (in the present volume), with specific reference to the 1636 French refusal, despite duress, to negotiate a "dishonourable" peace with Spain. Restrictive conditions applied to peace, as to war.

[13] Hermann Weber, "'Une bonne paix'. Richelieu's foreign policy and the peace of Christendom", in Joseph Bergin and Laurence Brockliss (eds), *Richelieu and his Age* (Oxford, 1992), pp. 46–7. As set out in Richelieu's *Instructions pour Messieurs les Ambassadeurs de France, envoyéez à Cologne pour le Traité de Paix générale*.

[14] Weber, "'Une bonne paix'. Richelieu's foreign policy and the peace of Christendom", p. 48.

[15] Weber, "'Une bonne paix'. Richelieu's foreign policy and the peace of Christendom", p. 51.

[16] Weber, "'Une bonne paix'. Richelieu's foreign policy and the peace of Christendom", p. 67.

In concrete political terms, fashioning a common front for peace against Spain entailed French *ad hoc* alliances with Protestant powers including England, Sweden and the Netherlands, and with certain Protestant States of the German Empire, not least Brandenburg. Strategic non-confessional "coalitions" thus underpinned this "first practical attempt at a peaceful solution for the whole of Europe".[17] Peace was not made contingent on first settling the intractable issue of religious truth.

Moreover, since "it was of decisive importance that the *state* of peace should last",[18] collective action for a secure peace did not end with a treaty ending the war. It was to be extended into a new arrangement whereby France as hegemon would guarantee future collective security in Christian Europe:

> The "paix sûre" thus had a triple basis: it required the participation of all the states of Christendom in setting up the treaty; it could rely on a guarantee based on international law and given by all the contending parties; it preserved the option of military intervention for France. In this manner lasting peace was to be established: peace for the whole of Christendom. Because the option of military intervention was preserved, the French king maintained his dominant role as the chief protector of Christendom – as it was unambiguously formulated in the preamble to the general directive.[19]

Such was the theory. In the event, the "whole of Christendom" did not sign up, nor did the two collective security "leagues" or blocs (German and Italian) envisaged by Richelieu come into being. Instead, despite intentions, Westphalia set the scene for territorial state independence.

Pufendorf's own overriding commitment to civil peace could therefore find its counterpart in essentials of Richelieu's peace policy: an exchange of obedience for protection by a hegemonic power, and a framework for a politically, and legally, grounded "ordered peace", enforceable by that power through the deliberative decision-making of Westphalia.

Yet given the political complexities of the German Empire, the disposition of a radically anti-Catholic territorial statist with absolutist leanings such as Pufendorf was never going to be simple. If Westphalia was a French-brokered pact whose political ordering of civil peace he endorsed, it nonetheless enabled foreign interventions into German affairs, as signalled in his 1667 *De statu imperii*

---

[17] Weber, "'Une bonne paix'. Richelieu's foreign policy and the peace of Christendom", p. 56.

[18] Weber, "'Une bonne paix'. Richelieu's foreign policy and the peace of Christendom", p. 57.

[19] Weber, "'Une bonne paix'. Richelieu's foreign policy and the peace of Christendom", pp. 60–61.

Germanici.[20] Here Pufendorf identified this risk to German states' territorial integrity with the ambivalent consequences of their capacity to enter into pacts with foreign powers:

> The Princes of *Germany* enter into Leagues, not only with one another, but with Foreign Princes too, and the more securely, because they have reserved to themselves a Liberty to do so in the Treaty of Westphalia, which not only divides the Princes of *Germany* into Factions, but gives those Strangers an Opportunity to mould *Germany* to their own particular Interest and Wills.[21]

This patriotic-xenophobic stance, however, found no echo in Pufendorf's history of the French state.

A positive Pufendorfian perspective on pre-1685 French hegemony could be further constructed through his characterisation of the *politiques* or his references to the Colloque de Poissy and the Edict of January. It would be a matter of recording the *politique* role of Gallican Catholic moderates in the Parlement de Paris, or the peace-broking initiatives of Charles IX's Chancellor, Michel de l'Hospital, who in the encroaching shadow of religious war put the case for civil peace. Speaking on 26 August 1561 to the States-General assembled at St-Germain-en-Laye, L'Hospital first recognised as fact the new "diversity of religions". Regretting the strife now flowing from this Christian division, he then indicated his wish to address "not the controversies of religion … but only what pertains to police, in order to contain the people in rest and tranquillity". Finally, L'Hospital proposed a civil logic that might govern religious plurality peacefully:

> The King does not want you to engage in dispute over which [religious] opinion is the best; for here it is not a question of establishing the faith, but of regulating the state. It is possible to be a citizen without being a Christian. Even the excommunicate does not cease to be a citizen. We can live in peace with those who hold to different opinions.[22]

---

[20] *De statu imperii Germanici* (*The Present State of Germany*) was published in 1667 under the pseudonym of Severinus de Monzambano, the author appearing in the guise of an Italian observer of the German Empire as an array of multiple competing mini-sovereignties marked by confessional disunity. Given the political weaknesses consequent upon this lack of unified sovereignty, Pufendorf contentiously assessed the Empire to be an "irregular" or "monstrous" state.

[21] Samuel Pufendorf [Severino de Manzambano], *De statu imperii Germanici /The Present State of Germany*, trans. E. Bohun (London, 1696), p. 182.

[22] Michel de L'Hospital, *Discours politiques, 1560–1568* (Clermont-Ferrand, 2001), p. 62.

The striking precept that "even the excommunicate does not cease to be a citizen" required the listeners to conceive a community of citizenship in the state as a neutral space of political governance, apart from the contested confessional domain. The following month at Poissy, facing forty Catholic clerics including the Cardinal of Lorraine and Diego Lainez, General of the Jesuits, and twelve Calvinists including the Genevan Théodore de Bèze, L'Hospital adopted again his pacificatory stance: "For the realm, peace is more important than dogma" (*Pour le royaume, la paix est plus importante que le dogme*). It could have been Samuel Pufendorf speaking, a century later.

Beyond Hegemony?

By 1687, Pufendorf's previous perspective on the rise of French power had sharply altered. Now the Protestant commentator in Brandenburg saw not a positive relation of force but the sectarian threat of a Franco-Catholic "universal monarchy". With this perceived mutation in the nature of French power came a conceptual question: At what point, theoretically speaking, does an ascending hegemon cross the threshold from being a Westphalian guarantor of a general peace in Christendom to become something else, a predatory *monarchia universalis* or, perhaps, a would-be "imperial" power? Hence my opening questions: Does this mutation signify a more intense exercise of hegemony, a difference of degree? Or does it signify a difference of kind, a different mode of domination exercised by a greater power over lesser states?

Reflection on a seventeenth-century state's mutation from protective hegemon to predatory universal monarchy is in part motivated by our own current experience. Like others here, I have lived under the military protectorate of the United States, first in London and later in Australia. The United States was the hegemonic power that had protected Europe against totalitarian threats – first the Nazis and then the post-war Soviet – and had established a general "ordered peace" by institutional means that included the United Nations, the Marshall Plan and Nato. More recently, the United States has seemed to many observers to have become something else: an omnipresent power that poses a general threat to peace by belligerent intervention everywhere. Hence the wholesale talk of "empire", "empire-lite", "liberal imperialism" and so on. How should this shift be characterised? Has an American hegemony become a more total domination, perhaps a current "unipolar" version of "universal monarchy" that employs war-making to improve the world in a domination reaching beyond the limits of protective hegemony?

But *comparaison ne fait pas raison*, particularly across centuries during which circumstances have greatly changed. While recognising that international law as such still has no enforcement mechanism against a hegemonic state, it would be anachronistic if not paranoiac to seek in today's geopolitical scene for exact equivalents to the modes of power exercised by seventeenth-century France. Better, then, return to the history of French hegemony and what, for Pufendorf, were its divergent projections of power.

In 1629 La Rochelle fell. With the Edict of Alès ending six years of war, Richelieu "demilitarised" the Huguenot party, voiding political-territorial entitlements granted to the latter under the Edict of Nantes. On the ground, inter-confessional tensions persisted: each sect disrupted the other's religious observances, a continuing battle of Calvinist psalms and Catholic church bells. There was mounting governmental action against "heretics". In 1665, the *Assemblée du clergé* submitted a consolidated list of demands for "anti-heretic" action to Louis XIV, whose personal rule had commenced only four years earlier. In 1676, King and clergy took a directly material approach to the problem of religious disunity: a *Caisse des conversions* would purchase the conversion of a Calvinist at a going rate of six *livres tournois* per turn. Paid apostasy proved not unsuccessful at least among the poor. By the early 1680s, with the *Assemblée du clergé* intensifying the demand for Catholic conformity, Louis moved from sweet commerce to coarse coercion as the better means to extirpate the Calvinist cult in France. The ferocity of the *dragonnades* (recorded in *De habitu*) became the savage emblem of this shift.

At Fontainebleau in October 1685 the order revoking the Edict of Nantes received the royal signature, its terms to go into effect immediately. Despite the apparent "toleration" granted in the twelfth and final article of the Edict of Fontainebleau, Huguenot abjurations followed and diaspora ensued.[23] The Edict and the King, its signatory, were celebrated by the great and the good, among them Racine, La Fontaine, Fénelon and Madame de Sévigné. In his January 1686 funeral oration for Le Tellier, Bishop Bossuet waxed hyperbolic in praise of the monarch: "Vous avez affermi la foi, vous avez exterminé les hérétiques: c'est le digne ouvrage de votre règne, c'en est le propre caractère. Par vous l'hérésie n'est plus: Dieu seul a pu faire cette merveille".[24] In the *intégriste* words of Louvois,

---

[23] The first clause of Article 12 of the Edict of Fontainebleau reads as follows:
Pourront au surplus lesdits de la R.P.R. [Religion Prétendue Réformée], en attendant qu'il plaise à Dieu de les éclairer comme les autres, de demeurer dans les villes et lieux de notre royaume, pays et terres de notre obéissance, y continuer leur commerce et jouir de leurs biens sans pouvoir être troublés ni empêchés sous prétexte de ladite R.P.R. à condition, comme il est dit, de ne point faire d'exercices ni de s'assembler sous prétexte de prières ou de culte de ladite religion de quelque nature qu'il soit, sous les peines ci-dessus de confiscation de corps et de biens.

In the the view of the Huguenots, the clause remained an empty formality.

[24] Bossuet, Jacques-Bénigne, *Oraisons funèbres de Bossuet* (Paris, 1837), p. 267.

Minister of State and of the *dragonnades*: "Tout est catholique". By 1687, Pufendorf's response to such claims of all-encompassing but coerced Catholic faith would find full-throated expression in the combative polemic of *De habitu*.

Not every voice in France remained so enraptured by the great event of 1685. Three decades later, the Duc de Saint-Simon reflected on the revocation of the Edict of Nantes with a disenchanted word on circumstances where "Le Roi était devenu dévot, et dévot dans la dernière ignorance".[25] The memorialist draws the picture of a Louis XIV blinded, by flattery and by his own religious pride, to Christ's way of converting heretics by love and teaching:

> On toucha un dévot de la douceur de faire au dépens d'autrui une pénitence facile, qu'on lui persuada sûre pour l'autre monde. On saisit l'orgueil d'un roi en lui montrant une action qui passait le pouvoir de tous ses prédécesseurs. ... On le détermina, lui qui se piquait si principalement de gouverner par lui-même, d'un chef-d'oeuvre tout à la fois de religion et de politique.[26]

In a precise reversal of the separation that Pufendorf endorsed, with the Edict of Fontainebleau the political was thus rejoined to the religious. In Saint-Simon's judgment, this was to the sharp detriment of the fortunes of the French state and its people. As for Louis XIV, "[il] s'applaudissait de sa puissance et de sa piété. Il se croyait au temps de la prédication des apôtres, et il s'en attribuait tout l'honneur".[27] Perhaps it is here, where a ruler is captured by messianic values and salvific voices appealing to his heightened sense of religious calling, that French political calculation favouring a European peace with honour fell victim to the counter imperative of a universal religious truth. At this threshold, with Samuel Pufendorf as contemporary witness, we could mark off a more predatory form of domination, with its resurgent universalist aspiration, from what had been a political exercise of protective hegemonic force.

---

[25] Duc de Saint-Simon, *Mémoires I* (Paris, 1990), p. 377.
[26] Saint-Simon, *Mémoires I*, pp. 378–9.
[27] Saint-Simon, *Mémoires I*, pp. 381–2.

Chapter 13
Colonial Design in European International Law of the Seventeenth Century[1]

Andrea Weindl

Introduction

Questioning the part played by non-European territories and peoples in the formation of international law of the seventeenth century, we may trace two different aspects. First, we will have to ask which role theoretical discussion in Europe provided for non-European political units within international law. This appears to be particularly worth pursuing with respect to the seventeenth century in view of the vivid discussion about the issue in the century before. Second, we may trace the political functionalising of non-European territories over which European states thought themselves to possess authority in interstate treaties within Europe.

In the following, I shall outline the main aspects of the issue. First, I give a short survey of the recognition of non-European political units as subjects of European international law that shows the extent to which European authorities concluded treaties with Non-European political leaders. Then I consider the theoretical discussion about the position of non-European peoples within European international law. Finally, I enlarge upon the development that brought the handling of non-European territories within the interstate policy inside Europe.

Non-European Political Units as Subjects of International Law

Although every now and then Europeans concluded treaties with political leaders in areas of the world discovered up to the seventeenth century, we may note different positions for different areas within European international law according to the degree of colonial penetration.

---

[1] For help in translating the German text into English, I am grateful to Mr Martin Steininger. I am of course fully responsible for any errors.

American societies were incorporated into the collective of Spanish or Portuguese subjects. They thereby lost their status as subjects of international law with their own scope. Although the respective colonial administrations in the course of protective legislation for the Indians restored some personal rights, the colonial administrations exercised all sovereign rights of indigenous societies. This was at least a claim of the Iberian powers directed against the expansive efforts of other European states, which was surely true in the Spanish American Empire's centres of power in Mexico and Peru. As a matter of fact, at the borders of the American Empire, the relationship between Europeans and American Indians were arranged according to the principles of interstate relations well until the era of independence. For example, in the south of their empire, the Spaniards fought for centuries against the Mapuche and concluded truces and peaces.[2] In their quarrels over Brazilian territories, Portuguese and Dutch depended on the support of Indian allies, and mainly the Portuguese underlined their pretensions with the argument of stable alliances with local peoples. Land seizures by the British, Dutch and French had to take place along with treaties about land ownership, settling rights and political alliances, precisely because they had to be enforced against Spanish claims. If necessary, European rivals of Spain also used arguments based on international law. Thus, in his attack on Spanish overseas territory, Cromwell used (among other things) the argument that the Spanish did not respect the rights of the Indians. For his part, Cromwell aimed at a kind of right of representation of Indian interests by combining this argument with that of the infringement of British trading interests in America.[3] This shows that Cromwell did not take the recognition of American political units as subjects of international law seriously.

Completely different conditions existed in the European relationship to African and Asian territories. In the course of the seventeenth century, the efforts

---

[2] In the year 1641, the Mapuche obtained acceptance as an independent nation in the Treaty of Quillin, which remained valid until the independence of Chile. Between 1861 and 1883, the Mapuche state was overthrown by the independent state of Chile. See Hugo Rosati Aguerre, "El imperio español y sus fronteras: Mapuches y Chichimecas en la segunda mitad del siglo XVI", *Historia* 29 (1995–96): 391–404. Armando de Ramón, *Breve historia de Chile. Desde la invasion incaica hasta nuestros días (1500–2000)* (Buenos Aires, 2001).

[3] Cromwell justified his attack on Spanish-American territories in the following words:

... since God hath made of one blood, all Nations of men, for to dwell on all the face of the Earth, and hath determined the times before appointed, and the bounds of their habitation; And certainly, at one time or another, by some hand or other, God will have an accompt of the Innocent Blood of so many Millions of Indians, so barbarously Butchered by the Spaniards, and of the Wrong and Injustice that hath been done unto them (Quoted in Bernd Klesmann, *Bellum Solemne* (Mainz, 2007), p. 155).

to develop overseas trade of most west European countries were connected with the establishment of trading posts on the coast of West Africa. In Africa there were no land seizures in the sense of colonial occupation. The Europeans rather founded trading posts, which they provided, if allowed, with forts. Both for the foundation and for the maintenance or possible defence of the forts, they depended on the support of the Africans, with whose political leaders they concluded treaties. Europeans tried to secure the loyalty of their African partners by regular donations, which may surely be seen as tribute payments. African leaders used their alliances with the Europeans within the local political system. We do not know exactly how far Africans and Europeans were able to understand each others' mechanisms of authority and representation, but there are hints that both sides were aware of the "international" character of their relationship. Thus African princes occasionally travelled to European courts in order to strengthen their alliances with a particular monarch. Further, cases are known in which Africans who had been sold as slaves in the Caribbean had to be escorted back to Africa because they were members of noble families and could not to be enslaved.[4]

We can also detect the recognition of African political units as subjects of international law in the practice and discussion of slave trade. Juan de Solórzano y Pereyra, a lawyer in the Spanish Indian council, declared that blacks were sold into slavery or volunteered or were taken as captives of just wars among themselves, so that it was legal to draw on their services in Spain or America.[5] This line of argument included the approval of African communities as subjects of international law and, in principle, all European states agreed on this attitude until the proscription of the slave trade in the nineteenth century.

---

[4] See, for example, Clarence J. Munford, *The Black Ordeal of Slavery and Slave Trading in the French West Indies 1625–1715* (2 vols, Lewiston, 1991), vol. I: "Slave trading in Africa", pp. 174–5; Peter Martin, *Schwarze Teufel, edle Mohren* (Hamburg, 1993), p. 86.

[5] In his own words:

A lo cual no contradice la práctica, que vemos tan asentada, é introducida de los esclavos Negros, que se traen de Guinéa, Cabo Verde, y otras Provincias, y rios, y pasan por tales sin escrupúlo en España, y en las Indias. Porque en estos vamos con buena fé, de que ellos se venden por su voluntad, ó tienen justas guerras entre sí, en que se cautivan unos á otros, y á estos cautivos los venden despues á los Portugueses, que nos los traen, que ellos llaman Pombeyros ó Tangomangos, como lo dicen Navarro, Molina, Revelo, Mercado, y otros Autores; concluyendo finalmente, que todavía tienen por harto peligrosa, escrupulosa, y cenagosa esta contratación, por los fraudes, que en ella de ordinario se suelen cometer, y cometen, pero éstas no les toca á los particulares averiguarlas (Juan de Solorzano y Pereyra, *Política Indiana* (Madrid, 1930 [1648]), vol. 1, p. 138).

A similar argument is made by an unknown speaker of the Indian Council, who in 1685 outlined the legal questions in connection with slavery. See Georges Scelle, *La Traite negrière aux Indes de Castille. Contrats et Traités d'assiento* (2 vols, Paris, 1906), vol. 1, Appendix Doc. 34: "Consulte du conseil des Indes sur la légitimité du trafic négrier".

In Asia, the European naval powers found an international system of "multiple staged relationships of tributes and vassals that resembled international relations formed by feudalism of the European middle ages".[6] For the permission to trade and to build trading posts in the sixteenth and seventeenth centuries, Europeans had to fit themselves into that system, so that from an Asian point of view Europeans entered into a kind of vassal relationship to them by paying tribute or obtaining unilateral privileges. In territories with a minor degree of political organisation, these relations could be inverted, as shown by the example of the Dutch policy of destruction and resettlement in some of the Molucca islands. Moreover, the Portuguese, according to their cartaz system, were able to bring a part of the maritime trade under tribute relations to their own benefit. Nevertheless, in general the Europeans had to adapt to the conditions of Asian international law. In European debates about international law, therefore, Asia mainly appeared in the context of granting a trade monopoly in certain areas against other European rivals or postulating the right to conclude treaties with local leaders in territories claimed by the Portuguese king.

The European Debate Over the Legal Status of Non-European Dominions

In general, legal titles for land seizures outside Europe were not at the centre of debates about international law in the seventeenth century. Even though not only Protestant powers[7] challenged the authority of the Pope over undiscovered territories, the claim to universality by Christendom or the mission to instruct the heathen remained the foundation for land seizures that were mainly carried out in America. In Europe, however, almost nobody questioned the right of the Spanish and Portuguese kings to rule over territories that their subjects had effectively taken possession of. Claims to the possession of territories not actually seized remained in dispute, that is, scholars and naval powers consistently denied the right to set up trade monopolies not only for certain trading posts but also

---

[6] Jörg Fisch, *Die europäische Expansion und das Völkerrecht* (Stuttgart, 1984), p. 37 (Transl. by A.W.).

[7] The fact that Portugal and Spain secured claims assigned by the Pope through an interstate treaty suggests the diminishing arbitral authority of the Vatican in the process of European state building. In another bill of 1506, however, the Pope approved the treaty of Tordesillas. See "Vertrag von Tordesillas 1494 VI 7, Spanien Portugal", in Heinz Duchhardt, Martin Peters (ed.), www.ieg-mainz.de/friedensvertraege (viewed 29 Feb. 2008). See Hans Jürgen Prien, "Las Bulas Alejandrinas de 1493", in Bernd Schröter, Karin Schüller (ed.), *Tordesillas y sus consecuencias. La política de las grandes potencias europeas respecto a América Latina (1494–1898)* (Frankfurt am Main, 1995), p. 18. France also questioned the Pope's power to dispose over territories not yet discovered.

for whole continents. In addition, in light of shrinking Spanish political and military power, overseas territories became entangled in European politics, so that northwestern European nations used different lines of argument depending upon their relationship to Spain.

Still, during the sixteenth century, the English crown had sent out expeditions to America to discover and settle new territories. The charters issued by the English crown were geared in principle to the language of the papal bull *Inter caetera*. Based on the English monarch's title as head of Anglican Church, the expeditions were sent with the command to preach to all nations and to colonise lands that were not occupied by other Christian princes. Apart from the disavowal of arbitration by the Pope, there was therefore no difference from the Iberian attitude. There existed a right (and the duty) to a Christian mission, namely where no other Christian prince performed this task.[8] Somewhat different were the efforts of some French Huguenot to found a colony in Brazil that would be safe from religious persecution. That they could be driven out very easily by the Portuguese may be attributed to lack of support from their mother country.[9]

Besides these land seizures, by which France and England challenged the right to claim whole continents under the title of a papal donation, it was mainly the American territories that were exposed to the vicissitudes of European politics from the beginning of the conquest. Until the peace of Cateau-Cambrésis (1559), the antagonism between Spain and France was accompanied by fierce attacks on Spanish settlements and trade ships in the Atlantic by French Corsairs. In their fight against domination by the Spanish Habsburgs, the Dutch also attacked Spanish overseas territories, a practice they were happy to extend to Portuguese territories in Africa, Asia and America after the union of the Iberian crowns. Politico-philosophical treatises written to support theoretical claims accompanied the military conflict, but, depending on the case, they could be diametrically opposed to reasons of state.

Thus Hugo Grotius's treatise *Mare liberum*, in which he advocated the freedom of the seas as a universal principle (that is, the right of all men to free navigation and trade), might be seen as a request, which different states pursued at most half-heartedly in regard to their own interests. The history of the book's origin and circulation already bears effective witness to this supposition: In 1603, a Dutch squadron captured the rich Portuguese carrack Santa Catarina in the Singapore Straits in reaction to various naval actions of the Portuguese against Dutch efforts to establish trade relations in the Far East. Crew and passengers were set free

---

[8] See James Muldoon, "Christendom, the Americas, and World Order", in Horst Pietschmann, *Atlantic History. History of the Atlantic System 1580–1830* (Göttingen, 2002), pp. 73–5.

[9] See Günther Kahle, *Lateinamerika in der Politik der europäischen Mächte 1492–1810* (Köln, Weimar, Wien, 1993), pp. 17–19.

and ship and freight were auctioned in the Netherlands at a great profit. On 9 September 1604, the Council of Admiralty decided that the capture of the Santa Catarina was lawful and that therefore the ship and freight were a "good prize". Notwithstanding, the lawfulness of the capture remained a topic of debate in the Netherlands. Some members of the United East Indian Company (VOC) resigned from the company because they objected to its militarisation. The VOC then commissioned the young lawyer Hugo Grotius to compose a legal opinion confirming the lawfulness of the prize capture. The Grotius's expert opinion formulated the principle of the freedom of the seas. Grotius acknowledged explicitly the sovereignty rights of East Indian princes. The Dutch VOC could conclude commercial treaties with East Asian princes only on the assumption that they were subjects of international law with equal rights, which could be enforced against Portuguese claims.[10]

The expert opinion written in 1604–1605 remained unpublished for about 300 years. Parts of it, however, were published in 1609 under the title *Mare liberum sive de jure quod Batavis competit ad Indicana commercia dissertatio* shortly after the conclusion of the twelve year truce between the United Provinces and Spain. Appealing to the *jus gentium*, Grotius reasoned that navigation and trade should be free and that neither on the grounds of being the first discoverers nor of papal donation, war, seizure, prescription or custom did the Portuguese have an exclusive right to possession of the East Indies, or to regulate navigation or to trade there.[11]

In the year of the treatise's publication, James I forbade its sale in England. Three years later the Spanish Inquisition placed the work on the Index. Grotius's treatise also provoked various objections. The Englishman John Selden advocated in 1635 the right of the states to rule over their surrounding waters. In connection with the later recognition of possession rights of non-European territories in inner European treaties, this argument led de facto to a vindication of overseas monopolies, even though Selden did not explicitly claim the lawfulness of dominion over non-European societies.[12] In a refutation of Grotius entitled *De justo imperio Lusitanorum Asiatico*, the Portuguese writer Seraphim de Freitas derived the right of the Portuguese to restrict the freedom of trade from the discovery of the sea routes, the treaties with local princes and the papal bulls. In this respect, the right to establish trading posts followed from the duty of Christian proselytising and the ability to fund this mission specified and sanctioned by the Pope. Interestingly, Freitas did not deny the Dutch a Protestant Christian right to

---

[10] See Fisch, *Die europäische Expansion und das Völkerrecht*, p. 251.

[11] See Jörg P. Hardegen "Einführung", in Seraphim de Freitas, *Über die rechtmässige Herrschaft der Portugiesen in Asien* ed. Jörg P. Hardegen (Kiel, 1976), pp. 18–29.

[12] See Jörg Fisch, *Die europäische Expansion und das Völkerrecht* (Stuttgart, 1984), pp. 251–2.

proselytise in principle; rather, he considered the Dutch mission in opposition to the papal instruction.[13]

With respect to entitlements of non-European peoples and states, Freitas's distinction between Spanish and Portuguese entitlements is striking. Although the:

> Indians [he means the American Indians, A.W.] were deprived of their goods and forcibly and tyrannically pressed by the military leaders to accept the dominion of the Spanish kings against the intention, the will and the instructions of the Pope and the Spanish kings ... the Spaniards were entitled to govern the Indian territories [because] empires conquered by armed force are acknowledged in the course of time through approbation of the people.[14]

By contrast, the Portuguese did not need to invoke (following Vitoria) their fundamental right to enforce the preaching of the gospel at gunpoint because they did not attempt to establish dominion over a broad area. They waged war against Asian princes on the grounds of the same criteria as they waged war in Europe, namely because of breach of agreements or support for threatened allies.[15] Freitas assumed a fundamental right to demand submission only from Muslim princes, because on the one hand in former times they occupied territories possessed by Christians, and because on the other hand Muslims were themselves always prepared to make war on Christians.[16]

More important than the question of the status of non-European peoples in European international law of the seventeenth century was the problem of handling territories to which any European nation might claim a right to dispose over, whether in the form of effectively executed dominion or of trade and sea route monopolies. In the following, therefore, I shall describe the treatment of overseas territories within inner European treaties from the time of Grotius's

---

[13] See Freitas, *Über die rechtmässige Herrschaft der Portugiesen in Asien*, chap. VIII, 40/41.

[14] *Ibid.*, chap. XII, 12, XII, 13 (Transl. by A.W.).

[15] See *ibid.*, chap. IX, 14–16.

[16] See *ibid.*, chap. IX, 10. For problems of international law between Muslim and Christian states that until now have been studied mainly with respect to the relationship between Europe and the Ottoman Empire, see Karl-Heinz Ziegler, "The peace Treaties of the Ottoman Empire with European Christian Powers", in Lesaffer, Randall, *Peace Treaties and International Law in European History* (Cambridge, 2004), pp. 338–61. Guido Komatsu, "Die Türkei und das europäische Staatensystem im 16. Jahrhundert. Untersuchungen zu Theorie und Praxis des frühneuzeitlichen Völkerrechts", in Christine Roll (ed.), *Recht und Reich im Zeitalter der Reformation: Festschrift für Horst Rabe* (Frankfurt am Main, 1997), pp. 121–44.

first formulation of the freedom of the seas to the Treaties of Utrecht, which provisionally ended the reshaping of global relationships of dominance.

Colonial Design in the Inner-European International Law

Up to the Peace of Westphalia, Spain had only a slight need to conclude agreements regarding overseas territories, since she was at war with the United Provinces as well as with France. One exception was the Twelve Year Truce, concluded with the States-General in 1609. The Truce was supposed to come into force in 1610, including in overseas territories. The trade with Spanish dominions in the East and West Indies was explicitly excluded from the freedom of trade broadly agreed upon. Indeed the States-General were able to stipulate a secret and separate article that allowed trade with princes outside Europe who issued a permit to this end. At the same time, the truce codified the right of the sovereigns to allow or forbid subjects of foreign powers to trade with their dominions outside Europe. This treaty admitted for the first time a monopoly trade with areas outside Europe to a non-Iberian power. Although at this time the United Provinces possessed only few bases overseas, the additional declaration (guaranteed by the French and English kings) amounted to the first recognition of non-Iberian trading posts.[17]

By contrast, in the treaty concluded between England and Spain in 1604 that ended the war started in the year of the Armada, overseas territories or the trade with them were not mentioned. The English side entered into negotiations demanding free trade in both Indies, but weakened this demand very quickly so as to receive permission to trade with territories not in Spanish possession, and finally settled for a formulation that omitted mention of overseas territories altogether. Trade was to be as free as before the war according to former treaties or "de uso y observancia".[18] Nevertheless, the treaty followed the inherent logic of

---

[17] See Corps *universel diplomatique du droit des gens; contenant un recueil des traitez d'alliance, de paix, de treve, de neutralité, de commerce, qui ont été faits en Europe, depuis le Règne de l'Empereur Charlemagne jusques présent* ed. J. Dumont (8 vols, 2 suppl., Den Haag, Amsterdam, 1739) vol. 5/2, p. 102. After forbidding the subjects of the States-General to trade in the Indian territories of the Spanish king without his permission, the declaration says: "Qu'il ne sera loisible aussi à ses Sujets [of the Catholic kings, A.W.] de trafiquer aux Ports, Lieux et Places que tiennent lesdits Sieurs Estats esdites Indes, si ce n'est avec leurs permission". Allegedly, the declaration was never ratified by the Spanish king. See Martine Julia Ittersum, *Profit and principle. Hugo Grotius, natural rights theories and the rise of Dutch power in the East Indies, 1595–1615* (Leiden, 2006), p. 357.

[18] This meant it was up to the English to prove that they had traded before the war with a place outside Europe. See Andrea Weindl, *Wer kleidet die Welt? Globale Märkte und merkantile Kräfte in der europäischen Politik der Frühen Neuzeit* (Mainz, 2007), pp. 87–93; "Tratado de Paz, Allianza y Comercio, entre el Senor Rey Catholico Don Phelipe III. y

English commercial interests in that the agreement admitted special conditions for English merchants with respect to intermediate trade to and from the Iberian Peninsula. They achieved an advantage in the trade with colonial goods over the merchants of the rebellious Dutch provinces, who suffered under trade embargos against Spain and Portugal. At this time the bulk of colonial goods from Asia and America were still brought to Seville and Lisbon and afterwards distributed via Antwerp or Amsterdam.[19] The importance of intermediate trade with Spain and Portugal by far outweighed any advantage to be gained by permission to sail to regions whose geographical position was not known exactly. Although the English argued against the binding character of the papal donation, they accepted the right of the princes to regulate the trade within their dominions. Even the line of argument used by Elisabeth I, namely that it was unintelligible why overseas territories should enjoy an exceptional position outside the general agreements about interstate trade, disappeared from the English conduct of negotiations.[20]

The treaty of 1604 was reinforced after a new military conflict between England and Spain in 1625–30, whereas the peace treaty of 1630 stipulated the same agreements for trade as sixteen years before. Indeed the treaty of 1630 extended the peace to American territories, that is, to territories beyond the Line of Demarcation.[21] Thus, along with the truce with the United Provinces eleven years before, this famous Line drawn in the middle of the Atlantic ocean, which had been bargained out in various treaties since the sixteenth century between Spain and France and which, according to Carl Schmitt, divided the world into a Europe ruled by international law and an unlegislated area to the west of the line, lost whatever significance it ever possessed. Of course Spain, threatened with the loss of its political and military power, reserved the right every now and then to ignore infringements in the American area in decisions about war and peace in Europe.[22] When the Spaniards considered themselves sufficiently

---

los Senores Archiduques Alberto, e Isabel Clara Eugenia sus Hermanos de una parte, y el Serenissimo Rey de Inglaterra Jacobo I. de la otra" Art. 9, in Joseph Antonio de Abreu y Bertodano, *Collección de los Tratados de Paz, Alianza, Neutralidad, Garantia, Protección, Tregua, Mediación, Accesion, Reglamento de Limites, Comercio, Navegación, &c. hechos por los Pueblos, Reyes y Principes de España* (25 vols, Madrid, 1740–1801), here vol. 1.

[19] See Oscar C. Gelderblom, "From Antwerp to Amsterdam, the contribution of merchants from the southern Netherlands to the commercial expansion of Amsterdam" (ca. 1540–1609), *Review* 26/3 (2003): 247–82.

[20] See (London) Public Record Office, State Papers 103/66/21.

[21] See "Tratado de Paz, Confederación, y Comercio entre el Rey D. Phelipe IV. y Carlos I. Rey de Gran Bretaña", 15.11.1630, Art. 2, in *Collección de los Tratados de Paz, Alianza, Neutralidad, Garantia ...*, vol. 2.

[22] The additional verbal agreement to the Treaty of Cateau Cambrésis 1559 or Vervins 1598 between France and Spain mentioned by Davenport, which limited the peace to Europe, should be seen in this context. Significantly, there exists no consensus as

strong, however, they connected American concerns with European politics. A truce with the Dutch at least had to slow up if not cut off the Dutch expansion in the East and West Indies. Otherwise it would be worthless to Spain. It would have meant ceding to the Dutch the trade with Spain that the Spanish administration looked upon as pivotal for Dutch economic prosperity, and at the same time opening overseas territories, which made this trade so important for Europe, to conquest.[23] This was also true for the relationship between Spain and England, as Spanish diplomats were to discover in the course of the century.[24] The phrase "no peace beyond the Line" was not relevant in the seventeenth century, even if in 1634 Richelieu approved permission for French subjects to attack Spanish and Portuguese ships beyond the Line.[25] Since the beginning of the century, America had been included in European peace treaties. Even breaches of the peace that could or should not be punished for political reasons did not change this fact.[26]

References to non-European territories in truces, peaces or alliances, by which the Dukes of Bragança accompanied the struggle for Portuguese independence after Portugal's defection from Spanish crown, were even more precise. Whenever necessary, the Portuguese administration bartered the recognition or sometimes the possession of overseas territories for an assumed or real support for Portuguese independence. For the naval powers, this turned out to be the gateway to possessions in Asia, Africa or America in accordance with the international law. It is no wonder then that mainly the naval powers were interested in Portuguese independence. Although the Dutch often attacked Portuguese overseas territories, the United Provinces, with their long fight for independence from the Spanish Habsburg,

---

to when this article was stipulated because it was never set forth in writing. See Fisch, *Die europäische Expansion und das Völkerrecht*, pp. 146–7; also Gundolf Fahl, *Der Grundsatz der Freiheit der Meere in der Staatenpraxis von 1493–1648* (Köln, 1969), pp. 54–63. Fahl mentions some indirect sources of reference to the line expressly stipulated.

[23] During the negotiations for a truce, the VOC advocated a continuation of war in the East Indies or total free trade. The Spanish administration could not agree with either proposal. See Martine Julia Ittersum, *Profit and principle. Hugo Grotius, natural rights theories and the rise of Dutch power in the East Indies, 1595–1615* (Leiden, 2006), p. 280. Kahle, *Lateinamerika in der Politik der europäischen Mächte*, pp. 12–16; Hans-Otto Kleinmann, "Der atlantische Raum als Problem des europäischen Staatensystems", *Jahrbuch für Geschichte von Staat, Wirtschaft und Gesellschaft Lateinamerikas* 38 (2001): 7–30. Jörg Fisch, *Die europäische Expansion und das Völkerrecht* (Stuttgart, 1984), pp. 25–8, 146–52.

[24] See Weindl, *Wer kleidet die Welt?*, p. 173.

[25] Fisch, *Die europäische Expansion und das Völkerrecht*, p. 117.

[26] It has to be admitted that only in 1684 did a treaty between France and Spain also stipulate a truce in America. See *European Treaties bearing on the History of the United States and its dependencies*, ed. by F.G. Davenport (4 vols, Washington, 1917–37), vol. I and II. See also the contribution of Luc Foisneau in this volume.

seemed natural allies to the Duke of Bragança in the Portuguese struggle. Both countries therefore concluded a commercial treaty in 1641, combining it with a truce concerning overseas possessions and an alliance in Europe. In this treaty the Portuguese accepted for the first time, even if only temporarily, Dutch colonies and trading posts in territories claimed by Portugal and thus bartered for military support in Europe.[27] Whereas France and Sweden, without interests in Portuguese territories, bartered their support for the Duke of Bragança in exchange for breaking up the Spanish trade embargos in Europe,[28] the treaty between Portugal and the United Provinces brought the keenest commercial rival of the latter into action. The peaceful use of American colonies by the Dutch resulted for the first time in the legal importation of American colonial goods directly to central Europe and endangered the position of English merchants in the European intermediate trade, which the English had secured through their previously mentioned treaties with Spain. Thus, although Charles I (already in a precarious political situation at home) did not achieve a sustainable success in his demand for free trade with Brazil and with the East Indies in Portuguese possession in his commercial treaty with Portugal of 1642, he did found a long-lasting Portuguese-English alliance that survived all domestic and external vicissitudes. Only a few years later this alliance secured the British grip on overseas territories in accordance with international law, because Great Britain largely succeeded in maintaining a good relationship with Portugal without being forced to war with Spain.

First, however, in the Peace of Westphalia the United Provinces compelled Spain to recognise all their possessions in America, Africa and Asia, while avoiding mention of their geographical situation. A European treaty was one thing; local facts could change very quickly. The treaty explicitly mentions only the territories in Brazil, which had been recaptured by the Portuguese and their allies in 1648,

---

[27] Although the Dutch Republic had to abandon their colonies in Brazil in 1654, most former Portuguese territories in Asia remained in Dutch hands. Responsible for the conquest were the Dutch overseas companies, whose claims were fixed in international treaties. See for example "Waffenstillstand und Beistandspakt von Den Haag, Generalstaaten, Portugal 1641 VI 12", in www.ieg-mainz.de/friedensvertraege (viewed 28 Feb. 2008).

[28] It seems that at the Munster negotiations France, Sweden and even the Netherlands sacrificed overseas interests in their efforts to reach an agreement with Spain, all the more so as Portuguese diplomats "had been instructed not to cede any part of the colonies. Nevertheless, on many occasions the Portuguese proposed the exchange of certain Brazilian territories for military assistance". Pedro Cardim, "'Portuguese Rebells' at Münster. The Diplomatic Self-Fashioning in mid-seventeeth Century European Politics", in Heinz Duchhardt (ed.), *Der Westfälische Friede* (München, 1998), p. 304.

and these were ceded to the Netherlands in a reciprocal demarcation of trading spheres.[29]

In a new treaty with Portugal thirteen years later, the Dutch definitely ceded their claims to Brazil for a compensation of four million cruzados (eight million florins), but compelled the Portuguese to permit them to trade between Portugal and Brazil and with all Portuguese trading posts in Africa. This resolved Dutch claims on Iberian states for overseas territories. Now the Dutch contest with Britain became more important. The treaties concluded after several naval wars between England and the Netherlands, settling quarrels about trade in connection with the Navigation Act and stipulated the transferring of some territory,[30] was a reflection of both the economic rivalry of the two naval powers and their treaties with Spain and Portugal, which wrested trade advantages from the Iberian powers.

The incorporation of overseas territories into European international law has to be examined against the background of the tensions among European nation states. After the Peace of Westphalia, the rivalry found its main protagonists in England and the United Provinces and had devolved, by the end of the century, on France and England. Agreements of one of these powers with a state of the Iberian Peninsula therefore necessarily brought about treaties initiated by the other powers with Spain or Portugal. The goal of international economic policy was not to obtain good conditions in certain markets; the goal of economic policy, which was to be enforced by the means of international law, was to obtain better conditions than one's rivals.

The Dutch agreements with Spain and Portugal between the years 1648 and 1661 made it incumbent on the British government to reshape its relationship with the states of the Iberian Peninsula. After the victorious revolution, London negotiated in parallel with both Portugal and Spain to conclude new peace treaties or to renew old ones. Portugal's support for Charles I caused military confrontation

---

[29] See *Recueil complet des traités, conventions, capitulations, armistices, autres actes diplomatiques de tous les états de l'Amérique latine ...: depuis l'année 1493 jusqu'à nos jours ... / par M. Charles Calvo* (11 vols. Paris, 1862–68), vol. 1, pp. 68–9. The agreement between the States General and the Portuguese king of the same year that obliged the latter to restore the conquered territories of Brazil and to make payments of compensation probably failed due to local conditions. See *ibid.*, pp. 75–99.

[30] Whereas in the treaty of Westminster of 1654 the Dutch were obliged to pay compensation for the Amboyna Massacre of 1623, to make annual payments to fish in English waters and to respect the Navigation Act (see Friedensvertrag von Westminster, 1654 IV 5), in the Treaty of Breda, Surinam was surrendered to the Dutch and New Amsterdam to the English. The treaty of Westminster of 1674 stipulated free passage of English settlers out of Surinam. Quarrels over East India were referred to arbitration, but the status quo of possessions was maintained. (See Friedensvertrag von Westminster, 1674 II 19, both: Großbritannien and Generalstaaten, in www.ieg-mainz.de/friedensvertraege, viewed 28 Feb. 2008).

between Portugal and the English Republic. Although Spain recognized the Republic, the English side urged the readjustment of the old commercial treaties of 1604 and 1630 in accordance with the changed conditions of the Westphalian Peace for the Dutch. Regarding overseas territories, English ministers placed at the centre of their negotiations the claim for free trade with English colonies in America, which were still situated in territories claimed by Spain. The English side must have been aware that complete free-trade, that is, including the Spanish-American colonies, was neither enforceable by maintaining the Navigation Act nor really desirable in view of some future most-favoured nation clauses in treaties between Spain and other powers.[31]

Simultaneously, London pressed its negotiations with Portugal. The small country at the western edge of Europe still needed English support to maintain its independence from Spain. In the treaty finally concluded between England and Portugal in 1654, Oliver Cromwell succeeded in achieving everything that had been denied the English in 1642. Portugal now allowed English subjects to trade between Portugal and Brazil and with the other Portuguese colonies in Africa and Asia.[32] Seven years later, Charles II provided himself with a very rich dowry through his marriage to the Portuguese princess Catharine. Portugal had to accept all the concessions of the previous treaty of 1642 again, hand over Tangier and Bombay to England, permit English subjects free trade with all its overseas territories, license the settlement of up to four British families at most trading posts and hand over in advance some East Indian territories to England in the case of their recapture from the Dutch. In return, England engaged to support Portugal militarily and not to conclude a treaty with Spain detrimental to Portugal.[33]

The treaty with Portugal of 1654 signed and sealed, Cromwell headed directly for a war with Spain, so that the Spanish administration very quickly recognised that the essence of his claims to open all trade with America to be a mere pretext for war.

We need not dwell here on the military conflict. Apart from the conquest of Jamaica, the British could chalk up little success. More interesting in the present context is that, between the end of the war shortly before the accession of Charles

---

[31] The Navigation Act of 1651 reserved the trade with English colonies to English ships and merchants. The act was aimed mainly against the Dutch intermediate trade. See J.E. Farnell, "The Navigation Act of 1651, the first Dutch war, and the London merchant community", *Economic History Review*, second ser. 16 (1963–64): 439–54.

[32] See Weindl, *Wer kleidet die Welt?*, pp. 147–56. Eventually the Portuguese king was forced to sign the treaty by sending an English fleet to the mouth of the Tejo. See Charles Boxer, "Second Thoughts on the Anglo-Portuguese Alliance, 1661–1808", *History Today* 36 (1986): 24.

[33] See Weindl, *Wer kleidet die Welt?*, pp. 162–3.

II to the throne and the conclusion of a new peace and commercial treaty between both countries eight years later, there prevailed a kind of "cold peace" between England and Spain, while their overseas relations came under a strictly separate heading. In the West Indies, a piracy war was raging, which the English argued could not be stopped because of the lack of a newly formulated peace treaty, although the reinstatement of the peace treaty of 1630 theoretically included a peace for America.

Based on the Spanish-English relationship of the 1660s, we can see very clearly the interrelationship between overseas interests and inner European peace policy, and its changed pattern in these years. For decades, Spain used the threat of interrupting European trade as a pawn. Spain was not always able to avoid war, but by blocking European trade it was always able to force England back to the negotiating table. Moreover, Spain always succeeded in gaining contractual recognition of its American trade monopoly in exchange for granting trade privileges in Europe. With reason, we can argue that for the overseas colonies of any European country there was nearly no difference if it traded with foreign nations in a legal or illegal manner. For a long time the Dutch, English and French had disputed provinces, harbours and places in the territories claimed by the Iberians. Trade between the colonies of different nations was probably as much a reality as the supplying of Spanish-America by Dutch, English and French merchants. We have to bear in mind that it made a fundamental difference for the power position of the European mother country if and how far overseas privileges for subjects of foreign nations could be negotiated or not. Claims to free trade with overseas territories were therefore not crucial for the English negotiations of the 1660s. The English had obtained the access they wanted some years before by their agreements with Portugal. On the contrary, because of Spain's the military weakness, English ministers feared the opening of American markets to all European nations. This would have brought about an undesirable rivalry. It is no wonder that when the Spanish trade monopoly seemed to be failing because of the lack of military power, a sole monopoly, namely that for the slave trade with Spanish America, found its way into the European international law. In the 1660s, English diplomats promised to ensure the Spanish trade monopoly for America in exchange for Spain's signing over the *Asiento de negros* to England. Accordingly, overseas territories were almost absent from the peace and commercial treaty finally concluded in 1667 between England and Spain. English subjects simply obtained the right to sell goods purchased on both sides of Cape of Good Hope in Spain without declaring their origin, which enabled them to sell goods coming from Portuguese overseas territories.[34] Apart from this, several detailed import regulations strengthened the position of English merchants in Spanish

---

[34] Considering Portugal as a rebellious province, the Spanish crown forbade this trade until a peace treaty was concluded with Portugal.

ports. Three years later another treaty cleared up the relationship in America, that is, both treaty partners were to retain his possessions and trade monopolies were to be mutually respected.[35] Only a peace in America offered the possibility of economic expansion in the West Indian possessions. Further, the Treaty of Breda (1667), which established the United Provinces as a predominant power in the East Indies and West Africa, and signed over territories on the American mainland (Surinam) to them, once more put the ball in Britain's court. In the following years, the Dutch West Indian Company (WIC) built up its slave depot in Curaçao, mainly to supply the *Asiento*. If English merchants wanted to use Barbados and Jamaica in a similar way, they would need a peace in the Caribbean. Against these advantages for trade, wishes to expand English possessions took a back seat.

The *Asiento de negros* finally became a part of international law through the quarrels over the Spanish succession. For being allowed to manage the *Asiento de negros*, first the French and then the British government ensured the Spanish monopoly for trade with America. The consolidation of possessions in all known continents entailed that no European power challenged the monopoly trade of another power, even though smuggling persisted. With the *Asiento de negros* in 1713, which was stipulated in an interstate treaty, Great Britain procured access to the Spanish monopoly system without opening this system to other rivals. Curiously enough, the General-states now pushed not for a share in legal trade with Spanish America, but for a codification that would maintain the Spanish monopolistic system in their peace and commercial treaty with Spain, with the exception of the *Asiento*, and promised to help in the enforcement of this monopoly.[36]

Conclusion

The call for the freedom of the seas, which was first heard on the occasion of quarrels over the East Indies between Portugal, Spain and the United Provinces, had fallen silent by the beginning of the eighteenth century. Apart from a few theoretical reflections and treatises, European international law regarding non-European territories was oriented throughout the seventeenth century towards the economic interests of the colonial powers.

The questions of the lawfulness of overseas land seizures discussed with varying emphasis since the beginning of the age of expansion took a back seat in seventeenth century to the handling of these territories in inner-European politics.

---

[35] See *Recueil complet des traités, conventions, capitulations, armistices, autres actes diplomatiques de tous les états de l'Amérique latine*, vol. 1, pp. 162–72.

[36] See "Friedens- und Handelsvertrag von Utrecht, Generalstaaten, Spanien 1714 VI 26", in www.ieg-mainz.de/friedensvertraege, Art. 31 (viewed 28 Feb. 2008).

The de facto position thus conceded to non-European political units within European international law reflects much more the real power relationships than the theoretical discussions of Spanish scholars of the sixteenth century.

PART VI
Conclusions and Perspectives

Chapter 14
Dynamics of Conflict and Illusions of Law: Making War and Thinking Peace in the Modern International System

Olaf Asbach

The Paradox of Modern World

A strange paradox has run through the modern European world since its origins: the processes of founding and institutionalising the conditions of secured peace and law go hand in hand with the expansion of conflict and war, of the violation and annihilation of individual and collective rights. The emergence of the modern state as a guarantee of law and peace, the expansion of *doux commerce* and the development of an international system regulated by international law and diplomacy: all these processes have been pushed through and mediated by means of conflict, war, expansionist force and exploitation. And this did not come to an end with the accomplishment of state building and of the capitalist world system.[1]

The continuity of this dialectics of conflict and order, war and peace, finds its reason in a twofold, and interconnected, relation between past and present. On the one hand, both the political and social institutions and structures and the concepts and ideas generated in the modern era have had a formative influence on today's political and social world; this concerns, so to speak, the dimension of social "objectivity". On the other hand, they have affected the way this world is perceived, grasped and judged; this is the dimension of "subjectivity". Exactly that is the reason many actual debates connect the diagnosis of a real or imagined crisis (or even the end) of modern states and state system with the quest for new concepts to understand and organize the world.[2] How can this continuity in fundamental structures and problems in society since the advent of early modern

---

[1] On the connection between war and state formation in early modern Europe, see Johannes Burkhardt in this volume. That peace will be realised when capitalism becomes globally dominant, has been asserted by Klaus Jürgen Gantzel, "Handel und Frieden. Ein klassischer Topos der Friedensbestrebungen und seine Bedeutung im Zeitalter der Globalisierung", in Ulrich Menzel (ed.), *Vom Ewigen Frieden und vom Wohlstand der Nationen* (Frankfurt am Main, 2000), esp. pp. 342–6.

[2] Cf. the manifold works that deal with the crisis or end of "Westphalian" state and/or state system, discussed under titles such as *Beyond Westphalia? State Sovereignty*

Europe be explained, and how far do actual institutions and concepts reproduce their contradictions? In order to avoid anachronistic arguments, ahistorical comparisons or projections, the following considerations will start with a short remark on the fundamental characteristics of the social order developed in modern Europe to which political and international discourses and practices reacted and whose persistence established the material conditions of their lasting relevance. Subsequently, I shall distinguish three pivotal currents of its perception, conceptualisation and organisation of this social order that became paradigmatic for concepts, discourses and practices up to now. In each case I ask how they try to manage theoretically and practically those new circumstances and problems, what their limits and inherent contradictions are and how far they may still be relevant to our understanding, criticism and management, or mismanagement, of today's globalised world.

Basic Structures and Dynamics of Conflicts in Modern Europe

How to explain the relevance and persistence of the theory and practice of modern politics and international law? They result from the emergence of a completely new, *modern* order, which was first generated in early modern Europe and is, despite all contemporary differences, still dominant at the present time.[3] It pervades and reconfigures the social world and generates new structures, dynamics and ways of acting and thinking. Generally speaking, modern society is characterised by the fact of *pluralisation*. It supersedes former social orders whose cohesion had been secured by the indisputable validity of given structures and belief-systems which guaranteed the unity of the social world and ascribed to everybody his or her respective social position, meaning and end. Such orders collapsed because of processes of social differentiation, leading to a plurality of social actors and interests competing and struggling for power, goods and recognition. When Hegel says that the "principle of the modern world as a whole is freedom of subjectivity",[4] he denotes the driving force of this new order, which is pervaded and sustained by heterogeneous interests, objectives, beliefs and the material and moral stakes of

---

and International Intervention, eds Gene M. Lyons and Michael Mastanduno (Baltimore, 1995).

[3] I cannot address here the issue of whether it is therefore a specifically *European* modernity. I discuss the fact that "Europe" itself, as a new sphere of action and communication, was "invented" in the modern era in Olaf Asbach, *Europa – Vom Mythos zur, "Imagined Community"? Studien zu Erforschung und Bedeutung des Europabegriffs* (Berlin, 2009).

[4] Georg Wilhelm Friedrich Hegel, *Philosophy of Right*, transl. and ed. T.M. Knox (Oxford, 1952), addition to § 273, p. 286 (transl. corrected).

different actors, groups and classes. This order is thus characterised ontologically by antagonism and conflict. Where the allocation of social, economic and political resources and positions and the validity of norms and values are left to the balancing of powers of competing actors and their relative stakes and capacities, it always runs the risk of turning into conflict and violence. This *systematic* structure of contingency, antagonism and conflict is at the same time the reason for and the result of the manifold conflicts and wars that have *historically* pervaded the modern era. The processes of differentiation, pluralisation and dynamisation of social actors and interests reciprocally intensified each other and led to a wide range of social, political and religious struggles and wars.[5]

The emergence of the modern state takes place via the institutionalisation of the capacities of organisation and regulation that are essential for maintaining and developing these new social structures. Sovereignty as the core of the modern state refers to precisely this function.[6] The state becomes the only legitimate authority to make and enforce law and to use physical violence in order to prevent social actors from pursuing their own interests and logic of action, from generating conflicts which can be solved only by means of subjective decisions about their respective claims and, in the last resort, by the use of force. This centralisation of the fields of force and media of right and violence produces and secures the sphere of activity required by plural actors and interests in modern societies.[7] Hence the

---

[5] This includes, to name just a few keywords, the religious struggles attendant upon the Reformation, the wars of state formation, and the political, social and cultural conflicts in the course of the rise of new socio-economic interests and classes or induced by the overseas expansion of the European powers.

[6] Cf. Olaf Asbach, "Sovereignty between Effectiveness and Legitimacy. Dimensions and Actual Relevance of Sovereignty in Bodin, Hobbes and Rousseau", *Eurostudia. Revue transatlantique de recherche sur l'Europe*, 2/2 (2006) (http://www.cceae.umontreal.ca/-revue-Eurostudia).

[7] Albeit the state has historically been developed in Europe in very different ways and has taken very different forms, it is impossible to distinguish between a pre-modern "personalized dynastic sovereignty" before 1800 and a modern "depersonalized sovereignty" since then, as Benno Teschke has suggested in *The Myth of 1648. Class, Geopolitics, and the Making of Modern International Relations* (London, 2003), pp. 10–12 and chap. V and VIII (see also his contribution in this volume). In the 1640s, Thomas Hobbes was already able to detect the general tendency and deep grammar of the modern state completely independent of its contingent empirical forms and representations, long before it was objectified and became an *impersonal* power in reality. Whatever the empirical figure of the sovereign was, the emerging state powers justified their position in early modern societies by their capacities to generate and enforce law and order on behalf of the common good. Through these discourses, even "*personalised* dynastic sovereignty" contributed to the early modern processes of generating a concept of and institutional structures for a *de-personalised* sovereignty; hence, attempts to set them in opposition by strict chronological

realisation of the modern – *Westphalian* – state and state system does not put an end to competition and conflict. Quite the contrary, state and state system establish a completely new form of generalized and perpetuated competition for political, economic and social power among a plurality of actors and interests on the social and international level. The modern state therefore is as much the *organiser* of as the *battleground* for competing social interests. The state is *organiser* insofar as it provides a society that is split by pluralisation, heterogeneity and power with a general will by which it is enabled to act, impose and enforce rules and guarantees non-violent forms of pursuing an actor's interests and resolving his or her conflicts. That is why the state is at the same time a *battleground*: as a central authority it necessarily brings about *particular* decisions on political and social rules, goods and power, which are *generalised* by its monopoly of the means of legitimate power. Consequently, the state has never been separated from society and the particular interests, conflicts and competing relations that act within it. On the contrary, precisely by assuming a separate existence, the state becomes an element and a medium of these political, social and economic aspirations and interests in internal and external relations.

The Dialectics of War and Peace in the Modern Era

The state based and state centred *Westphalian* order that emerged in modern Europe and was subsequently globalised was *not*, as has been shown, an order in which States have been the only important actors in the sense that they were completely autonomous in their structure, functioning and logic of action. Modern states rather emerged as new forms of organisation and nodes of differentiating modern societies, which are in principle marked by antagonistic social relations and interests on all levels, with regard to political, social, economic, cultural, religious and other dimensions. Thus, being institutionalised as well as imagined systems, states emerge, persist and work as imaginary but permanently substantiated "actors" in concrete situations, as "unities of action and effect" in questions of internal and external relevance.[8] They work as agencies of organisation and mediation for a plurality of social actors and actor constellations, and exactly this, so to speak, sets social actors free to pursue their particular interests, values and aims on the national as well as on the transnational level. Consequently, territorial and national borders have been transgressed since the beginning of the formation

---

limits (such as before or after 1800) or by territorial or national borders (such as France versus England) promote a rather ahistorical and abstract point of view.

[8] Cf. Hermann Heller, *Staatslehre* (Tübingen, 1983), pp. 259 and 269–79 (my translation).

of modern states in fifteenth- and sixteenth-century Europe.[9] The global as well as the social dimensions are inscribed in the so-called Westphalian state system from its onset, just as, vice versa, in the globalised world states are and remain central relay stations of the organisation, the guarantee and the enforcement of political, social and economic interests and power.

In this *condition moderne*, understanding, theorising and organising law and peace is faced with a paradoxical situation. On the one hand, there is an intrinsic quest for law and peace. To the extent that modern societies lead to a pluralisation of competing social, economic and cultural actors, interests and value systems, new ways of understanding and institutionalising law and peace are indispensable for the functioning of this complex social and international system. On the other hand, there are intrinsic dynamics of conflict. To the extent that states act as organisers and guarantors of the conditions of law and peace, they generate and reproduce at the same time relations of competition, conflict and lack of peace: both domestically and abroad, states always advocate particular political decisions, claims and interests and therefore necessarily negate alternative interests and legal claims of other actors. This problem has driven theory and practice in modern politics and international relations and stimulated attempts to get a clear understanding of the emerging political and social conditions at the national and international level, its principles and problems in finding institutional and normative concepts to achieve peace and stable order in internal and external affairs. Notwithstanding all differences, there ensued a tradition of political and social discourses and action that has been effective theoretically and practically in political, cultural and social practice ever since. In the following sections, I shall distinguish and discuss the structure and problems of three main currents of thinking and organising modern international relations in order to secure stability, self-preservation and the pursuit of interests under the conditions of the modern world: attempts to organise them by means of politically balancing and coordinating a plurality of actors by institutionalising international law and diplomacy, or by the construction of a global order, including a monopolisation of the means of violence.

---

[9] The analytical distinction between a "world of states" and a "world of societies" should therefore neither be ontologised nor historicised in the sense that the former has only recently been transformed into the latter (Ernst-Otto Czempiel, *Kluge Macht. Außenpolitik für das 21. Jahrhundert* (Munich, 1999), p. 11 and chap. I, pp. 17–101 passim). The social as well as transnational and global dimensions of the early modern processes of – European – state building can be identified from its beginnings, including and depending on the construction of trade routes and monopolies, the constitution of national and regional markets and customs barriers, of internal and external legal relationships and so on.

Peace by Balance of Power and International Cooperation?

The first current of modern political theory and practice aims at achieving a balance of power in order to secure peace and stability. This concept implies the general secularisation and rationalisation of the structures of the political system as well as political action.[10] Modern international relations are characterised by the dynamics and problems of mediation resulting from a system of states which, on the one hand, are correlated to each other as free and competing actors and, on the other hand, are themselves the result as well as the agents of specific social and economic interests at the internal and at the transnational level. Thus the international system is a highly complex, dynamic and fragile net of relations: the conditions required for maintaining and stabilising the whole and its members are not given by all-embracing norms or religious beliefs,[11] but emerge as a resultant of constellations of interests and power. This is why modern political theory and practice are confronted with the task of developing reliable and binding rules and mechanisms for such a constellation of basically equal actors, since the calculability of relations in the international system is a major constituent of sustaining and pursuing both the interests of states and those of social and economic actors that are directly or indirectly connected with or dependent on this system. The stability is to be achieved by balancing and interrelating the interests and power of the actors in the international system or by connecting them through alliances and negotiation systems in such a way that they no longer harm or threaten each other. Since Machiavelli, political theory has made this a subject of discussion under the heading of the "raison" or "interest of the state" in internal and external affairs or in the "balance" among states.[12] In political practice, the existence of a plurality of competing (state) actors, as the point of departure in international relations, was increasingly recognised in the period between the peace treaties of Westphalia in 1648 and Utrecht in 1713, pursuing international security and

---

[10] Secularisation does not necessarily apply to the contents and the aims of political action, but to the *structure* of the political, so that to achieve political success it is "better to concentrate on what really happens rather than on theories or speculations" (Niccolò Machiavelli, *The Prince*, transl. and ed. Quentin Skinner and Russell Price (Cambridge, 1988), chap. XV, p. 54).

[11] Even if all relevant actors conceive of themselves as good Christians and adhering to the same religious belief and norm system, after the breakdown of the *respublica christiana* they are all accountable only to themselves for their interpretations and the actions following from them, and they necessarily regard anybody else as actual or potential competitors.

[12] Cf. Friedrich Meinecke, *Machiavellism: the doctrine of Raison d'État and its place in modern history*, ed. W. Stark (Epping, 1984).

order by varying systems of balance and "convenance" of powers, by concerts of Great or Super-Powers or by bi- or multi-polar systems.[13]

The problems of these ways of organising international relations are evident. A balance of power system where the whole is nothing but the functional net of pure quanta of power is necessarily characterized by competition, conflict and a possible recourse to violence in order to enforce particular interests. This conflictual dynamics is thus not accidental but results from the structural contingency of the modern international system. It is always up to the calculations of the actors themselves to decide what the respective interests and power relations in the international system are and what the effects of the reciprocal perceptions, assessments and supposed long-term consequences of actions are going to be. This system therefore systematically excludes the possibility of permanent enforcement and the guarantee of secured conditions of peace and law. Thomas Hobbes expressed this logic of action with precision when he demonstrated that the state of nature *is in itself* a state of war – and that it does not *become* one only for auxiliary reasons such as human malice, scarce resources or historical decline.[14] In a system of actors that are in principle free and equal, conflicts of rights and interests are logically inevitable because of the *structure* of their relations of will and appropriation. Even if the quest for peace and secured right is a necessary condition of self-preservation, prosperity and progress,[15] as long as the action structure of free, unrestricted and competing actors without a general coercive power persists, it is possible at any given moment that conflicts of action, right and property should swing to violence, the application of force and, finally, war.

Critiques of the concept of a balance of power between states that can easily plunge into turmoil and collapse are as old as this system itself. In a phrase that

---

[13] Cf. Michael Sheehan, *The Balance of Power: History and Theory* (London, 2000).

[14] In the state of nature – between individuals as well as between states – everybody "hath a right to make use of, and to do all whatsoever he shall judge requisite for his preservation"; Thomas Hobbes, *Philosophical Rudiments Concerning Government and Society*, English Works, ed. Molesworth, vol. II (London, 1841), I.10 note, p. 10; and because this right necessarily harms the rights of the other actors, the state of nature is as such a state of war (cf. *ibid.*, I.12, p. 11).

[15] This is even true for Hobbes, who declares that the law of nature commands, "that peace is to be sought after, where it may be found", "to perform contracts, or to keep trust" and so on, and that those "laws of nature are immutable, and eternal; what they forbid, can never be lawful; what they command, can never be unlawful" (Hobbes, *Philosophical Rudiments*, II.2, III.1 and III.29, pp. 16, 29 and 46); and who demonstrates that even the strictest commands cannot alone guarantee peace and legally organised relations as long as they are addressed only to the individual conscience, the *foro interno*, and do not bind actors *in foro externo*; see Thomas Hobbes, *Leviathan Or The Matter, Forme, & Power Of A Common-Wealth Ecclesiastical And Civill*, English Works, ed. Molesworth, vol. III (London, 1839), chap. XV, pp. 145–6.

became famous, Emmanuel Kant, in 1793, ironically called the hope of "a lasting universal Peace on the basis of the so-called *Balance of Power in Europe*" as "a mere fantasy": "like Swift's house that the builder had constructed in such perfect accord with all the laws of equilibrium that it collapsed as soon as a sparrow alighted upon it".[16] But this appraisal is only the latest in a long series of comparable verdicts by European political theorists since the late seventeenth and throughout the eighteenth century. Be it Fénelon or Saint-Pierre, Justi, Rousseau or Mably, they all agreed on the fact that the balance of power system was prone to permanent struggles rather than being a guarantee of peace and stability.[17] And, in fact, this logic of political rationality was never intended to strive unconditionally for peace or even the abolishment of war in itself. Balance of power politics is a *modus operandi* of moving and subsisting *in* the given order of the international state of nature. The core and telos of political action are thus not peace and law as ends in themselves, but as conditional means of self-preservation, self-determination and self-development under conditions of general competition and conflictual relations with others – other actors, other proprietors, other states, other systems of belief and values and so on. And as long as this is the case, there will always be the possibility of the recourse to power, violence and war.

It would be naïve to suppose that this dynamics has been overcome in the twenty-first century. The increase of inter-, trans- and supranational interdependencies, integration and cooperation is borne by a plurality of actors, interests and powers that perpetuate the dynamics of competition and conflict. The globalisation of neo-liberal politics in the last decades has demonstrated how these structures and platforms of alleged post-national cooperation serve as medias for the enforcement of the particular interests of national or transnational, private or public, actors. This yields paradoxical results: the extension of market economy, commerce and cooperation is running under the banner of peace and law and goes hand in hand with a constant extension of the domain of struggles between private and public powers; the alleged processes of de-nationalisation and internationalisation of

---

[16] Immanuel Kant, "On the common saying: That may be correct in theory, but it is of no use in practice" [1793], in Kant, *Practical Philosophy*, transl. and ed. Mary J. Gregor (Cambridge, 1996), p. 309.

[17] Thus, the physiocrat Pierre-Paul Le Mercier de la Rivière argues that "le systême de *la balance* de l'Europe … est peu propre à prévenir les guerres parmi les Puissances de l'Europe; il semble plutôt servir d'occasion, ou de prétexte; car tous les jours ils se font la guerre pour maintenir la balance; les peuples ainsi s'entr'égorgent, armés les uns contre les autres par un système imaginé pour les empecher de s'entr'égorger." (*L'ordre naturel et essentiel des sociétés politiques* (2 vols, London and Paris, 1767), vol. 2, pp. 228–9) For a closer look at Saint-Pierre and Rousseau, see Olaf Asbach: *Die Zähmung der Leviathane. Die Idee einer Rechtsordnung zwischen Staaten bei Abbé de Saint-Pierre und Jean-Jacques Rousseau* (Berlin, 2002), pp. 113–16 and 228–33.

sovereignty are accompanied by the strengthening of the executives of powerful states and by nationalist, ethnic and separatist nation building processes "from below" as well as "from outside". The construction of trans- and supranational institutions as for example the *European Union* does not cancel the logic and dynamics of the international state of nature and its intrinsic element of force and war. What may be seen and described as a supranational network of cooperation to organise the problems of globalised markets, or even as a "peace project",[18] has its Janus face in creating new global players and political regimes reproducing the mechanisms of regional and global competition, inclusion and exclusion.[19] They always serve as agencies and driving forces of particular interests, dynamics and contradictions and constitute new actors in international competition, bound up with potentials of military, economic and other forms of the use of power and force.[20]

Peace by International Law?

A second current in modern political theory and practice relies on the law of nations. It can be said that this tradition works as a *legal* complement to the previously outlined approaches for stabilising and sustaining modern states and state system by *political* means. In the modern era, the idea of a legal unity of the *respublica christiana* was replaced by a plurality of states claiming sovereignty, that is, to be the only legitimate power in public and international law.[21] In connection with the formation of the European power system and overseas expansion, Spanish Scholastics, Grotius and others initiated a new legal discourse on the law of nations. Although marked by fundamental differences, whether seeing the law of nations justified by nature, by reason or by positive acts, custom and consent, those taking this tendency agree on one crucial point that the only ultimate authority about

---

[18] See Dieter Senghaas: *Friedensprojekt Europa* (Frankfurt am Main, 2002).

[19] This transformation and reconfiguration of sovereignty "does not circumvent the inside/outside divide associated with statehood" (David Boucher, "Resurrecting Pufendorf and capturing the Westphalian moment", *Review of International Studies* 27 (2001): 576); rather it reproduces it at a new level – with all its effects concerning the inclusion and exclusion of other actors and interests.

[20] It is illuminating to see that Jürgen Habermas, trying to legitimate the European Union as a new actor and global player in the so-called "postnational constellation" (so the title of his book, Cambridge, 2001), converges with the theory of a post-sovereign spatial world order composed of continental geopolitical unities as they were promoted by Habermas's proclaimed political opponent, Carl Schmitt; see Schmitt's *Staat – Großraum – Nomos* (Berlin, 1995).

[21] On this concept, see Asbach, "Sovereignty between Effectiveness and Legitimacy" (chap. 2).

what is accepted and enforced as international law is the will of free and sovereign actors.[22] This is the real meaning of the *Myth of 1648*: it serves as an imaginary point of reference for an actually emerging order of international law whose *raison d'être* is the existence and free development of the plural actors, and as such it is of practical importance.[23] The mutual recognition of territorial integrity ensures the self-preservation of its members in the international system and their equality in legal relations, while the network of diplomacy and negotiations creates and maintains common legal interactions and respective independence. In all the various forms of this modern law of nations it is always a question of a legal structure in which the restraints on free action are left to the will of the actors in this international system, to their moral insight and political decisions.

Nevertheless, this attempt to tame the modern state system by the construction of a common *inter-national* law not only shows up internal limits and contradictions; it moreover provokes a new dynamics of competition and conflict. Most modern theoreticians and practitioners of the law of nations either disregard these problems or else see no problem at all, contenting themselves instead with deducing the rules and validity of the law of nations and showing its supposed practicability and binding character. Only a few criticise the law of

---

[22] The decisive move of all modern international law can be identified *in nuce* in Francisco de Vitoria's observation that neither the Pope nor the emperor can claim to be "the lord of the whole world" (Vitoria: De indis, II.1 and 3), and in his shift from the traditional *ius gentium* to the *ius inter gentes*, that is, to the primacy of "the rulers and magistrates to whom the commonwealth has delegated its powers and offices"; Vitoria, "On Civil Power", in *Political Writings*, tansl. and ed. Anthony Pagden and Jeremy Lawrance (Cambridge, New York, 1991), I.5, p. 12. The whole range of different and opposing interpretations of the origins and validity of this law of nations, whether given by god, nature, reason, consent or tradition, from sixteenth century onwards, are little more than variations *within* this new paradigm of a *ius gentium* as a "law-of-what-free-actors-decide-to-be-law", and this according to what *they* judge to be, or are able to enforce as, the true grounds and contents of law in international relations.

[23] It certainly is a myth that the peace of Westphalia in 1648 historically realised the specifically modern principles of international relations such as sovereignty, territorial integrity, legal equality, the principle of non-intervention and so on (see Teschke, *The Myth of 1648*, pp. 215–16). Nevertheless, it is important to distinguish, as Boucher does ("Resurrecting Pufendorf", pp. 560–62), between the *historical* and the *emblematic* character of "1648". As an important point of departure and point of reference in the following political thinking and acting, 1648 *became*, precisely *as* a myth, a formative factor in the construction of the modern state system; cf. Heinz Schilling, "Der Westfälische Friede und das neuzeitliche Profil Europas", in Heinz Duchhardt (ed.), *Der Westfälische Friede. Diplomatiepolitische Zäsur – Kulturelles Umfeld – Rezeptionsgeschichte* (Historische Zeitschrift. Beiheft 26) (München, 1998), pp. 3–32, esp. 22–4. On the Westphalian system between myth and reality, cf. Matthias Zimmer, *Moderne, Staat und Internationale Politik* (Wiesbaden, 2008), pp. 37–53.

nations as necessarily stumbling before the hurdle of the "modern" principle of subjectivity – for the subjective right to decide what is right and wrong, just and unjust, is at the same time the guarantee of freedom *and* the reason of conflicts. As long as it remains up to the actors themselves to operate as the ultimate authority and decide upon what is right, on the validity of contracts and alliances and so on, there can be no such thing as Law *sensu strictu*.[24] The existence of a "real" international law would require what is definitively nonexistent in the state of nature: a clear and legally enforceable differentiation of the respective rights and spheres of action and freedom of the manifold actors. That is why exponents of modern law of nations, in the eyes of Hobbes, Saint-Pierre, Rousseau or Kant, are nothing but – as the latter put it – "miserable consolers", insofar they speak of law where it has no binding force, thus providing to those who have the power and interests to use it the opportunity "for the *justification* of an outbreak of war".[25] They produce, so to speak, the illusion of international law and the illusion of the existence of objective limits and restraints to warfare, but de facto they only conceal in this way the impossibility of realising, under these circumstances, secured conditions of law and peace.

What seems to be a paradox and a failure, however, is actually in full accordance with the demands on the theory and practice of the modern law of nations. The law of nations emerges as a form of organisation of a plurality of actors in a new European world system, of states, corporations and companies, competing for territories and markets, trade and sea routes, resources and men – to enslave or convert them.[26] The modern law of nations never aimed at the categorically eliminating force and war: the law of nations has therefore always comprised the laws of war, specifying the conditions of the state's right and duty to declare, conduct and end wars. In the modern social as well as the international system

---

[24] As Hobbes has put it, in a condition where everybody has the right to judge what is just and unjust, right and wrong, "the effects of this right are the same, almost, as if there had been no right at all" (Hobbes: *Rudiments*, I.11, p. 11). Hence, no international law between sovereign states and actors is possible, or as the Abbé de Saint-Pierre put it: "il n'y a aucun *Droit* dans la signification précise du terme, *Droit*, du terme, *Jus*". Abbé de Saint-Pierre, *Mémoire pour diminuer le nombre des procès* (Paris, 1725), pp. 393–5.

[25] Immanuel Kant: "Toward perpetual peace. A philosophical project" [1795], in Kant, *Practical Philosophy*, tansl. and ed. Mary J. Gregor (Cambridge, 1996) second definitive article, p. 326.

[26] The successive formation of the early modern *Ius Publicum Europaeum* in the Spanish and French Age (cf. Wilhelm G. Grewe: *The Epochs of International Law* (Berlin, 2000), part II and III) was always part of the movement to legitimise and secure the conditions of and rights to territorial possessions and acquisitions in Europe and overseas. Its major aim was thus to found and reproduce the structures of pursuing particular interests of (*European*) states and other actors and interest groups. And this always included the possibility as well as the reality of manifold conflicts and wars.

of competing actors, freely determining their interests and ends, law is always an element and expression of extra-legal interests and power relations. These interests and power relations are not external to it, but rather constitute its fundament and core. Consequently, they charge law with conflict potential.

In recent years, the theory and practice of international law have often been described as a success story, even if a delayed one, that has finally overcome its contradictions and bellicist implications by outlawing war, undermining the principle of sovereignty, and establishing networks of international rules and obligations, thus producing the hope that historical developments in international and humanitarian law and institutions will ultimately turn out to be guarantees of the general rule of peace and law.[27] There are reasons, however, to doubt this interpretation. *In the first place*, all this does not cancel the fundamental contradiction of rights in international relations: the international system is and remains a plurality of state, trans- and supranational actors that decide on the validity and enforcement of what is considered to be justice – actors that, depending on opportunity and their respective positions of power, are able to enforce their own particular interests. This is why liberal and democratic concepts, with their reference to a law of nations enforcing peace and rights, easily become instruments spreading and accelerating conflicts to the point of military force. They provide a set of *universal* normative arguments, principles and values that serves to feed the arsenal of necessarily *particular* actors in a global state of nature. Thus, and *secondly*, even the alleged universality of international law always reveals some particular dimension. Under the given conditions of a fragmentised world of interests and powers competing at the transnational and global level, it functions as a driving force for pushing through specific interests, whether "egoistic" or "universalist", and so itself tends to provoke and justify conflicts and wars. What comes along in terms of the universal law of nations and is executed in its name always includes the aspect of particularity, of power and the right of the strongest. And such a "right" necessarily provokes resistance, with in turn its claim to its own right.[28] Therefore, *thirdly*, it proves to be highly dangerous and consequently

---

[27] G.I.A. Draper concludes that, "after 150 years of its development", a remarkable "progress of the humanitarian law of war" has been achieved ("Humanitarianism in the Modern Law of Armed Conflicts", *International Relations* 8 (1985): 394). And, following numerous corresponding accounts, Habermas reconstructs a kind of successive formation process of a global legal order, which has come about, despite all reversals, since the end of the First World War; for more detail, see Olaf Asbach, "Jenseits des internationalen Naturzustands? Habermas und die Transformation des neuzeitlichen Völkerrechts", in Gary S. Schaal (ed.), *Das Staatsverständnis von Jürgen Habermas* (Baden-Baden, 2009), pp. 223–8.

[28] This confirms Hobbes's insight that in such a state of nature the competing "rights" provoke a state of war and the negation of any right because everybody "hath a

politically inadvisable simply to rely on the historical continuity of actual processes of juridification, including their alleged preconditions of democracy and market economy, processes that are proclaimed to be afoot in international law and in the international system.[29] To do so would result in a fatal dialectic, consisting on the one hand in the spread of these developments under the aegis of a doubly "good" conscience, because now backed by both history *and* reason, and assisted if necessary by military force, and on the other hand in the thereby generated resistance that sees itself as legitimately founded in the right to self-preservation and self-determination against the latest manifestations of the old European and western aspiration for hegemony;[30] and together, feeding one another, they would herald the proliferation of conflicts and wars among the plurality of actors at the international and regional levels.

Peace by Institutions of Global Law?

A third tendency tries to end the international state of nature by means of global institutions. From seventeenth century onwards, it was developed mainly by political philosophers in what has often been called projects of *perpetual peace*.[31]

---

right to make use, of and to doe all whatsoever he shall judge requisite for his preservation: wherefore by the judgement of him that doth it, the thing done is either right, or wrong; and therefore right" (Hobbes, *Philosophical Rudiments*, I.10 note, p. 10).

[29] Even – or precisely – "critical" peace researchers and cosmopolitan thinkers as Habermas, Pogge, Senghaas and others (cf. above, note 1 and 18) tend to suppose that the fulfilment of the holy trinity of (initially *European* or *Western*) capitalism, democracy and legal systems will guarantee general peace, law and wealth on earth. This is not only dubious for systematic reasons, but also in the light of the fact that this is inevitably a historically specific – *European* or *Western* – form of political, economic and social organisation and thus exclusive of all other ways of living and thinking.

[30] "For those we exclude, and even for a lot of those we wish to include, ... all this is a horrible déjà vu: The white man rides again. Since the Middle Ages, the West has struggled to make the world happy by imposing its values upon the rest. It is like a Russian babushka doll" that leads from actual cosmopolitanism back to the imperialist *mission civilisatrice*, Spanish missionaries and Christian crusaders: "For us, cosmopolitan justice seems to be rather a break with this past. For most of the rest of the world, it is an old pattern in a new disguise: The inexorable drive by the white Western man to impose himself on the globe"; Harald Müller, "What we are fighting for: Why the Quest for Universal Justice Might Mean Perpetual War", unpubl. conference paper (Frankfurt am Main, 2007).

[31] The first important works of this tradition are Éméric de Cruce's *Le nouveau Cynée ou Discours des occasions et moyens d'établir une paix générale et la liberté du commerce par tout le monde* (1623) and William Penn's Essay *Towards the Present and Future Peace of Europe, by the Establishment of an European Dyet, Parliament, or Estates* (1693). For a brief

Unlike pre-modern or humanist peace theories, which try to revoke the ongoing processes of political, social and economic differentiation and its specific conflict structures, these theories aim at founding and rationally as well as functionally organising a politico-institutional order capable of regulating the competing wills and interests of particular (state and other) actors that cannot be pacified by means of the political balance of power or the classical law of nations. By creating general institutions, they try to prevent violence among actors without eliminating their freedom of action. Following the arguments of modern contractualist theory from Hobbes on, theorists such as Saint-Pierre, Rousseau or Kant tried to demonstrate that the antagonistic structure of the modern state system can be pacified only if this state of nature is abandoned. The stability of peace is the function and the result of an institutionally guaranteed system that constitutes and ensures the subjective rights of its members by a system of objective law afforded by common institutions (such as a parliament of representatives of the member states, a court of justice and so on) with the capacities to enforce them. No member state retains the right and the means to enforce its private claims and interpretations of the law against the other's will, and is instead contained within common institutions and their means of legitimate violence. Although states are thus subordinated to a superior power, they are subjected not to an external will but only to their own will, since they themselves create and sustain the general institutions that make and enforce law.[32]

In the recent decades, these ideas of the European enlightenment have experienced a certain revival in political theory and practice. This suggests that plans of "perpetual peace" by global institutions are more than simple chimeras of naive philosophers and refer to real problems of the modern world. The current phenomena of globalisation seem to attest to the actual relevance and modernity of these plans. Institutions that are capable of dealing effectively with regulations, problems and crisis of a more and more complex and interwoven world system prove to be decisive conditions of an order of actors who pursue their self-preservation, political, economic and other interests and ends within a global system of competition and accumulation of power and capital, and therefore have to secure its preconditions – free markets, commodity production, private appropriation, personal freedom and property rights at the national and transnational levels. Moreover, the idea of transnational and global institutions guaranteeing peace and law as they can be recognised in at least rudimentary forms

---

overview, see Olaf Asbach, "Friedensutopien", in *Enzyklopädie der Neuzeit*, ed. *Horst Carl and Christoph Kampmann*, vol. 4 (Stuttgart, Weimar, 2006), pp. 27–34.

[32] Concerning the concrete forms, feasibility and desirability of such common law giving and enforcing institutions, the different authors have varying opinions; on Saint-Pierre and Rousseau, see Asbach, *Zähmung der Leviathane*; for Kant see Otfried Höffe, *Kant's Cosmopolitan Theory of Law and Peace* (Cambridge, 2006), chaps 10–12.

in institutions such as the United Nations or the European Union, sometimes seems to have become a kind of central theme or prevailing ideology during the last decade. This is particularly the case in the "old Europe", whose proponents fight for the primacy of global juridification by common institutions so as to direct power and the pursuit of interests into the channels of legal organisation and conflict resolution.[33] But, paradoxically, these attempts to subordinate power to law and to prevent the use of force and war by means of common institutions often provoke new forms of exercising power, of conflict, violence and war. Two remarks on the reasons for this dark side of global institutions of peace and law may go some way in accounting for this.

In the first place, this conception of globalising peace and law-enforcing institutions is tied to the specific, conflict-generating dialectics of right and power to which Rousseau and Kant already pointed when they spoke of the threat of a new despotism.[34] The abstractness and effectiveness of global institutions imply that only few actors – primarily the national, international and transnational elites – have access to them and dispose of the necessary resources to bring in and to enforce their interests as global players. Such a configuration of global institutions thus increases the given inequalities and conflicts of powers. Despite and because of their formal universality and impartiality, these institutions act as media of the competition between actors who, provided with different degrees of political, economic and social power, fight for the generalisation and enforcement of their respective particular interests and values; so that these forms of global governance contain "a consistent bias in favour of interests well-represented in international institutions and actors with sufficient resources to carry out their policy choices".[35] This in turn evokes resistance, conflicts and wars against these national, regional or global institutions or against the agents of this global order that are felt to be repressive and heteronomous.

---

[33] "We, citizens of the European Union, Paradise", as Martti Koskenniemi ("Global Governance and Public International Law", *Kritische Justiz* 37 (2004), pp. 241–2) ironically put it, "share an intuition about how the world – the international world – is and how it will be in the future. We think it will be like we are". And this "quintessentially European reading of public international law" follows "the image of the law of the nation-state" with Multilateral treaties as legislation and international courts "as an independent judiciary. And they do proliferate".

[34] This is why they both finally rejected the idea of global institutions with a law-enforcing monopoly of the means of violence and opted for democratisation of nation states and the principle of national autonomy and non-intervention.

[35] Koskenniemi, "Global Governance", p. 451. Examples are legion; one has only to consider institutions such as the WTO or the World Bank and their power to influence or direct national economic and social policies and enforce the reconstruction of public and private sectors of many states and regions all over the globe in a specific direction during recent decades.

Secondly, and at the same time, this points out the problems of such institutions in light of the claims of democratic self-determination. Despite all existing mechanisms of influence by national or sectoral actors, publics and interest groups, such institutions tend to produce a kind of "geo-governance without democracy".[36] Political decisions are made far away from concrete situations, problems and interests that are culturally, politically and economically highly disparate, so that to many of the affected nations they appear to be the dictates of a foreign power. This situation would not be rectified by the most honest attempts to exclude partial interests and power relations, or even by restricting the competences of global institutions purely to the protection of peace and human rights.[37] Since the realisation of peace and human rights necessarily depends on complex political, economic and cultural factors and their specific interpretation, any such decision involves far-reaching interventions into the respective relations of power, interests and cultural traditions.[38] All this gives rise to new clashes of interest and resistance, new divisions and concepts of the enemy: some feel they are being patronised and are a pawn in the hands of powerful and foreign interests, while others act in the full consciousness of their responsibility to protect peace, human rights and their preconditions and, if necessary, to enforce them by "just wars" proclaimed by institutions whose generality and neutrality are sharply contested. Even if these institutions are not vehicles for enforcing western systems of values and world order, capitalist structures or the interests of powerful actors, under the given conditions, a global order for making and enforcing law and peace runs the risk to initiating a never-ending chain of conflicts and wars: wars for peace, wars for human rights, wars for humanitarian aid – and all the resistance, divisions, conflicts and old and new wars that this will provoke.

---

[36] Cf. Mark Imber, "Geo-governance without democracy? Reforming the UN system", in Anthony McGrew (ed.), *The Transformation of Democracy? Globalization and Territorial Democracy* (London, 1997), pp. 201–30; Michael Th. Greven, "Some Considerations on Participation and Participatory Governance", in Beate Kohler-Koch, Berthold Rittberger (eds), *Debating the Democratic Legitimacy of the European Union* (Lanham, 2007), pp. 233–48.

[37] See, for example, Jürgen Habermas: *The Postnational Constellation. Political Essays* (London, 2001), chap. V.

[38] It is a sad irony that the – correct – understanding of the complex conditions of the realisation of peace and human rights is often deduced from the *particular* European and Western experiences and, abstracted and naively understood as *universal*, can be used as an argument and weapon for its imposition, violating just those conditions of peace and human rights that it presumes to protect.

War, Peace and Self-Criticism of Modernity

Pointing to the manifold international institutions, forms of cooperation and governance, processes of denationalisation and transnationalisation of law, the rise of NGOs, proclamations of human rights and international law, many contemporary scholars and political activists convey the impression that we are near to a global *post-histoire*. We already know the ways, the axis and the practices of what is good and true, and we have only to overcome the trouble of teething and other imperfections before realising and imposing it. Looking back on the theory and practice of international politics and law in and since the early modern age, however, shows that it would be naïve and dangerous to suppress the inherent problems and contradictions. This holds for all the currents forming and organising the conditions of global peace and law in the modern and contemporary world that have been sketched here. They invariably tend to provoke new forms of exclusion and repression – sometimes even when they are paradoxically proclaiming democracy, peace or human rights. Repressing those problems that have been inherent in the different ways of seeking peace and the juridification of conflicts in the modern world would forgo the opportunity to identify, and possibly to overcome, the contradictions that are reproduced by well-intentioned concepts and activities. Only if critical analysis does not deceive itself with the achieved progress in the theories and practices of pacifying international relations will it be capable of identifying the reasons for their conflict-generating consequences. Constant criticism of these developments and their dark sides, and self-criticism, is an indispensable condition to prevent the threatening – and too often actual – relapse from modernity and enlightened reason into barbarism.

Index

9/11 141

absolutism 41, 49–52, 57, 58
Africa and Africans
    international law 232–3, 240–45
        passim
    international relations 109, 128, 139
    terra nullius 64, 70, 76
Agincourt, Battle of 109
Ailianos 108
Alès, Edict of 229
Alexander VI, Pope 174
Althusius, Johannes 114, 121
American Independence, War of 57
American Indians
    international law 177, 232, 237
    terra nullius 64, 71–2, 73, 74, 75–6, 77–82
Americas
    international law 172–80 *passim*, 232, 234–5, 237, 238–45 *passim*
    terra nullius 63, 64, 71–2, 73, 74, 75–6, 82
anarchism 105–6
Anderson, Perry 43
Anglicanism and Anglicans 235
Aquinas, St Thomas 119
Aristotelianism 114–16, 125, 139, 143, 156, 183, 192
Arnisaeus, Henning 114
Arnold, Thomas 78
Asia and Asians
    international law 234, 236, 237, 239–43 *passim*
    international relations 109, 128
Asiento de negros 244–5
Association of Southeast Asian Nations (ASEAN) 133
asymmetrical wars 17
Atabalipa, King 180

atheism and atheists 101–2
Augsburg, Treaty of 202, 203, 213
Augustinian peace theology 116, 125
Austin, John L. 148
Australia 64, 70, 75, 79
Australian Aboriginals 64, 70, 75, 79
Austria and Austrians 30, 57
autonomy of states, lack of 32–3
Ayala, Balthazar 71, 72

Baldus de Ubaldis 102
Barbados 245
Barbeyrac, Jean 177, 213–14
    natural law and religion 67
Bärwalde, Treaty of 203
Bavaria 203, 209
Bean, Richard 37
Benedict XVI, Pope 63
Bèze, Théodore de 228
biologism 105
Bireley, Robert 198
Blockmans, Wim 38
Bodin, Jean 88
Bohemia and Bohemians 19, 27–8, 199–200
Bohemian Revolt/Uprising 27, 199–200
Bonney, Richard 38, 45
Borch, Merete 70
Borghia, Cardinal 203
Borkenau, Franz 176, 177
Bosse, Abraham 178
Bossuet, Jacques-Bénigne 229–30
Botero, Giovanni 88
Bragança, Catharine of 243
Bragança, Dukes of 240–41
Brandenburg 28, 39, 226
Brazil 232, 235, 241–2, 243
Breda, Treaty of 245
Brenner, Robert 47
Brewer, John 37, 42, 55

Brockmann, Thomas 198, 202
Brunner, Otto 46
Burlamqui, Jean Jacques 67, 68, 69

Cabbot, John 74
Calvinism and Calvinists 126, 212, 214, 222–3, 228, 229
Canada 57
capitalism 40, 41, 42, 45, 53–7, 58–9
Carr, E.H. 103
Cateau-Cambrésis, Peace of 235
Catharine of Bragança 243
Catholic League 126
Catholicism and Catholics 212
    after revocation of Edict of Nantes 211, 214–23, 228, 229–30
    before revocation of Edict of Nantes 223–8, 229
    and Huguenots 84, 99–100, 216, 219–21, 223–4, 229
    inter-state relations 99–100, 102, 167, 174
    legal status of non-European dominions 234–7
    Machiavelli on 94
    state jurisdiction 192
    terra nullius 63
    Thirty Years' War 201–3, 204
    Treaty of Westphalia 213–14, 223–8
Charles I, King 241, 242
Charles II, King 243–4
Charles V, Emperor 26
Charles IX, King 227
Chesne, Legier du 84
Chigi, Fabio 200
China 40
Christianity and Christians 117, 158
    after revocation of Edict of Nantes 214–23, 228, 229–30
    before revocation of Edict of Nantes 223–8, 229
    inter-state relations 83–4, 165
    legal status of non-European dominions 234–7
    origins of capitalism 41
    terra nullius 63, 64, 66, 76, 77

Christine, Queen 22, 24
Cicero 95–9, 144
Colloque de Poissy 224, 227, 228
Connor, Michael 70
Constantinople, conquest of 41
Contamine, Philippe 38
Contarini, Alvise 200
contractualism 113–14, 118, 120–22
    see also social contracts
Council of Trent 83
Cromwell, Oliver 232, 243
Crucé, Emeric de 114, 117

Danish War 201
Davenport, F.G. 174
Derrida, Jacques 151
Dickmann, Fritz 207
Duchhardt, Heinz 197–8, 199, 204, 205
Duffy, Michael 37
Dutch East India Company 109–10, 139, 236
Dutch Revolt 28–9, 84, 113–14, 118, 121, 122
Dutch West India Company 245

East Indies 236, 238–45 *passim*
Edict of Alès 229
Edict of Fontainbleau 230
Edict of January (1562) 224, 227
Edict of Nantes 211, 214, 220, 222, 224, 229–30
Eighty Years' War 107–14
Elizabeth I, Queen 84, 192, 239
England and the English 191–2, 226
    capitalism 39, 45, 48, 53–7
    colonialism 235, 236, 238–45 *passim*
    state formation 37, 39, 41, 45, 48, 53–7
English Civil War 183
English Revolution 191
equality of states, lack of 31
Erasmus of Rotterdam 117
Euclid 181
Europa Regina 19–20
European Convention on Human Rights 133

European Union 135, 257, 263

Fénelon, François 229, 256
Ferdinand II, Emperor 198, 199–200, 201–2, 207–9
Ferdinand III, Emperor 22, 24, 209
Financial Revolution 37, 54
Fiscal Revolution 54
Florida 57
Fontainbleau, Edict of 230
France and the French 57, 167, 174
    absolutism 41, 49–52, 58
    after revocation of Edict of Nantes 214–23, 228, 229–30
    before revocation of Edict of Nantes 223–8, 229
    capitalism 39, 48
    colonialism 232, 235, 238–45 *passim*
    hegemony and Westphalia 211–14, 223–8
    and Huguenots 84–6, 216, 219–21, 223–4, 229
    republicanism 93
    state formation 26–7, 30, 39, 40, 41, 44, 48, 49–52, 58
    Thirty Years' War 22, 198–205 *passim*, 206–9
    visual representation of 19, 22, 26–7
François II, King 224
Frederician wars 32
Frederick II, King (Frederick the Great) 30, 31
Frederick V, Elector Palatine 28
Freitas, Seraphim de 236–7
French Revolution 52, 191
Friedrich-Wilhelm, Prince Elector of Brandenburg 215, 216, 220, 222
Frisch, Michael 202
Frontinus 108

Genet, Jean-Philipe 38
Gentili, Alberico
    inter-state relations and religion 83–93, 99–102
    republicanism 93–9
    terra nullius 71, 72, 74

Germany and Germans 19, 56, 93–4, 164, 205, 214, 222, 226–7
global governance 134, 140, 152
global lines 165, 172–80
globalisation 5–6, 134, 256–7, 262–3
    and global lines 173–4
    and social contracts 137–42, 151–2
    and sovereignty 135–7
Glorious Revolution 37, 54, 56
Great Britain and the British 27, 79, 81
    colonialism 232, 238–45 *passim*
Griffin, James
    natural law and religion 65
Grotius, Hugo 107, 108, 131–5, 163
    freedom of the seas 235–6
    governance 140, 152
    language 146–7, 149, 150–52
    law of nations 133, 257
    natural law 145
    natural law and religion 65, 67–8, 69, 89, 150
    personal rights 138–9
    pluralism 144–5
    positive law 145
    promising 146–52
    property 78, 80, 137–8, 140
    punishment 139–40
    self-constraint 125
    social contracts 137–46, 151–2
    sovereignty 135–7
    speech 147–9, 150–52
    terra nullius 73, 74
    utility 144
Guicciardini, Francesco 84
Guise massacre of Huguenots 224
Gustavus Adolphus, King 19, 21, 126, 201, 203, 210

Habermas, Jürgen 46, 147–8, 150
Habsburgs 19, 22, 26, 27, 28, 128, 202, 214, 225, 235, 240
Hanovers 55, 56
Hartmann, Anja V. 199
Heckel, Martin 202
Henry IV, King 224
Hintze, Otto 11, 17, 35

Hobbes, Thomas 17, 69, 112, 255, 259
  imperialism 172–80
  inter-state relations 99, 194
  philosophy 181, 183–4
  political sovereignty 181–2, 186–93
  reason of state 156, 158
  religious sovereignty 191–2
  security 163–5
  social contracts 137, 142, 182, 184–5, 262
  terra nullius 74
  war as a duel 166–72
Holland, *see* Netherlands and the Dutch
Holy Roman Empire 19, 53, 58, 214
  Thirty Years' War 199–205 *passim*, 207–9
Hooker, Richard 65, 121
hostages 102
Huguenots
  colonialism 235
  inter-state relations 84–6, 99–101
  revocation of Edict of Nantes 216, 219–21, 223–4, 229

imperialism 172–80
  see also terra nullius
India 57, 139
Innocent X, Pope 201
institutional stability of states, lack of 31–2
International Court of Justice 133
International Criminal Court (ICC) 140
Isidore of Seville 72
Islam and Muslims 41, 237
Italy and Italians 19, 39, 48, 93–4, 109, 128

Jacobins 191
Jamaica 243, 245
James I, King 236
Jesuits 101, 228
Johann VII, Count 127
John of Salisbury 65
Justi, Johann 256

Kant, Immanuel 3, 143, 152, 191, 256, 259, 262, 263

Keckermann, Bartholomaeus 115, 116
Kennedy, Paul 37, 43
Koller, Alexander 203
König, René 159
Krippendorf, Ekkehard 17
Kyoto Protocol 138

l'Hospital, Michel de 227–8
La Fontaine, Jean de 229
Lainez, Diego 228
Langewiesche, Dieter 17
language 146–7, 149, 150–52
law of nations 63, 64, 66, 70–71, 76–7, 132, 133, 194
  and peace 257–61
Lesaffer, Randall 199
liberalism 35–6, 43
Lipsius, Justus 84, 88, 108, 111, 115
  contractualism 118, 120–22
  self-constraint 117–25
Locke, John 170, 190
  natural law and religion 65
  property 78–9, 138
  terra nullius 71, 72, 74, 77, 78–9, 80, 81
Lorraine, Cardinal of 228
Louis XIII, King 174, 207, 224
Louis XIV, King 22, 24, 27, 51, 215, 216, 219–22, 223, 224, 229–30
Louisiana 57
Lutheran Protestantism and Lutherans 202, 212, 222–3

Mably, Gabriel Bonnot de 256
Machiavelli, Niccolò 84, 108, 119, 124, 144, 163, 179, 254
  inter-state relations 86–90, 92–3, 98–102
  rationalism 157
  reason of state 155–61
  republicanism 93–9, 192
Malcolm, Noel 164
Malettke, Klaus 207
Mann, Michael 11, 40–42, 48, 58
Māoris 79–80
Mapuche 232

Mariana, Juan de 101, 121
Marshall, John, Chief Justice 73
Marshall Plan 228
Marxism and Marxists 35–6, 43, 47–8
Maurice of Orange 123
Maximilian I, Emperor 117
McGrade, A.S. 65
Meinecke, Friedrich 158–9
Mexico 232
Middle East 138
Military Revolution 37, 41, 54
militiamen 107–9
Mills, Charles 74–5
Molucca islands 234
Monarchomachs 100
Monroe doctrine 173
Moore, Barrington 43
More, Thomas 72, 74
multiple social contracts 137–42, 152
Münkler, Herfried 17
Münster, Treaty of 3, 209
Muslims, *see* Islam and Muslims

Nantes, Edict of 211, 214, 220, 222, 224, 229–30
NATO 228
natural law 63, 64, 89, 145
    and religion 65–9, 77, 150
    and *terra nullius* 75–6
natural rights 64
    and religion 65–9
    and *terra nullius* 75–6
neo-Hintzeanism 36–42, 43, 44, 48, 58
neo-Stoicism 125
Netherlands and the Dutch
    capitalism 39, 48
    colonialism 232–7 *passim*, 238–45 *passim*
    contractualism 121–4
    Dutch Revolt 28–9, 84, 113–14, 118, 122
    Eighty Years' War 107–14, 126–8
    state formation 39, 41, 48, 53
    Thirty Years' War 200–201, 204, 226
    see also United Provinces
new wars 8–9, 17–18

Nietzsche, Friedrich 157
Nine Years' War 27
North American Free Trade Agreement (NAFTA) 133
North Carolina 82
Nouvelle, Claude 84–5
Nussbaum, Arthur 65, 68

Öhmann, Jenny 199, 210
Olivares, Gaspar de Guzmán y Pimentel, Count-Duke of 204
OPEC 138
Orange, House of 110, 123, 124
    military reforms 111–14, 126–8
Orthodox Christianity 41
Osnabrück, Treaty of 3, 223
Ottoman Empire 27, 91–2, 100, 117

Panizza, Diego 84
Parker, Charles 37
Parker, Geoffrey 111
Pascal, Blaise 178
Pateman, Carole 75, 77
Patrizi, Francesco 108
Paul, St 66
Paul III, Pope 63
peace 116–17, 152
    by balance of power 254–7
    by institutions of global law 261–4
    by international law 257–61
    and war 152, 252–3
    visual representation of 22, 25
Peru 180, 232
Peter the Great 27
Philip II, King 84
pluralisation 250–52
pluralism 144–5
Poland 58
Polybios 108
Portugal and the Portuguese 110, 173–4
    colonialism 232–7 *passim*, 238–45 *passim*
promising 146–52
property
    and social contracts 137–8, 140
    and *terra nullius* 63, 64, 78–80

see also social property relations
Protestants
    after revocation of Edict of Nantes
        211, 214–23, 228, 229–30
    before revocation of Edict of Nantes
        212, 214, 223–8, 229
    inter-state relations 89, 101, 102, 167, 174
    legal status of non-European dominions 234–7
    Thirty Years' War 126, 201–3, 204
Prussia 28–30, 57, 179
Pufendorf, Samuel von 177
    Catholicism and Protestantism 214–23, 223–8, 229–30
    church and state 214–23
    French post-1685 hegemony 214–23, 228, 229–30
    French pre-1685 hegemony 223–8, 229
    natural law and religion 65, 67, 68, 150
    terra nullius 80
punishment 139–40

Rachel, Samuel
    law of nations 71
    natural law and religion 65, 67, 68, 69
Racine, John 229
reason of state 155–61
Reinhard, Wolfgang 17, 18, 38
republicanism 93–9
Reynolds, Henry 70
Rhineland-Palatinate 28
Ribadeneyra, Pedro 88, 92–3, 100–102
Richelieu, Cardinal 204, 206–8, 224–7, 229, 240
Roberts, Michael 37
Rohrschneider, Michael 198
Rousseau, Jean-Jacques 93, 98, 137, 256, 259, 262, 263
Rudolf II, Emperor 19
Russia and Russians 27, 30, 39, 40, 57

Saint-Pierre, Bernardin de 256, 259, 262
Saint-Simon, Duc de 230
Sallust 108

Savoy 28
Saxony 209
Scandinavia 19
Schilling, Heinz 198
Schmitt, Carl 164–5
    global lines 165, 172–80, 239
    imperialism 172–80
    war as a duel 166–72
Scholasticism and Scholastics 116, 131, 143, 257
Searle, John 147–8
Seldon, John 236
self-constraint 125–8
Sepúlveda, Juan Ginés de 76–7
Seven Years' War 30, 44–5, 56, 57
Sévigné, Madame de 229
Skocpol, Theda 40, 42, 58
Smith, Adam 48, 81, 125
social contracts 137–46, 151–2, 182, 184–5
    and promising 146–52
social property relations 36, 47–59
Solórzano y Pereyra, Juan de 233
South Africa 140
Spain and the Spanish
    Asiento de negros 244–5
    colonialism 76, 90, 180, 232–7 *passim*, 238–45 *passim*
    Dutch Revolt 84, 121
    Eighty Years' War 107–11
    inter-state relations 90, 93, 173–4
    republicanism 93
    Thirty Years' War 198–205 *passim*, 208, 226
    visual representation of 19, 26
Spanish Inquisition 236
Spanish Succession, War of 27
speech 147–9, 150–52
St Bartholomew's Day massacres 84, 88, 224
Stoicism and Stoics 115, 132
    see also neo-Stoicism
Story, Joseph 81
Strauss, Leo 176, 177
Stuarts 54
Suarez, Francisco 65, 121
    law of nations 70–71

terra nullius 71
Surinam 245
Sweden and Swedes 19, 22, 26, 211, 241
    Thirty Years' War 199, 203, 209–10, 226
Swiss Confederates 27
Switzerland 53

Tacitus 72, 93, 123–4
Taylor, Charles
    natural law and religion 66
terra nullius
    and husbandry 77–80
    idea of 64–9
    implications for 69–77
    and sovereignty 80–82
Textor, Johann Wolfgang
    natural law and religion 65, 67, 68–9
    terra nullius 76
Thirty Years' War 3, 22, 127, 132, 198–9
    diplomatic relations during 199–201
    as a "Holy War" 201–3
    and *Pax honesta* 205–10
    and state formation 26, 27–8, 167
    and universal monarchy 203–4
    see also Dutch Revolt
Thomson, Erik 199
Thucydides 163
Tilly, Charles 11, 39–40, 44, 48, 52
Tilly, Johann Tserclaes, Count of 201
Tönnies, Ferdinand 176
Tordesillas, Treaty of 174
Trained Bands 107–9, 112
TRIPS Agreement 138
Truth Commissions 140
Tuck, Richard 177
Tully, James 74–5, 77
Twelve Year Truce 238
tyrants 100–101

United Nations 133, 228, 263
United Provinces 139, 238–42 *passim*, 245
    see also Netherlands and the Dutch
United States 73, 74, 168, 173, 212, 228
Urban VIII, Pope 203
Utrecht, Treaty of 56, 118, 254

Vattel, Emer
    natural law and religion 66
    terra nullius 70, 71, 72–3, 74, 79
Vegetius 108
Versailles, Treaty of 168, 170
Vienna Settlement 57
Vitoria, Francisco 168, 176, 237
    terra nullius 71–2, 76
VOC (Vereenigde Oost-Indische Compagnie), *see* Dutch East India Company

Wallenstein, Albrecht von 201
Wallerstein, Immanuel 43, 48
Wallhausen, Johann Jakobi von, Captain 127
Waterloo, Battle of 57
Weber, Hermann 207, 225
Weber, Max 44, 58
West Indies 238, 240, 244, 245
Westphalia, Peace Treaty of 198, 200–201, 209, 254
    and colonialism 241–2, 243
    and French hegemony 211, 212–14, 223–8
    Grotius' influence on 132
    and sovereignty 192
    and state / state system formation 4, 22, 26, 53, 254
    visual representation of 22
Westphalian order 4, 9, 52–3, 57, 106, 252, 253
    creation of 22–7
    upheavals within 7–9
White Mountain, Battle of 27
WIC (Westindische Compagnie), *see* Dutch West India Company
Williams, Michael 177–8
Wittgenstein, Ludwig 142
Wolff, Christian 71, 72, 80–82
World Trade Organization (WTO) 138
World War I 168
World War II 212

Yugoslavia Tribunal 140